WATER LOGICS

UNDER THE SIGN OF NATURE:
EXPLORATIONS IN
ENVIRONMENTAL HUMANITIES
Sarah Dimick, Alison Glassie, and Jesse Oak Taylor, editors

WATER LOGICS

MATERIALIST EPISTEMOLOGIES FOR THE ENVIRONMENTAL HUMANITIES

EDITED BY
YASSER ELHARIRY AND EDWIGE TAMALET TALBAYEV

UNIVERSITY OF VIRGINIA PRESS
Charlottesville and London

The University of Virginia Press is situated on the traditional lands of the Monacan Nation, and the Commonwealth of Virginia was and is home to many other Indigenous people. We pay our respect to all of them, past and present. We also honor the enslaved African and African American people who built the University of Virginia, and we recognize their descendants. We commit to fostering voices from these communities through our publications and to deepening our collective understanding of their histories and contributions.

University of Virginia Press
© 2026 by the Rector and Visitors of the University of Virginia
All rights reserved
Printed in the United States of America on acid-free paper

First published 2026

1 3 5 7 9 8 6 4 2

ISBN 978-0-8139-5420-2 (hardback)
ISBN 978-0-8139-5421-9 (paperback)
ISBN 978-0-8139-5422-6 (ebook)

Library of Congress Cataloging-in-Publication Data is available for this title.

Cover art: Detail of *Curtain Waterfall*, Pat Steir, 1991.
(© Pat Steir, courtesy the artist and Hauser & Wirth)
Cover design: Cecilia Sorochin

CONTENTS

Acknowledgments | vii

Watermarks: Toward a Water Logics   1
yasser elhariry and Edwige Tamalet Talbayev

Of Flood and Drought: Water Logics and the
Shaping of Odessa and New Orleans   21
Olivia Irena Durand

Wave Lab Logic   50
Stefan Helmreich

The Wave as an Epistemological Challenge Today   72
Nathalie Roelens

Thinking from Multiple Oceans: Historical and
Elemental Lineages and Futures of Ocean
Geography(s)   94
Philip Steinberg

Mo(u)rning in the Mediterranean: Liquid Mortuaries
and the Arts of Re-Membering   123
Supriya M. Nair

Water Necropolitics   142
Edwige Tamalet Talbayev

From Surveillance to Contestation: The Ebb and Flow
of the Mediterranean Frontier's Aesthetic Regime   **159**
*An Interview with Charles Heller, by Marie Sandoz and
Anne-Katrin Weber, translated by Nicole Horne*

Coralization: Coral Materiality in Khal Torabully's
Poetry   **177**
Shanaaz Mohammed

Is the Sea History? The Marine Life of Recent
Haitian Fiction   **197**
Martin Munro

Liquid Language   **214**
Aaron Pinnix

Between the Mountains and the Sea: Currents and
Currency of Terrestrial Waters and Aqueous Idioms
in Morocco   **233**
Matthew Brauer

Towards a Romantic Hydrocommons: Victor Hugo,
Humanity, and Hydrology   **255**
Bradley Stephens

"Forever Folding and Unfolding": The Critical Depths
of David Gascoyne's Poetics   **276**
Isabelle Keller-Privat

Afterword: Logics of Port Cities   **301**
Brian T. Edwards

Notes on Contributors | 311

Index | 317

ACKNOWLEDGMENTS

This volume bears the mark of conversations and arguments developed at the *Water Logics* international conference held at Tulane University in New Orleans on April 11–12, 2019. For their generous support of the event, we wish to thank our sponsors at Tulane—the Carol Lavin Bernick Faculty Grant Program, Kathryn B. Gore Chair in French, the New Orleans Center for the Gulf South, the Department of French and Italian, and the School of Liberal Arts. We owe a debt of gratitude to Sanela Frasch and Jéda McGlothan, whose dedication and efforts were instrumental in ensuring the success of our event. Our appreciation goes to Ben Depp, whose poignant photographic opus *Bayou's End* left its indelible mark on our ruminations during the conference and beyond.

At University of Virginia Press, we extend our gratitude to Angie Hogan for her sterling guidance and staunch support of the project from our first contact, and to Fernando Campos for his competent stewardship. Publication was made possible by a subvention from the Associate Dean for the Arts and Humanities at Dartmouth College, Samuel Levey. We also wish to thank the two anonymous peer reviewers, whose insightful comments and constructive feedback contributed to sharpening the focus of the book.

WATER LOGICS

WATERMARKS

Toward a Water Logics

YASSER ELHARIRY AND EDWIGE TAMALET TALBAYEV

We are scholars of literature, specialists of riddling tongues and foreign languages, of postcolonialisms, migrations, and movements, of poetry and poetics, rhetoric and manipulation. In our lives, in our practice, we turn to works of art, objects, and artifacts. As critics, we are receivers, at tail ends of creative and generative processes. As editors and conveners of gatherings, we hear ideas and read essays through the many phases of their life cycles. In our public-facing personas, we present as stewards. In practice, it is as though we were medium, mediums, or mediators. The words and writings of others pass through us. They touch us. Then they go away, repeat what they did to us, to others, after us, far from us.

> Futurity
> no more than duration
> Of a wave's rise, fall, rebound
> Against the shingles, in ever repeated mutation (Zukofsky 2011, 3)

Upon the first touch, words and waves leave no mark. Repetitive, they run amok. In unstoppable transferential blasts, they act like free agents. It is only afterward, in their ensuing afterglow, that we find ourselves sated by the ever-repeated memory of the events. We bear witness to the ideas. They came from afar. They were with us. They went. We are left with memory. The memory of an object. The subject within the object. The subject that gave us the object. The object that passed through the subject before passing through us. Its echo. Its mark. Or, in the ecology of this book, its *water*mark.

We call watermark the material imprint of water on humanistic and social-scientific inquiry and writing, in the style of wavelike rhythms—their "rise, fall, rebound." For watermarks are everywhere. If only we could recognize them, we would then be able to deduce the water logics that follows. We would be cognizant of the coimplication of matter and meaning, of their relational imbrication, in the spirit of the critical insights of material ecocriticism. In Karen Barad's powerful ascription, "the relationship between the material and the discursive is one of mutual entailment. Neither discursive practices nor material phenomena are ontologically or epistemologically prior. Neither can be explained in terms of the other. Neither is reducible to the other. Neither has privileged status in determining the other. Neither is articulated or articulable in the absence of the other; matter and meaning are mutually articulated" (2007, 152). And so, we approach the materiality intrinsic to considerations of the maritime with a sensitivity to the nuances of water's riveting indiscipline. Brian T. Edwards speaks directly to the complexities of maritime transitions and translations, writing in his coda to this book that "water teaches us that we cannot contain it, just as we cannot contain thinking and human expression within the academic disciplines that have formed to organize our thinking. Water and ports thus connect the disciplines and overwhelm them at the same time. They require an interdisciplinarity—perhaps even an 'indisciplinarity.'"

Yet *Water Logics* as a book seeks more than the marks—lingual, medial, material, scholarly, scientific—left by water on the wide array of primary sources discussed here, more than the merely invisible marks of water on language. *Water Logics* pursues the marks of water on thought itself. Taking our cue from characterizations of bodies of water as "site[s] of intellection" and "imaginative projection" (Wigen 2007), we underscore throughout *Water Logics* the cultural, geographic, historical, literary, and philosophical inquiries underlying the production, performance, and dissemination of knowledge through hydrological constructs. With an eye on the "material condition and praxis of the maritime world" (Blum 2010, 670), this book reorients theoretical methodologies within the humanities and social sciences alike toward a water logics—a water-based, comparative critical practice where water comes to set the boundaries of a new materialist epistemology.[1]

Our last book, *Critically Mediterranean*, paid particular attention to the histories of one sea. The book homed in on a "sedimented, gaping present . . . the basis of a jerky, fragmented, unsynchronized" time in the Mediterranean (elhariry and Talbayev 2018, 4), whose "unique texture renders it a privileged site for its reconsideration as a discursive space marked by multiple concurrent temporalities" (8). In our reading, the sea "conjure[d] . . . innumerable trajectories, and any number of potential histories, both micro and macro" (10). Mediating the time of the Mediterranean required attending to "singular knottings of subjective experiences of time following from moments of undoing . . . bearing in mind the layered temporalities" that thinking about a specific body of water, like the Mediterranean Sea, entails (Talbayev 2018, 264).

In *Water Logics*, we take a step beyond the singular Mediterranean water mass and its plural imaginaries. By bringing multiple spaces and places of water as discrete points of inquiry within a larger interconnected hydrology, *Water Logics* rethinks the aqueous both within and beyond its contiguity with landed logics. In these pages, we turn our attention to the hydrological shaping of border cities, waves, wave labs, liquid mortuaries, water necropolitics, forensic oceanography, corals, marine life, water molecules, and terrestrial waters—that is, to water writ large as materially interconnected on the global levels of society, culture, history, and politics. In all cases, water emerges as a medium for something else, other than itself. And unsurprisingly so. Seas and oceans, rivers and lakes have historically been construed as areas of deployment for processes of division, conquest, and globalization from the early days of empire. Their existence nevertheless transcends their status as repositories for the examination of the small-scale effects of macrolevel dynamics such as race and capitalism, or the flexing of sovereign, settler, and colonial powers.

For these reasons, water has been attracting renewed attention in twenty-first-century scholarship, which alternates in its understanding of water as conducive to and constitutive of both space and place. Water, seascapes, and the oceanic loom increasingly large over all our collective and individuated disciplinary constructs. They complement and enrich academic taxonomies rooted in the fragmented, exclusive terrains of national literatures, teleological narratives, and other land-bound theoretical constructs (Wampole 2016; Döring and Horden 2018). Beyond dominant transit tropes (the sea as an expanse to be traversed or bridged in a series of physical, metaphorical, and historical transitions), what kinds of materialisms, transnationalisms, knowledge transfers, and translational practices specific to water can we devise once diverging, geographically disparate aqueous sites of knowledge production are brought into contact? These are some of the questions asked by the critical literature, which stresses the social construction of seas and oceans (Steinberg 2001) and calls for closer attention to the material, instrumental conditions of maritime environments (Blum 2008, 2019; Steinberg 2013; Jue 2020). Other approaches resist cultural, metaphorical readings by recasting bodies of water in the light of anthropogenesis (Yusoff 2016), that is, sediments, signatures, or traces of the "ruptures in the human relationship to the planet, a way of reckoning ecological modernity" (DeLoughrey 2019, 8). Foreign, othered, even alien (Helmreich 2009), bodies of water exceed and frustrate the literal and imaginary limits placed upon them (Hofmeyr et al. 2022).

To espouse a water logics means facing up to water's many fundamental contradictions, bearing them in mind, at all times. Alongside the body of work in hydrocriticism, we draw, in the remainder of this introduction, on what we know best—literature and philosophy—to define water logics as a critical methodology at the intersection of medium, matter, and memory, with far-reaching implications for disciplines as varied as anthropology, cultural geography, continental philosophy, and literary studies. Although water may be material first and foremost, its molecularity remains inseparable from less literal associations. We cannot help but drift from material to immaterial bodies, from molecules to memory. Still, somehow, as we seek concrete emplacements and material sites of memorialization, we inevitably seem to find our way back to matter. Therein lies the perennial challenge of shape-shifting liquid. How do we give form to formless, liquid bodies?

The liquid bodies that emerge in these pages—ever-growing bodies of hydrocritical scholarship, but also bodies of water, human bodies that dissolve in bodies of water, bodies of monetized and expendable matter, organic and inorganic matter, bodies of writing that seek to give form to ungraspable phenomena, unspeakable experiences, or shapeless matter—all gesture toward the plural contours of a water logics. The narrative arc of this volume's single sequence of essays flows alongside the constant shifting of water's logics, between emplacement and evanescence. *Water Logics* begins with the artificially scaled-down and shape-giving containments of laboratory experiments, the sandbox delimitations of philosophical figures of thought, and the geographic realities of socioeconomic human formations around bodies of water. But such seemingly constrictive points of departure swiftly fade into expansive questions of scale, they open up to the temporal dimensions inherent in the progressive undoing and dissolution of matter in water. The two poles of extreme delimitation and infinite unfurling galvanize an extensive range of hardenings and pseudohardenings, such as the development of historical records and fictional narratives; the complex interplay between the organic and mineral accretions unique to corals; or the imprint of water on poetics, language, and theories of language, which molds thought and imbues it with form, however fleeting, on the page. A water logics sets thought aswirl amidst liquid bodies. And so, we may now begin to delineate water logics through a new epistemology that combines water's specificity as medium, matter, and a bearer of memory.

MEDIUM

Let us, for a moment, dwell on ourselves, on language, on scholarship, and on water as medium. A logic of ephemerality and capture emerges out of their intersection. Let us zero in on the concept of the medium as a "physical material . . . used for recording or reproducing data, images, or sound" or ideas; as "an intervening substance through which a force acts on objects at a distance or through which impressions are conveyed to the senses"; as "any substance considered with regard to its properties as a vehicle of light or sound"; even as a "person believed to be in contact with the spirits of the dead and to communicate between the living and the dead . . . a clairvoyant, a person under hypnotic control."[2] If water can be the medium for a host of hydrological and nonhydrological concerns, what becomes of the medium of water itself? What is the medium to apprehend the medium? Arrest, seize, perceive it? Capture its logics?

Here, the congruence between water and sound proves illuminating. For yasser elhariry, "the word produces sound, but sound is like writing on water" (2021, 48). The diffusive ephemerality of sound and water, their elusive reverberation, marks them as intractably "unintegrated and unintegratable . . . unfixed and unfixable" (48)—in other words, entropic. Rey Chow and James A. Steintrager highlight the evanescence of sound waves, defining sonic capture as "the capture of that which is lost. More succinctly put, sound is always capture, and capture is always loss" (2011, 4). At stake in any medium's existence is the promise to capture, record, or transmit, through a process that leaves "an aperture for interventional creativity" (Chow 2012, 54). Louis Zukofsky, for instance, once attempted to capture water's continual transformation in these lines of verse.

> It's hard to see but think of a sea
> Condensed into a speck.
> ....
> alternations that escape,
> So many waves of a speck of sea or what,
> Or a graph the curve of a wave beyond all sound,
> An open circuit where no action
> Like that of the retina made human by light
> Is recorded otherwise
> Than having taken a desired path a little way
> And tho infinitely a mote to be uncontained for
>   ever. (2011, 82)

See into sea, speck into mote: the first couplet isolates the act of seeing and identifies the sea, then "condense[s]" the act and the object, twice, "into a speck . . . a speck of sea." Condensation compresses ethereal vapor into viscous liquid, but the condensation, in turn, constantly decompresses the speck, now "a mote," and "uncontained for/ever." The extreme reduction of all watery expanse into a microscopic particle, compressed into another, then another again, or into as discrete an area as "the retina made human by light," boils down to "a mote," the vanishing point, which, one day, may "infinitely" expand back to noncontainment, to uncontainable, sealike expanse. The heavy, ungainly syntax of Zukofsky's long second sentence—choppy line breaks, clashing nouns unseparated by punctuation, clausal accumulations, a plurality of parsing possibilities—places the question of medium and its constant transformation front and center. Ourselves, water, language: one medium (our physical senses, "to see"), marked and grafted by another medium ("the sea"), both of which mark our language as medium (the graphemic, "a graph the curve"). As an example of Chow's "interventional creativity," Zukofsky's verse seeks to capture the transformation of the sea as medium, just as each of the chapters in *Water Logics* homes in on and "record[s] otherwise" one of water's states.

In a very real sense, then, water dictates the writing throughout *Water Logics*. No longer formless, submissive, and in need of construction, water operates as a shape-giver, a shape-maker for thought, as we see in the volume's essays. In doing so, *Water Logics* builds on feminist and queer strands of ecocriticism that have reversed long-standing gendered hierarchies and geographical biases associated with water, liquids, and viscosity (Pierce 2000; Tinsley 2008; Tinsley 2012; Freed-Thall and Cadieu 2021; Freed-Thall 2023). For "water makes the network of my nerves crackle," in the words of the radical lesbian and material feminist Monique Wittig, and "water dripping from the leaves of the trees" now is and always has been capable of imbuing them with "shape . . . even . . . colour," to such a degree that "luminous water-spouts burst over m/e, *I* don't know whether it is the storm outside or messages from my brain from the eyes that *I* cannot open, hundreds of orange globes a second depart and reprecipitate there, the intensity is too great, *I* feel *I* cannot stand it, *I* faint away, but not before m/y saphenous nerves are touched" (Wittig 1975, 61).[3] Where Zukofsky sees compression, where he seeks form, where he attempts to control water and the evasiveness of its perspectival shape-shifting, Wittig embraces the extreme physical reconfigurations, corporeal shattering, and the profound loss of self that water renders palpable. "In this encounter with water," writes Bradley Stephens in his essay, "the humanist mind-body dualism gives way to a more fundamental interrelationship between cognizance and materiality, and between self and other."

Importantly, Stephens critiques Gaston Bachelard's 1942 essay *Water Dreams* for its "patriarchal undercurrents since water conspicuously risks being subjugated to a reasoned masculine knowledge." The gendered subjugation of bodies of water represents an approach long critiqued by oceanic geographers such as Philip Steinberg, and previously suspected by Gilles Deleuze and Félix Guattari, who write, in an arresting illustration of Pierre Boulez's twinned concept of smoothness and striation (Boulez 1971, 84–85), that "one of the reasons for the hegemony of the West was the power of its State apparatuses to striate the sea by combining the technologies of the North and the Mediterranean and by annexing the Atlantic. But this undertaking had the most unexpected result: the multiplication of relative movements, the intensification of relative speeds in striated space, ended up reconstituting a smooth space or absolute movement" (Deleuze and Guattari 2010, 52). Water, then, is not merely shapeless and transparent, conforming to the contours, color, and opacity of its surroundings. It defies the most powerful, the most systematically deployed forms of state-sponsored division, conquest, and violence. As Isabelle Keller-Privat illustrates in these pages, water, "far from being a stylistic ploy, operates as a hermeneutic metaphor that displaces and challenges our viewpoint," any attempt at subjugation. The process that Keller-Privat dubs a "hydrologics" ends up "mapping out a new reading of the world that encompasses the impending arrival of what lies beyond—the unknowable and uncontrollable that defeats the logics of appropriation and domination—and which, through the sheer power of the word, is brought closer."

Out of this troubled waterscape, Shanaaz Mohammed extracts the notion of coralization, which gives water's resistive logics a specific figure, in the niche register of poetics. Coralization "prompts a material understanding of corals as actively and independently constituting their own agentic vibrancy that affects human and nonhuman life alike while also intertwining with the past, present, and future." Such a poetics undergirds the Mauritian poet Khal Torabully's "coralline architexture and anthropomorphic representations of corals," which allows Mohammed to argue "that corals are not mere metaphors but rather profound underwater networks of material relations, which, together with their oceanic environment, connect with the materiality of human lives."

Water Logics complements the general ethos of resistance to metaphor—a recurrent thread in the contributors' multifaceted attempts to write about and capture water as medium—with the figure of the watermark. Keith Waldrop writes in his poem *Water Marks*:

> From certain angles, one may see
> what the water reflects and
> also the bottom of the lake—like a world and its
> memory—(1987, 17)

What is above and what is beneath: medium paves the way for many such dualities, infinitely refracted, like memory, as implied by the logics of seeing, contemplating, and feeling sustained by water. So, if we think of water as medium, what medium do we have at our disposal to grasp and think of water? Watching, then writing about the waters and waves of seas serves to shape our sensorial perceptions of the world, in the world. An absence of movement (waves) would ring the medium's collective death knell. Movement occurs in the material passage of water from one state to another, including written states, the literal water mark of liquid ink on the page. Nathalie Roelens meditates upon water's liquid transience, writing in her essay here that "scientists question the wave's liquid substance, which passes from one state to another (water, droplets, foam), accelerates (swell, splash, torrent, cataract, geyser), or slows down (surf, fresh water)." The logics of movement imprints upon water its form, its rhythm. It heralds mutation, an encounter between multiple elements: "In the making of waves, first the air 'deforms' the water, which then begins to 'perturb' the flow of air across it; and it is out of this delicate intercourse . . . that the wave is born" (Raban 1999, 164; qtd. in Steinberg and Peters 2015, 250). In the interactive water logics of the wave, the forming and reforming of the bulging sea reveals the elemental weft of the sea, giving body and density to the elusive medium. In the swirling vortex, molecules assemble in shifting convergence of motion and matter. They lend form, shape the watermark. Within the swelling of each wave, "a superimposition of the real and the ideal, the actual and virtual," takes hold, as Stefan Helmreich writes in his essay for this volume, prompting a consideration of the "unfurling of fluid processes [that] might inform as well as yield to *scientific logic*, a set of abstract formal and symbolic theories and methods for perceiving and representing regularities in the phenomenal world." For Helmreich, the water logics of the wave further invites a reflection on the transposability (motile, unfixed) of any model of intellection onto the world. It implies acquiescence to the spectral presence of failure (of representation, of scale modeling, of human attempts at any degree of mastery) inherent in any impetus toward a water logics.

MATTER

Philip Steinberg coined the expression "the world-ocean" (2001, 1) to denote the historical forms of striation used to control the oceanic expanse, "a surface to be crossed," "a provider," partitioned into "a set of discrete locations" (2–3), a checkered "repository of fragile, global nature, to be stewarded" (207). Water, he posits in this book, thus "exists [only] to be ignored": if water were thought of as a substance rather than a striable surface, space, or place, it would suddenly appear uncontrollable, whereas the management of the world-ocean animates Steinberg's engagement with how societies have constructed it. For him, the world-ocean represents not so much "a formless void *between* societies but rather a unique and specifically constructed space *within* society" (23). From a biopolitical perspective, the outsize watery expanse that Steinberg dubs "ocean-space" operates as a "force-field," "a space in which battles are waged but also a space across which power is projected," and which "is dependent upon an idealization of the sea as an unmanaged and unmanageable surface" (17). When considered in this fashion, water-as-medium becomes especially evasive. It is difficult to mark. It is difficult to leave a mark on it. "*Stewardship* for this unclaimable space" has been historically dubious (65), and, in contemporary realpolitik, contested from national-sovereign perspectives (Steinberg et al. 2015, 19). Indeed, how can a territorial claim to an unclaimable medium be staked? The physical properties of the medium of water—dense but unstable, everywhere but unlocatable, in constant transferential and transformative motion—render any control or mastery, firm knowledge or affirmations about its expanse, difficult. Desirable and necessary in controlled quantities, water, in excess of the human scale, rapidly becomes a most formidable and foreboding opponent—tidal, beyond capture, beyond rule, a medium beyond medium. On the human scale, in a world marked by ever-repeated cycles of catastrophes and natural disasters, matter eclipses medium.

Poetics and language, literary and nonliterary alike, animate the fraught sociopolitical confrontations over water-matter, as outlined by Steinberg. Aaron Pinnix, who looks at water and literature on a material level, writes in these pages that "water molecules and words function within a global matrix of shifting relationships with other water molecules or words, each gaining their meaning within this larger web of shifting intensities." Verbal assemblages—such as the inescapable metaphors forged around the sea, made possible by thinking through the logics of a medium like water, and coalescing a rallying cry for many arbiters of oceanic studies (Blum 2010; Steinberg 2013)—provide a vantage point for complementing sociocultural and sociopolitical models for thinking about a water logics. Take Elizabeth Bishop's "The Map," the first poem of her 1946 collection *North and South*.

> Does land lean down to lift the sea from under,
> drawing it unperturbed around itself?

Along the fine tan sandy shelf
is the land tugging at the sea from under? (2011, 5)

Bishop's lines "reveal the iterability of signs, or how language refuses to ossify or solidify into any singular meaning," as Pinnix would say in his contribution, just as they "show how both language and the ocean are dynamic spaces of persistent change that function through an interplay of fluid convergence and deliquescence that locates meaning within constantly shifting networks of molecules that are constantly in motion." Pinnix anchors his model in the idea of deliquescence, which always involves matter. Deliquescence implies melting, solubility, dissolution; and water's remarkable capacity to dissolve, absorb, and preserve other matter—material and memorial, organic and inorganic—emerges as one of its most ethereal qualities as medium.

The medium is strewn with and suspends matter. Edwige Tamalet Talbayev has shown, for instance, how, in the context of lethal trans-Mediterranean migrations, "the process of human dissolution under the influence of seawater alongside the alteration of the marine environment that it causes reveals the reciprocal agency of material bodies, be they biotic or non-biotic," identifying in the churning brew a "dissolutive ontology . . . premised on loss and decomposition that blurs the discrete categories of subject and object into an enmeshed form of intimacy" (2021, 208). Such an attention to the broader, more-than-human world of overwhelming matter, "composes" a transcorporeality out of many "discontinuous pieces" (Latour 2010, 122; quoted in Alaimo 2012, 490). For Stacy Alaimo, transcorporeality "traces the material interchanges across human bodies, animal bodies, and the wider material world," which conceives of the human subject as "substantially and perpetually interconnected with the flows of substances and the agencies of environments" (476). Joseph Pugliese's *Biopolitics of the More-than-Human* trains its critical lens on matter, or, to be more precise, "different entities (soil, water, trees, animals) that, under existing forms of Euro-anthropocentric law, possess no jural life and thus remain outside the purview of justiciability" (2020, 33). His work redirects our attention to Indigenous views such as the Yarralin people's law where "non-human beings are active members of society. Animals, soil, water, and plants, in this Indigenous view, are constitutive of human subjectivities and cultures, rather than passive matter that is only ever acted on by humans" (34; see also Ingersoll 2016).

Pinnix and Talbayev build on Alaimo and Pugliese, all while heeding Steinberg's admonition against ignoring water. They share the move away from water as an inanimate, nonhuman repository, and highlight the multiple imbrications underlying the co-constitutive relation between human and more-than-human. As argued by Talbayev in these pages, water-suffused "matter endures over *longue durée* timelines—incarnating, decomposing, reincorporating in an endless cycle of molecular becoming marked by mutations and re-formations." The aqueous medium carries within its folds the material traces as well as the memory of derogation and violence. It churns with the traces of past losses and decompositions. Its "heavy waters" (DeLoughrey 2010) open themselves to the mediation of a "seascape epistemology," in Karen Amimoto Ingersoll's formulation, an Indigenous form of oceanic knowledge remarkable for its embodied, "organic nature, its inability to be mapped absolutely, and its required interaction with the intangible sea" (2016, 6). Over ocean-worlds, striation, and social construction, which lead to power grabs, fixity, and idealization, a water logics foregrounds water as a medium beyond medium, as matter imbricated with and in excess of medium, and, above all, as a memorial site of infinite mutability, with no real emplacement.

MEMORY

A water logics progressively leaves behind the shoreline, that mutable, shape-shifting edge, the meeting point and demarcation. The liminal threshold, ever a "reminder of the permeability between land and sea" (DeLoughrey 2018, 93), finds an echo in Elizabeth Bishop's cartographic contemplation—does land lift and tug at the sea from under?—which exceeds and undoes the oculocentric impulse to striate, acquire, and control memory. Bishop stresses instead the ephemerality not just of medium but of the matter of the medium. Her poem goes beyond mere looking and seeing, far beyond liminality, in-betweenness, hesitation, doubt, taking a deep-end plunge into unknowing wonder. Bishop marvels at the sheer magnitude of the orogenetic pressures exerted by land leaning on water, as much as by water on land. With one geological shelf against another, she initiates us into how "the interaction of the ocean's 'unstable cascades' should be understood not simply as the movement of water but as the mutation of atmosphere—space and time—as assembled from multiple elements" (Steinberg and Peters 2015, 250; quoting Serres 1995, 13).

Shape-shifting boundaries and dynamic geographies lie at the core of an understanding of memory shaped by tidalectics, Kamau Brathwaite's term for countering how dialectical "Western Philosophy has assumed people's lives should be" (1999, 34). Tidalectics has inspired new paradigms for grappling with alternative, fluid histories and memories unbound by land. In *Routes and Roots*, Elizabeth DeLoughrey turns to tidalectics as "a methodological tool that foregrounds how a dynamic model of geography can elucidate island history and cultural production, providing the framework for exploring the complex and shifting entanglement between sea and land, diaspora and indigeneity, and routes and roots" (2009, 2; see DeLoughrey 2018, 94). As Stefanie Hessler notes, tidalectics "delves into deeper layers of meaning, involving a variety of different readings and interpretations," "assumes the shape of an unresolved cycle rather than a forward-directed argument or progression," and "allows us to think of hybridity, cross-cultural syncretism, incompleteness, and fragmentation" (2018, 33–34). Martin Munro expands upon Brathwaite, DeLoughrey, and Hessler's multifaceted approaches to history and memory in his essay for *Water Logics*, as he outlines the remarkable way by which land has been steadily receding from view in recent Haitian fiction. "The land is marked by historical absence," writes Munro, whereas "the sea in Caribbean literature and thought is often the means by which connections are made, physically, culturally, and historically."

Thus memory is shaped and reshaped "along the fine tan sandy shelf." On the ground beneath our feet, there remain unseen, uncomprehended, incomprehensible natural phenomena as simple as water lapping land, land noshing water, coastline paradoxes, and the irresolvable tensions between one and the other borne of their unlocatable, labile points of contact. Olivia Durand's notion of "edge habitat," explored in these pages as a "transition zone between different natural and social ecosystems," limns the contiguity and porousness of the shore while shining light on the "malleability" of water as an interface between nature's sovereign agency and human efforts at managing it. In Durand's perspective, "intransigent borders between the elements of earth and water can be deceptive. Such infusions also signal contested 'ownership' of water bodies, generally assumed to be more of a 'commons' than terra firma, where borders can be more rigidly demarcated."

The intellective process of apprehending and rendering such mutable, shape-shifting memories poses the question of the modalities of their capture. For Matthew Brauer in this volume, the capture of water can be conceived as an interruption of an infinite sequence of liminal states, though one might concurrently add to this the notion of transitory states. The labile morphology of water belies any attempt at pinpointing and therefore stabilizing it. Any capture of the variable time of water requires its apprehension through truncation, through the segmentation and reification of a moment in what is otherwise an unending process of circulation.

A liquid repository of melancholic traces, water functions as a memorial medium, though one that only memorializes absence (Loichot 2020). Watery graves trace the lineaments of vanishing bodies, those of the migrant or enslaved bodies drowned at sea, and of evanescent matter. Water coheres as an amorphous repository that underpins the multifold transitions marking the passage from life to death, from being to nonbeing. The sea forms the outside edge of a "chalk [outline] on the bloody pavement," in the haunting *excipit* of Margaret Mazzantini's novel *Morning Sea* (2015, 143) dexterously parsed in Supriya Nair's contribution to this volume. In Nair's essay, the sea contains, delimits, yet points only to vacuity—a mediatic substance, the muted diffraction of the absent object's lingering form bearing witness to its endurance. Plato's *Timaeus* outlines such a receptacle through the concept of the *khôra*, mobilized by Nair, as a substratum, an interval, an interloping expanse that sustains the Forms in their transformation toward the sensible.[4] We here rethink the *khôra*, a motherly presence in Plato, in terms closer to the logics of a matrix, with an eye toward issues of duplication and deformation, cyclicity and (re)generation—the matrix of a differential water logics.

Water mediates a "testamentary desire" for the trace (Nair), and lends itself to another form of intellection, one attuned to markings, inscriptions, and deposited memories, however intangible or seemingly inaccessible they may be to the human sensorium. Hewing closer to the molecular level means engaging in the "attention to details" ingrained in the nonrepresentationalist methodology advocated by Karen Barad under the concept of "diffraction," a model that the philosopher likens to a "performative . . . mode" that "does not concern homologies but attends to specific material engagements" (2007, 88).[5] Such a model adopts an "onto-epistem-ology" (89) attentive to "marks on bodies" (90), but it is also an acknowledgment of humans' intra-active[6] entanglement with the world and its becoming, to the marks left behind by bodies—the alterations surging in their wake, in this *khôra*-like space awash with remanent forms of being.

Water Logics reveals how water as medium acts as a repository for the memory enshrined in matter, a presence-absence awaiting deciphering, filtering, re-membering. Given the challenge of accessing, composing, creating, re-composing, and re-creating intangible forms of transcorporeality, the sociocultural archive gathered in these pages may be productively accessed at a mediated remove, for example through "critical forensic practices" (Heller 2022, 92), such as the one articulated by Charles Heller and Lorenzo Pezzani—a specific political and jural form of forensic oceanography (Heller and Pezzani 2020) that seeks to counter how the sea "effaces all traces," a process abetted by forms of state-sponsored "liquid violence" that intentionally buttresses the medium's penchant for material effacement (Heller 2022, 89). Critical forensic practices, in turn, seek to rupture the hegemonic regime of disappearance, and its accompanying politics of visibility and invisibility. Charles Heller explains in his interview here that forensic oceanography "renegotiate[s] the in/visibility structuring the maritime space," as it questions how "the in/visible and in/audible structure the practices and policies of all the actors implicated in the control or transgression of . . . borders." In other words, forensic oceanography engages in practices of imperfect and hypothetical memories. Beyond the material focus of Heller and Pezzani's investigative regime, *Water Logics* takes aim at what lies beyond the remains.

As we've been thinking about water from the specific material configuration of its dissolution, we've been struck by its diffractive logics. Water as medium and matter morphs into an ever-evolving heuristic tool used to map and probe the suppressed echoes of memories and past losses. "From certain angles," to intone, once more, Keith Waldrop's penetrating lines, "one may see/what the water reflects and/also the bottom of the lake—like a world and its/memory—" (1987, 17). Like evanescent sound rebounding back onto itself, loss is enclosed, shimmering under the destabilizing blur of its recapture—a restitution of sorts, which, as Jacques Rancière contends, is "always already a new gesture of capture" (2006, 116). Most significant in its ellipses, ever intangible, water logics materializes at the intersection of loss and restoration, of memorial density and material vacuousness. It retains events long after the afterlife of its hollowed-out remains fades away. It reactivates traces, relentlessly redirecting them. It reinvigorates the awareness of our immersion into orders of magnitude far exceeding the human. It carries forth our reconnection to the world, the redefinition of the very trappings of our (in)humanity.

NOTES

1. Our movement toward a "water logics" amplifies the labile, unbounded, irresolvable quality of intellectual endeavors sustained through water against any univocal, prescriptive Western philosophical concept of "logic"—as logos, reason or speech. Our adoption of the substantive "logics"—as a singular—to coalesce our reflections on water thus pulses with the same resistance to normativity and linearity that animates Kamau Brathwaite's concept of a "tidalectics" to which we return below.
2. *Oxford English Dictionary*, "medium (n. & adj.)," June 2025, https://doi.org/10.1093/OED/1069470442.
3. On Monique Wittig's idiosyncratic usage of personal pronouns, see Crosland 1975, 7; Cadieu and Kim 2023.
4. "So likewise it is right that the substance which is to be fitted to receive frequently over its whole extent the copies of all things intelligible and eternal should itself, of its own nature, be void of all the forms. Wherefore, let us not speak of her that is the Mother and Receptacle of this generated world, which is perceptible by sight and all the senses, by the name of earth or air or fire or water, or any aggregates or constituents thereof: rather, if we describe her as a Kind invisible and unshaped, all-receptive, and in some most perplexing and most baffling way partaking of the intelligible" (Plato 1925, 51a).
5. Drawing on Donna Haraway's concept, Karen Barad writes of diffraction: "whereas reflection is about mirroring and sameness, diffraction attends to patterns of difference . . . Haraway notes that '[reflexivity or reflection] invites the illusion of essential, fixed position, while [diffraction] trains us to more subtle vision' (1992)" (2007, 29).
6. Writing on "intra-activity," Barad reveals how "human bodies, like all other bodies, are not entities with inherent boundaries and properties but phenomena that acquire specific boundaries and properties through the open-ended dynamics of intra-activity. Humans are part of the world-body space in its dynamic structuration" (2007, 172).

WORKS CITED

Alaimo, Stacy. 2012. "States of Suspension: Trans-Corporeality at Sea." *Interdisciplinary Studies in Literature and Environment* 19 (3): 476–93.

Barad, Karen. 2007. *Meeting the Universe Halfway: Quantum Physics and the Entanglement of Matter and Meaning*. Duke University Press.

Bishop, Elizabeth. 2011. "The Map," from *North and South*. In *Poems*, 5. Farrar, Straus and Giroux.

Blum, Hester. 2008. *The View from the Masthead: Maritime Imagination and Antebellum American Sea Narratives*. University of North Carolina Press.

Blum, Hester. 2010. "The Prospect of Oceanic Studies." *PMLA* 125 (3): 670–77.

Blum, Hester. 2019. *The News at the End of the Earth: The Print Cultures of Polar Exploration*. Duke University Press.

Boulez, Pierre. 1971. *Boulez on Music Today*. Translated by Susan Bradshaw and Richard Rodney Bennett. Faber and Faber.

Brathwaite, Kamau. 1999. *ConVERSations with Nathaniel Mackey*. New York: Web Press.

Cadieu, Morgane, and Annabel L. Kim. 2023. "Lesbian Materialism: The Life and Work of Monique Wittig." Special issue, *Yale French Studies*, no. 142.

Chow, Rey. 2012. *Entanglements, or Intermedial Thinking About Capture*. Duke University Press.

Chow, Rey, and James A. Steintrager. 2011. "In Pursuit of the Object of Sound: An Introduction." In "The Sense of Sound," edited by Rey James A. Steintrager, special issue, *Differences* 22 (2–3): 1–9.

Crosland, Margaret. 1975. Introduction to *The Lesbian Body*, by Monique Wittig. Translated by David Le Vay. William Morrow and Company.

Deleuze, Gilles, and Félix Guattari. 2010. *Nomadology: The War Machine*. Translated by Brian Massumi. Wormwood Distribution.

DeLoughrey, Elizabeth M. 2009. *Routes and Roots: Navigating Caribbean and Pacific Island Literatures*. University of Hawai'i Press.

DeLoughrey, Elizabeth M. 2010. "Heavy Waters: Waste and Atlantic Modernity." *PMLA* 125 (3): 703–12.

DeLoughrey, Elizabeth M. 2018. "Revisiting Tidalectics: Irma/José/Maria 2017." In *Tidalectics: Imagining an Oceanic Worldview Through Art and Science*, edited by Stefanie Hessler, 93–101. TBA21–Academy.

DeLoughrey, Elizabeth M. 2019. *Allegories of the Anthropocene*. Duke University Press.

Döring, Annika, and Peregrine Horden. 2018. "Heidegger as Mediterraneanist." In *Critically Mediterranean: Temporalities, Aesthetics, and Deployments of a Sea in Crisis*, edited by yasser elhariry and Edwige Tamalet Talbayev. Palgrave.

elhariry, yasser. 2021. "Unsound French." In *Sounds Senses*, edited by yasser elhariry. Liverpool University Press.

elhariry, yasser, and Edwige Tamalet Talbayev. 2018. "Critically Mediterranean: An Introduction." In *Critically Mediterranean: Temporalities, Aesthetics, and Deployments of a Sea in Crisis*, edited by yasser elhariry and Edwige Tamalet Talbayev. Palgrave.

Freed-Thall, Hannah. 2023. *Modernism at the Beach: Queer Ecologies and the Coastal Commons*. Columbia University Press.

Freed-Thall, Hannah, and Morgane Cadieu, eds. 2021. "Beaches and Ports." Special Issue, *Comparative Literature* 73 (2).

Haraway, Donna. 1992. "The Promises of Monsters: A Regenerative Politics for Inappropriate/d Others." In *Cultural Studies*, edited by Lawrence Grossberg, Cary Nelson, and Paula Treichler. Routledge.

Heller, Charles. 2022. "De la surveillance à la contestation: Flux et reflux du régime esthétique de la frontière en Méditerranée; Marie Sandoz et Anne-Katrin Weber, en conversation avec Charles Heller." In "L'Image verticale: Politiques de la vue aérienne," edited by Marie Sandoz and Anne-Katrin Weber. Special issue, *Transbordeur: Photographie, Histoire, Société* no. 6, 88–97. https://journals.openedition.org/transbordeur/945.

Heller, Charles, and Lorenzo Pezzani. 2020. "Forensic Oceanography: Tracing Violence Within and Against the Mediterranean Frontier's Aesthetic Regime." In *The Handbook of Displacement*, edited by Peter Adey, Janet C. Bowstead, Katherine Brickell, et al. Palgrave.

Helmreich, Stefan. 2009. *Alien Ocean: Anthropological Voyages in Microbial Seas*. University of California Press.

Hessler, Stefanie. 2018. "*Tidalectics:* Imagining an Oceanic Worldview Through Art and Science." In *Tidalectics: Imagining an Oceanic Worldview Through Art and Science*, edited by Stefanie Hessler. TBAS21–Academy.

Hofmeyr, Isabel, Sarah Nuttall, and Charne Lavery. 2022. "Reading for Water." Special issue of *Interventions* 24 (3).

Ingersoll, Karin Amimoto. 2016. *Waves of Knowing: A Seascape Epistemology*. Duke University Press.

Jue, Melody. 2020. *Wild Blue Media: Thinking Through Seawater*. Duke University Press.

Latour, Bruno. 2010. *On the Modern Cult of the Factish Gods*. Duke University Press.

Loichot, Valérie. 2020. *Water Graves: The Art of the Unritual in the Greater Caribbean*. University of Virginia Press.

Mazzantini, Margaret. 2015. *Morning Sea*. Translated by Ann Gagliardi. One World.

Pierce, Christine. 2000. "Holes and Slime: Sexism in Sartre's Psychoanalysis." In *Immovable Laws, Irresistible Rights: Natural Law, Moral Rights, and Feminist Ethics*. University Press of Kansas.

Plato. 1925. *Plato in Twelve Volumes.* Vol. 9, translated by W. R. M. Lamb. Harvard University Press.

Pugliese, Joseph. 2020. *Biopolitics of the More-than-Human: Forensic Ecologies of Violence.* Duke University Press.

Raban, Jonathan. 1999. *Passage to Juneau: A Sea and Its Meanings.* Picador.

Rancière, Jacques. 2006. *Film Fables.* Translated by Emiliano Battista. Berg.

Serres, Michel. 1995. *Genesis.* Translated by Geneviève James and James Nielson. University of Michigan Press.

Steinberg, Philip E. 2001. *The Social Construction of the Ocean.* Cambridge University Press.

Steinberg, Philip E. 2013. "Of Other Seas: Metaphors and Materialities in Maritime Regions." *Atlantic Studies* 10 (2): 156–69.

Steinberg, Philip E., and Kimberley Peters. 2015. "Wet Ontologies, Fluid Spaces: Giving Depth to Volume Through Oceanic Thinking." *Environment and Planning D: Society & Space,* no. 33, 247–264.

Steinberg, Philip E., Jeremy Tasch, and Hannes Gerhardt. 2015. *Contesting the Arctic: Politics and Imaginaries in the Circumpolar North.* I. B. Tauris.

Talbayev, Edwige Tamalet. 2018. "Afterward: Critical Mediterranean Times." In *Critically Mediterranean: Temporalities, Aesthetics, and Deployments of a Sea in Crisis,* edited by yasser elhariry and Edwige Tamalet Talbayev. Palgrave.

Talbayev, Edwige Tamalet. 2021. "Seawater." *Contemporary French and Francophone Studies: SITES* 25 (2): 207–17.

Tinsley, Omise'eke Natasha. 2008. "Black Atlantic, Queer Atlantic: Queer Imaginings of the Middle Passage." *GLQ: A Journal of Lesbian and Gay Studies* 14 (2–3): 191–215.

Tinsley, Omise'eke Natasha. 2012. "Extract from *Water, Shoulders, into the Black Pacific.*" *GLQ: A Journal of Lesbian and Gay Studies* 18 (2–3): 263–76.

Waldrop, Keith. 1987. *Water Marks.* Underwhich Editions.

Wampole, Christy. 2016. *Rootedness: The Ramifications of a Metaphor.* University of Chicago Press.

Wigen, Kären. 2007. Introduction to *Seascapes: Maritime Histories, Littoral Cultures, and Transoceanic Exchanges,* edited by Jerry H. Bentley, Renate Bridenthal, and Kären Wigen. University of Hawai'i Press.

Wittig, Monique. 1975. *The Lesbian Body.* Translated by David Le Vay. William Morrow and Company.

Yusoff, Kathryn. 2016. "Anthropogenesis: Origins and Endings of the Anthropocene." *Theory, Culture & Society* 33 (2): 3–28.

Zukofsky, Louis. 2011. *Anew: Complete Shorter Poetry.* New Directions.

OF FLOOD AND DROUGHT

Water Logics and the Shaping of Odessa and New Orleans
OLIVIA IRENA DURAND

> [The river] was so mighty and so unsubdued all the time that I could not help fancying she would some day take the matter into her own hands again, and if so, farewell to New Orleans.
> —FRANCES MILTON TROLLOPE

> Two of the most indispensable necessaries of life, Odessa, unfortunately, is ill-supplied with: the water in the wells is brackish; and the surrounding country, an elevated plain of immeasurable extent, without tree or shrub, cannot, of course, furnish fuel.
> —EDMUND SPENCER

The ports of Odessa and New Orleans, located across oceans and on contrasting shores, share a surprising story of parallel rise and transformation.[1] Shaped by distinct geopolitical contexts in the 1800s, the two burgeoning metropolises were nonetheless bound together by networks of trade, themselves contingent on the cities' proximity to water. Geography played a pivotal role in their founding, defining their significance within expanding imperial formations. At the dawn of the nineteenth century, both the United States and the Russian Empire went through territorial transformations that accelerated their evolution into widespread continental empires. On the Pontic steppe, Russian forces concluded three decades of conflict with the Ottoman Empire by conquering the northern shores of the Black Sea in 1789. These victories secured Russia access to a lucrative maritime trade with European nations, a pathway to the Mediterranean, and a new fertile agricultural frontier on Ukrainian lands. Meanwhile, across the Atlantic, the United States purchased the Louisiana Territory in 1803, effectively eliminating Spain and a waning French colonial empire as serious competitors for control over the Mississippi. This gain also set the stage for American westward migration. In both cases, aspirations to control promising trade routes and exploit commercial opportunities drove arguments for expansion. The economic potential vested in the Black Sea and the Mississippi Delta was inseparable from access to their shores. Yet conquest and acquisition marked only the beginning of a complex historical process of territorial integration and alteration. Central to this process were two rapidly growing urban centers. The region comprising the southern Ukrainian steppes, rebranded as "New Russia," was soon dominated by Odessa, a city founded in 1794. Similarly, New Orleans, once a minor colonial outpost under French and Spanish rule, became one of North America's most important harbors. By the mid-nineteenth century, both cities had cemented their status as critical hubs: New Orleans became the third-largest city of the United States, while Odessa held the same rank within the Russian Empire.[2]

By adopting a comparative framework, this essay sheds light on the practical processes, underlying rationale, and prevailing arguments involved in the founding of Odessa and refounding of New Orleans. It examines how their waterborne environments—maritime and riverine shores—durably framed their destinies. The emphasis on water control and management, as well as its far-reaching social and political consequences, foregrounds the environment's role in the development of these comparably large and newly emerging port cities. The lens of water reveals a shared process: in both cases, the early growth of these cities was fundamentally articulated by the tension between human occupation and aquatic surroundings. While settlement and trade were pivotal to their rapid economic ascent, water rendered them contested spaces—both within their respective imperial systems and in their interactions with the natural world. This focus on "water logics" calls for a hydrocentric analysis, one that moves beyond the conventional territorial primacy of empire while still intersecting with it. By employing a comparative approach, this essay resists the exceptionalist narratives that at times characterize single-case studies of Odessa and New Orleans. Instead, it highlights the crucial role of environmental factors in transforming these cities into ports of global significance. The abundance or scarcity of water—manifested through cycles of floods and droughts, aquatic connectivity and landed isolation—emerged as a central determinant of their growth and success. As agents of both permanence and adaptation, water logics defined the evolving relationship of New Orleans and Odessa within the imperial systems to which they belonged.

Water, as an element, evokes notions of porousness and liminality. This essay engages with these ideas by deploying and testing the conceptual frameworks of edge habitats and ecotones in the environmental histories of New Orleans and Odessa. Derived from ecological sciences, the term "edge habitats" describes transition zones between distinct natural ecosystems, often marked by heightened biological diversity. Similarly, "ecotones" denote areas of transition between ecological communities, where normally separate groups converge and undergo processes of creolization.[3] Historian Thomas Barrett adapted this ecological perspective to the Russian Empire, reinterpreting its territorial expansion through the lens of borderland edge habitats.[4] His approach nuanced the American concept of the frontier, emphasizing the social diversity that characterized borderlands. Transposed to human history, edge zones become spaces of cultural complexity, social exchange, and stratification. Viewing Odessa and New Orleans as edge zones underscores the transnational and transimperial dimensions of their early histories, shaped profoundly by their waterborne environments. The concept of water logics—defined by porosity and adaptability—highlights how these locations fostered the emergence of new communities at the edges of empires. The urban development of Odessa and New Orleans within imperial borderlands also reflected their settler colonial transformation, as local environments were modified to meet the demands of empire building: in this context, water represented both an element and a space. Considering the role of water invites reflection on the adaptability of these societies and their strategies for negotiating their aquatic environments. Both a risk factor and an opportunity, water enabled the development of urban centers on the geographic and conceptual peripheries of continental empires.

This essay examines how the ports of New Orleans and Odessa evolved through their reciprocal relationships with distinct water environments, overflow in the former and scarcity in the latter. These contrasting conditions imposed enduring constraints that influenced their urban history. The analysis begins by considering how water, through its proximity and the connections it facilitated, influenced the founding of both cities and determined their geographical significance. In the American and Russian contexts alike, water logics often disrupted traditional landed logics, necessitating strategies to control and integrate these port cities into broader continental and national systems—a process only partially successful. The discussion then focuses on the local implications of water management for residents of New Orleans and Odessa, highlighting how water logics were integral to their early urban histories. Positioned on imperial watersheds, these cities became zones of coexistence for diverse port societies, navigating fluid spaces fraught with both risk and opportunity. Water governed trade and migration, its abundance or scarcity alternately sustaining and devastating populations. At the same time, the cities' water horizons directed gazes outward, situating New Orleans and Odessa within liminal spaces—on the peripheries of empires, yet connected to broader seascapes. Their dual roles as imperial edges and maritime nodes underscore the centrality of water in shaping their destinies.

THE RECIPROCAL RELATIONSHIP BETWEEN THE PORTS OF NEW ORLEANS AND ODESSA AND THEIR WATER ENVIRONMENT

Water logics—conceived as both asset and constraint—were fundamental in the conquest, settlement, and further development of New Orleans and Odessa. New Orleans, initially a French colonial town, commanded the strategic Mississippi River and its porous delta, and thus virtually controlled the bulk of North American interior trade prior to the development of the railway—providing its eastern seaboard with supplies of provisions such as cereals and meat, and raw goods for foreign factories, like cotton. The port also acted as an interface with the wealthy Gulf of Mexico and the high-capital Caribbean islands, a nexus of the international slave trade that produced prized commodities such as sugar and tobacco.[5] The strategic city was ensconced between the young United States, the Spanish American empire, and vast distances of Indigenous lands. In another seascape, Odessa offered a southern outlet towards the Black Sea, with further access to the straits of the Bosphorus and the Mediterranean, connecting them with the north-oriented Russian Empire. Its site had been known since the fourteenth century as Khadjibey, a Tatar fort later controlled by the Ottomans. There as well, interactions with ancient and populous trading routes and the sale of staple goods conferred primacy to the city's geographical situation. As emblems of blue-water colonialism, ports like New Orleans and Odessa served as points of contact between land and sea, sites from where colonial control could be extended inland. The proximity of water and its mastery were fundamental in choosing the location of both Odessa and New Orleans, positioning them centrally within edges between distinct societies and environments. While the question of geographical situation was foremost in determining their settlement, the suitability of the site and its topography often came second. Reassessing the role of water anchors this analysis into each city's local ecologies, nuancing sea-focused colonialism with land-based considerations.

New Orleans was founded in 1718 by a group of French colonists, led by Jean-Baptiste Le Moyne, sieur de Bienville, on an elevated natural levee—the site that was the most accessible for the easy portage of goods between the Mississippi River and the estuarial Lake Pontchartrain.[6] In a mostly flat or even below-sea-level landscape, the site of New Orleans had been originally inhabited by Indigenous nations (chiefly Chitimacha, Houma, Choctaw, and Biloxi) because they found that it was a safer location for a small settlement—the first place coming from the Gulf of Mexico where ships could anchor easily and stock goods.[7] Yet it was a site subjected to water risks, as it was situated in the midst of an extensive floodplain. In another seascape, Odessa was founded in 1794 alongside other Russian ports on the northern banks of the Black Sea, in the aftermath of Catherine II's campaigns against the Ottoman Empire and the Crimean Khanate. The territory surrounding it was known as Yedisan, or Western Nogai, referencing the Nogai Tatar horde that roamed the area. The city was established on the Khadjibey fortress site, surrounded by a preexisting fishing settlement. However, if the place was good for defense and anchorage, it was on dry and friable ground, subject to droughts and distant from substantial freshwater sources, and exposed to the northern winds that swept the steppes and dried the land. Other new Black Sea port creations, such as Kherson or Nikolaev (Mykolaiv), were initially favored by the Russian government, because they offered better water connections with the interior. Odessa ultimately took precedence due to its natural harbor and how its population negotiated the water advantages and restrictions of the new port city. In the case of Odessa as in New Orleans, the fate of these new port cities was consequently shaped by water—its overflow and abundance as well as its scarcity and salinity. While water connected the ports to their transnational maritime surroundings through trade and immigration, it was also an important source of geographical liminality. Indeed, water logics mirrored altered landed logics: the cities' seaward and transnational connectivity clashed with the inward-facing demands of empire and nation-building. Water transformed the domestic significance of Odessa and New Orleans: it made them evolving imperial watersheds, continental edges where porous societies were formed.

Both cities commanded fluid geographies. In New Orleans, urban development had to contend with the territorial shifts that affected the Mississippi watercourse. In the past, the unpredictability of the Mississippi River had made its valley a permeable and unreliable boundary. Although the Louisiana Purchase changed the Mississippi's function from a natural interimperial border to an integrated transportation corridor, representations of its course as a territorial limit persisted. By 1803, most of the northern regions of the Territory of Louisiana had been only sparsely settled by European colonists and belonged to Indigenous nations. However, the lower Mississippi Delta had been settled and cultivated for almost a century by pockets of colonial subjects of two distant European empires: France and Spain. Abruptly, and with little notice, these colonists became members of an independent Republic. At the time of the Purchase, the question of the imagined and concrete spatial integrity of the territory was the object of intense diplomatic discussions, especially as Louisiana's boundaries were negotiated between Paris and Madrid.[8] The Floridas had once been part of Spanish Louisiana, but these colonies were regained by Spain during the American War of Independence and thus not included in the Purchase agreement. Lying on the east bank of the Mississippi Delta, West and East Florida (eventually gained by the US in 1810 and 1822), created for a time another border, just across from New Orleans. Consequently, the city's position in relation to—and within—the

United States changed multiple times and was only stabilized in the 1840s, after the annexation of the southwestern lands of Texas (1845), at a tipping point when the focus on the Mississippi watercourse was displaced by further Western expansion. The centrality of New Orleans in the Caribbean trade and in the Mississippi basin stood in contradiction with the city's geographical marginality—first at the edge of the French and Spanish American empires, then of the United States. On land New Orleans was a contested center, subject to territorial shifts and reconfigurations; but on water its significance was more indisputable. Situated at the intersection of diverse environments and imperial formations, New Orleans became a convergence point for the cultural and historical sediments left by waves of conquest, settlement, and immigration. Its fluctuating prominence and unique position within the United States were deeply influenced by water's dual nature as a boundary and a connector.

Water not only shaped the city's function but also heightened the exclusionary tensions at the crossroads of national and transnational networks. This dynamic invites a water-centric reinterpretation of economic globalization and political assimilation—patterns that are similarly evident in the case of Odessa. Although located in a very different geopolitical context, Odessa's rise as a new port city and its evolving role between land and sea were likewise affected by aquatic logics of integration, opportunity, and permeability. Located in a newly conquered territory in southern Ukraine (also known then as "New Russia," or *Novorossiya*), Odessa was founded as the result of the empire's most recent expansionist wars over the Ukrainian steppe frontier (Kodharkovsky 2004; McNeill 2011). Initially established as a Russian border outpost on the site of a former military fort, Odessa remained loosely connected to the centers of imperial power. It lacked both reliable overland routes and direct maritime access to the capitals. This limited inland connectivity was a challenge that Odessa shared with New Orleans, as the United States and Russia had comparably few established highway roads at the time. In both countries, before the advent of railroads, cities located on navigable waterways served as gateways, bridging outward spaces with their respective interior (Burghardt 1971). Charles Sicard, a trader from Marseilles and a local resident, underscored this dynamic in his writings on Odessa's early trade history, emphasizing its significant aquatic advantages: "All [of Odessa's] possessions at this time consisted of a small Tartar fort, and a few miserable huts; but the bay had, from time immemorial, proved a secure haven to winter in, for vessels navigating these waters" (Sicard and Stevens 1819, 5). And indeed, the site of Odessa benefited from environmental advantages, including a natural deep-sea harbor and stable banks, while its southern location provided ice-free waters for most months of the year. However, Odessa was not directly located on a river, making communications with the interior difficult.[9] About one hundred miles away, the nearest prominent river, the Dnieper, was shallow and not navigable by large boats. The Dniester remained a secondary watercourse linking back to western Ukraine, while the Danube, with its estuary further south on the Black Sea coast and outside of Russian control, fostered connections with Central and Western Europe rather than the centers of Russian government. Notwithstanding its lack of inland connections, Odessa was viewed by traders as a maritime interface between Europe and Asia, "the grand entrepôt" of an intercontinental system, connected through the waters of the Black Sea and of the Mediterranean (Sicard and Stevens 1819, 12). A frontier city at the edge of the Russian Empire, coalescing distinct geographies, Odessa was very much a crucial node for transnational trade, its own growth conditioned by local and regional water logics. Odessa's position on the Black Sea transformed the port into an economic and social ecotone, where the Russian Empire's continental ambitions met maritime trade networks, prompting adaptation and innovation.

The geographical significance of Odessa and New Orleans could have predisposed them to remain secondary port towns with subordinate hinterlands, perpetually lacking strong connections to the centers of power. However, because the cities bordered major riverine and maritime bodies, water logics widened the scope of their influence and located each city at the heart of hydrocentric and interimperial systems. While the movement of exported goods and provisions was a key feature of the two ports, New Orleans and Odessa grew into large cities through the continuous settlement of individuals coming in, in turn creating a growing local market and consumer base for their urban development. In this relationship, water was key: its control regulated trade and migration, its supply both nurtured and decimated its population, and its horizons embedded the city within transnational and liminal spaces.

Port and city mutually reinforced one another: the prosperity of one was closely tied to the success of the other. The interplay between their roles as international trade hubs and regional centers of commerce profoundly influenced their urban and demographic growth. Both Odessa and New Orleans were key nodes for exporting agricultural products harvested from newly acquired agrarian hinterlands, emerging during an era of transformative expansion in the scale and reach of global trade. They also served as gateways for the influx of new populations and capital. The two ports relied heavily on trade with Western European states for the majority of their revenue. While the boom in cotton production and steamship navigation gradually diversified New Orleans's export economy beyond provisions, both cities remained central for the redistribution of grain and other foodstuffs. As international trade surged in the 1830s and 1840s, the strategic access to waterways elevated the status of Odessa and New Orleans within their respective nations.

In the case of New Orleans, it was specifically the port's position on the Mississippi River that had made the Louisiana Purchase the "greatest real estate deal in history." In the words of Thomas Jefferson, "with Boston, Baltimore, New York, and Philadelphia on the left; Mexico on the right; Havana in front, and the immense valley of the Mississippi in the rear, no such position for the accumulation and perpetuity of wealth and power [had] ever existed" (Thomas Jefferson to W. C. C. Claiborne, qtd. in United States Department of the Treasury 1888, 185). This reasoning had driven the US president's efforts to acquire New Orleans, and with it the entire Louisiana Territory. But more than land, though key for settler expansion, it was the control of water that made New Orleans such a precious acquisition: the Mississippi Delta ensured the transformation of the town into a global port. Yet Jefferson, in the long run, proved to be wrong, and New Orleans's economic and trade history demonstrated that relying solely on this natural advantage could not ensure the city's long-term prosperity, and these shortcomings will be discussed in the next section.

Odessa, lacking New Orleans's temporary dominance over a major water inlet, had to find other ways to bolster its port, especially as, until the advent of the railroads in the 1860s, trade with the hinterland relied on the ceaseless work of Ukrainian *chumaks*, or wagon-carriers on foot. Odessa residents, before those of New Orleans, felt the need to innovate and develop artificial urban advantages to get ahead of other Russian Black Sea ports: the active pursuit and eventual establishment of a free-port status provided the city with a unique position in the Black Sea. From 1819 to 1859, the importation of merchandise was authorized with a duty representing only one fifth of the usual amount paid in other ports of the Russian Empire.[10] In turn, this duty was then "employed to defray the annual expenses which [were] spent for the benefit of this City, such as pavements, footpaths, repairing streets, lights, government buildings, and for the expenses of all local administrations" (USNA II M459, vol. 2, f. 195, January 1, 1854). The port and its maritime trade were thus instrumental to the growth and improvement of the city, strengthening Odessa's access to the sea with legal advantages. Many articles that could not be imported into the Russian Empire or were hard to acquire because of high duties (such as tea, printed cottons, and silk) were consumed cheaply within the limits of the free port, thus influencing the mixed type of urbanity and social practices that developed in the port city.[11] This legal apparatus also offered undeniable advantages for local development. However, as in New Orleans, the delays in Odessa's technical advancement to control land routes in addition to water spaces eventually hindered the city's chances at long-term prosperity. While water was fundamental in shaping the foundation and early appeal of the two ports, these natural advantages increased the cities' separateness and tested their integration as territorial margins.

AQUATIC ADVANTAGES AND LANDED SHORTCOMINGS: THE LIMITS OF TERRITORIAL INTEGRATION

The fluidity of water networks connected New Orleans and Odessa to urban archipelagoes beyond their national anchor: their situation as imperial edges ensured that, through water, the two cities became spaces of friction, innovation, and exchange. New Orleans's economic boom was associated with the introduction of steamship navigation on the Mississippi River, which enabled greater control over this central water route. Steamboat activity on the Mississippi began in 1812, each vessel carrying up to eight hundred bales of cotton and fifty to sixty passengers; by 1817, with improved engines, they could reach as far as St. Louis when navigating upriver (AMAE 227CCC/01, April 10, 1812).[12] The advent of steam power granted New Orleans dominance over its North American hinterland, coinciding with a shift from its earlier outward connections with Europe and its colonies to a stronger focus on national demands. Steamship technology was a critical catalyst for the cotton boom, securing New Orleans's economic prosperity and drawing both immigrants and capital to the city. It was mastery over water, rather than land, that proved fundamental to the city's success, underscoring the central role of water management in driving urban growth.

In southern Russia, the use of steamships developed later than on the Mississippi, with sail remaining the primary mode of transportation until mid-century. By 1857, the United States Consul to Odessa reported that a Russian company, comprising forty-five to fifty boats, started operating regular journeys to different ports of the Black Sea, as well as to the main ports of the Mediterranean (including Constantinople, Athens, and Marseilles), and even beyond, to London.[13] The Russian government itself invested in the company to ensure the carrying of its official mail. However, if steamships revolutionized transportation on the Black Sea, they only fully developed as backup competitive advantages after the expiration of Odessa's free-port privileges in 1859. Although its free port had given Odessa a distinct advantage in international trade, in the Black Sea region—prone to sudden storms and cold winters—only technological advancements could ensure consistent prosperity throughout the year.[14] If proximity to water had presided over the founding and singularity of both Odessa and New Orleans, their success ultimately depended on human control over their waterways. At the same time, their over-reliance on aquatic routes fostered a growing disconnect from land-based networks.

Just like with steamships, the development of railroads became commonplace around the Black Sea only after the end of the Crimean War, in an equally slow and frustrating process.[15] Contemporary observers lamented that Russia's conservative government limited entrepreneurial attempts at building roadways, and that it would be a likely be an anomaly "if a railway should connect Moscow and Odessa in the absence of any macadamised road between the two; and one nonetheless striking, because only to be found elsewhere in America" (Oliphant 1854, 334). The US consul, conscious of southern Ukraine's competitivity in the grain trade, reported regularly on plans to build railroads in the northern Black Sea; in 1857, he conveyed the rumor "that the establishment is all arranged, and that the lines are to go through 3700 versts . . . and are to be finished in the course of ten years" (USNA II M459, vol. 2, f. 152, January 1859). Still, the city of Feodosia in the Crimean Peninsula was then in preference, at a time when the Russian

Empire was completing the military conquest of the Caucasus. During the 1853–1856 war, Britain had also built the Grand Crimean Central Railway between their military camp and the port of Balaclava to provide supplies to the troops. Odessa, having been eliminated from the outset of the conflict and occupied until 1856, had to wait its turn to be integrated in the southern railroad network. While the port was a central hub on water, it was sidelined on a continental plane.

The first section of the railway to Odessa was finally completed in December 1865, but it took an additional thirteen years for that railroad to be merged into the wider national network, from its limited regional run.[16] By 1872, it was finally possible to travel all the way to Moscow by train, yet the repeated delays in the construction and integration of the railway system meant that Odessa was initially more connected to its surrounding maritime region than to the Russian interior, especially with the much earlier development of sail and steamship connections. As a result, the development of the region surrounding Odessa displayed two conflicting logics: the initial, port-oriented, aquatic logic, opposed to a more centralized, national logic. Where water logics highlighted the transnational potential of Odessa as an edge habitat, landed logics made it a periphery and implied more imperial demands—a situation correspondingly visible in New Orleans, notwithstanding its republican context. The map of the railroad tracks mirrored that tension, as Russia's defense strategies were more important than commercial and migration considerations in tracing their routes (Herlihy 2019, 232–33). The development of the railroads also meant that access to the port and water, while remaining "key factors" for Odessa, started losing importance and influence in the urban community (Sifneos 2017, 26).

Railroads, just like steamships, prompted the rise to prominence of new ports around the Black Sea—such as Batumi in Georgia. In the second half of the nineteenth century, Odessa started to look more inward, supporting the development of its local industrial sector, and no longer exclusively dependent on water. The increased mobility provided by steamships also contributed to level the reputation of the different centers of trade around the Black Sea, while that enclosed maritime space started losing its geographical prominence with the opening of the Suez Canal in 1869, which facilitated direct maritime trade with Asia. Ultimately, technological integration brought Odessa closer to the landed centers of Russian imperial power, enabling easier trade and communication with the interior, yet that connection underpinned the relative decline of the city. A similar transition transformed the shores of the Mississippi, as its basin shifted from an economic and settlement highway of national importance to a subsidiary regional center.

The site of New Orleans initially provided the best transshipment point before reaching open seas, its location on a meander of the Mississippi River, guaranteeing its economic prominence.[17] Aquatic mobility made New Orleans a central site for global exchanges (of goods and people, immigrants and enslaved), a role that reframes the history of the United States toward its Gulf South. This prominence seemed evident to contemporaries, who lauded the location of the city, and its position as the nexus of far-reaching maritime and riverine networks: "Standing on the extreme point of the longest river in the world, New Orleans commands all the commerce of the immense territory of the Mississippi, being the staple posited out by nature for the countries watered by this stream—a territory exceeding a million of square miles. . . . New Orleans is beyond a doubt the most important commercial point on the face of the earth" (Sealsfield 1828, 165–66). The rhetoric about New Orleans thus insisted on its incomparable situation at the intersection between land and water, which was only confirmed by the city's extraordinary economic and demographic growth within a few decades of American rule. Yet, because the port benefited from such a valuable natural advantage, it lacked backup technical, infrastructural, or legislative assets. The absolute reliance upon the Mississippi fostered a rather conservative approach to trade and business—the city, in the words of a local journalist, "[contented itself] with contemplating the Mississippi."[18] In other parts of the country, transport was undergoing tremendous transformations, which challenged the water logics that had given New Orleans its early prominence. The Erie Canal opened in 1825 and other artificial waterways and railways were built across the Eastern seaboard and in the trans-Appalachian region. Therefore, relying solely on the Mississippi's commanding course was not enough for the port of New Orleans to stay ahead, and the erosion of its natural advantages was soon visible. According to Richard Campanella, while in 1840 about 80 percent of western shipments went through New Orleans, by 1858 only 18 percent used that route (2008, 229–32).[19]

New Orleans's integration of water and landed routes suffered from delays because of the city's overreliance on the primacy of the Mississippi River. The first railway was eventually chartered in 1856, and construction began in earnest two years later. Although the construction of the railroad had only just begun, it was celebrated as a national event that would bring Louisiana closer into the fold of the national territory, by making it the end point of a cross-national journey: "The metropolis of the Nation has been linked to the metropolis of the South. The 'magnificent distances' of Washington terminate in the beaming 'crescent' of New Orleans!" (Ayres 1858, 5). Even as the port city was associated with the nation's capital, New Orleans, like Odessa, was also reframed as a peripheral capital, a terminus at the fringe of the continental nation. Once operational, the railroad was first connected to Houston rather than to the East Coast centers of political power. The route of the railroad progressively isolated New Orleans by removing it from the main axes of communication, previously embodied by the river, and further demoting the city in the center-periphery dialectic. The porosity of the Mississippi Delta, and its function as an edge habitat, also meant that New Orleans was a place where American identities were challenged and adapted, making it a disputed center within the United States.

If the Mississippi had been fundamental in the city's former preeminence, the river had also concealed the delays in acquiring railroad services by upholding momentarily the city's natural competitiveness. Nationwide, the development of railroads operated a cardinal change, with an east-west orientation supplementing the north-south natural axis of the Mississippi River basin. Eastern urban centers could now be directly supplied with produce originating from the Midwest and the western frontier, and although New Orleans's trade remained important in absolute numbers, its preeminence declined comparatively (Campanella 2008, 230).[20] By supplementing traditional riverine and marine connections, the increased technological connectivity contributed to the relative geographical and economic demotion of New Orleans, and contradicted earlier water logics. The third-largest city in the United States in 1840, New Orleans was only the sixth largest at the start of the 1860s, and never regained such a high rank. If anything, these new technological assets isolated New Orleans geographically and economically, rather than acting as a factor of integration.

Ultimately, technological change brought increased mobility to both New Orleans and Odessa, but it also eroded their unique features and position, making their waterborne position—the very same asset on which both cities had built their early commercial power—less relevant. The development of railroads further emphasized the advantages and shortcomings of the cities' integration into a broader region. While water, through its porosity, created convergence and supported the development of ecotones in the urban settings of Odessa as in New Orleans, that same fluidity eventually increased their territorial marginality. At a local level, regulating water was just as important for the vitality and morbidity of the two cities: beyond imperial integration, water logics—droughts and floods, with all their associated risks—conditioned their early urban settlements.

LIFE AND DEATH ON THE BLACK SEA AND THE MISSISSIPPI: WATER IN URBAN HISTORY

While the sites of Odessa and New Orleans had been chosen for the advantages they provided for the expansion of trade, their waterborne location and respective ecological context created infrastructural weaknesses and endemic hazards that plagued their first decades of existence and adversely impacted the lives of their inhabitants. From the absence of nearby rivers and springs in Odessa to the seasonal hurricanes and flooding in New Orleans, urban life had to contend with significant water-related challenges, themselves the source of persistent risks. New Orleans's history—both early and contemporary—has been punctuated by deadly floods that spread diseases, destroyed neighborhoods, displaced populations, and prompted extensive infrastructural efforts to mitigate waterborne risks (Powell 2013). Odessa, as a settlement project, had to contend with the growing population and activity tied to its maritime port. While its location was ideal to establish a commercial harbor, droughts, dust storms, and failed forage operations created obstacles to the development of a large metropolis. Thus, human control over water environments was essential to the expansion of both cities. The mastery of water and its alteration to align with land-based imperatives sought to meet the local demands of growing commercial cities embedded in transnational trade pressures, while also serving the national ambitions of increasingly integrated domestic marketplaces.

The fast development of Odessa, predicated on proximity to the sea, was paradoxically met with the daunting task of securing water suitable for consumption and use. As the city was not located directly on a river course, provision of clear water proved increasingly difficult, especially as the city grew spatially and demographically. The absence of nearby natural sources of drinkable water, combined with the dry and windy environment of the Ukrainian steppes, created droughts that were the source of constant worries for the municipal authorities and the imperial government of the southern provinces. Contemporaries repeatedly mentioned dust storms and concurred on the general filth of the new city, describing, in the absence of water, "whirlwinds of dust exactly like waterspouts in all but the material composing them, [which] darkened the air every moment, and swept the ground with incredible fury" (Hommaire De Hell and Hommaire De Hell 1847, 6).

To address persistent drought, foreign experts were brought in to locate artesian wells, but the city's elevated site—two hundred feet above sea level—made successful drilling nearly impossible (Spencer 1837; Gervits 2024). In the absence of an aqueduct, "people would generally use water coming from public wells," which barely sufficed to meet the needs of the population and the cattle that hauled wheat-laden carts into Odessa (Saint-Joseph 1820, 60). The water shortage hindered both urban growth and trade, as oxen-drawn carts remained essential for transporting agricultural produce to the port until mid-century. The nearest springs, located several kilometers from the city center, were "guarded as treasures," turning water carrying into a lucrative profession. Local historian Apollon A. Skalkovsky noted that that by 1839 water trade evolved into an entire branch of urban and suburban industry, with some entrepreneurs earning up to a thousand rubles annually by monopolizing scarce water sources and driving prices higher (Skalkovsky 1839, 23, 35–36). In response to the scarcity, residents resorted to rooftop cisterns to collect rainwater, but the water's often poor quality contributed to outbreaks of infectious diseases (Skinner 1973; Herlihy 1978). Any solution, as imperfect as it was, was welcome.

Throughout Odessa's early decades, ambitious plans to address the city's hydraulic problems were announced with great fanfare in local newspapers. For example, in 1833, the discovery of promising wells south of the city prompted the immediate construction of a reservoir tank and pump on the site (ONSL 971, 1833, no. 48, June 16 and 28). Yet these victories proved short-lived, and it was not until the completion of a canal to the Dniester River by the Odessa Waterworks Company in 1873 that clean water was reliably supplied. Despite this milestone, infrastructural improvements had limited effect, as the city's rapid population growth exacerbated persistent issues, including severe dust in summer, mud in winter, and inadequate sewage disposal.[21] An English traveler passing through Odessa described it as "in wet weather the dirtiest place [she] ever saw; and in summer the dust [was] as intolerable as the dirt in winter" (Holderness 1823, 78). The lack of fresh water compounded these issues, contributing to urban insalubrity, even though sanitation challenges were a common feature of urban modernity. Such environmental problems quickly tarnished Odessa's reputation, with newspapers regularly publishing similar accounts—the following humorously detailing the dire state of the city as late as 1840: "Being exposed to the most sudden changes of temperature and to violent gusts of wind, the dust is intolerable at times, and other times the mud runs in rivers or lies like stagnant lakes. A wit sketched a coat of arms for Odessa, and wrote for the motto, *qui trotte se crotte* [who trots about soils themselves].... not many years ago, individuals were drowned in the mud of the Greek Bazaar in winter" (Slade 1840, 327–28).

While on the arid Black Sea steppes water scarcity was a dominant concern, it was water abundance that posed challenges on the banks of the Mississippi River, chiefly because New Orleans developed in an alluvial plain that was, in some places, beneath river level. Only a frail levy protected the city from inundations. Cyclically, as snow in the northern regions melted away, accounts reported "the river [rising] higher than usual, and the levee not being able to resist the current and the force of the water, [bursting] and [inundating] the streets and houses to a height of more than four feet" (Robertson and Alliot 1911, 62). New Orleans had to contend with the abundance and excess of water, most often because of regular hurricane-induced floods. This situation was made more complex by the absence of an efficient water-management system.

The building of the successive city districts was shaped by reactions and responses to the difficult containment of these waters. Historian Lawrence Powell described New Orleans as an "accidental city" and contemporaries commonly referred to the city as *Île d'Orléans*, or Orleans Island, because it was more surrounded by water than by land (Powell 2013, 67). At the turn of the nineteenth century, American New Orleans had very little to do with its toponymic predecessor, *La Nouvelle Orléans*: little remained of the French colonial city following a widespread fire in 1788, and at the time of the 1803 Purchase, large parts of the city had not yet been rebuilt. The population growth had also remained quite modest, with only eight thousand inhabitants over eighty years after the settlement of the city, half of them enslaved. The start of American rule in 1803 drove immigration from other parts of the United States, while the arrival of thousands of refugees coming from the Caribbean, primarily from Haiti, more than doubled the population of the city within ten years of the Louisiana Purchase.[22] The transformation of the urban population itself resulted from the contiguity fostered by water spaces, a feature of New Orleans's edge habitat.

This rapid demographic development of American New Orleans into a large city put an unprecedented pressure on the natural site of what had been, up to that point, a large town at best.[23] More than anything, it was water that seasonally endangered the city: the combination of heavy rains, hurricanes, and floods brought chaos and death to a city nicknamed the "Necropolis of the South" (Campanella 2008, 281). Concerns arose over limited space for safe neighborhood expansion, as "the whole city [was] upon almost a dead level," making urban development "no easy matter" (Nichols 1864, 182). In contrast to Odessa's water scarcity, New Orleans grappled with the ominous challenges posed by water's abundance. In both cities, environmental pitfalls directed and often trumped settlement endeavors. In New Orleans, the powerful Mississippi River and its dynamic delta repeatedly destroyed neighborhoods and took lives, turning the city into a contested edge between competing human and ecological habitats.

Despite being a source of commercial prosperity and ascendency, the river was a constant threat and could very well sound New Orleans's death knell, as a visitor observed: "It rushes along through the busy region, seeming to be touched with mercy, or to disdain its power of mischief. It might overwhelm in an instant the swarming inhabitants of the boundless level: it looks as if it could scarcely avoid doing so; yet it rolls on within its banks so steadily, that the citizens forget their insecurity" (Martineau [1838] 2000, 134). Most of such deadly episodes were the consequence of bank erosion, spring flooding, and autumn tropical storms, while further overbank flooding also originated from Lake Pontchartrain, located on the northern limit of the city. The city was partially inundated in 1791, 1799, 1816, 1849, and 1865. As a result, the development of new neighborhoods to cope with demographic growth, such as Marigny and the Garden district, was significantly influenced by this omnipresent aquatic environment. Initially, Anglo-American newcomers constructed traditional East Coast–style houses, but they soon adapted to local ecological constraints, erecting taller structures that were built in higher density and on elevated terrain. Adaptability and innovation were a direct response to local water imperatives in this urban ecotone. And there was a good reason for it, because water not only surrounded New Orleans but also infiltrated its foundations, embedding porousness into the very structures of the city: "No attempt has been made at filling up, for there was nothing to fill with. There is no such thing as a cellar or a well, or any sort of excavation—not even a grave, as I can learn, in all New Orleans. One foot below the surface, and the mud is full of water" (Nichols 1864, 182). This contemporary writer concluded that "these may be the 'waters under the earth,' spoken of in the Scriptures," thus linking the environmental plague assailing the city to the physiological one (Nichols 1864, 182).[24] This conclusion was not completely foregone; flooding brought not only destruction to the city, but also an array of lethal diseases.

The tension between human settlement and water logics durably impacted urban cycles of life and death, to the point that New Orleans was sometimes described as a "wet grave" (Sealsfield 1828, 144). Paul Alliot, a French physician living in Louisiana at the turn of the nineteenth century, observed: "If New Orleans is not at all healthful, and if the bad air that its inhabitants breathe occasions fatal diseases, the reason is due in part . . . to the abundance of stagnant water, which for lack of drainage, lies the whole year round in the cypress groves which surround the city, and corrupts the air, which becoming putrid, poisons all who live there. On the other hand, during the rainy season, the streets are in a frightful state" (Alliot and Robertson 1911, 63). Alliot reported that a flood episode in the early 1800s left New Orleans' streets cluttered with rotten fish, causing the death of up to 3,000 residents. Overall, between 1796 and 1812, the city also endured eight yellow fever epidemics, nearly one every other year ("Quelques réflexions faites sur la Nouvelle Orléans par le Citoyen Alliot médecin adressées au Citoyen Laussat, préfet colonial de la Louisiane," HNOC MSS.125, f.128, April 14, 1803; hereafter MSS.125). Seasonal floods during the rainy months coincided with the summer heat, while rapid urban growth accelerated land clearing: the combination of these factors fostered the creation of prime breeding spots for mosquitoes and facilitated the spread of yellow fever.[25] Despite this health crisis, city leadership often resisted implementing federally administered quarantines, unlike other American ports, which enforced strict confinement and frequently refused cotton and other goods coming from New Orleans.[26] Despite New Orleans's commercial successes, its economic destinies were linked to its physiological health, with yellow fever representing a major "drawback upon its prosperity." As described by a contemporary health activist: "Once in three years on an average, for fifty years, the yellow fever—the dreaded vomito of the West Indies, Yellow Jack of the sailors, the most fatal of tropical epidemics—has visited New Orleans" (Nichols 1864, 197). Although survivors acquired immunity to the disease, its fatality rates still ranged between 40 and 50 percent. This disease disproportionately killed the city's vulnerable and transient populations of refugees, immigrants, and newly arrived enslaved people, while Americans from the northern states left the city in the summer if they could afford it.

Odessa, much like New Orleans, grappled with water management issues that were intertwined with sanitary challenges, as urban expansion exacerbated waterborne problems. A growing population heightened the demand for fresh water, while worsening existing issues caused by drought, dust, and the enduring absence of a sewage system. As discussed earlier, the water carted into the city was expensive and often of dubious quality, while rooftop rainwater collection contributed to outbreaks of bacterial diseases. Cholera, particularly during the second pandemic of the 1830s, significantly increased urban morbidity, while overcrowded living conditions further elevated health risks.[27] Although Odessa's southern location attracted those seeking relief in its supposedly favorable climate, the city's role as a seaport also facilitated the spread of lethal contagious diseases, including malaria, plague, and typhus—key vector-borne illnesses. Urban expansion in Odessa involved draining nearby marshes to accommodate its growing population. This effort reduced mosquito breeding grounds and mitigated malarial outbreaks—in contrast with New Orleans, where land clearing had the opposite effect. Additionally, the planting of trees also became a systematic policy to protect the soils from wind-induced erosion ("Plantation d'arbres sur le Pérésip pour le raffermir—Avis," ONSL 971, 1832, no. 26, March 30 and April 18).

As a port city, Odessa faced significant public health challenges, as its grain silos often harbored rat populations carrying fleas and incoming ships exposed the city to infections from abroad. In 1812, Europe's last major plague outbreak left 4,038 residents infected and claimed 2,632 lives out of a population of 20,000—about 10 percent of Odessa's urban population—marking one of the city's foundational hardships. Despite slow infrastructural improvements, a subsequent plague outbreak in 1829 still resulted in 2,458 victims (Herlihy 2019, 100–113). Odessa's role as a gateway city into the Russian empire heightened concerns about contagion due to its integration into the "seaside world." Port cities like Odessa and New

Orleans were often viewed with suspicion, seen as vulnerable to foreign influences and as conduits for both dangerous ideas and infectious diseases (Rothschild 2005). To mitigate these threats, Odessa introduced early isolation measures. Devastating epidemics led to the establishment of a mandatory quarantine lasting thirty to forty days for all merchants and visitors at Odessa's new lazaret, despite opposition from merchant guilds advocating for the abolition of such conservative rules.[28] While epidemics and diseases were a hallmark of Odessa's frontier identity, they notably did not incite pogroms or social unrest. Nevertheless water, the source of the city's prosperity, came with significant drawbacks. The sea and port were conduits for disease, while the lack of natural water springs and effective drainage systems facilitated contamination, compounding the city's health crises.

Odessa's local dearth of water and dusty environment meant that the city's mortality rates were higher among its young and older residents.[29] In the late 1830s, a foreign physician observed that in Odessa, endemic "dysentery prevail[ed], particularly among children, to an extent . . . unparalleled in any other country, proving fatal to at least one-third under four years of age" (Spencer 1837, 131). It is in response to high urban mortality rates that Odessa's government initiated infrastructural improvements such as modern hospital facilities and infrastructural work for water and sewage later in the century. While Odessa's mortality was initially higher than comparably dense cities—notably Berlin or London[30]—these measures proved successful in the long run: Patricia Herlihy notes that by the end of the nineteenth century, Odessa's death rate became lower than that of Moscow, St. Petersburg and other European cities such as Liverpool, Manchester, and Budapest (Herlihy 1978, 432).

The physical extension of Odessa's districts, as in New Orleans, was conditioned by efforts to mitigate the risk factors associated with water and diseases, along with the overall enhancement of its urban infrastructure. In 1856, quarantine regulations were abolished to facilitate business, and reflected a new epoch in the city's development and its mastery over its natural site.[31] Ultimately, water-related ecological constraints produced disease environments that framed the early histories of Odessa and New Orleans and characterized the complex and evolving connection between their sites and situation. Located on the geographical edges of large continental empires, the unstable nature of these emerging ports exemplified the centrality of water logics as an analytical tool, overlapping both local infrastructural concerns and transnational commercial aspirations. A hydrocentric perspective on their histories disrupts simplistic narratives of geographic determinism and inevitable commercial success, highlighting instead the influence of contingent events and factors.

As much as the existence of a port depends on its location along the shore of a body of water, the concept of water logics in urban history offers a multilevel framework for examining cities from both global and local perspectives. This essay applied this lens to the early histories of Odessa and New Orleans, comparing their role as emerging ports and human settlements situated on territorial edges. Through this transnational and environmental analysis, focusing on water informs intersections with and divergences from the units of empire. In regions as far apart as the Mississippi Delta and the Black Sea, water logics emphasize the uneasy and evolving connection between site and situation, revealing how cities in novel environments function as ecotones—zones that foster transformation and adaptation. This perspective challenges the typical view of these cities as peripheral within their imperial formations, repositioning them at the heart of aquatic geographies that connect land and sea.

New Orleans and Odessa offer valuable case studies for this analysis because their early urban trajectories exhibit notable similarities: both emerged as new urban centers distant from the political cores of their empires, competing as the outlets for agricultural frontiers, with rising and international populations. By focusing on the challenges posed by water, the essay shifts attention to how these cities defied conventional center-periphery dynamics and underscores the critical role of environmental factors in shaping their development. Despite significant differences in their hydrological conditions—New Orleans contending with an overabundance of water and Odessa with its scarcity—both cities faced volatile environments that profoundly influenced their destinies, reputations, and identities. Cycles of droughts, floods, and disease underscored the tension between human ambition and natural constraints. As ecotones on the edge of water, these cities became porous societies where the dynamics of adaptation and survival were continually negotiated. By framing New Orleans and Odessa through the lens of water logics, the essay not only aimed to highlight their shared struggles and innovations but also to invite a reevaluation of the broader interplay between urban development, environmental challenges, and imperial frameworks.

NOTES

This chapter grew out of a presentation and subsequent conversations that began six years ago at Tulane University in New Orleans, during an inspiring interdisciplinary conference on Water Logics that laid the groundwork for this edited volume. First conceived while I was still a doctoral candidate, this essay—through its many drafts and revisions—has accompanied me from the University of Oxford to Freie Universität Berlin, and now to my current academic home at the Institute of Historical Research in London, each version shaped by the evolution of my own research interests. I am deeply grateful to the volume's editors, yasser elhariry and Edwige Tamalet Talbayev, for their patient guidance over the years. I am also especially thankful to Marie Puysségur and Hitesh Dhorajiwala, who at various stages offered invaluable feedback on earlier versions of this essay—their careful reading and brutally honest comments exemplified peer support at its best.

Translation note: Unless otherwise indicated, all translations of quoted material from French or Russian are by the author.

1. In this essay, the Russian name "Odessa" will be employed in the context of its historical use in the eighteenth- and nineteenth-century documents, instead of the contemporary Ukrainian "Odesa." Similarly, some geographical landmarks, such as the Dnipro and Dnister River, will be referred to as Dnieper and Dniester for coherence with texts quoted. This choice does not reflect the author's views on current issues and toponymy.
2. The rapid urban development of Odessa and New Orleans was characteristic of settler cities located on new agrarian frontiers, attracting settlers. In addition to cotton, Louisiana became a key transit space for exports of cereal and provisions from the Midwest, while Odessa was the main port through which Ukrainian and Polish grain was traded.
3. The concept of ecotones, as developed by Lacroix et al. in the 2015–2020 conference cycle of the same name, contains an environmental nuance that adds complexity to the idea of edge habitat and underscores the critical potential of using water logics as an analytical tool by emphasizing porosity, risk, and adaptability.
4. As Thomas M. Barrett writes, "all of Russian history is presented as frontier history, beginning with Kiev and ending with Siberia. . . . Or, the Russian frontier is simply equated with the American one: Kazan becomes St. Louis, the

conquest of Novgorod is likened to the acquisition of Ohio from Britain, and the conquest of Ukraine is Russia's Louisiana purchase" (1999, 2).

5. After the abolition of the international slave trade by the US in 1808, New Orleans also became the main market for the domestic trade in enslaved people. See Johnson 2016.
6. "Resolved to establish, thirty leagues up the river, a burg which should be called New Orleans, where landing would be possible from either the river or Lake Pontchartrain" (Company of the West ledger, September 1717, qtd. in Campanella 2008, 97).
7. The name of the site was known in Choctaw as Bulbancha, "the place of other tongues," illustrating its early role as a trading hub.
8. Letter from Louis André Pichon, French *chargé d'affaires* (ambassador), Georgetown, to Pierre Clément Laussat (Historic New Orleans Collection; hereafter HNOC MSS.125, f. 458, January 15, 1804).
9. Other ports had been created by Russia on the northern shores of the Black Sea. Kherson, founded in 1778, was located on the estuary of the Dnieper River, Ukraine's largest waterway, crossing it from North to South while Nikolaev (Mykolaiv), on the Southern Bug River, had been instrumental in the building of a Russian fleet in the Black Sea, a major undertaking in the context of regular conflicts with the Ottoman Empire. Despite its lack of riverine connections, Odessa's site had other advantages for a trading port—the city was strikingly located on a cliff two hundred feet high, thus benefiting from a large and natural harbor. Rival harbors had additional problems linked to site and climate. Although Kherson was located on the Dnieper River, a major fluvial route across Ukraine, large boats could only sail upstream for a short distance, and the river's shallow waters remained frozen for several months.
10. Odessa received officially free-port privileges in 1817 (implemented in 1819), a unique status within the economically conservative Russian Empire. This status was renewed several times and lasted until 1859.
11. "The importation of all kinds of Merchandise is allowed even those articles which are prohibited at all other Ports of the Empire, but which are not allowed to be transported in the Interior from hence, as tea, refined sugars, strong spirits, cloths black and green, printed cottons, silks, and wools" (USNA II M459, vol. 2, f. 195).
12. Between 1815 and 1817, only 10 steamships were built, "compared to 69 in the next three years" (Belich 2010, 98). The port followed an explosive pattern of growth: in 1802, 256 vessels entered the Mississippi; by 1816 the number had grown to 1,867 vessels including 6 steamboats, with 87,670 tons of freight.

During the year 1836–37, 1,372 steamboats arrived, with the freight handled amounting to 401,500 tons (Winston 1924, 201–2).

13. "The Russian Steam Navigation and Trading Company has . . . now Steamers running to all the Ports of the Crimea, to all the principal Ports on the East Coast of the Black Sea, one weekly to Galtz, one weekly to Constantinople, a line to Jaffa, a line to Marseilles (tho this is not yet regular) a line to London conjointly with an English Company, besides occasional Steamers running to Athens and other Ports of the Mediterranean" (USNA II M459, vol. 2, f. 152, January 1857 and October 1859).

14. Additionally, the Black Sea trade was subjected to the regulations of the Ottoman authorities over the Bosphorus straits, which at times altered maritime navigation to Odessa.

15. "The more the quantity of products has increased, the more sensitive becomes, year after year, the necessity to improve communications between the villages and cities in the interior and the ports of the Black Sea" (ONSL 971, 1844, no. 58, July 2 and August 2).

16. It then became part of the joint stock company Southwestern Railways.

17. "We have been accustomed to look to the Mississippi as the protector of our greatness. We have thought that as long as the mighty . . . Father of Waters continues to roll past our city, our superiority in a commercial point of view, never can be successfully attacked" (NOPL, *Daily Picayune*, September 8, 1850, 2).

18. "Time, the corrector of all errors, has demonstrated the fallacy of our belief. It has shown us that we are by no means impregnable; that our situation, unequalled though it may be, can be made useless to us, when railroads and canals, intersecting the valley of the Mississippi in every direction, offer to the producer a cheaper and readier transit. . . . In the meantime, New Orleans has contented herself with contemplating the Mississippi, boasting of their magnificent position and unbounded resources, and yet has done nothing at all to preserve the advantages which nature has conferred to her" (NOPL, *Daily Picayune*, September 8, 1850, 2).

19. Richard Campanella writes that "New Orleans controlled over 99 percent of trans-Appalachian shipping up to 1825, but only 80 to 90 percent in the 1830s, 60 to 70 percent in the 1840s, and around 50 percent in the 1850s" (2008, 229–32).

20. After the 1830s, canals diverted a growing share of western produce directly eastward, but New Orleans's rapid growth initially masked its declining prominence. The expansion of railroads further deepened this divergence, and even the late addition of rail lines in New Orleans could not overcome its

geographical isolation or the denser rail networks connecting the Midwest to the East (Campanella 2008, 229–33).

21. "We are not used here to follow the police rules and to keep the streets in the state of cleanliness needed for their upkeep; that the indulgence granted ordinarily to the inhabitants of a new city has spoiled us" (ONSL 971, 1832, no. 19, March 4 and 16). Odessa only acquired a sewage system in 1878, while New Orleans only began to lay down sewer pipes in 1903 (Herlihy 2019, 107–8).
22. The population of New Orleans in 1803 was of about 8,000 inhabitants, with almost equal parts enslaved, free and formerly enslaved people of color, and white people. By 1812, the urban population neared 25,000.
23. Comparatively, Odessa already counted about 8,000 inhabitants ten years after its creation, even if it had faced difficult beginnings. Yet a large portion of this number was made up of members of the garrison—while in New Orleans, almost half of the urban population was enslaved.
24. See also Ermus 2018 and Solnit and Snedeker 2013.
25. Charles Sealsfield commented, "The years 1811, 1814, and 1823 were the most terrible of any for New Orleans. From sixty to eighty persons were buried every day, and nothing was to be seen but coffins carried about on all sides. Whole streets in the upper suburb, (inhabited chiefly by Americans and Germans) were cleared of their inhabitants, and New Orleans was literally one vast cemetery" (1828, 193).
26. It was not until 1900 that mosquitoes were isolated as a carrier of the yellow fever virus—initially they were just seen as a warning sign, and quarantine regulations were applied to products as well as to humans.
27. These epidemics inspired the composition of a large-scale medical report in 1834.
28. In Edward Morton's words, "the advantages, however, to be so gained would be but trifling, and the disadvantages numerous: among which an increased tendency to the propagation of contagion cannot be considered as the least: for it should be constantly borne in mind, that Odessa, from its locality, is always liable to the introduction of the plague" (1830, 198).
29. In 1832, the Odessa council of physicians found that about a third of deaths were newborns under a month old (ONSL 971, 1832, no. 37, May 6 and 18).
30. "You will see that mortality is much greater here than in many capital cities, because while in Petersburg the proportion of deaths in the population is about 1 to 25, in Moscow 1 to 32, in Berlin 1 to 36, in London 1 to 39 etc. in Odessa, 1 resident out of 24 dies annually" (ONSL 971, 1843, no. 7, January 22, and February 3).

31. "The abolition of the Quarantine regulations has greatly facilitated business, and if not imposed again, and when the projected railroads are also established, I look forward to Odessa reaching a very high rank among the Commercial Cities of Europe" (USNA II M459, vol. 2, f. 147, September 30 and October 12, 1856).

ARCHIVAL SOURCES

ARCHIVES DU MINISTÈRE DES AFFAIRES ETRANGÈRES, PARIS (AMAE)

227CCC: Nouvelle Orléans, Correspondance Consulaire at Commerciale
230CCC: Odessa, Correspondance Consulaire at Commerciale

HISTORIC NEW ORLEANS COLLECTION, NEW ORLEANS, LA (HNOC)

MSS.125: Pierre Clément de Laussat Papers

ODESSA NATIONAL SCIENTIFIC LIBRARY (ONSL)

898: *Courrier de la Nouvelle Russie*
971: *Journal d'Odessa*

NEW ORLEANS PUBLIC LIBRARY, CITY ARCHIVES (NOPL)

Daily Picayune

UNITED STATES NATIONAL ARCHIVES (II) AND RECORDS ADMINISTRATION AT COLLEGE PARK (USNA II)

M459: US Consulate, Odessa, Russia

WORKS CITED

Ayres, George B. 1858. *Descriptive Railroad Hand-Book of the Great Southern Route Between New Orleans and Washington*. G. B. Ayres.

Barrett, Thomas M. 1999. *At the Edge of Empire: The Terek Cossacks and the North Caucasus Frontier, 1700–1860*. Westview Press.

Belich, James. 2009. *Replenishing the Earth: The Settler Revolution and the Rise of the Anglo-World, 1783–1939*. Oxford University Press.

Burghardt, A. F. 1971. "A Hypothesis About Gateway Cities." *Annals of the Association of American Geographers* 61 (2): 269–85.

Campanella, Richard. 2008. *Bienville's Dilemma: A Historical Geography of New Orleans*. Center for Louisiana Studies, University of Louisiana at Lafayette.

Ermus, Cindy, ed. 2018. *Environmental Disaster in the Gulf South: Two Centuries of Catastrophe, Risk, and Resilience*. Louisiana State University Press.

Gervits, Maya. 2024. "Plague, Quarantine, and Environmental Design." *Planning Perspectives*, no. 39, 131–52.

Herlihy, Patricia. 1978. "Death in Odessa: A Study of Population Movements in a Nineteenth-Century City." *Journal of Urban History* 4 (4): 417–42.

Herlihy, Patricia. 2019. *Odessa Recollected: The Port and the People*. Harvard Ukrainian Research Institute; Brighton, MA: Academic Studies Press.

Holderness, Mary. 1823. *New Russia: Journey from Riga to the Crimea, by Way of Kiev*. Sherwood, Jones and Co.

Hommaire De Hell, Adèle, and Xavier Hommaire De Hell. 1847. *Travels in the Steppes of the Caspian Sea, the Crimea, the Caucasus, &c*. Chapman and Hall.

Johnson, Rashauna. 2016. *Slavery's Metropolis: Unfree Labor in New Orleans During the Age of Revolutions*. Cambridge University Press.

Khodarkovsky, Michael. 2004. *Russia's Steppe Frontier: The Making of a Colonial Empire, 1500–1800*. Bloomington: Indiana University Press.

Lacroix, Thomas, Judith Misrahi-Barak, and Jill Didur. 2019. *Ecotones #6: Post/Colonial Ports: Place and Nonplace in the Ecotone*. Concordia University. https://jilldidur.ca/home/projects/ecotones-post-colonial-ports-place-and-nonplace-in-the-ecotone/.

Lacroix, Thomas, Judith Misrahi-Barak, and Maggi Morehouse. 2014. Program. *Ecotones: Encounters, Crossings, and Communities, 2015–2020*. Université Paul-Valéry-Montpellier 3.

Martineau, Harriet. (1838) 2000. *Retrospect of Western Travel*. M. E. Sharpe.

McNeill, William Hardy. 2011. *Europe's Steppe Frontier, 1500–1800*. University of Chicago Press.

Morton, Edward. 1830. *Travels in Russia, and a Residence at St. Petersburg and Odessa, in the Years 1827–1829*. Longman, Rees, Orme, Brown, and Green.

Nichols, Thomas Low. 1864. *Forty Years of American Life*. Vol. 1. J. Maxwell and Company.

Oliphant, Laurence. 1854. *The Russian Shores of the Black Sea in the Autumn of 1852*. 4th ed. William Blackwood & Sons.

Powell, Lawrence N. 2013. *The Accidental City: Improvising New Orleans*. Harvard University Press.

Robertson, James Alexander, and Paul Alliot. 1911. *Louisiana Under the Rule of Spain, France, and the United States, 1785–1807*. A. H. Clark.

Rothschild, Emma. 2005. "Language and Empire, C. 1800." *Historical Research: The Bulletin of the Institute of Historical Research* 78 (200): 208–29.

Saint-Joseph, François Anthoine, de. 1820. *Essai historique sur le commerce et la navigation de la Mer-Noire; ou, Voyage et entreprises pour établir des rapports commerciaux et maritimes entre les ports de la Mer-Noire et ceux de la Méditerranée*. H. Hagasse.

Sealsfield, Charles. 1828. *The Americans as They Are: Described in a Tour Through the Valley of the Mississippi*. Vol. 2. Hurst, Chance and Co.

Sicard, Charles, and Stevens, Robert. 1819. *An Account of Odessa: Translated from the French, with Some Reflections, Showing the Benefits of the Trade of the Black Sea to the United States of America, and the Advantages of a Commercial Treaty with Turkey*. William Simons.

Sifneos, Evrydiki. 2017. *Imperial Odessa: People, Spaces, Identities*. Brill.

Skalkovsky, Apollon Alexandrovych. 1839. *Istorichesko-statisticheskii opyt o torgovykh i promyshlennykh silakh Odessy* [A historical and statistical study of the commercial and industrial forces of Odessa]. Odessa.

Skinner, Frederick. 1973. "City Planning in Russia: The Development of Odessa, 1789–1892." PhD diss., Princeton University.

Slade, Adolphus. 1840. *Travels in Germany and Russia: Including a Steam Voyage by the Danube and the Euxine from Vienna to Constantinople, in 1838–39*. Longman, Orme, Brown, Green, and Longmans.

Solnit, Rebecca, and Rebecca Snedeker. 2013. *Unfathomable City: A New Orleans Atlas*. University of California Press.

Spencer, Edmund. 1837. *Travels in Circassia*. Krim Tartary & Co.

Trollope, Frances Milton. 1832. *Domestic Manners of the Americans*. 4th ed. Whittaker, Treacher & Co.

United States Department of the Treasury Bureau of Statistic. 1888. *Commerce and Navigation*. Vol. 2 of *Annual Report and Statements of the Chief of the Bureau of Statistics on Commerce and Navigation of the United States for the Fiscal Year Ended on 30 June 1887; Internal Commerce of the United States*. Government Printing Office.

Winston, James E. 1924. "Notes on the Economic History of New Orleans, 1803–1836." *The Mississippi Valley Historical Review* 11 (2): 200–26.

WAVE LAB LOGIC

STEFAN HELMREICH

Begin with waves in a box. Figure 1 pictures an engineer surfing in a wave flume, a long, rectangular container made of concrete that serves as a narrow swimming pool–like channel down which wave scientists can mechanically generate waves of specified heights and periods. The photo, with its juxtaposition of Pacific Northwest surf culture and civil engineering enterprise, documents a circa 1974 publicity stunt undertaken to advertise the then-under-construction O. H. Hinsdale Wave Research Laboratory, a site at Oregon State University (OSU) where oceanographers, civil engineers, and others would, over the coming decades, study the patterns and properties of waves made to order, watery waves that could be designed to be set against scale models of coastal and maritime structures.

The wave flume (360 feet long, 12 feet wide, 15 feet deep) was the first infrastructural piece of a facility inaugurated in 1972 by Oregonian coastal engineers invested in building breakwaters at the mouth of the Columbia River, the largest river in the Pacific Northwest of North America. The Large Wave Flume, as the container came to be called, was built to test hydrodynamics relevant to that river-meets-the-sea purpose; wave modeling here was in early days all about learning to read and rewrite parts of the Columbia River—a river that environmental historian Richard White (1995) has called an "organic machine"—in order to ease waterway navigation for the Oregonian logging industry.[1] In 1989, the Hinsdale lab garnered funds from the United States Office of Naval Research to construct a Directional Wave Basin, a 300,000-gallon wave pool (160 feet long, 87 feet wide, 4½ feet at its

Fig. 1 Surfing in the wave flume at the early O. H. Hinsdale Wave Research Laboratory site, Corvallis, Oregon, circa 1974. (Hinsdale Wave Research Laboratory)

deep end) that could model not just one wave train at a time, but whole wave fields, and, significantly, and eventually, tsunamis, which have a different pulse and profile. After the Indian Ocean tsunami of 2004, the Directional Wave Basin came to be known, in connection with National Science Foundation (NSF) funding, as the Tsunami Wave Basin (see figure 2)

The lab, then, is equipped to tackle a range of wave problems. Scientists may come to the Hinsdale with NSF grants to investigate the effects of wave action on specific shorelines. Civil engineers may want to know how bridges will weather a storm. Oil companies may come with funds to test an oil platform model. Clients order up different species of waves—and those desires can be read, historically, for what they say about which waves are interesting to whom, when, and for what.

I visited the lab for an extended stay in 2015, encountering it at the edge of the OSU campus as a covered, airplane hangar–sized facility sited next to the scrubby pastures of the university's Department of Animal and Rangeland

Fig. 2 The O. H. Hinsdale Wave Research Laboratory Directional Wave Basin (known as the Tsunami Wave Basin from 2001–2011), 2015. (Photo by the author)

Sciences. Walking past sheep grazing at the border of the building's parking lot, I passed a sign that read "Entering Tsunami Hazard Zone"—a dry joke, since, at fifty miles from the Oregon coast, the city of Corvallis is far from any such watery danger. Still, as a center of tsunami research, the wave lab has become a site for working out, through scale models, how scientifically to grapple with all of those things: tsunamis, hazards, and zones. In the aftermath of the Tōhoku earthquake off the coast of Japan in 2011, the basin's designation as the world's largest tsunami tank kept Hinsdale central for studying those fast, long-wavelength waves generated by sudden displacements of water caused by undersea earthquakes or landslides. OSU faculty who use the Hinsdale maintain links to colleagues in Japan; one had been working as a visiting scholar at the Disaster Prevention Research Institute in Kyoto when the Tōhoku tsunami hit, and visited the surrounds of the devastated Fukushima Daiichi Nuclear Power Plant just afterward, the site of a disaster that unfolded at such a scale as to make the very notion of scale fail—setting into disorder in-place sociotechnical calibrations of human lives and infrastructures to the massive forces of the oceanic—a theme to which I will return.

On one of the first mornings of my fieldwork at Hinsdale, I found the lab's Education and Outreach Coordinator telling a visiting middle school class about the possibility of a calamitous tsunami arriving to Oregon's shores, a wave that, she informed the students, would arrive if there were to be a fracturing slip in the nearby Cascadia fault, an underwater subduction zone just seventy or so miles off the coast, where the Juan de Fuca, Explorer, and Gorda tectonic plates press against one another. The last Cascadia quake happened in the year 1700, but with geologists figuring a recurrence interval at about 250 years, there is growing worry that the Northwest may be due for another, maybe soon (Cascadia Region Earthquake Workgroup 2005; Henderson 2014; Schulz 2015). She showed the students a video of a 1:50 scale model of the coastal city of Seaside, Oregon, a color-coded, boxy mock-up of this tourist town constructed on the concrete shore of the tsunami basin. I joined the students in watching the miniature city inundated by a twenty-centimeter pulse of water meant to stand for a ten-meter tsunami.[2] Some students laughed, some gasped, and one asked, with a mix of anxiety and defiance, "Are we all going to die?" Most everyone was amused to learn that on-foot evacuation plans may be aided by adapting the *Zombies, Run!* fitness app, which tracks a person's movement with a blue dot on a smartphone map, helping them outrun virtually imagined waves of the undead. Uneasy laughter at this scale model indexes the unimaginable character of what it might herald.

What kinds of accounts, for planning and preparedness, do wave modeling and prediction—and not always or only about tsunamis—make it possible to assemble in this laboratory setting? How do scientists and engineers adjust and adjudicate the logic of scale, both for waves and for humans, at interacting and always-political state, coastal, community, neighborhood, and individual levels? How do they grapple with similitude—with discerning likenesses, making comparisons across scales of waves? What defines a "wave" or "waves" in a simulation circumstance in which mechanically produced waves exist both as physical processes in real water and as computationally described instantiations of established wave theories and models—as, that is, a superimposition of the real and the ideal, the actual and virtual? As researchers conjure their composite waves, they must discern which aspects of their waves are effects, artifacts, or confounds resulting from their model and which may be transposable to the world. Under construction are their ideas about watery agency and their views about how and whether humans can intervene to apprehend or control such agency—how *water logic* as the unfurling of fluid processes might inform as well as yield to *scientific logic*, a set of abstract formal and symbolic theories and methods for perceiving and representing regularities in the phenomenal world.[3]

Such ideas are formed in *practice.* In generating understudies for real waves, researchers must develop transformed perceptions of space and time, shifting their senses of speed and proportion in ways that have more than a little in common with cinematographic special effects thinking. When necessary, they must also learn to think backwards—to hypothesize, from wave observations in world and lab, what causal forces might have produced the phenomena they see, so that they might better reproduce these in the lab. In this essay, I argue that ordering the space and time of models is to make claims about which social aspects—and historical conditionings—of future coastal risks, hazards, and disasters, in Oregon and elsewhere, are significant and to whom. Waves, ordered and disordered (for example, disastrous waves in the world), become vehicles for thinking about the boundaries—scientific, technical, political, social—between control and calamity where sea meets land.

WAVES *IN AQUA:* MAKING FORM AND MATERIAL

When, by prior arrangement, I arrived at the Hinsdale in July 2015, Director Pedro Lomónaco was ready for me with some assigned reading. He handed me a copy of Robert G. Dean and Robert A. Dalrymple's *Water Wave Mechanics for Engineers and Scientists,* from 1991. This text contains canonical mathematical descriptions of waves and serves as an instruction manual for people interested in artificially generating waves using assemblies of powered pistons and paddles in wave tanks. It is one foundational text at the Corvallis Lab, a book of waves to consult when generating waves in the Large Wave Flume or in the Directional (Tsunami) Wave Basin. It contains a compendium of wavemaker theory, theory not so much about what generates waves in the wild (wind, earthquakes) as about how to reverse engineer, from desired outcomes, laboratory waves that imitate, that look similar to real-world waves.

Laboratories are sites where what scientists call "nature" is at once imitated, isolated, partitioned into processes of interest and noninterest, modulated into extremes, and, in such processes, summoned forth in technically and culturally constructed form (Knorr-Cetina 1995). The logic of such lab nature is realized through processes of simplification that take measured and abstracted parts to stand for complex wholes (for example, isolated DNA to stand for inheritance, subatomic particle collisions to stand for nuclear reactions in stars), and that record the interactions of such parts through what Bruno Latour and Steve Woolgar (1986) describe as inscription, the recording and reproduction of traces that stand for findings about the world. Lomónaco affirmed to me that "most of the time we are trying to reproduce something that is in nature—or our *representation*[it was audio recording conducted in July 2015] of nature. Sometimes we make sinusoidal waves—which are not natural, not something you see on the ocean, but which can be very good representations of our mathematical understanding of waves." He went on, saying that lab waves "are always a simplification of nature. You have to simplify turbulence, you have to simplify viscosity, and you have to simplify three-dimensionalities." And, he said, "You cannot actually do tsunamis. Not real tsunamis. You can try to reproduce some pieces of the big picture. The bore, or the wave itself, or forces, or just the beginning of those forces, and then you assume that the rest is not what you care about. So, you simplify your system, and then you generate the tsunami, you generate the wave that resembles a moment of the tsunami, or just some fractions in the forces of the tsunami." He told me that, in spite of 1990s worries that computer simulations would replace physical wave tanks, facilities like Hinsdale continue to have utility, especially since the qualities of the materials that waves hit—rocks, trees, sand, concrete, mixes of these—are difficult to capture in computer models. If wave basins have been imagined as the "laboratory" to the ocean's "field," they have more lately also became sites of "field testing" for computer models.[4] What counts as "lab" or "field" is not prespecified but rather the result of motivated framings.

Lomónaco was a generous guide into the world of wave tank modeling. He had just in 2015 taken up directorship of the lab after twenty years as the director of a similar facility at the University of Cantabria in Spain, after education in his native Mexico and in the Netherlands, at the Delft University of Technology. He was eager to talk, and had already become a practiced ambassador for this facility. Almost as soon as we sat down in person for the first time, I heard a loud crash just down from his second-floor office—the rushing collapse of a wave generated in the Wave Flume. The noise took me a bit by surprise with its emphatic whoomp (I later learned that the Flume generally runs 5-foot tall waves at 12 feet per second, quite fast). Hearing a crashing wave indoors was strange, and I immediately wanted to know what chain of human and machine and watery agency had created this plunging splash of water on concrete. Lomónaco took me to the control room. There, a research associate at a computer initiated wave impulses using a Windows interface that would permit him to choose such features as wave height and speed. A lot of the work here is automated; in fact, the lab itself has only four permanent staff—the director, a research associate (managing the software, hardware, and infrastructure at the lab), an education outreach coordinator, and a maintenance person. Scientists at a range of departments at OSU, as well as visitors from other institutions, work with the lab, but not every day.

The wave-inaugurating software I saw in action was written in a numerical computing environment and programming language called MATLAB and is tuned to interface with the wave paddles. Together, the software and hardware instantiate the wavemaker theory about which Lomónaco had told me.

Over the next few weeks, scientists told me more about how they conjured the waves they wanted in the laboratory. I came across a poster in the Hinsdale hallway that helped me think about the *water logics* in play in this lab (figure 3). This image, read left to right, morphs Katsushika Hokusai's famous 1829 woodblock print "Under the Wave off Kanagawa" into a digitized, scientific wave, suggesting a wave in the world being formally dissected and rematerialized in a computer.[5] In this transposition, it is worth noting, the fishers in the boats vanish (the people who are "under the wave"—for whom, in the image, the wave was most immediately significant), leaving a manageable, bitmapped nature, a promise of science spiriting away danger and terror. At the Hinsdale, there's a next step of transformation, of course, which is that mathematized waves are rematerialized in water, which then makes them "real" again, now as technical, rather than unpredictable things. They become entities around which engineers and planners might work. What is happening when impulses are pressed through water in wave tanks, then, is that particular mathematical models—abstractions—of wave action are giving shape to new waves. Any wave in the tank is thus a kind of artificial-natural hybrid, an "ideal" wave form made manifest in the material of a "real" wave.

Fig. 3 *The Wave of the Future,* by Judy Kirpisch and Alex Berry, 1981.

Software that realizes formulations in wavemaker theory is a switching point where models of wave action are set into operational motion, ready to be imparted to water. Such mathematical and computational models, of course, have a history to them: they enfold established, community-certified, peer-reviewed knowledge about wave dynamics. The shaping of such knowledge makes me think of similarities with, and differences from, the knowledge of waves documented by such scholars as Karin Amimoto Ingersoll, who in her *Waves of Knowing: A Seascape Epistemology* (2016) documents how *kānaka ʻōiwi* in Hawaiʻi come to know waves through oral history, chants, and surfing (see also Walker 2011)—a mode of fully social epistemology that is muted in dominant scientific and calculative approaches that emphasize formalisms and views of waves from outside or above. Scientists, of course, have their own embodied intuitions, including some from surfing, though these are usually treated as anecdotal or personal, rather than part of a corpus of authorized community knowledge.

I met up with Solomon Yim, a structural engineer at OSU since the late 1980s. He summarized the question before wave modelers seeking to imitate real-world phenomena in the lab: "How do you infer from a known wave pattern what it was that initiated it?" This is, he told me, an inverse problem, taking a known outcome and trying to reverse engineer an answer to what may have led to that outcome. In the case of making waves in the lab, it may sometimes be that a known wave outcome can be produced mechanically (through the mathematical and computational activation of wave pistons and boards) in ways that are simply similar, but not necessarily identical, to real-world causes.

What goes into modeling a wave? Yim reminded me that waves are characterized by their spectra, by the frequencies of which they are made up. Yim told me that making artificial waves meant imparting to water a suite of energies that recreate a desired spectrum. One of the artificial features of these spectra in the wave tank is that while waves in the ocean acquire their energy largely from the wind that creates waves, in this lab, there is no wind; spectral parameters in a model artificially fold wind effects into the substance of an artificially generated wave (fitting, perhaps, that, in the "Wave of the Future" image, Hokusai's clouds also disappear as the wave goes digital; note that other wave labs do use wind, which introduces additional calculations to do with scale and similitude and the composition of air).

Such spectra, Yim emphasized, are mathematical descriptions and, as such, are conceptual tools that change as mathematical and oceanographic communities fine-tune them. And the theories installed in wavemaker algorithms are only up-to-date as far as the 1980s, even as oceanographic theory has moved on. So, I asked Yim this: "Does that mean that if engineers today are working with wave spectra that were well characterized in the 1980s, that they are creating 1980s waves in 2015 water?" Are they still playing Madonna songs in an age of Beyoncé? His answer was an emphatic *yes*. I thought of 1980s vinyl recordings being transcoded into 2015 digital streaming files (see Sterne 2012). Matters started to snap into focus: wave machines *animate* equations, even theories—authorized and inherited community knowledge. What then happens is that the physics of the water and the tank itself become the *media* for theory—and in ways that, scientists hope, do not interfere or produce lab artifacts added on top of the target waves (on water as media, see Peters 2015 and Jue 2020). *Artificial waves become a superimposition of theory and reality,* a chimera, a thought experiment made water. Yim gave me a more down-to-earth reading: "Mother Nature still governs the lab, too, right? The laws of physics still apply in the lab." An artificial model of a real wave is still itself a real, physical, wave.

Still, any given model may be deficient. Make the analogy, he now instructed me, of waves to *animals* and consider that the task of wave modelers might be to replicate the diversity of the animal world, to create models, say, of both cats and dogs. Current wavemaker theory, he suggested, could only make "cats," when we know that there are also "dogs" out there. Some tweaking can be done to make some of the cats look more like dogs, but, in general, he told me, "wavemaker theory is really only cat theory; the linear wave theory is our common shorthair American tabby." But there are, he said, many more interesting nonlinear waves—dogs—out there. I could not help but think of these domestic animal analogies as pitching artificial waves as entities to be sculpted, even carved down to size, by human enterprise (see Helmreich 2019). Mechanically made waves install the formalisms of the people whose work is reflected in them, a realization I attach, fancifully, to the lab's press image of one of its open-house events (figure 4).

Yim then arrived at another metaphor. The lab, he told me, is engaged in the *3D printing* of waves, in water.[6] When I relayed this metaphor to Lomónaco, he ran with it, telling me, "Right, so when you print a picture with a dot matrix printer, you can tell it's correct, but it's not exactly the same. It's blurry. It's imperfect. But when you have a color laser printer, you will have a very nice picture that is very close. So, yes, that analogy applies." Scientists know that their waves are artifactual and that modeling choices—which pick out which dimensions of waves are significant and to whom—then provide limits on how faithfully they can render lab waves similar to real-world ones. They are producing likeness, not sameness, and they know that media

Fig. 4 Attendees at an open house for the Hinsdale lab, reflected in a wave traveling down the Directional Wave Basin. (Photo by Sol Neeman)

matter. I began to see the waves in the wave tanks not just as mathematical texts written in water but as pictures—even moving pictures, maybe even animated 3D movies.

WAVES AS CINEMA: SPACE AND TIME

The mechanically produced waves in the Hinsdale basins are images, images in motion. Waves, taken as visible objects, are portioned into instants and reassembled in the space-time of the viewer, who comes to see lab waves as at once empirical things and as a kind of animation. Experienced and interpreted from outside, such waves make me think of philosopher Henri Bergson's early twentieth-century concept of the *movement-image,* a notion he theorized to reflect on the effect of the then-new technology of cinema: "instead of attaching ourselves to the inner becoming of things, we place ourselves outside them in order to recompose their becoming artificially" (1907, 332; see Deleuze 1986).

How do scientists interpret these images? One day, a video crew arrived to gather footage for a web documentary on tsunami modeling. They shuttled lights around, setting themselves up to film some half-meter waves speeding across the Directional Wave Basin. The tank's concrete shore hosted a 1.5-foot-tall model of a building (which researchers dubbed a "hotel"), giving the incoming waves a scale (as one of the researchers told me: "you have to have a model to have a scale!"). The video team zoomed in on the mechanical paddles that generate waves, paddles that they had been informed were set in motion by a person at a computer in a control room perched above the shore side of the basin. As that person looked down out of a small window, he reminded me of nothing so much as a movie projectionist peeking out from an overhead booth. The scientists on the lab floor communicated with him via walkie-talkies, asking him to "run some waves."

When a member of the visiting film crew was given control of the walkie-talkie, she offered overlapping jargon: "roll 'em!" I could not help but think, then, of these waves as 3D movies, movies in a material—water—that, like that once-upon-a-time illuminated celluloid, has its particular affordances and resistances. This was a coincidence between *real waves* and *reel waves*. Not so much, now, the book of waves I was given at the beginning of my visit, *Water Wave Mechanics for Engineers and Scientists*, but a *cinema of waves*.

That coincidence between the real and the reel, however, has a strange temporal logic. All is not linear, frame-to-frame time here. There is something hidden from the untrained eye about "time" as it exists in the scale model. When wave scientists make a 1:100 scale model of a tsunami, space scales down at a different rate than time. This is because the molecular structure of water and the force of gravity cannot themselves be miniaturized (it is also the case that the tank does not use salt water, since that wears on the infrastructure; as one engineer told me, "We have to use all kinds of fancy math to calibrate"). And so, modeling a 10-meter-tall tsunami by generating a lab wave that is 100 times smaller (10 centimeters tall) does not yield dynamics that unfold 100 times faster, as one might think (nor, as some might also think, at the same speed). Rather, the temporal unfolding of such a wave will be described by the ratio

$v\sqrt{gd}$

where v = the velocity of flow

g = gravitational acceleration

d = depth of water

to account for those aspects of water that are not scaled down (compare with Jue 2014). The ratio—proposed by nineteenth-century English hydrodynamicist William Froude—suggests that if one wants to watch a real-time film of a 1:100 scale model tsunami and have it "look" anything like a "real-world" event, it needs to be slowed down by 10, not 100 times. Hollywood filmmakers know this well and do such calculations whenever they destroy a scale model city with a wave of real water, whenever they summon what environmental historian Gregg Mitman (1990), in his analysis of nature films, might call *reel nature*. To watch a video replay of a wave run in the lab, *reel time* needs to be slowed down by the inverse of the square root of gravity times depth—the Froude similitude (said out loud, these words rhyme)—in order to give the impression of *real time*, which, recursively, is only available through such *reel time*.[7] What is in play here is similitude, the similarity, as legible through geometry and dynamics, of a phenomenon at one scale with a phenomenon at another.

So, if making waves and filming them is, perhaps, to quote anthropologist of cinema Anand Pandian, "participating in the creative process and potential of a larger universe beyond the human" (2015, 8), that *beyondness* may sometimes be wrestled back into sensorial access by media technique—though, as I will discuss in connection with human experiences of tsunamis, such beyondness often never goes away, remaining in the register of the traumatic, sometimes unspeakable, terror-sublime. The agency of water—immanent water logic—cannot be fully filtered through the logic of formal wave models.

Viewers of artificial waves, of time-corrected video of such waves, and of footage of real-world tsunamis often gather their sensibilities about how to compare these phenomena through experiences across screens—cinematic, computer-y, and documentary. They develop what anthropologist Cristina Grasseni (2014) calls "skilled vision," a hybrid viewing that permits them to see in physical objects those features that might be modulated by technical action (Grasseni's examples are from the biological world, having to do with how breeders learn to see different potentials in the cattle they domesticate). Pandian writes that "vectors of experience . . . undo the very distinction between subjects and objects of human action" (2015, 272). That is certainly the case here in the wave lab, as waves as objects become infused with, mirror, subjective human purpose. The vector of experience into which I was being initiated as I began to see a slice of the world through a mathematical formula made me see these waves differently. The scientists around me now struck me as science fiction aliens able to see in two temporalities at the same "time," a skilled vision that permitted them to see the waves as hybrids, natural, and artificial. Lomónaco told me this: "You get used to that. Because everything is relative, you get used to having a picture in your head. Things are happening at a different pace than you expect. So, when you see a wave in the lab that is moving very fast, and you see these model boats rocking very fast, you know, in your head, you reproduce that image, and you know everything you see should be happening in slow motion." Some of this is about speed as a sensation, "not sheer velocity as such but the impression of shifting from one velocity into another" (Pandian 2015, 222)—where such impressions, for wave scientists, require not just tuning for "exaggerated speed and slow-motion torpor" (226) but, back to the equation above, knowing how to move through exponential, not linear, time. That back-and-forth perceptual movement is the result of researchers asking themselves constantly to see water logic through scientific logic, with scientific logic demanding attention to scale, a quality-quantity that is always an abstraction, not immanent in water "itself."

WAVES TO ORDER: PARAMETERS AND ARTIFACTS

When the lab is not running waves for television documentaries, what sorts of waves does it model? That depends on the clients for whom they are doing their work.

Lomónaco told me that after early work on river waves, the lab saw a number of projects on "biofouling," the accretion of unwanted organisms—algae, animals—on wet marine structures such as piers. The question was how wave action on such conglomerations might put measurable pressures on marine infrastructures. Then, in the first decade and a half of the century, tsunamis came into focus—the National Science Foundation in 2001 designated the lab as a key location for tsunami research—and some ninety-or-so percent of lab work was on these sorts of waves (Briggs et al. 2010). When that dedicated tsunami grant ran out, around 2014, a new public rhetoric of relevance appeared: "multiple hazards"—the tank was now pressed to account for waves not just from tsunamis but also from hurricanes (even though wind is not a physical input into the models but is folded into the generating wavemaker equations). "Resilience," Lomónaco said, became the new watchword, with hurricanes Katrina and Sandy as reference points. Most recently, another set of interests has emerged that has turned to the wave lab to explore *wave energy*, the mechanical extraction of power from the rise and fall of ocean waves. Waves, then, belong to their historical moment, approached, on the one hand, as dangers and, on another, as promising energy infrastructure. Think of the lab, again, as a film studio, with clients contracting the facility to produce movies to order, for audiences whose demands and preferences change over time.

Getting model waves in the lab to behave in ways that scientists and clients want takes negotiation. Clients might order a certain periodicity—a wave every eight seconds, for example—or a reliable height. Or they might want a more general picture. Lomónaco drew a distinction for me:

If you have a single wave, you can analyze all the details of the shape of that particular wave. But if you have a sequence of one thousand waves, you cannot study all the details of them. You have to represent that into a single parameter, significant wave height, so you kind of average what's going on. You don't care about the details. I approach one case like I care about the shape of individual waves, and another like I care about the spectrum and the probability distribution of the waves.

It is not always easy to meet client desires. The lab facilities have idiosyncratic parameters and it takes time to set up experiments, to fill the wave tank with water as well as to set in place measuring instruments. Former director Dan Cox told me: "People come to the lab with certain demands, or they want a certain spectrum, or they want a certain frequency, or a certain kind of set of profiles for wave things, and then you come back to them and say, 'yes, we can do that,' or 'we can kind of do that . . .'" Some clients rush in after having done models on computers and then expect the in-water world to behave the same way. They may assume that waves will break at a particular point because the mathematics they have done gives them that expectation. As Cox told me,

> So, if they do a lot of numerical work first, they kind of synthesize a certain sea state. And then we'll generate waves, and just naturally they'll break, and they'll come out a little bit small. And then the client is very unhappy that the waves are too small. And you have to explain to them, "You're never gonna get 'em," right? Just because the numerical models and textbooks tell you you're going to have a wave break when it reaches 0.78 of the stable height . . . it's not reality. Because waves will break sooner than that!

There may also be cases when "you've got larger waves moving faster than these smaller waves, sometimes they'll superimpose here, and they'll start to trip and break. There're just so many factors that come into play."

Lab engineers may argue with clients about the model they are after, too. Scale is not a given but a discussion. As one engineer at OSU told me,

> In a recent proposal, I was reproducing a fraction of a port in one-in-fifty scale, which is about the limits of what you can do with scaling when you are studying the stability of breakwaters. Sometimes you can go one in

sixty, but it depends. And the client says, "Can you do this in one in forty? Because I don't like one in fifty." And then I, well, take a look at it, and say, "I think I can, but there is a trade-off. I cannot reproduce all of the breakwaters you want to reproduce, it's gonna be smaller. And you will have some other effects."

The wave basins also have properties that need to be taken into account, properties that sometimes lead to artifacts in the data. As Cox told me,

> a whole other part of the problem is that the laboratory itself introduces artificial walls. There's re-reflection, and limitations on what the wavemakers can do. These are all effects of being in a laboratory. The most notorious one is the current. In the ocean, currents are just going to go along the coast or out to sea, but we're in a box, and those currents are just coming back in. And if you keep running things for a long time, it's just a soup of currents.

So, there are physical features of the wave tanks that need to be taken into account in any simulation. Lomónaco told me, too, that sometimes it is possible to superimpose one client's project on another, taking advantage of a common wave field. Getting a wave experiment set up requires physical and social engineering, and thinking, too, from the scale of the lab to matters of concern in the world.

WAVE MODELS MEET THE SEASIDE

Take the Hinsdale laboratory's work on a scale model of the coastal Oregon town of Seaside, a hamlet of about seven thousand people just south of the mouth of the Columbia River. Dan Cox, who was lab director when the Indian Ocean tsunami hit, told me how that disaster had prompted efforts to model tsunami inundation effects in Oregon. He and his colleagues had the idea of modeling a generic coastal city, a black and grey checkerboard with blocks of different heights. When that effort did not get funded, they added color coding to call out residences, commercial sites, parking lots. And when *that* did not get funded, they decided to model a specific city, with recognizable landmarks, hoping to make the local relevance of their science crystal clear. They selected the city of Seaside because, with its largely flat shore and downtown, it was dramatically vulnerable to a tsunami coming from the Cascadia subduction zone, with a possible wave arriving in just twenty minutes. Cox told me some people in Seaside worried that the town would lose tourist revenue with the public attention that might come from this project—and there were instances of residents taking tsunami warning signs down to protect their town's image as a safe harbor. Eventually, most residents embraced their new status, with some even making light of their newly described locale with restaurant names like Tsunami Sandwich Company or Tsunami Bar and Grill.

One of the papers Cox and colleagues published (in early 2011, before the Japan tsunami) about the Seaside model, "Optical Measurements of Tsunami Inundation Through an Urban Waterfront Modeled in a Large-Scale Laboratory Basin," illustrates a few things about working with scale and similitude. First, that, from the scientists' point of view, the entity to be modeled may already offer the possibility of scaling well. The paper spells out the reasons for choosing Seaside: "First, the constructed environment (seawall, hotel, residential and commercial buildings) were [sic] typical of coastal communities at risk to tsunamis with populations concentrated within the first 200m of shoreline. Second, the bathymetry at Seaside was fairly easy to construct, with uniform, shore-parallel contours and a relatively flat spit on which the buildings were constructed. Third, the USGS report gave reasonable guidance for the expected tsunami height triggered by a Cascadia Subduction Zone event" (Rueben et al. 2011, 230). Second, that the choice of scale brings some things into focus and not others. The model was built at 1:50 scale, a degree of resolution that, the article points out, unlike previous 1:200 scale models, permitted researchers to grapple with such things as the effect of building shapes and densities—here, "eight large hotels and five large commercial buildings" as well as "residential structures"—on the flow of a tsunami across land, while leaving out "vegetation, small-scale roughness, debris or sediments" (a subject for another scale and, indeed, one that my one-week office-mate at Hinsdale was working on). They learned, Cox told me, about how large buildings at the shore affect smaller buildings farther away: "At first, we thought that the large buildings would provide sheltering from the wave, but it turned out that some areas further back were subjected to flow convergence—it seemed that the forces could increase because of larger buildings," which, spaced close together, might focus wave energy.

With respect to the modeled wave, different aspects of wave behavior had to be weighed against one another: "The biggest scale effect is the wavelength. Tsunamis inundate the coast for several minutes and this continuous inundation is very hard to reproduce in the lab, so we focus on the leading edge." So, arguing that a single, solitary pulse from the lab's wavemaker might create a wave that was too neat, too symmetrical, and might underestimate durations of inundation, Cox and company sought to create a bit of noise, or error, around the "solitary wave algorithm" they used to generate the model tsunami. Such error had to be distinguished from "short term variations due to [lab] building vibration or wind response and long term variations due to thermal expansion or building creep" (Rueben et al. 2011, 232). They might also, at the inundation point, switch to computer modeling.

Getting information out of the model required technologies not only of photography and digital video, but also techniques that could bring into visual relief "the leading edge of the tsunami front," which turned out to require converting "color images to intensity images, assigning each pixel a scalar value that represents its overall brightness, instead of the three values (red, green, and blue) required for color images" (Rueben et al. 2011, 233). Video images of waves, in other words, had to be treated to bring into visibility what people who needed to run away from a wave front would need to know. Revaluing the pixels in the video also permitted researchers to see patterns of turbulence, and wake areas behind hotels—something Cox told me he saw evidence of when he looked at the aftermath of 3/11. Running the experiment over and over again (136 times) generated a spread of likely wave fronts ("an algorithm was developed to detect the landward-most statistically significant bright point and then a polynomial curve was fitted to the raw edge, producing an initial estimate of the wave edge" [Rueben et al. 2011: 235]), which could then be looped into evacuation planning. Visits to Seaside "to look at building stock, to talk to the city engineer and some of the building owners to get a sense of the structural integrity of the buildings," provided knowledge to be fed back into the physical model.

One of Cox's colleagues, Oregon State University civil engineer Harry Yeh, reflected on the back-and-forth between such models and the world:

> Tsunamis interact with intermediate scales of bathymetry and topography, and so, scale effects are a crucial issue for studying tsunami dynamics. But our lack of field data can make this difficult. Tsunamis are rare, and so we

do not have a sufficient empirical "feeling" for the phenomenon. Prior to the 2004 Great Indian Ocean event, video footage of real tsunamis was almost nonexistent. So, we attempt to understand tsunami behaviors in the controlled laboratory environment. The large tsunami basin in Hinsdale is often used to simulate tsunamis, but there are still potentially substantial scale effects we can't see.

Just one month after the work on the 1:50 model of Seaside was published in *Coastal Engineering,* the Tōhoku earthquake off the coast of Japan generated the tsunami that devastated the Miyagi, Iwate, and Fukushima prefectures on March 11, 2011. Cox was in Japan and visited the Tōhoku region:

> I was not prepared for how much of an impact it had on me when I went there for the first time. I had been at the museum at Hiroshima the previous week, but still I would say that the most immediate thing was how different photographs are from reality. We think photographs are kind of like a bit of reality, but it's totally different. You know, once you're there, you're looking around, you're looking up, and it's like, "I can't believe this happened." I was not prepared for what I saw—I was a textbook wave guy, not really prepared for that first field visit.

The 2011 Japan tsunami now hovered as a cautionary tale, an event revisited again and again as both potentially similar to and different from what might happen sometime in the next decades in cities like Seaside all along the northwest North American coast. Cox pointed me to some differences:

> Thinking back to the Japan tsunami of 2011, there were a lot of regions that were affected that had different coastlines. Some of the most heavily impacted areas were along Japan's ria coast, which is quite different from what we have here in the Northwest. The ria coasts were formed from drowned river valleys and look more like fjords, with deep, narrow embayments that funneled a lot of water into the towns. The Sendai plain was wide and fairly flat, so the local tsunami run-up was a lot lower and the tsunami inundated that area for several kilometers. Even in the "same" event, local conditions made a huge difference. So, for the Pacific Northwest, we would also need to really look at each area carefully.

Yeh pointed to similarities between eastern Japan and the Pacific Northwest: "The source of the 2011 tsunami was approximately five to six hundred kilometers long and two hundred kilometers wide. Tsunami-affected coasts are larger than the source because tsunamis propagate. A potential Cascadia event could be similar, with large affected coastal areas, from British Columbia to northern California. This is quite different from hurricane or earthquake hazards, which are more local." Thinking at different scales, in other words, makes similarities and differences slide in and out of view; scale-making is similarity-and-difference-making. And it sometimes fails, as effects from one scale spill over or inflect another (Clark 2012).

The water logics and scientific logics in action at the Hinsdale wave lab, then, sit within nested sets of concerns—local, regional, oceanic—and they are calibrated to those scales through work that is all at once technical, embodied, abstract, civic, industry-minded, and more. The next time you see a wave breaking on a built-up shore, think of how many times its imitation predecessors have been tested for their form, force, and logic.

NOTES

1. The logging industry arrived in the 1880s, along with white American westward settler colonialism, which displaced Oregon Indians to reservations such as Grand Ronde, Siletz, Warm Springs, and Klamath. Oregonian businessman O. H. Hinsdale, for whom the OSU lab is named, hailed from a family that once owned the Umpqua River Steam Navigation Company, which was involved in the timber business (with the name "Umpqua" lifted from dispossessed Native inhabitants). The Hinsdale webpage features a poem about him, written by friend Peggy Hoecker, part of which reads: "A generous philanthropist,/O. H. Hinsdale had a dream,/Of recreating ocean waves by the use of a machine" (https://wave.oregonstate.edu/history).
2. For a report on the experiment, see Rueben et al. 2011.
3. If the figure of the wave offers what literary theorist Nathalie Roelens describes as "revolving movement as the unveiling of a latency," this is always "implicit against Euclidian geometry" (2019). In her 1999 book on waves, Marie Darrieussecq writes, "the wave is by its essence a formal modification of matter, with its creation of froth, vapor, sprays, breaks and shocks" ([1999] 2014, 29–30).

4. On the substitution of computer simulations for physical experiments, see, to begin, Galison 1997 and Winsberg 2010. On the lab-versus-field distinction more generally, see Kohler 2002.
5. Interestingly, this poster is a 1981 ad for a software company, and the pixel images in its middle were rendered by hand, in pencil.
6. The printing idiom may be fitting, since Corvallis, Oregon, is the home of that segment of the Hewlett-Packard Company, responsible for inventing the inkjet printer.
7. See Weston 2002 and Riles 2004 for more on "real time."

WORKS CITED

Bergson, Henri. (1907) 1911. *Creative Evolution*. Translated by Arthur Mitchell. Henry Holt and Company.

Briggs, Michael J., Harry Yeh, and Daniel T. Cox. 2010. "Physical Modeling of Tsunami Waves." In *Handbook of Coastal and Ocean Engineering*, edited by Young C. Kim, 1073–105. World Scientific Publishing Company.

Cascadia Region Earthquake Workgroup. 2005. "Cascadia Subduction Zone Earthquakes: A Magnitude 9.0 Earthquake Scenario." Cascadia Region Earthquake Workgroup. https://www.oregongeology.org/pubs/ofr/O-05-05.pdf.

Clark, Timothy. 2012. "Scale." In *Telemorphosis: Theory in the Era of Climate Change*, vol. 1, edited by Tom Cohen. Open Humanities Press.

Darrieussecq, Marie. (1999) 2014. *On Waves*. Translated by Peter Schulman. VVV.

Dean, Robert G., and Robert A. Dalrymple. 1991. *Water Wave Mechanics for Engineers and Scientists*. World Scientific Publishing Company.

Deleuze, Gilles. 1986. *Cinema 1: The Movement Image*. Translated by Hugh Tomlinson and Barbara Habberjam. University of Minnesota Press.

Galison, Peter. 1997. *Image and Logic: A Material Culture of Microphysics*. University of Chicago Press.

Grasseni, Cristina. 2014. "Skilled Vision: An Apprenticeship in Breeding Aesthetics." *Social Anthropology*, no. 12, 41–55.

Helmreich, Stefan. 2019. "Domesticating Waves in the Netherlands." *BOMB*, no. 146, 153–58.

Henderson, Bonnie. 2014. *The Next Tsunami: Living on a Restless Coast*. Oregon State University Press.

Ingersoll, Karin Amimoto. 2016. *Waves of Knowing: A Seascape Epistemology*. Duke University Press.

Jue, Melody. 2014. "Proteus and the Digital: Scalar Transformations of Seawater's Materiality in Ocean Animations." *Animation: An Interdisciplinary Journal* 9 (2): 245–60.

Jue, Melody. 2020. *Wild Blue Media: Thinking Through Seawater*. Duke University Press.

Knorr Cetina, Karin. 1995. "Laboratory Studies: The Cultural Approach to the Study of Science." In *Handbook of Science and Technology Studies,* ed. Sheila Jasanoff, Gerald E. Markle, James C. Peterson, and Trevor Pinch, 140–66. SAGE Publications.

Kohler, Robert. 2002. *Labscapes and Landscapes: Exploring the Lab-Field Border in Biology*. University of Chicago Press.

Latour, Bruno, and Steve Woolgar. 1986. *Laboratory Life: The Construction of Scientific Facts*. Princeton University Press.

Mitman, Gregg. 1999. *Reel Nature: America's Romance with Wildlife on Film*. Harvard University Press.

Pandian, Anand. 2015. *Reel World: An Anthropology of Creation*. Duke University Press.

Peters, John Durham. 2015. *The Marvelous Clouds: Towards a Philosophy of Elemental Media*. University of Chicago Press.

Riles, Annelise. 2004. "Real Time: Unwinding Technocratic and Anthropological Knowledge." *American Ethnologist*, no. 31, 392–405.

Roelens, Nathalie. 2019. "The Wave as an Epistemological Challenge Today." Paper presented at Water Logics, Tulane University, New Orleans, LA, April 11–12.

Rueben, Matthew, Robert A. Holman, D. Cox, Sungwon Shin, Jason R. Killian, and J. Stanley. 2011. "Optical Measurements of Tsunami Inundation Through an Urban Waterfront Modeled in a Large-Scale Laboratory Basin." *Coastal Engineering*, no. 58, 229–38.

Schulz, Kathryn. 2015. "The Really Big One." *The New Yorker,* July 20. https://www.newyorker.com/magazine/2015/07/20/the-really-big-one.

Sterne, Jonathan. 2012. *MP3: The Meaning of a Format*. Duke University Press.

Walker, Isaiah Helekunihi. 2011. *Waves of Resistance: Surfing and History in Twentieth-Century Hawai'i*. University of Hawai'i Press.

Weston, Kath. 2002. *Gender in Real Time: Power and Transience in a Visual Age*. Routledge.

White, Richard. 1995. *The Organic Machine: The Remaking of the Columbia River*. Hill and Wang.

Winsberg, Eric. 2010. *Science in the Age of Computer Simulation*. University of Chicago Press.

THE WAVE AS AN EPISTEMOLOGICAL CHALLENGE TODAY

NATHALIE ROELENS

> The human being who comes to scrutinize these breaths and waves
> —If spectators for these profound things exist—
> Feels himself mingled with this quivering,
> And in this enormous rut vaguely attracted . . .
> —VICTOR HUGO, "Dieu, fragments," 1857[1]

INTRODUCTION

Within the marine episteme, the pattern of the wave deserves special attention. This turbulent object leads to an epistemological challenge since it requires complex thinking, resorting to a synergy between exact and human sciences to circumscribe its fluidity and its hidden structure. Today the phantasm of domesticating the wave is a reality: tidal power plants and new techniques for converting wave energy are spreading rapidly. Besides, the wave entails dreams of the unknown and produces charming and monstrous chimeras. As a hypostasis of experience, the wave figures the unpredictable and dismantles established values. My hypothesis is that artworks that represent waves or their collateral effects, as they shed new light on them and reshape their contours, could emphasize the need to recognize "wave studies" and to raise awareness of the "hydric stress" of countries with submersible areas. This assumption is in line with the findings of philosopher Jean-Jacques Wunenburger, who, facing the epistemological dilemma between scientific intelligence and poetic imagination, distinguishes three ages of water: (1) poetic and symbolic, (2) productive and positive, and (3) sustainable. As a close disciple of Gaston Bachelard, Wunenburger notices that in the sustainable age, "anxious urgency is still mixed with images, symbols and myths, clearly assumed as a communicative medium, or latent in the imaginations of ecologists . . . who use poetic categories: clear and dead water, wild waters, domestic waters." The semiotic object "wave" in all its regimes of intelligibility—aesthetics, science, politics, ethics—and emblematic of the unknowable nature of water, seems to condense the topic of water logics. In short, this essay aims to propose the wave as a candidate item for a new field of studies, beyond science and culture.

THE WAVE AS A CATALYST OF THE UNKNOWN, THE ALMIGHTINESS OF NATURE

The wave has embodied the indomitable, untamable, and sacred essence of the sea. Even if the Scriptures describe the Flood as a heavy rain—"the fountains of the great deep were broken up, and the floodgates of heaven were opened" (Genesis 7.11)—its iconography often focuses on the surges that it generates and especially on the human bodies struggling with it. The human becomes a survivor or a victim at the mercy of God. The etymon of the Hebrew word for sea, *yam*, was linked to *roaring*, which stresses its impetuosity and violence, whereas the sea became benevolent in the Gospels (walking on water, for example, or miraculous fishing). Throughout antiquity and the Middle Ages, Thalassa (the female deity) was associated with the relative placidity of the Mediterranean, and Pontos (the male deity) with the agitation and fury of the Atlantic Ocean, which was relegated behind the Pillars of Hercules as an enigma, the realm of the forbidden. Homer's Ulysses, with his decade-long "poor cabotage" (Cassano [1996] 2005, 46), belongs to the first paradigm, whereas Dante's Ulysses, in canto 26 of the *Inferno*, inaugurates the Atlantic paradigm, since he defies the limits of knowledge. His fearlessness and ardor incite him to surpass the Strait of Gibraltar, thus realizing "the jump between a sea that remains between the land and the infinite expanse of the ocean" (23), and expose him to divine punishment: a wirlwind and drowning. Moreover, the Atlantic "sea of Darkness" became in the Renaissance the "sea of conquests," and while the Meridian moved from Jerusalem to the Canary Islands (1634) and later on to Greenwich (1884), it failed to curb the unmappable ocean (Roelens 2018).

Even secularized, stripped of its mythical aura, the unknown resists. Unsurprisingly, the wave became an emblem of the sublime, which elevates the beholder to the overwhelming omnipotence of nature. Whereas according to Edmund Burke, the dread that one experiences in front of the sublime is due to an instinct of survival, for Immanuel Kant, the sublime of the raging ocean inspires a respectful and controllable anxiety, under the condition that the viewer as a "cultural being" is in security on the shore: "But if we find ourselves safe, the spectacle is all the more attractive because it is capable of inciting fear, and we gladly name these sublime objects, because they elevate the forces of the soul above the usual average and . . . give us the courage to measure ourselves with the omnipotence of nature" (Kant [1790] 1993, §28).

In the wake of this terrifying sea that devours boats, the pre-romantic topos of drowning, though deprived of "cultural" distance and shelter, links shipwreck to destiny, as in William Falconer's poem "The Shipwreck": "Awhile they bore th' o'erwhelming billows' rage,/Unequal combat with their fate to wage" (1769, vv. 35–36). Hans Blumenberg sees in the demonization of the sea the tropism of man in search of a fatal slope or existential sinking. The shipwreck is "the figure of an inaugural philosophical experiment" ([1979] 1994, 15) inherent in our human condition, as it engages what Gaston Bachelard calls "irrational adhesion" or "the active invitation of the stream," the appeal of the liquid element that demands "a total gift, an intimate gift" ([1942] 1993, 187). This appeal participates not of a *libido sciendi* but of a *libido tout court*.

THE WAVE AS AN AESTHETIC PUZZLE

"What is more complex than a wave, this phenomenon that Vitruvius struggled to fit into thinking?" claimed Kenneth White (1994, 355), hearkening back to *De architectura* (first century CE), which was already imagining the possibility of maritime protective works or wave-breakers. Throughout history painters, writers, and filmmakers have struggled with this representational challenge, as if the wave inflected their artistic technique.

Leonardo da Vinci, both painter and engineer, undertook a series of drawings entitled *A Deluge* (1517–18; figure 1), which feature cataclysmic visions accompanying experiments of water-braking systems for flood control in the city of Florence, then threatened by the Arno River. The twenty works represent all forms of swirls: "Leonardo da Vinci dipped a twig in the water, so, on either side of the small branch exerting a 'water brake,' a whirlwind formed, which did not account for the matter 'it's water,' but the dynamic

Fig. 1 Leonardo da Vinci, *A Deluge,* 1517–18, ink drawing. (The Royal Collection at Windsor Castle, © Royal Collection Enterprises Limited 2024 | Royal Collection Trust)

'it's a current.' Even if the movement of the current is weak and virtually invisible to humans, the small vortex that forms around the stick shows that 'water flows'" (Keiji 2012, 161). Yet the profusion of drawings testifies to the complexity of seizing a single swirl of a wave.

Another giant who tried to take up this challenge is Victor Hugo. Art historian and philosopher Georges Didi-Huberman devoted a whole essay to Hugo's attempts to draw a wave full of pathos and tormented desire during his eighteen years of exile in Jersey and Guernsey. According to Didi-Huberman, Hugo's graphic work thematizes the link between internal *torment* (*turba*, emotion of the *psyche*), and *turmoil* (*turbatio*, motion of the *physis*)—in other words, between *anima* (soul) and *animation*. Turmoil is thus both an emotional state and an external climatic phenomenon, ontological and morphologic, human and natural. Didi-Huberman considers Hugo to be a seismograph of the rhythm of waves (sea pulse) and the tempest (sea spasms) and concludes that no ontological difference separates wind waves from the ripples of draperies or the romantic corrugation of the mood. He calls this immanent matrix of universal analogies a "milieu": "It is a material-place in movement. It is a scattering intensity. It is a continuum where folds, waves, vortices, exceptions proliferate. It is a fluid stirred by the surf or storm, and that makes everything anadyomene: disappearances and reappearances, engulfments and resurfacing, darkness and glimmers, dreams that plunge and realities that emerge" (2017, 23-24). This milieu functions as a "poetic principle, a generalized aesthetics" (57). If we examine Hugo's ink wash *My Destiny*, which frames in close-up an impending wave just about to break (figure 2), we notice that the challenge consists in giving form to the formless, to capture the agitation of elemental energy in a still image.

All these attempts to represent a volume (three dimensions) and motion thematize a question from Lessing's *Laocoon* (1766), which defines, against Horace's *ut pictura poesis* dogma, the specificity of time and space in art: how to capture in a simultaneous medium such as painting a wave which is a continuum? To paraphrase wave anthropologist Stefan Helmreich (2018): Which moment is the most appropriate to freeze, the swelling, the cresting, the breaking, the imminent collapse, the splashing of water, or the foam? This interrogation is legitimate, but the range of plastic choices seems also determined by the available techniques within the visual arts themselves. In sixteenth-century engravings for Pantagruel's travels in François Rabelais's *Tiers livre* (figure 3), the waves look solidified due to the stylet cuts.

Fig. 2 Victor Hugo, *My Destiny*, 1857, feather, brown ink wash and gouache on vellum paper, 17.4 cm × 25.9 cm. (Paris, Maison de Victor Hugo)

Fig. 3 Pantagruel's travels in François Rabelais, *Tiers livre des faictz, et dictz heroiques du noble Pantagruel* (C. La Ville, 1547), p. 252, woodcut. (Bibliothèque nationale de France)

Analogously, even three centuries later, Utagawa Hiroshige's wave woodcuts give a solid impression of an arch or a canopy (figure 4). On the contrary, in William Turner's watercolors or gouaches (figure 5) and Hugo's ink washes (figure 2), the paper itself is wetted, soaked in the fluid material where form and content melt together: "Thematically, the material can be the water of

Fig. 4 Utagawa Hiroshige, *The Cave at Enoshima in Sagami Province (Sôshû Enoshima iwaya no zu)*, from the series Famous Places in Our Country *(Honchô meisho)*, 1832, woodcut, 24.3 cm × 37.2 cm. (© Museum of Fine Arts Boston)

Fig. 5 William Turner, *Bell Rock Lighthouse,* 1819, watercolor and gouache with scratching out, 30.6 cm × 45.5 cm. (© National Gallery of Scotland)

torment, the wind of hurricanes, the scent of ghosts, the crowd of revolutions or the drapery of an erotic mink. Technically, in almost all cases, this material is *ink*, the one whose 'Ocean Man' covered so many manuscripts and drowned so many drawing sheets" (Didi-Huberman 2017, 24). Finally, James Ensor, in his sarcastic drawing *Baths at Ostend* (1890; figure 6), uses the expressionist sinusoid line in both the small wind waves and the threatening clouds. This sinuousness responds to the moral deviance of the petit bourgeois resort community. Hence, the topic, the painting technique, and the medium are tightly interrelated.

Literature, in contrast, due to its intrinsically sequential nature, focuses on the wave's movement itself, on the metastable phenomenon of ebb and flow. But a problem arises when it comes to a wave's beginning and end. In the liminal short story of the eponymous book, Mr. Palomar, Italo Calvino's metaphysical alter ego, tries to "read" a single wave through mere observation. The challenge is to isolate one wave from the others, to see it as different from and equal to the others at the same time. Palomar is puzzled by the tension between order and disorder—"There are shapes and sequences that repeat themselves, even though they are irregularly distributed in space and time" (Calvino 1983, 6)—and by the "alternating overlap" and "thrusts and counterthrusts" (9) that language is unable to grasp. However, despite

Fig. 6 James Ensor, *The Baths at Ostend*, etching, heightened, paper, 21.3 cm × 22 cm, 1899. (Museum of Fine Arts, Ghent)

this epistemological defeat, the text offers a whole syntax through which to parse a wave's growing and ebbing: "Mr. Palomar sees a wave springing up, grow, approach, change shape and color, wrap itself, break, vanish, flow back" (5). To describe the limit between sand and wave, Calvino resorts to sedimented metaphors: "white carpet," "the wave splits into two wings," "sand tongues" (7). In short, Palomar's failure is emblematic of the evanescent essence of water in general. As Helmreich states: "You need to define what a wave is before you can measure it" (2014, 271).

In turn, in Alessandro Baricco's novel *Ocean Sea* (1993) set in a mythical sea resort "on the world's ultimate ledge" (48), the character Bartleboom plans to write an "Encyclopaedia of Observable Limits in Nature." He isolates a frame in which the profile of the wave shows a "fringe hemmed with a delicate beading" (41) before it retreats. But, like Calvino's Palomar, Bartleboom has to surrender: he must realize that it is impossible to stop this flow, "this continual alternation of creation and destruction," because of "the moving uncertainty of this back-and-forth that cradled and flouted any scientific view" (42). Another character, the portrait painter Plasson, paints the sea with seawater, leaving nothing more than mere liquid brushstrokes on a perfectly white canvas . . . The verbal and the visual fail to reach the unseizable essence of the wave. Is film better equipped? Is there a medium-bound propensity to represent fluidity?

Drawing on Gilles Deleuze's "movement-image" and Henri Bergson's "duration," Stefan Helmreich suggests that film would be the best medium to represent or, at least, to address a wave, which is "always implicitly, inexorably in motion" (2018, 504): "Towering waves in film have operated, in shifting ratios and phases, as emblems of (a) the elemental power of cosmic, inhuman, arbitrary forces, (b) the return of the social-environmental repressed, with waves as moral messengers paying humanity back for sins against the orders of nature or social justice, and (c) the fantastic power and limits of cinematic media themselves" (495). "The wave," he states, "is a narrative force" (500). The paradox of animation is that recent disaster fiction movies prefer using the older techniques of real water over digital-only technology to re-create tsunamis (502). Hence, "what is true of the art was also true of science: when you represent what a wave is, you can only do it partially" (Helmreich 2014, 277). The epistemological challenge indeed overlaps with an aesthetic and a scientific one.

A WAVE OF SHOCK

The energy of waves knew other applications. With the development of sea resorts at the end of the eighteenth century, vigorous hydrotherapy using blade baths (*bain à la lame*; figure 7) became frequent in the English Channel, first in Bristol and later along the facing shores in Dieppe and Boulogne-sur-Mer. This treatment by immersion in the open sea, directly inspired by antiquity and the torment of the ordeal, was first recommended for health reasons by the physician Richard Russell to cure all kind of diseases, glandular affections, and rabies, something like a premise of thalassotherapy. Russell ran an establishment in Bristol where the patients were provided with "jury guides," excellent swimmers appointed by the administration, who were responsible for leading them into the water. The patient was left underwater for the duration of an Ave Maria (Vincent 2007). In the early days of clinical psychology, the baths were supposed to heal not only of corporeal diseases but mental diseases, nervous exhaustion, and insomnia. The patients were taken to the open sea, and simply thrown into the water, after tying them up with a rope. Baricco's novel alludes in this context to the Madman of Brixton, a clinical case forcibly immersed in the icy water stirred by the waves, and who did not withstand the treatment: "digested by the

Fig. 7 Gustave Doré, *Sea Bathing*, woodcut, *Dessinateurs et humoristes: Gustave Doré*, vol. 1, 1858-73. (Bibliothèque nationale de France)

large aquatic intestine and never returned to the beach, spewed out . . . in the form of a livid and grotesque bladder" (1993, 58). No one ever came to claim this sought-after corpse, as if the sea transforming the bodies erases any trace: "The sea is without explication" (62). This aphorism finds an echo in the stranded bodies washed up on the beaches during the "migrant crisis." In the novel *The Sea Drinkers,* Amine Elalamy focuses on the trauma of a mother discovering the dead corpse of her son. The sea spews him onto the shore he had left some days earlier, bringing an interruption to his dream of Eldorado: "The sea that took her child from her, turned her head, drank him all of a sudden. Spit him out on the sand. Who would dare fighting the sea?" (2008, 57).

This metabolism of the sea through the movement of the wave can also be understood as an opportunity. As we saw with Victor Hugo, the wave is a "matrix of the possible" (Didi-Huberman 2017, 122). Philosopher Peter Sloterdijk argues that foam has a political—even democratic—value, since the wave, due to its "revolving" nature, embodies the unveiling of a latency, allowing "revolution." Through the "equation between foam and dream" (2005, 29), Sloterdijk opposes the *sferology,* referring to the immunity of the Divine monosphere, to the *aphrology* of foam (Aphrodite, born from foam, *aphros* in Greek). The wave is an epiphanic event that engenders *anadyomene* nymphs, emerging from the sea. In this respect, Stefan Helmreich quotes the personified waves of Norse mythology, the alluring and destructive "wave maidens" (2017, 33). It helps also to understand the uncanny pictorial fable *Alpha and Omega* (1910) by Edvard Munch, which gives graphic evidence of this ambivalence: the wave as a source of life and death, pleasure and displeasure. The twenty-two black-and-white lithographs and the accompanying narration, created in the clinic where Munch was interned after his mental breakdown, offer a rewriting of Genesis. Alpha and Omega are the first people on an Eden-like island. Alpha discovers Omega erotically entangled with a snake and other animals in the forest. When Omega decides to leave their secluded life behind, an anxious Alpha is left alone with a group of her half-breeds. The story ends in violence. Eventually Omega returns, emerging from the sea, and approaches her former lover. Alpha responds with anger, beating her to death (figure 8). Munch privileges the moment before Omega's emergence out of the sea through convulsionary lines and curvilinear forms that invade the beach, the sky (airwaves), the sea (waves), and the internal fear of Alpha, whose reminiscence of the famous *Scream,* painted almost two

Fig. 8 Edvard Munch, *Alpha's Despair*, 1908-9, lithographic image. (Photo © Munchmuseet)

decades earlier, operates the same morphological homology between body and mind seen in Hugo. What we retain is the insistence on the unpredictable when the wave is invoked, or, in our era, the returned of the repressed of "human arrogance" (Helmreich 2018, 506).

THE WAVE AS A "COMPLEX OBJECT"

Scientists question the wave's liquid substance, which passes from one state to another (water, droplets, foam), accelerates (swell, splash, torrent, cataract, geyser), or slows down (surf, fresh water). As a vital principle, the wave has always struck thinkers (in chemistry, physics, optics) with its energy and eternal fluence or motion, belonging to a prediscursive world requiring a phenomenological approach. Stefan Helmreich is curious "about how people employ such hybrid onto-epistemo-forms as 'waves' to think across domains" (2014, 267). Addressing both the theoretical and the empirical, swells and tides, flux and reflux, waves remain a scientific enigma, unpredictable and hard to model and to measure. Helmreich calls them "epistemic hybrids":

"while waves are material, they are also abstractions that take form depending on how oscillation is conceived, observed, modelled" (2014, 271).

This is not surprising since a wave itself belongs to the "complex paradigm." This leads us to extend the concept of the "wave" to other power effects of seawater—the current, the vortex, the maelstrom—and to relate waves with other spiraling momentums, like shells or dance pirouettes, all physical manifestations of rotational dynamics and dispersive forces. According to Edgar Morin, a complex phenomenon is one whose structure remains equal although the components are changing: a whirlpool, the flame of a candle, but also our organism and, in the case of the wave, manifestations of rotational dynamics. Even though the water molecules are in continuous motion, the Gestalt remains a wave. The "complexity" of the wave lies also in the fact that it oscillates between disorder (a turbulence) and order (a vortex): "Often, in a meeting between a flux and an obstacle, a whirl is created, i.e. a constant organized form that recomposes itself continuously: the union between the flux and the counter-flux produces indefinitely this organized form. This means that an organizational whirl can sprout out of a process that produces disorder (turbulence)" (Morin 1990, 83). Utagawa Hiroshige excels in representing this duality inside a single image (figure 9): in the background of his *Naruto Whirlpool* (1855), we distinguish chaotic turbulences (vertical, impending); on the foreground, a counterclockwise vortex (horizontal, flat, but rotating under the surface). The latter may be more mysterious than a *revolving* one, because it creates an *involution*, endowed with a dreadful swallowing power. What is striking here is that the visible does not coincide with the impetus behind it. Order can be more threatening than disorder. In any case, if there is a relation between force and shape, artists and philosophers are not outdone by scientists; rather, they often anticipate mathematic insights. Through representation, they reveal the inner patterns behind a natural phenomenon: spiral, circle, rhythm.

Vertigo and spiral impulses are homologized by Paul Valéry in his short treatise *The Man and the Shell* (1937). Valéry takes the pretext of the radial force of a mollusk that "secretes its shell" to develop an aesthetic and a poetics. The shell's "swirling grace" also leads to epistemological considerations endowing the shell with a "generating power" that ignores the separations between classical Euclidean geometry and modern physics (Einstein's relativity theory), since this "simple gastropod" makes us see "perfection in art," exceeding all tools and objects that a potter could shape

Fig. 9 Utagawa Hiroshige, *Naruto Whirlpool, Awa Province*, from the series *Views of Famous Places in the Sixty-Odd Provinces*, 1853, colored woodblock print, 35.6 cm × 24.4 cm. (Metropolitan Museum of Art)

(Valéry 1957, 887). The arrangement of curves and ribbons of color hints at the existence of a "field of forces" whose action imprints upon the growth of the shell the irresistible twist and rhythmic progress that we observe in the product.

In *The Soul and Dance* (1923), Valéry turns this swirling force into the essence of the dance, hence the transcendental, the condition of possibility of all art. This dialectic between the constraints of the frame (here, the body) and the ubiquity and amplitude of the shapeless vital force is embodied by the dancer Athikté, who vibrates and turns in front of the guests, leaps out of her form, and reforms. Devoured by countless figures, a perplexed Athikté explains where she returns from: "Asylum, asylum, O my asylum, O Whirlwind! I was in you, O movement, apart from all things" (1960, 176). This vital impulse embraces a *rythmaesthetics* hearkening back to the original meaning of *rhuthmos* < *rhein*: to flow, "a special way of flowing" (Maldiney 2012, 155; figure 10).

Fig. 10 Patrick Steen, *Dancing Waves*, 2009. (Photo by the author)

Italo Calvino illustrates this *natura naturans*, or form-giving phenomenon, in "The Spiral," a small tale of *Cosmicomics*, where he evokes the secretion of the mollusk as a desire to create, but also to please the female, whose special vibrations the male feels in the tepid, "undifferentiated soup" (Calvino 1965, 174) that is seawater. The formal impulse turns into libido: "And in this mode of expression I put all the thoughts I had for her" (176). In sum, art allows us to rethink natural products as a shell or a wave by envisioning them as susceptible to transformations and malleability. The wave and its curving motion serve as a constant reminder that "waves are physical and cultural objects" (Helmreich 2014, 272), "icons of rhythmic and predictable motion as well as of chaos and destruction" (2017, 29).

This intrinsic ambivalence of the object requires disciplinary ecumenism more than interdisciplinarity, not only using several disciplines but finding a common ground to align their methods. Roger Caillois called "diagonal sciences" those that overarch the clear separation of the domains—human, animal, plant, and mineral. In the wake of his observations in the luxurious environment of South America, Caillois postulated an interconnection within the architecture of the world, or "deep unity." He noticed the unexpected similarities between the shapes of certain human-made objects and the puzzling manifestations of what he calls the "natural fantasy," such as the fabulous face in the livery of a butterfly or the abdomen of a spider.

These "ceiled recurrences" are based on the assumption of a finite, but nevertheless "abundant," world (Caillois 1970, 71). Caillois advocates for a poetic "method" that would "identify the elusive" and establish "indirect and just relationships" (254) between the world's data. The result is the conviction that certain analogies provided by the poetic imagination can be "right," revealing "an unexpected relationship, a new connivance in the network of the inextricable universe" (218), where "correctness" does not mean fidelity but rather the way natural and cultural phenomena are anchored in the complexity of the world. Once again, this brings us back to Hugo's universal analogies as emphasized by Didi-Huberman: "between the outside and the concealed inside, a kind of interface rhythmically undulates, a fascinating wave, a whole extra world stirring the milieu: hair, draperies, fluent patterns of ornamentation, washed-out material of the expanding ink wash" (2017, 36).

Katsushika Hokusai's *The Great Wave of Kanagawa* (1831; figure 11) best embodies the polarity between order and disorder, culture and nature, the immobility of framing and the dissipation of energy. Some critics pay more attention to the small wave on the foreground, whose outline resembles that of Mount Fuji itself, comparable to a solidified wave. Erik Orsenna reaches the same insight in his essay on the Gulf Stream: "Seafarers and mountainfarers look alike. What is a mountain, if not a long-frozen wave? What is

Fig. 11 Katsushika Hokusai, *The Great Wave of Kanagawa*, 1831, print on paper, 26 cm × 38 cm. (New York Metropolitan Museum of Art)

navigation, if not horizontal mountaineering?" (2005, 202). Yet "The Great Wave" legitimizes other approaches, a mathematical and a sustainable one. A multiple gestational power indeed generates new curves everywhere (similar but of a smaller scale), which is precisely the definition of Benoît Mandelbrot's *fractality*. Fractality is a mathematical finding that also has a sustainable impact, since fractal coastlines are more subjected to submersion and erosion. With his "coastline paradox" (1967), Mandelbrot had already pointed to the crumbly nature of the Breton coastline and cliffs. The more you approach the line, the longer it becomes. In the same way, Hokusai's wave proposes an ecological reading of a threatened humanity, provoking the *tsu-namis* and "hydric stress" of countries with submersible areas. The "wave," more precisely *nami ura* ("under the wave"), phonetically echoes *tsu-nami* ("the wave front"). How to understand this conjunction between fisher-folk and the "rogue" wave? According to a nefarious Western reading (from left to right, following the direction of writing), the boats are victims of the gigantic, overwhelming wave, deified on account of its hugeness. According to an auspicious Eastern reading (from right to left), the boats are crossing, almost indifferent to the wave. Moreover, speaking about a "rogue" wave is already an act of *biomorphism* (Komárek 2009, 108), or describing material nature through analogies with living organisms or humans and endowing them with intentionality.

The "wave Anthropocene" or "climate-change-induced flooding Anthropocene" (Helmreich 2014, 504) raises one last issue. Whereas wind waves are predictable, tsunamis are detectable but not predictable. Their stochastic nature complicates statistical prediction and forecasting prognosis. In other words, their randomness promotes nature's *potestas* against the nation's *auctoritas* (Agamben 2003, 135), in addition to humans' ecocidal and arrogant behavior during the Anthropocene. Helmreich explains that "buoys are *political* objects," inside jurisdictions, and wonders if waves have "legal lives" (2014, 273). The difficulty of predicting rogue waves has to do with the politics of wave-watching and measuring average wavelengths, "how to model and manage hazardous wave activity, particularly the kind on the rise with climate change, including storm surges consequent upon hurricanes" (271), despite the observation that "the patterns and shapes of waves themselves are also transmuting" (267). Long before any climate change concerns, Herman Melville, a sailor himself, had already meditated upon this unpredictability: "As the profound calm which only apparently precedes and prophesies of the storm, is perhaps more awful than the storm itself; for, indeed, the calm is but the wrapper and envelope of the storm; and contains it in itself, as the seemingly harmless rifle holds the fatal powder, and the ball, and the explosion" (1851, 254). As an artistic illustration of this sudden transition between calm and storm, *The Raft* by Bill Viola, a video installation created in 2004,[2] shows in slow motion a group of nineteen people dramatically subjected to and knocked over by an unpredicted sudden breaker, a flood. At first, they appear calm as they wait in line, but a sudden flow of water comes to disturb this serenity. The faces reveal the anguish and desperation to survive, and the bodies cling to each other. Redemption, however, is suggested: just as the water storm had begun, it stops suddenly. *The Deluge,* also by Viola, created in 2002, and perhaps recalling 9/11, insists on the din and velocity of the deflagration, and has even more resonances with the Noachian flood, and with the question of taming surging water.

The unforeseeable is also inherent in the metaphorization of the wave: a *wave* of migrants, or the *waves* of a pandemic. For his cartoon *Wave of Migration* (2009),[3] Popa Matamula echoes the morphology of one of Hokusai's waves, *Kaijo no fuji* (1834), with the same left-right orientation, diffracted in birds-foam. The foam bodies are propelled towards other horizons westward. This deliberately ambiguous drawing carries two narratives: either populist (the "flow" of migrants has to be dyked or contained), or humanistic (the flow of migrants has to be welcomed). This metaphorization addresses connections between upcoming tsunamis and waves of climate refugees. "Rogue waves," writes Stefan Helmreich, "are spectres, materializations of the inhuman human . . . like the rogue states of which their name must remind us" (2014, 275–76). In rapidly changing climactic conditions, the *significant wave height* (the highest third of the average wave height, measured from trough to crest) is increasing, and rogue waves (waves of over twice the significant wave height) proliferate yet remain unpredictable, raising meteorological rather than oceanographic questions.

A WAVE OF CONCERN

The relationship between wave and fauna should also be addressed, considering that what happens beneath the sea surface is as important as what is visible. Helmreich's anthropological approach, which is invested in the materiality of the nonhuman world, should then be complemented by Timo Maran's semiological approach, which insists on the significant modeling and shaping activities of organisms on their environments. Following this reasoning, we could ask not only if a wave has an advantage for fish, but also if it has a meaning. Maran warns against the "incapacity of an organism to recognize and categorize correctly" (2017, 14). In our case, we could say that the whole of fauna is lost and lives in a nonsensical world. Fauna is no longer able to understand the environment altered by humans. It does not know how to react to floods, rogue waves, and tsunamis with lethal consequences. Maran evokes the idea of herring gulls, which, though they have adapted to life in some European cities and are capable of nesting on roofs, sometimes crash into glass walls, committing a semiotic error (16).

We should then ask ourselves: Do fish receive the wave as an "affordance"? According to James Gibson, the affordances of the environment are "what it offers the animal, what it provides or furnishes, either for good or ill" (1979, 127). The answer is a sustainable one since we know that fish need gyres in order to feed. A gyre (from late Latin *gyrare*, "turn," and *gyrus*, "a ring," from Greek *guros*) is a circular pattern of ocean currents running in large rotational loops. As mentioned above, I include all rotating aqueous phenomena inside the concept of *wave*. The most famous are the two large gyre systems around Antarctica, the Weddel Sea and the Ross Sea. They constitute an ecological niche with either harms or benefits depending on the densest concentrations of krill or zooplankton. In his *Portrait of the Gulf Stream* (2005), Erik Orsenna warns against lack of respect for the Gulf Stream and the gyres. Both are natural pumps and fertilizers that are now endangered due to the melting of fjords. The fresh water released by this melting is lighter than saltwater and thus causes the slowing down of the warm-water current coming from the Gulf of Mexico. In addition, new gyres now occupy the oceans since rivers of plastic objects are carried by ocean currents along the north Pacific Rim into the gyre: "there's a *lot* more ocean, uninterrupted, in the south, which means the proportion of the ocean suffused by swells—waves no longer driven by wind—is much higher. . . . [T]here's less particulate plant matter in the near-sea atmosphere because there's less land. . . . [T]here is a larger area of *ice* in the southern oceans" (Orsenna 2005,148). The installation *Des bouteilles à la mer* (Messages in a Bottle), by the French-Luxembourgish artist Nathalie Adam (2014; figure 12), is an artistic alarm call, featuring a small

Fig. 12 Nathalie Adam, *Des bouteilles à la mer*, 2016, installation, glass and ultramarine pigment, variable size, 2016. (Photo courtesy of the artist)

still life (*nature morte*) made of bottles that were abandoned by unscrupulous humans but, once polished by erosion, have become pebbles again. The shameless usurpation of nature by culture practiced in the Anthropocene undergoes a mutation: culture is once again reduced to nature. The animal, the vegetal, and the mineral fuse symbolically on this small artificial beach: Do they offer hope or suspicious serenity?

Arts prompt science and politics to reconsider what seems obvious, and raise the awareness that resources are limited and that the perpetuation of life itself is dependent on a holistic view of the world. Recent climatic deregulations show the urgency of considering waves, approaching them, representing them, stemming and controlling them. In other words, whereas the interest of the human sciences in waves (myths, shapes, beauty) contributes to curbing the scientific impasse, which is only focused on the measurable, mathematical and geometric insights tend to reveal hidden, isomorphic structures in natural phenomena. Ecology is located at the intersection of these two domains. Being all part of a whole, we are all concerned. It is obvious that the field of "wave studies" hasn't said its last word yet.

NOTES

1. Unattributed translations are mine.
2. The video may be viewed at https://youtu.be/3ktdKhNa9LM.
3. The cartoon may be viewed at https://cartoonmovement.com/cartoon/wave-migration.

WORKS CITED

Agamben, Giorgio. 2003. *État d'exception*. Translated by Joël Gayraud. Seuil.
Bachelard, Gaston. (1942) 1993. *L'Eau et les rêves*. Corti.
Barrico, Stefano. 1993. *Oceano mare*. Feltrinelli.
Blumenberg, Hans. (1979) 1994. *Naufrage avec spectateur: Paradigme d'une métaphore de l'existence*. Translated by Laurence Cassagnau. L'Arche.
Caillois, Roger. 1970. *Cases d'un échiquier*. Gallimard.
Calvino, Italo. 1965. "La spirale." In *Le Cosmicomiche*. Einaudi.
Calvino, Italo. 1983. *Palomar*. Einaudi.
Cassano, Franco. (1996) 2005. *Il pensiero meridiano*. Laterza.
Didi-Huberman, Georges. 2017. *Ninfa profunda: Essai sur le drapé-tourmente*. Gallimard.
Elalamy, Youssouf Amine. 2008. *Two Novellas by YAE: A Moroccan in New York; and Sea Drinkers*. Translated by John Liechty. Lexington Books.
Falconer, William. 1769. *The Shipwreck*. https://www.bartleby.com/360/5/298.html.
Gibson, James J. 1979. *The Ecological Approach to Visual Perception*. Houghton Mifflin Harcourt.
Helmreich, Stefan. 2014. "Waves: An Anthropology of Scientific Things." *HAU: Journal of Ethnographic Theory* 4 (3): 265–84.
Helmreich, Stefan. 2017. "The Gender of Waves." *WSQ: Women's Studies Quarterly* 45 (1–2): 29–51.
Helmreich, Stefan. 2018. "Massive Movie Waves and the Anthropic Ocean." *Social Science Information* 57 (3): 494–521.
Hugo, Victor. (1857) 1990. "Dieu, fragments." In *Œuvres complètes: Chantiers*. Robert Laffont.
Kant, Immanuel. (1790) 1993. *Critique of Judgment*. Translated by J. H. Bernard. Macmillan.

Keiji, Usami. 2012. "Freinages et déluges." In *L'Archipel des séismes: Écrits du Japon après le 11 mars 2011*, edited by Corrine Quentin and Cécile Sakai. Philippe Picquier.

Komárek, Stanislav. 2009. *Nature and Culture: The World of Phenomena and the World of Interpretation*. Lincom.

Maldiney, Henri. 1973 *Regard, parole, espace*. Cerf.

Mandelbrot, Benoit. 1967. "How Long Is the Coast of Britain? Statistical Self-Similarity and Fractional Dimension." *Science*, no. 156, 636–38.

Maran, Timo. 2017. "La sémiotisation de la matière: Une zone hybride entre l'écocritique matérielle et la biosémiotique." *Cygne noir*, no. 5. https://doi.org/10.7202/1089938ar.

Melville, Herman. 1851. *Moby-Dick; or, the Whale*. Harper and Brother.

Morin, Edgar. 1990. *Introduction à la pensée complexe*. ESF.

Orsenna, Erik. 2005. *Portrait du Gulf Stream: Éloge des courants*. Seuil.

Roelens, Nathalie. 2018. "L'Incartographiable." In *Cartographier: Regards croisés sur des pratiques littéraires et philosophiques contemporaines*, edited by Isabelle Ost. Presses de l'Université Saint-Louis.

Sloterdijk, Peter. 2013. *Écumes: Sphérologie plurielle*. Translated by Olivier Mannoni. Pluriel.

Valéry, Paul. 1960. *L'Âme et la danse*. In *Œuvres complètes, II*, edited by Jean Hytier. Gallimard.

Valéry, Paul. 1957. *L'Homme et la coquille*. In *Œuvres complètes, I*, edited by Jean Hytier. Gallimard.

Vincent, Johan. 2007. *L'Intrusion balnéaire: Les Populations littorales bretonnes et vendéennes face au tourisme, 1800–1945*. Presses universitaires de Rennes.

White, Kenneth. 1994. *Le Plateau de l'albatros: Introduction à la géopoétique*. Grasset.

Wunenburger, Jean-Jacques. 2017. "Les Trois âges de l'eau." In *Écologie politique de l'eau: Rationalités, usages et imaginaires*, edited by Jean-Philippe Pierron. Hermann.

THINKING FROM MULTIPLE OCEANS

Historical and Elemental Lineages and Futures of Ocean Geography(s)

PHILIP STEINBERG

How does one tell a sea story? Or, to restate the question: How does one put the sea in the center of a story without fetishizing it in its alterity, reducing it to a metaphor, diminishing it to an environment that provides resources, or bypassing it as an intervening space in the middle? How does one bring the ocean to the foreground without elevating its materiality and its affordances—its opacity, its fluidity, its repetitive churn, its dangerous unpredictability, its emotive power, its embedded memories—into something that they are not? How does one tell a story *with* the sea—as a space that, in its difference from the normative space of land that has "grounded" much of social theory, can challenge understandings of the temporalities that are assumed to characterize relations between humans and their more-than-human environments—while also honoring histories that emerge *from* the sea, through encounters between marine subjects that generate traumas, hopes, and relational identities?[1]

I often reflect on these questions when I'm flying in an airplane over the ocean, squeezed into an economy seat, trying to work on my laptop without spilling a drink on the individual who has had the misfortune of being seated next to me. I'm tempted to close the window shade; the sun casts a glare on my screen. But, I resist the urge: I had requested a window seat for a reason.

As someone who writes about the ocean and who writes about how others write about the ocean, I want to cherish this rare opportunity to experience the ocean in all its enormity: as nothing but a vast expanse of water.

As I stare at the seascape, though, it occurs to me that I have no idea how to concentrate my vision. First my eyes, and then my mind, start wandering. I try to focus on something more tangible than the uninterrupted, feature-free surface presented below. I find myself looking for ships, wind towers, navigational aids, coastlines . . . anything to break up the ocean's monotony. I search for discrete objects that I can then recombine to tell *my* story of the sea.

I am hardly the first to face this dilemma. Just weeks after completing his epic poem *Rime of the Ancient Mariner*, Samuel Taylor Coleridge embarked on a ferry from Yarmouth to Hamburg and found himself, for the first time in his life, beyond sight of land. Reflecting on the "feeling of immensity" that he had ascribed to the ocean in his recently completed allegory, Coleridge wrote that now that he was confronted with the actual ocean, he found himself "exceedingly disappointed . . . at the narrowness and nearness, as it were, of the horizon [and] that round objectless desert of water" (cited in Raban 2023, 94). Flailing for a narrative that he could construct from this "objectless" space, Coleridge was left to concentrate on the only object he could recognize: "a single solitary wild duck."

If Coleridge had spent longer at sea, he might have changed his view. If he were on a voyage lasting weeks or months, ploughing the ocean's waves and feeling its swell, he might have had a much greater sense of the ocean's differentiation, its rhythms, the way it dynamically moves in both space and time. But even then, I'm not sure that he would really know how to put the ocean and, crucially, its temporalities, and the meanings that adhere to those temporalities, into the foreground. As Kimberley Peters and Mike Brown (2017) write, there is a tension between what they call thinking *with* and thinking *from* the sea. When one thinks *with* the sea, they argue, the distanced, "God's eye" observer turns to the sea as an epistemological crutch, focusing on the ocean's geophysical properties (e.g., flow, volume, turbulence), but also the visual impression of vast, blue nothingness. Thinking with the sea allows the romantic to develop new perspectives on the world, beyond the (apparent) fixed boundaries and linear temporalities of land. When thinking with the sea, the ocean is mobilized as a scaffold that masculinized, distanced intellectuals can stand on to exercise their mental powers. This is the perspective that left Coleridge, confronted by the reality of the "objectless" ocean, with no option but to draw narrative from a duck. Furthermore, thinking with the sea as a space of difference can result in obscuring the significant differences in how various humans (and other species), with their differentiated and entangled histories and levels of power, encounter ocean space. At its extreme, as Elizabeth Povinelli warns, thinking with the ocean can bury political critique and historic experience beneath an "absorptive, relations-erasing universalism" (Povinelli 2020, 2). The alternative, for Peters and Brown, is to think *from* the sea, engaging its waters as an encountered, inhabited, felt, and sensed space of more-than-human livelihoods. Thinking *from* the sea, it is a space where histories are made and remembered. It is less a space for romantic imagination than for confronting the spatiotemporalities that bind pasts with futures.

Like most conceptual binaries, this one begins to collapse when encountered in practice. To give just one example, waves, which are often mobilized by scholars thinking with the sea to illustrate its "difference," themselves reflect and impart temporalities of encounter, including the political valences of different ocean knowledge systems and the politics of modern wave science (Helmreich 2023). Indeed, Peters and Brown demonstrate through a conversation between the two coauthors that productive dialogue is possible. However, the divide persists in different starting points: between those who work from the ocean as an encountered space (i.e., in the histories and present-day livelihoods of coastal peoples, islanders, and transoceanic diasporas for whom the ocean has a special place in cultural practices, memories, and identities) and those who use it as a geographic scaffold for thinking (i.e., artists and scholars who use the ocean's "difference" from land—its geophysical dynamism, position outside state boundaries, persistence as a global commons, etc.—to destabilize normative categories). As critical scholars, it behooves us to keep this tension in mind as we interrogate the "work" that oceanic writing can (and cannot) do in revealing dynamics of intersectionality, memory, and global interconnectivity as well as the hierarchies, traumas, and hopes that prevail within.

THE POSITION OF POSITIONALITY

At root, this is an essay about positionality: the possibilities that are opened and closed when one assumes a position of thinking with the ocean versus thinking from the ocean; when one looks on the ocean from above, as from an airplane, versus when one submerges oneself in its historical, spatial, inhabited depths. Although selection of one position or another (or an intermediate position) is made strategically to support an argument, it is not *just* strategic. One's position also reflects where one comes from: one's cultural heritage, one's academic training, one's scholarly networks, as well as the history of doors that have been opened and closed over the course of one's personal and professional development. Therefore, a discussion about critical positionalities is inevitably immersed in questions about the position of the individual initiating that discussion, as well as questions about that individual's authority to do so.

In my case, I am a white, male, heterosexual geographer trained in a social science tradition that, very broadly, links aspects of political economy with an attentiveness to the materiality of environments. Although my academic training is as a social scientist, and specifically a geographer, I recognize a commonality with many scholars in the "blue humanities" (e.g., Mentz 2023) and I frequently draw on and contribute to this literature. Crucially, it is this heritage and training as a scholar of the social sciences and humanities, and the research questions that emerge from this heritage, that originally motivated my turn to the sea. This contrasts with others who have been inspired by, for instance, their embodied encounters with the ocean, or the tangible place of the ocean in their everyday practices, or the references to the ocean made by their ancestors to transmit memories and knowledges through generations. My heritage, inevitably, continues to shape my perspective on the ocean, even as I am aware of its limits.

Here, as I work from my position as an ocean geographer to think through tensions inherent in thinking with and from the ocean, I engage with a select sample of perspectives emanating from a Black critical tradition, a tradition that looks to the ocean as a historically specific space of memory, meaning, and transcontinental connections animated, most starkly, by the Middle Passage and the long shadow that it has left in its wake. To be clear, my aim is not to build a "bridge" between the two traditions. As someone located on one "side" of the bridge—in terms of identity, experience, and academic training—it is not my place to unilaterally propose that a bridge should be built. Furthermore, much "bridging" has already been done by Black geographers who, to varying degrees, turn to the ocean or, more broadly, "aquatic space"[2] to elaborate on the geography of the Black experience (for just a few examples that speak directly from or to the discipline of geography, see McKittrick 2006; Noxolo 2016; T. L. King 2019; Wright 2020; Proglio et al. 2021; R. Walcott 2021; Winston 2021; Hawthorne 2023). A call to build a "bridge" would not only be arrogant; it also would reify the idea that there are two (and just two) delimited and homogenous "critical ocean geographies" out there: a "white" one and a "Black" one. This is, of course, an oversimplification. And yet, there are strikingly few references shared between, on the one hand, scholars who have found their way to the ocean from an appreciation of its role in capitalism or empire-building, or in its unique geophysical, ecological, or affective properties, and, on the other hand, scholars whose starting point has been the role of the ocean (and, more broadly, "aquatic space") in Black lives and livelihoods, including Black histories and Black futures.[3]

Rather than seeking to build a bridge between these literatures, this chapter is rooted in a different bridging: between the perspectives of thinking with and thinking from the ocean. In the process, though, the Black critical tradition looms large, as this tradition has long turned to the ocean as both a space of lived history and one of imagined futures. In the chapter that follows, I respectfully engage this literature to enhance my own critical thinking, not as an act of appropriation (for I am not claiming it as *my* subjective analysis) but as a moment of learning. I would hope that with an appropriate level of humility and respect we can all gain insights into our inevitably entangled histories, even as we encounter those histories through distinct subjectivities. Indeed, that, in large part, is what this chapter is about.

THINKING WITH AND FROM THE OCEAN

To begin to answer the question raised at the beginning of this chapter, there are a number of ways that one can tell a sea story. One route is to critically evaluate the rhetorics and rules applied by a society as it constructs the ocean as an ordered space in the middle: as a space to be crossed, to be utilized for its resource potential, to absorb the externalized costs of capitalism. Working from this perspective, one can go on to explore how the ocean serves as a pathway for influences, and out of such stories one can begin to understand the forces that underpin attempts at engineering the ocean as a space seemingly external, but actually quite internal, to society. This is the approach frequently taken in ocean-region studies, as well as in global ocean studies that seek to reveal the ocean's central role in the spatiality of capitalism (e.g., Steinberg 2001; Campling and Colás 2021).

This approach, however, has some limits. A story about how the ocean is socially constructed presupposes, in the first instance, an ontological separation between land and sea, where explanation emanates from land and the social forces that prevail there. In retrospect, it is telling that I titled my first book *The Social Construction of the Ocean* (Steinberg 2001) and not *The Oceanic Construction of the Social*. Likewise, it is telling that Liam Campling and Alejandro Colás titled their 2021 book *Capitalism and the Sea*, which assumes two distinct subjects, rather than *Capitalism in the Sea*.

Also, the ocean is a vast and varied space, and different regions are encountered in different ways, leading to different stories. If one focuses on the coast, the power of the imaginary of a vast watery world can get lost amidst a dense web of land-sea interactions, near-shore fisheries and resource extraction opportunities, marine hazards, and the place of the ocean in coastal people's livelihoods and cultural systems. Space, in all its richness, not just as points of encounter but as a field of dreams, futures, and traumas, risks becoming subsumed in the anthropology of coastal livelihoods. By contrast, if one focuses on the deep sea, the *longue durée*, real and imagined, takes over. As the ocean's presence emerges as a repository of historic episodes, traumas, and aspirations, one risks losing sight of the ways in which most coastal people actually experience the sea: in the moment, in their livelihoods, as interspecies, dynamic spaces of life and death, forces and objects.

Just as there are ways to bridge the gap between thinking with and thinking from the sea, there are numerous ways to tell stories of the sea that challenge the dichotomy that divides an inhabited coastal region of societies and encounters from an abstracted deep sea of embedded histories and projected dreams. Some human livelihoods persist in distant, deep waters. Merchant mariners, offshore oil rig workers, and deep-sea fishers, for instance, all spend significant time away from the coast. Time at sea can have a devastating impact on migrants and enslaved persons crossing oceanic divides. For all these individuals, the sea, even distant from the coast, is a space of human habitation and, to varying degrees, carcerality and dehumanization (Khalili 2021). And yet, all too often, ship-based life is idealized as occurring *in spite* of the ocean. After all, the whole point of navigation (at least in Western navigation) is to transcend the ocean's geophysical properties so that the ocean simply becomes a platform for the ship on which social life (including mobility) occurs. That is, the ocean exists to be ignored. The result is that stories of "life at sea" become those of "life on ship," as the sea recedes into the background (Mack 2011). There are stories that deviate from this dichotomy—from science fiction that brings the ocean's rhythms into the daily lives of marine colonizers (e.g., Slonczewski 1986), to research on the ways in which the ocean's materiality becomes a presence against the will of those who would wish it away (e.g., Peters 2012), to the stories of migrants whose boats, tragically, become one with the water (e.g., Heller and Pezzani, n.d.)—but this scholarship is the exception.

Another alternative is to start from the ocean's geophysical properties: its "wet ontology" (Steinberg and Peters 2015). This approach seeks to take the ocean seriously as a geophysical space with its own mobilities, dimensions, and temporalities. In my work with Kimberley Peters, we have suggested that when one adopts a perspective that places the ocean's geophysicality at its center, one is led to rework some of the foundational concepts typically employed to understand society—such as place, solidity, permanence, repetition, temporality, surface, and volume. A further iteration of this approach suggests that when one begins from the ocean's geophysical properties, one necessarily extends analysis well beyond the blue space depicted on a map as "ocean," because the ocean's materiality and its meaning is so deeply imbricated in the forcings of the earth system (Peters and Steinberg 2019).

Thinking with the ocean to the point that it exceeds its geographic boundaries and material wetness can be highly productive for generating new modes of geographic reasoning that rework, and ultimately undermine, prevailing binaries that distinguish land from sea and, within the sea, coastal from distant regions. However, it can also direct us away from the livelihoods of those—human and nonhuman—who engage with the sea on a daily basis, and from honoring the meanings that they attribute to and derive from oceanic spaces (Povinelli 2020; Reid 2020). A contrasting approach begins by examining the ways in which livelihoods are entangled with the sea—its meanings, its forces, its flows, its creatures, as well as, as Peters and Steinberg (2019) would have it, its "extensions." This perspective reveals that the ocean is neither a fecund environment of resources nor an empty surface to be traversed. Rather, it is a space of *different* ontological understandings, *different* legal systems, *different* conceptualizations of the relationship between land and water, humans and nonhumans. This approach requires not just a critique of the Western, temperate, continentalist, masculinist tradition; it also requires that one go beyond that tradition to listen to the understandings of those who experience water—whether near-shore or distant; proximate, historical, or aspirational; as a tactile moment or as a historical memory—as saturated by the flows and currents that churn traumas, toxins, migrants, and ideas, as well as, of course, water itself and the countless biota that turn it into a multispecies habitus.

This, in turn, begins to move scholarship from a perspective of "thinking with" to "thinking from," or that, perhaps, uses "thinking from" to "think with" better. It directs us, for instance, to the "seascape epistemology" of Karin Amimoto Ingersoll (2016), whose understanding of the role of the ocean's various mobilities in the historic (and ongoing) imperial and military conquest of the Pacific islands and its peoples is inseparable from her practice of surfing, that, as a Native Hawaiʻian, connects her with the ocean's movements through space and time. The ocean, for Amimoto Ingersoll, is thus both a source of specific knowledge that shapes and reflects her identity and environment *and* a disruptive space that one can productively think with to undermine masculine, land-centered, statist norms. Similarly, Edward Kamau Brathwaite's (1981) concept of "tidalectics" "foregrounds not only the diverse temporalities of oceanic space [which can be used to reframe historiography] but also what he calls the 'submerged mothers' that must be recuperated in regional history" (DeLoughrey and Flores 2020, 134; see also DeLoughrey 2007; Hessler 2018). As DeLoughrey and Flores stress, the general analytic perspective that Brathwaite advocates for thinking with the sea is possible only due to his immersion in both oceanic time and oceanic space as seen from his Afro-Caribbean vantage point. The traffic between "thinking with" and "thinking from" goes in the other direction as well. Alexis Pauline Gumbs (2020) enters the world of marine mammals to gain perspectives on survival, adaptation, and love that she deploys to interpret and nurture the persistence of an African diaspora that is connected to, but also exceeds, the strictly aquatic. If Amimoto Ingersoll and Brathwaite are thinking *from* the ocean in order to think *with* it better, then Gumbs is thinking *with* the ocean in order to think *from* it better.

The examples of Amimoto Ingersoll, Brathwaite, and Gumbs, and those of countless others writing from positions as islanders, coastal dwellers, members of Indigenous nations, or descendants of transoceanic slavery, often also informed by feminist, decolonial, posthumanist, or queer thinking, impart the message that simply bringing the ocean into our narratives is not enough. It is all too easy to integrate the ocean into our stories much as we view it from the airplane: as a scaffold for thinking. But the ocean, as a space, is not just imagined, or thought with; the ocean (like every space) is *practiced*, and practicing the ocean involves deriving meaning from and assigning meaning to its forces. It involves acknowledging and advancing the histories that emerge from the entanglement of human and more-than-human life-forms in its volume and across its expansive borders.

THE ELIDED OCEAN IN *MOBY-DICK*

To dive further into questions of positionality and epistemology in oceanic thinking, I turn to the mid-nineteenth-century American novelist Herman Melville and, in particular, his classic ocean novel, *Moby-Dick*. This might seem like an odd focus for a chapter on positionality in critical ocean geography, but Melville, and in particular *Moby-Dick*, is selected here because the novel is in some senses the literary equivalent of the view from the airplane: thinking with but not from the ocean. And yet, as I suggest below, by engaging with some of the ways that Black literary scholars have encountered Melville, we can gain insights that might assist critical ocean geographers, and others who think with the sea, to combine their thinking with perspectives from the sea, developing a perspective on the ocean that is both *more historical* and *more elemental*.

The ocean permeates *Moby-Dick*. Almost the entire novel takes place at sea, on board the *Pequod*. Even in the chapters set on land, the focus is on individuals who are somehow connected to the sea, whether as a source of their livelihoods (e.g., the proprietor of the Spouter Inn, frequented by whaler crews) or their dreams (e.g., land-bound Manhattanites gazing to sea from the shoreline). That said, in *Moby-Dick* the ocean, or, more broadly, the maritime world, is not a *space* in the sense that the term is understood in contemporary geographic thought, where geographic differentiation is integrated with temporal change and encountered in ongoing processes of co-constitution and becoming (see e.g., Elden 2004; Massey 2004). Rather, in *Moby-Dick* the ocean is *context*, an inert environmental platform (or container) that hosts meaning-laden events, objects, and creatures.

Although Melville provides detailed descriptions of whales, the analysis is more anatomical and behavioral than ecological. The water is background, not just for the whaling ship but for the whale. The ocean establishes a metric of distance and difference, a platform on which the microcosmic civilization of the ship is floated, and an environment for staging the agonistic struggles between order, passion, progress, and nature that permeate the novel. However, Melville's depiction of the ocean fails to capture the underlying processes and dynamisms that give it its unique character as the fulcrum of a biogeophysical hydrospherical system whose elemental properties—wetness, churn, repetition, unpredictability, volume, depth, invisibility—generate specific material states, geophysical phenomena, and affective responses.

When Melville does describe the ocean's water, it is depicted as featureless and timeless, valuable for its function as a reliable host for specific creatures, metaphors, and movements, but not particularly present as a thing in itself. Foreshadowing the statement made a hundred years later by Carl Schmitt, that "the sea has no *character*. . . . [O]n the waves there is nothing but waves" (Schmitt [1950] 2003, 42–43; emphasis in original), Melville writes in chapter 13 ("Wheelbarrow") that "the magnanimity of the sea . . . will permit no records" (Melville [1851] 1922, 52), and this attitude is reiterated by several of the novel's characters. In chapter 16 ("The Ship"), when Ishmael applies to ship out on the *Pequod*, he tells Peleg that he wants to see the world, to which Peleg, pointing at the water, responds that the only "world" that he will see when whaling is what he sees before him, and if that is the case, then he might as well stay put since all water looks the same. Contra Derek Walcott (1986), for Melville the sea is *not* history.

A similar depiction of the ocean appears in the very last line of the book (before the epilogue): "The great shroud of the sea rolled on as it rolled five thousand years ago" (Melville [1851] 1922, 491; see also chapter 111 ["The Pacific"]). For Melville's characters, the waters of the sea are timeless. They also are apparently featureless. Although the novel includes a brief discussion of marine microorganisms and their role in revealing and obscuring the presence of larger creatures (chapter 58 ["Brit"]), little attention is paid to how these microorganisms actually move in, or are moved by, the ocean's water. Likewise, although the ship has a log line that can be used to generate knowledge of the ocean's depths and, more broadly, the volumetric characteristics of the oceanic environment, we learn in chapter 125 ("The Log and Line") that the instrument largely goes unused. When the ocean's depth *is* described, it is mobilized (in chapter 93 ["The Castaway"]) as a metaphor for unknowability: a pathway into the mysterious unknowns into which Pip's soul has sunk, not as an actual volume of water (Publicover 2017).

Mid-nineteenth-century Western sailors were largely ignorant of the sea's geophysics (Rozwadowski 2018), and so, in one sense, the omission of oceanographic curiosity among Ahab and his crew is understandable. Indeed, Ishmael notes in chapter 41 ("Moby Dick") that "the secrets of the currents in the seas have never yet been divulged" (Melville [1851] 1922, 156–57).[4] However, sailors certainly were cognizant of the weather. And yet, for a novel suffused with an abundance (some would say an overabundance) of scientific digressions, the weather, including the oceanic component of earth-ocean-atmosphere relations, is described in only the broadest terms. Richard King elaborates on this absence:

> What's perhaps most notable about the way that Melville crafted his heavy weather events in this novel is that he did so with so little of the meteorological detail or grand frothy-plumed descriptions that most twenty-first-century readers expect in a sea story. Melville described no grueling, sublime, lengthy scenes of crashing around Cape Horn or heeling through hurricanes. . . . Ishmael barely warns of portentous calms or any approaching meteorological signs that foretell this bad weather. Ishmael never describes a specific wave height or wind speed. He does not mention changes in barometric pressure or air temperature. He does not discuss strategies for steering or sail plans. In his storms in *Moby-Dick*, which include Father Mapple's multi-layered storm sermon on Jonah and the squall in "Forecastle—Midnight," Ishmael does not describe the characteristics of clouds. He barely describes the sound of storms, beyond a few words of roaring and thunder and cracking lightning. (R. J. King 2019, 271–73)

Ultimately, for all his interest in the ocean's creatures, Melville has little interest in the ocean (or the hydrosphere) as an actual *space*. Indeed, in chapter 45 ("The Affidavit"), when Chace recounts his night floating alone at sea after the *Essex* was wrecked by a whale, he explicitly disparages those who would see the ocean's water or its forces as sources of danger: "The dark ocean and swelling waters were nothing; the fears of being swallowed up by some dreadful tempest, or dashed upon hidden rocks, with all the other ordinary subjects of fearful contemplation, seem scarcely entitled to a moment's thought; the dismal looking wreck and *the horrid aspect and revenge of the whale*, wholly engrossed my reflections until day again made its appearance" (Melville [1851] 1922, 179; emphasis in original).

In fact, to the extent that the novel features characters' struggle against a central element, that element is not water but fire. C. L. R. James elaborates on this in one of his first reflections on *Moby-Dick* in *Mariners, Renegades and Castaways:*

> Ahab, a true son of nineteenth-century America, worshipped fire but he was struck by it (probably lightning) and was marked from head to foot.
>
> Living all his life away from civilization, hunting whales in remotest seas, looking up at stars at night, and thinking his own thoughts, he gradually began to discard the ideas of his times and to think independently. This is what he arrived at.
>
> Fire, power, the civilization of material progress, was a mighty creative force. But its creativity was mechanical. Mechanical is a word he will use many times. It is this which is destroying his life as a human being. And he will fight it. . . . [W]hen the thunder and lightning of a frightful storm are flashing around his ship and magnetic lights are burning on the masts. (James [1953] 1978, 16)

At another point in *Mariners, Renegades and Castaways,* James references analogous literary antiheroes to elaborate on this image of the solitary Ahab consumed by fire even as he is surrounded by water:

> When Ahab defies the spirit of fire, he is way out in distant seas, thousands of miles away from civilization, standing on the deck of the *Pequod*, with the meanest mariners, renegades and castaways around him. When Prometheus defies Zeus, he is chained to a rock on a wild expanse of land at the very ends of the earth. . . . When [King] Lear defies the thunder and the lightning, the most powerful manifestations of the forces of Nature, he is also on an open heath. . . . Zeus hurls Prometheus and his followers into the lower regions with the thunderbolts and lightning of a great storm. Lear

is driven mad by the thunder and lightning.... Ahab escapes the lightning and the thunder and the corpusants only to fall victim to his own madness. At times the three characters use almost the same words. These similarities cannot possibly be accidental. (James [1953] 1978, 124)

Two things are notable in these passages. First, the environment in which Ahab, Lear, and Prometheus undergo their tests is characterized by its distance from "civilization." It is that very distance, that sense of being beyond, that allows for the construction of an environment in which personal struggles—against nature, against social institutions and expectations, and against oneself—can be played out. Indeed, it is the very externality of these spaces to human society—as alter-natures—that allows them to be interchangeable as sites of agonistic struggle: Ahab's ocean, Lear's heath, and Prometheus's wasteland all present essentially the same challenge, and it is a challenge facilitated by distance and difference rather than by any specific elementality. That is, the environment is characterized by what it is not (solid, civilized territory) and by the way that it broadly facilitates the sublime, rather than by any geophysical properties that are directly encountered, resisted, and incorporated into one's worldview.[5]

Secondly, and relatedly, these are not fundamentally stories, or spaces, of navigation. Of course, there are scenes of Ahab literally navigating, poring over his charts and the like, but this is presented as an unproblematic activity, one of the few moments in *Moby-Dick* where science and rationality unquestionably triumph over passions of the human soul. Missing is the idea of navigation as an encounter, where the mobile protagonist ascribes meaning to places, engaging in a series of processes that would, to varying degrees, reaffirm, question, or co-opt the ocean's otherness through a territorializing dialectic that alternately reduces the ocean to an undifferentiated surface to be crossed (deterritorialization) and reclaims it as a space with nature, character, and differentiation (reterritorialization).[6] When Ahab (and Lear and Prometheus) find themselves in an uncomfortably "wild" environment, they do not try to tame it and territorialize it. Rather the environment's affect goes straight to the protagonist's soul, leading to angst-ridden cycles of internalization and repulsion. As James writes:

> This is modern man, one with Nature, master of technology, all personal individuality freely subordinated to the excitement of achieving a

common goal. They have reached it at last by the complete integration of the ship and the wind and the sea and their own activity. . . .

[As Melville writes in *White-Jacket*], "the sense of fear is annihilated in the unutterable sights that fill all the eye, and the sounds that fill all the ear. You become identified with the tempest; your insignificance is lost in the riot of the stormy universe around." . . . Nature is not a background to men's activity or something to be conquered and used. It is a part of man, at every turn physically, intellectually and emotionally, and man is a part of it. And if man does not integrate his daily life with his natural surroundings and his technical achievements, they will turn on him and destroy him. (James [1953] 1978, 74, 100–101)

As James elaborates so well, this drama between the characters and their hostile but increasingly regularized environment is mobilized to signal the modern subject's struggle with the social institutions and norms that, in the mid-nineteenth century, were coming to characterize white, male, bourgeois civilization (see also Casarino 2002) and within which, through appeals to the romanticism of technology and transcendence of the rational self, James identifies gathering storm clouds of fascism.[7] The ocean here is not so much reduced to metaphor as it is elevated to allegory (see also Blum 2010; Steinberg 2013; DeLoughrey 2019a). However, as the oceanic encounter is endowed with a surfeit of meaning, the ocean itself—the ocean that is key to this transformation of modernity—remains undertheorized.[8]

Although not directly engaging James's work, psychoanalytic scholar Sarah Ackerman (2017) develops a complementary line of argument in her reading of *Moby-Dick*. Ackerman argues that the novel can be read as a "treatise"[9] on Sigmund Freud's concept of the "oceanic feeling," a condition where one finds oneself in an environment without the bearings that one normally uses to locate one's ego:

> The ocean is hypnotic, according to Ishmael, and draws men to it in a spontaneous, instinctual way. Like Narcissus, we see our unreachable selves in the water. Looking out before setting sail, Ishmael observes that "the prospect was unlimited, but exceedingly monotonous and forbidding; not the slightest variety that I could see." This monotony invites men to lose themselves in the vastness of the water. (Ackerman 2017, 12)

Ishmael "loses himself" by taking on a studied indifference. The ocean becomes an arena for a historic drama from which he detaches himself as observer. Ahab, by contrast, "loses himself" by projecting his (angry) ego onto specific environmental elements: the storm, the lightning, and, of course, the whale, descending into a nihilistic rage that is both predatory and suicidal.

Recognizing the nihilism inherent in the oceanic feeling, Freud advised against pursuing it in psychoanalytic practice for fear that it could nourish suicidal tendencies (Ackerman 2017). In contrast, Fred Moten (2013) and Jackie Wang (2016) have suggested that, in the context of intergenerational traumas that have denied Black subjectivity, an embrace of the oceanic can provide a means for reorientating and relocating Black livelihoods (see also Sharpe 2016; Gumbs 2020). For Melville's characters, though, the ocean provides only *dis*location, as the ocean is reduced to a scaffold for something else: the directionless dreams of a disengaged sailor or the angry outbursts of a captain's tortured soul. This is not a space to think *with*; it is a space to think *without*, and thus it is certainly not a space to think *from*. That is why, for both characters, the ocean's defining geographic characteristic, its water, is interchangeable with other, equally unattainable elements—immersive fire that rains down from the heavens, for Ahab; endless, undulating expanses of farmland, for Ishmael—just as the struggles of Ahab, Prometheus, and King Lear are interchangeable despite the very different demons that they seek to conquer.

FROM WHAT OCEAN DO WE THINK, WHEN WE THINK FROM THE OCEAN?

To summarize, as Melville reduces the ocean's nature to a signifying environment that hosts emotive elements and psychological dramas, he distracts the reader from the ocean's practiced meanings in the maritime world of the nineteenth century, even as he seeks, more broadly, to engage that world. Paul Gilroy, in *The Black Atlantic* (1993), takes a somewhat different tack, as he mobilizes the ocean less as an arena for psychological reckonings than for spatial imaginings. Gilroy essentially uses the term "Black Atlantic" as shorthand for the Atlantic world that is constructed by the African diaspora and symbolized by the Middle Passage and subsequent acts of crossing. In the process, as he focuses on various Middle Passages, he largely bypasses the liquid, voluminous materiality of the Atlantic Ocean, as well as the work of writers such as Walcott and Brathwaite whose writings on the Atlantic (and Caribbean) directly engage the ocean's materiality.

There is an ongoing debate regarding whether Gilroy's use of the Atlantic Ocean as a touchstone for a broader Atlantic region of peoples, memories, objects, and maritime passages is an elision of the ocean's geographic presence or an extension of it; whether it is a rejection of the turbulent, felt space of flows that underpins the Atlantic world or a thoughtful reimagining of it; whether Gilroy is missing an opportunity to place the ocean's liquidity at the heart of his imagination of Black postnationalism or whether he is constructing a Black Atlantic geography that persists "in excess" of that liquidity.[10] For Katherine McKittrick (2006), "*The Black Atlantic* works to loosen the naturalization of (black) identities and place, arguing for the ways in which a different sense of place, and different geographic landmarks, might fit into our historically present spatial organization" (13). Drawing on relational concepts of space proffered by thinkers like Édouard Glissant ([1990] 1997) and Sylvia Wynter (McKittrick 2015), for McKittrick, Gilroy's oceanic explodes the space of the African diaspora into a fractal of places, objects, and memories that exist across temporal and spatial scales. Such a project, for McKittrick, gets to the essence of geography through a Black reconfiguration of space. By contrast, Joan Dayan (1996) has suggested that in reducing the ocean, its artifacts, and encounters from materiality to metaphor, Gilroy has produced an a-geographic text. According to this critique, the *space* of the ocean—the liquid, churning, dynamic, fluid, four-dimensional space of incessant movement and recomposition that is simultaneously both transparent and opaque, and that is encountered by those who voluntarily or involuntarily encounter its depths—fades from view, as geography is replaced by a dis-placed historical referent (see also DeLoughrey 2007; Steinberg 2013). Entering into this debate, Omise'eke Natasha Tinsley (2008) takes an intermediate position when she writes with reference to Gilroy and others who point to the Atlantic as a metaphor to animate Black thinking: "My point is never that we should strip theory of watery metaphors but that we should return to the materiality of water to make its metaphors mean more complexly, shaking off setting into frozen figures" (212).

From one perspective, this debate can be seen as an iteration of the debate between the relative primacy of thinking with versus thinking from the ocean. McKittrick sees Gilroy's oceanic thinking as establishing a geography that one can think with, expanding one's viewpoint to a world that exceeds the strictly oceanic. For Dayan, by contrast, Gilroy's failure to think from material oceanic practices and spaces leads him to abrogate the potential for the ocean to be a space to think with. To (over)simplify, McKittrick places primacy on thinking *with* conceptualized oceanic geographies so that one can then think *from* the places of Black experience; Dayan places primacy on thinking *from* the encountered, material ocean so that one can think *with* the oceanic to understand diasporic experiences and identities.

From another perspective, though, this heuristic binary between thinking with and thinking from reveals that the two sides are not that far apart. Both sides are attempting to engage the ocean's materiality and the moments of present and historical encounter *and* the ways in which the ocean, as a social construction, can spur reimaginings of space. The challenge, to refer back to Tinsley, is to do this in a way that retains the ocean's provocative alterity *and* the historical contingency (and even the phenomenology) of oceanic encounters.

To address this challenge further, it is useful to return to Gilroy. Some twenty years after publishing *The Black Atlantic,* when asked to address "geographies of the Anthropocene," Gilroy used the opportunity to criticize the posthumanist turn that characterizes much of social, and, in particular, geographic, thought. Gilroy's argument is that any understanding of the African experience has always, necessarily, required a consideration of the more-than-human. In part this is because objects have always been enrolled in efforts to oppress Africans, but also, perhaps more profoundly, it is because that oppression has always involved the association of Africans with an "infrahuman" nature. Thus, Gilroy writes:

> Before the steady rise of object ontologies reached its apogee, nobody who has been party to the urgent conversations that have reproduced and extended the "black radical tradition" needed to be re-acquainted with the manifold problems arising from the social life of objects or the complexities of interacting with things and nature. The slaves from many parts of Africa who were exchanged for rum, cloth, guns, salt-cod and other commodities recoiled from their own brutal reification as labour, as capital and as brute. (Gilroy 2018, 4–5)

Crucial for Gilroy is that these historic processes that have rescripted Africans as infrahuman objects—reworking relations between natural forces, nonhuman objects, and sentient humans—have engaged the seemingly external space of the ocean, the extraterritorial space of the ship, and the liminal spaces of the coast and the shipwreck to rework (and reproduce) received human-nature dichotomies. To make this case, Gilroy turns to Melville (*Benito Cereno* as well as *Moby-Dick*) and, in particular, to James's reading of Melville. Gilroy writes approvingly of:

> Herman Melville's passionate planetary ontology of labouring humans, marine life, weather, capital and objects which, against the expectations of many scholastic guardians of his work, secretes in its poetics an argument about the elemental significance of racism and modern racial orders.... Slavery's pelagic theatre of power reveals its hidden character in a grey, watery confrontation between the properly human and the supposedly infrahuman. (Gilroy 2018, 5–6)

Gilroy concludes on a note of hope that the ocean, notwithstanding its central place in "slavery's pelagic theatre of power," can be a site where that power is reworked. He proposes that at the oceanic point of encounter, the agonistic struggle between humans and nature, and between humans and the individuals who have been constructed as their "infrahuman others," can be reconstructed around new dimensions that build a common humanity out of shared, if not necessarily identical, experiences, fears, and hopes. The ocean, Gilroy proposes, has particular purchase as a nature that suggests potential for a transcendent "offshore humanism" based on the reflection that comes from shared engagement with a hostile element, even if that sharing is not undertaken as equals. Gilroy suggests that if nature has been used to rationalize human hierarchies perhaps a reengagement with nature in all its messiness (and, in particular, the exceptionally messy nature of the ocean) may be used to disentangle these hierarchies and build new solidarities.

FROM AN OCEAN MORE ELEMENTAL . . . AND MORE HISTORICAL

Gilroy's argument is compelling, and his work on "offshore humanism" does much to "return to the materiality of water to make its metaphors mean more complexly" (Tinsley 2008, 212). And yet, even as Gilroy focuses on the power of the oceanic environment to rework new relationships between humans and nature (and between humans and humans), his focus on points of contact—the port, the coast, the beach, the ship, the shipwreck—leaves the underlying forces of the ocean, its geophysical and geopolitical liveliness, subsumed by the moment of the encounter and by the entities that they produce. My argument is not that we should turn away from points of oceanic encounter. Indeed, encounters provide crucial moments where one can achieve the goal of thinking both from and with the oceanic environment. Rather, echoing Tinsley's admonition with regard to the ocean metaphor, I want to propose that when we explore the encounter, we adopt a perspective that is both *more elemental* and *more historical,* thereby fusing Melville's attentiveness to the emotive properties of the marine environment as a site of agonistic struggle with Gilroy's focus on the ways in which that struggle shapes (and has the potential to reshape) human-human and human-nature hierarchies. Following McKittrick, this suggests a reorientation of geographies.

Turning first to the "more elemental," while Melville focuses on specific objects at sea—the ship, the whale, the crew member, the captain, and the symbiotic relationship between them—I want to argue that this ecological understanding be extended to the ocean itself. This mandates a foregrounding of its geophysical forces. The result is not simply a world of waves, currents, depths, and continual re-formation. It is also one that necessarily exceeds its liquidity, as atmospheric and land forces are understood as constitutive of, and constituted by, the marine environment (Peters and Steinberg 2019). Although an elemental perspective might seem to reduce the ocean to a different kind of abstraction—molecular objects that can be used only to think with—scholars have demonstrated than an attention to the ocean's elementality can, in fact, open up worlds of relationality (Anderson 2019), complexity (Engelmann 2019), and more-than-human agency (Bear 2019). It also can draw attention to the properties that the ocean shares with other instances of "aquatic space" (Oslender 2016) as well as to social entanglements that span interrelated but oppositional substances, like the intertwined worlds of fire and water (Peters 2024). Likewise, although a focus on the ocean as a spectral property, such as the color blue that anchors the notion of a "blue humanities," can depoliticize and dehistoricize analysis by reducing the ocean to an abstraction and to the lens through which it is viewed, conversely a focus on conditions and perceptions of "blueness" can direct attention to the role of the ocean in valuing and devaluing humans and nature and in projecting power over space (DeLoughrey 2019b; Ferwerda 2024; see also Alaimo 2013).

Consider how, for example, when the ocean is understood as an arena of molecules—perpetually mobile in four dimensions—the very concept of "place" as static and determinate is challenged. Is a "place" in the ocean a latitude-longitude coordinate, a latitude-longitude-depth coordinate, or, perhaps, a molecule that retains its identity even as it moves around a three-dimensional plane? And what of that molecule when it evaporates into air or freezes into ice? Is it then, still, a "place in the ocean?" In other words, do time or physical condition limit the continuity of "place" in a marine context? Of course, these are not questions that can be definitively answered—although how one answers them does influence one's approach to modeling or managing the resources of ocean-space (Lehman 2020; Peters 2020; Steinberg et al. 2020). But even asking these questions forces us to revisit our understanding of various "places" in the ocean—ships, shipping channels, ports, as well as individual geophysical features such as waves and ice floes—that are both constant and continually being re-formed, at one moment revealed and then at another reabsorbed within the ocean's incessant flow.

Since notions of place incorporate understandings of time (Tuan 1977; Massey 2004), and time makes possible the accrual of meaning (Nora 1989), how we approach these questions—how we approach the ocean as a space, and how we think both *from* and *with* it—impacts the understandings that we take from our encounters with the ocean in our lives and in our histories, and in others' lives and histories as well. An attentiveness to both oceanic histories and oceanic materialities enables Christina Sharpe's (2016) suggestion that the fate of enslaved African people cast off ships should lead to a focus not only on their burial ground at the bottom of the sea but also on how their bodies have decomposed, how they have been transformed and moved in space and time by organic and inorganic forces and processes, as molecules transported around the world, through the hydrosphere, entering the food chain, and ultimately becoming parts of our livelihoods and bodies, persisting, as Sharpe notes, in "residence time."

Reading Sharpe's discussion of "residence time" through a perspective informed by Gilroy's "offshore humanism," there is a point where we all, in a sense, become one with the Black Atlantic. To be clear, I am not proposing that we would all have the same subjectivities in this "excessive" Black Atlantic world: the position of the descendent of enslaved persons whose racialization is reproduced through contemporary hierarchies is very different from that of the descendant of the enslaver, or from that of the person whose connections are solely through contemporary economic hierarchies (see also Hartman 2008). Indeed, I share Povinelli's (2020) concern about a "critical ocean studies ... which annihilates the specificity of how entanglements produce difference in order to erase the specific ancestral present" (3). Rather, an attention to the oceanic, informed by the works of Black scholars thinking both with and from the ocean, can help to elucidate how the historical and contemporary oceanic entangles us all in the history of transcontinental trafficking in enslaved persons, and through its resonances in contemporary political economy and structures of racialized hierarchy, in different ways. The "offshore humanism" of the Black Atlantic extends in time and space so that, in the end, no one is absolved of responsibility

DESCENDING FROM 35,000 FEET

Thinking with (and, to varying degrees, from) the sea, (primarily white) critical ocean geographers and their allies in other areas of critical ocean theory have proposed that the ocean suggests a *different* spatiotemporality: one in which space and time are recomposed amidst continual turbulence and reformation and in which movement takes on a different character because the background itself is not stable (e.g., Lehman et al. 2021). Critical Black scholars, looking out at the sea and considering its role in producing the history and contemporary condition of the African diaspora, have developed perspectives that bear some striking similarities (e.g., Brathwaite 1981). Noting this co-incidence, it would be easy to suggest that the time is ripe for scholars from various backgrounds to join forces and consider, for instance, ways that the ocean can be mobilized to tell stories of racialization that incorporate the temporalities of the Black experience, in memories, hopes, rootings, and oceanic crossings, while also relying on modernist tropes that denigrate the ocean as an empty "other" (e.g., Steinberg 2022). It also would be easy to suggest that the time is ripe for engaging Black temporalities to shed light on the oceanic world that extends to all of our lives (e.g., Pugh 2016).

While this chapter holds out hope for building these bridges and making translations across literatures, it also suggests that tensions remain, in all critical traditions, between the starting points of *thinking with* and *thinking from* the ocean. At the beginning of this chapter, I illustrated this with the extreme example of the "God's eye" view from the airplane. Staring down from 35,000 feet, blankly surveying a flat field of water without any visible features, the ocean and the airplane both appear immobile. With an absence of reference points to map space to time, the journey is both brilliantly fast and agonizingly slow. The ocean is both enticingly close and incalculably far away. Experiencing the "oceanic feeling," the distant theorist, viewing from above, looks inward, leaning toward the ocean as a space to think with, to make sense of what one cannot really know, below.

But this is a caricature. Few scholars work from such distanced heights. Even the frustrated, aloof narrator at the beginning of this chapter was looking for a story, and even Melville found his, as the violence of the marine environment seeped its way into the livelihoods of the men on board the *Pequod*. Whether engaging historic narratives, scientific knowledges, cultural productions, everyday practices, embedded memories, or embodied encounters, most oceanic thought engages at least some aspect of thinking *from* as well as *with* the ocean.

The question, then, is less that of whether one thinks *with* or *from* the ocean than that of *what* ocean one thinks from and *how*. This is arguably where the greatest potential lies for engagement between the critical ocean geography and Black studies traditions (and their various points of intersection), as theorists, regardless of their starting point, search for ways to conceive of the ocean as a space that is simultaneously one of experience, history, memorialization, theorizing, healing, life, death, dreams, and so much more. Nonetheless, challenges remain when thinking across traditions and positionalities. Gumbs's (2020) work here is instructive. On the one hand, as she notes (with reference to marine mammals as well as humans) we all breathe, we all find ways to survive, we all find love in oceanic darkness.

On the other hand, as she also stresses, we all do so in different ways, so that the very definition of "we" becomes associated less with group identification according to specific properties or experiences (what she calls "identification" [romanized]) than with what she calls "*identification*" (italicized, 8): feelings of kinship and solidarity that emerge amidst adversity and struggle. Gumbs's ocean is thus an ocean of empathy that echoes Gilroy's appeal to an "offshore humanism" even as, for her, it extends beyond the human.

In short, searching for ways to think both with and from the ocean may assist us in building dialogue between different lineages of ocean studies. Within our respective traditions, we are doing this anyway as we integrate the ocean into our analyses, as history, as matter, as space, as a scaffold for thinking. However, stories told through analogs, metaphors, histories, and encounters are inevitably partial, and thus the stories that we tell when thinking from the ocean will always be multiple, encouraging a further round of thinking with the ocean's affordances and meanings. The dialectic between thinking with and from, and the entanglements of different analytic lineages, productive as they may be, may never resolve. In the end, we may find that, indeed, we swim in different seas, even as they are connected in one world-ocean.

NOTES

1. This chapter originally appeared in *Social & Cultural Geography* and is reprinted here with permission. Much earlier versions of this paper were presented at the 3ROceans seminar series at NTNU, Trondheim (2018); the Mariners, Renegades, and Capitalism conference at New York University (2018); the Water Logics conference at Tulane University (2019); and the Annual Conference of the Royal Geographical Society (2024). I am grateful for feedback from individuals at all these venues, as well as from Kimberley Peters and Lawrence Publicover. Finally, I am grateful for incredibly helpful input from yasser elhariry, Michele Lobo, Edwige Tamalet Talbayev, and the four anonymous reviewers at *Social & Cultural Geography*.
2. "Aquatic space" is a term used by Ulrich Oslender (2016) to describe the watery environments that both characterize and rework Afro-Colombians' sense of place.
3. There are, of course, exceptions. Paul Gilroy's (1993) *The Black Atlantic* and several works by Marcus Rediker (e.g., Rediker 2007) are widely cited across

genres, as are writings by key thinkers who have engaged with the ocean in postcolonial theory (e.g., Glissant [1990] 1997; Hau'ofa 2008). A simplified genealogy of "white" and "Black" ocean geographies also skips over those who have approached the ocean from perspectives informed by feminist theory (e.g., Neimanis 2017) as well as a large body of work on perspectives of the ocean held by Indigenous peoples, coastal peoples, and islanders that, in some (but certainly not all) cases, resonates with Black oceanic experiences (e.g., DeLoughrey 2007; Shilliam 2015). It also overlooks (white) geographers who have drawn on the Black ocean geography literature (and the broader corpus of Black oceanic theory) to aid in their conceptualization of the ocean as a space of memory and forgetting (e.g., Steinberg 2022; Pugh and Chandler 2023).

4. In fact, there was some intellectual traffic between mid-nineteenth-century ocean scientists and marine authors; for instance, Helen Rozwadowski (2018) notes that Melville revised his chapter "The Chart" (chapter 44) after learning that Matthew Fontaine Maury was developing a global whale chart. Furthermore, as Rozwadowski also notes, this knowledge flowed in both directions, with oceanographers following in the wake of novelists and explorers as well as the other way around.

5. There are parallels here with Melville's depiction of the three main non-white characters in *Moby-Dick*: Queequeg, Tashtego, and Daggoo. While each, as Melville scholars have noted, contributes to a critique of prevailing norms of racial hierarchy (see, e.g., Freeburg 2012; Blum 2022), each is also a "noble savage" who, as a harpoonist, exhibits a closeness to the ocean and its different and distant nature, and an essential distance from civilization, not shared by their white sailor colleagues (Steinberg 2001).

6. Here, I build on Deleuze and Guattari's ([1980] 1987) dialectical conceptualization of territorialization, which they develop with reference to oceanic navigation in chapter 14 ("1440: The Smooth and the Striated").

7. James wrote *Mariners, Renegades and Castaways* as an appeal to the United States government, while he was being held in custody awaiting deportation as a suspected communist.

8. For a survey of alternate perspectives, where materialities that differ from the terrestrial norm are understood not as empty spaces wherein individuals establish *extra*-territories but rather as spaces for the establishment of *different* territories, see Peters et al. (2018).

9. Since *Moby-Dick* was written before Freud's birth, Ackerman does not mean this literally. Rather, she argues that *Moby-Dick* can be read as an exploration of the same egoistic state that Freud later came to define as an "oceanic feeling."

10. For the concept of an "ocean in excess," see Peters and Steinberg (2019).

WORKS CITED

Ackerman, Sarah. 2017. "Exploring Freud's Resistance to the Oceanic Feeling." *Journal of the American Psychoanalytic Association* 65 (1): 9–31.

Alaimo, Stacy. 2013. "Violet-Black." In *Prismatic Ecologies: Ecotheory Beyond Green*, edited by Jeffrey Jerome Cohen. University of Minnesota Press.

Amimoto Ingersoll, Karin. 2016. *Waves of Knowing: A Seascape Epistemology*. Duke University Press.

Anderson, Jon. 2019. "The Aquatic as Elemental Excess." *Dialogues in Human Geography* 9 (3): 320–24.

Bear, Christopher. 2019. "The Ocean Exceeded: Fish, Flows and Forces." *Dialogues in Human Geography* 9 (3): 329–32.

Blum, Hester. 2010. "The Prospect of Oceanic Studies." *PMLA* 125 (3): 670–77.

Blum, Hester. 2022. Introduction to *Herman Melville: Moby-Dick*, edited by Hester Blum. Oxford University Press.

Brathwaite, Edward Kamau. 1981. *The Arrivants: A New World Trilogy*. Oxford University Press.

Campling, Liam, and Alejandro Colás. 2021. *Capitalism and the Sea: The Maritime Factor in the Making of the Modern World*. Verso.

Casarino, Cesare. 2002. *Modernity at Sea: Melville, Marx, Conrad in Crisis*. University of Minnesota Press.

Dayan, Joan. 1996. "Paul Gilroy's Slaves, Ships, and Routes: The Middle Passage as Metaphor." *Research in African Literatures* 27 (4): 7–14.

Deleuze, Gilles, and Félix Guattari. (1980) 1987. *One Thousand Plateaus: Capitalism and Schizophrenia*. Translated by Brian Massumi. University of Minnesota Press.

DeLoughrey, Elizabeth. 2007. *Routes and Roots: Navigating Caribbean and Pacific Island Literatures*. University of Hawai'i Press.

DeLoughrey, Elizabeth. 2019a. *Allegories of the Anthropocene*. Duke University Press.

DeLoughrey, Elizabeth. 2019b. "Toward a Critical Ocean Studies for the Anthropocene." *English Notes* 57 (1): 21–36.

DeLoughrey, Elizabeth, and T. Flores. 2020. "Submerged Bodies: The Tidalectics of Representability and the Sea in Caribbean Art." *Environmental Humanities* 12 (1): 132–66.

Elden, Stuart. 2004. *Understanding Henri Lefebvre: Theory and the Possible*. Continuum.

Engelmann, Sasha. 2019. "Adrift in the Etheric Ocean." *Dialogues in Human Geography* 9 (3): 325–28.

Ferwerda, Susanne. 2024. "Blue Humanities and the Color of Colonialism." *Environmental Humanities* 16 (1): 1–18.

Freeburg, Christopher. 2012. *Melville and the Idea of Blackness: Race and Imperialism in Nineteenth-Century America*. Cambridge University Press.

Gilroy, Paul. 1993. *The Black Atlantic: Modernity and Double-Consciousness*. Harvard University Press.

Gilroy, Paul. 2018. "'Where Every Breeze Speaks of Courage and Liberty': Offshore Humanism and Marine Xenology; or, Racism and the Problem of Critique at Sea Level." *Antipode* 50 (1): 3–22.

Glissant, Édouard. (1990) 1997. *Poetics of Relation*. Translated by Betsy Wing. University of Michigan Press.

Gumbs, Alexis Pauline. 2020. *Undrowned: Black Feminist Lessons from Marine Mammals*. AK Press.

Hartman, Saidiya. 2008. *Lose Your Mother: A Journey Along the Atlantic Slave Route*. Farrar, Straus and Giroux.

Hau'ofa, Epeli. 2008. *We Are the Ocean: Selected Works*. University of Hawai'i Press.

Hawthorne, Camilla. 2023. Black Mediterranean Geographies: Translation and the Mattering of Black Life in Italy. *Gender, Place & Culture* 30 (3): 484–507.

Heller, Charles, and Lorenzo Pezzani. n.d. *The Left-to-Die Boat*. https://forensic-architecture.org/investigation/the-left-to-die-boat. Accessed June 16, 2025.

Helmreich, Stefan. 2023. *A Book of Waves*. Duke University Press.

Hessler, Stefanie, ed. 2018. *Tidalectics: Imagining an Oceanic Worldview Through Art and Science*. TBA21–Academy.

James, C. L. R. (1953) 1978. *Mariners, Renegades and Castaways: The Story of Herman Melville and the World We Live In*. 2nd ed. Bewick.

Khalili, Laleh. 2021. "Carceral Sea." *Millennium: Journal of International Studies* 49 (3): 462–71.

King, Richard J. 2019. *Ahab's Rolling Sea: A Natural History of Moby-Dick*. University of Chicago Press.

King, Tiffany Lethabo. 2019. *The Black Shoals: Offshore Formations of Black and Native Studies*. Duke University Press.

Lehman, Jessica. 2020. "The Technopolitics of Ocean Sensing." In *Blue Legalities: The Life and Laws of the Sea*, edited by Irus Braverman and Elizabeth R. Johnson. Duke University Press.

Lehman, Jessica, Philip Steinberg, and Elizabeth R. Johnson. 2021. "Turbulent Waters in Three Parts." *Theory and Event* 24 (1): 192–219.

Mack, John. 2011. *The Sea: A Cultural History*. Reaktion.

Massey, Doreen. 2004. *For Space*. Sage.

McKittrick, Katherine. 2006. *Demonic Grounds: Black Women and the Cartographies of Struggle*. University of Minnesota Press.

McKittrick, Katherine, ed. 2015. *Sylvia Wynter: On Being Human as Praxis*. Duke University Press.

Melville, Heman. (1851) 1922. *Moby-Dick; or, the Whale*. Sampson Low, Marston.

Mentz, Steve. 2023. *An Introduction to the Blue Humanities*. Routledge.

Moten, Fred. 2013. "Blackness and Nothingness (Mysticism in the Flesh)." *South Atlantic Quarterly* 112 (4): 737–80.

Neimanis, Astrida. 2017. *Bodies of Water: Posthuman Feminist Phenomenology*. Bloomsbury.

Nora, Pierre. 1989. "Between Memory and History: Les Lieux de Mémoire." *Representations*, no. 26, 7–24.

Noxolo, Pat. 2016. "A Shape Which Represents an Eternity of Riddles: Fractals and Scale in the Work of Wilson Harris." *cultural geographies* 23 (3): 373–85.

Oslender, Ulrich. 2016. *The Geographies of Social Movements: Afro-Colombian Mobilization and the Aquatic Space*. Duke University Press.

Peters, Kimberley. 2012. "Manipulating Material Hydro-Worlds: Rethinking Human and More-than-Human Relationality Through Offshore Radio Piracy." *Environment and Planning A* 44 (5): 1241–54.

Peters, Kimberley. 2020. "The Territories of Governance: Unpacking the Ontologies and Geophilosophies of Fixed to Flexible Ocean Management, and Beyond." *Philosophical Transactions of the Royal Society B* 375 (1814). https://doi.org/10.1030/rstb.2019.0458.

Peters, Kimberley. 2024. "Geography H_2O: Compounding Water Studies." *North West Geography* 24 (1): 14–26.

Peters, Kimberley, and Mike Brown. 2017. "Writing *with* the Sea: Reflections on In/Experienced Encounters with Ocean Space." *cultural geographies* 24 (4): 617–24.

Peters, Kimberley, and Philip Steinberg. 2019. "The Ocean in Excess: Towards a More-than-Wet Ontology." *Dialogues in Human Geography* 9 (3): 293–307.

Peters, Kimberley, Philip Steinberg, and Elaine Stratford, eds. 2018. *Territory Beyond Terra*. London: Rowman & Littlefield.

Povinelli, Elizabeth A. 2020. "The Ancestral Present of Oceanic Illusions: Connected and Differentiated in Late Toxic Liberalism." *E-Flux*, no. 112, 1–11, https://www.e-flux.com/journal/112/352823/the-ancestral-present-of-oceanic-illusions-connected-and-differentiated-in-late-toxic-liberalism.

Proglio, Gabriele, Camilla Hawthorne, Ida Danewid, et al., eds. 2021. *The Black Mediterranean: Bodies, Borders and Citizenship*. Springer Nature; Palgrave Macmillan.

Publicover, Laurence. 2018. "The Invisibility of the Sea." In *The Invisibility of the Sea*, edited by M. Pieraccini and L. Publicover. Brigstow Institute, University of Bristol. https://cpb-eu-w2.wpmucdn.com/blogs.bristol.ac.uk/dist/8/543/files/2020/04/The-Invisibility-of-the-Sea-working-paper.pdf.

Pugh, Jonathan. 2016. "The Relational Turn in Island Geographies: Bringing Together Island, Sea, and Ship Relations and the Case of the Landship." *Social & Cultural Geography* 17 (8): 1040–59.

Pugh, Jonathan, and David Chandler. 2023. *The World as Abyss: The Caribbean and Critical Thought in the Anthropocene*. University of Westminster Press.

Raban, Jonathan. 2023. *Father and Son: A Memoir About Family, the Past and Mortality*. Picador.

Rediker, Marcus. 2007. *The Slave Ship: A Human History*. John Murray.

Reid, Susan. 2020. "Solwara 1 and the Sessile Ones." In *Blue Legalities: The Life and Laws of the Sea*, edited by Irus Braverman and Elizabeth R. Johnson. Duke University Press.

Rozwadowski, Helen M. 2018. *Vast Expanses: A History of the Ocean*. Reaktion.

Schmitt, Carl. (1950) 2003. *The Nomos of the Earth in the International Law of Jus Publicum Europaeum*. Translated by G. L. Ulmen. Telos.

Sharpe, Christina. 2016. *In the Wake: On Blackness and Being*. Duke University Press.

Shilliam, Robbie. 2015. *The Black Pacific: Anti-Colonial Struggles and Oceanic Connections*. Bloomsbury.

Slonczewski, Joan. 1986. *A Door into Ocean*. Avon.

Steinberg, Philip. 2001. *The Social Construction of the Ocean*. Cambridge University Press.

Steinberg, Philip. 2013. "Of Other Seas: Metaphors and Materialities in Maritime Regions." *Atlantic Studies* 10 (2): 156–69.

Steinberg, Philip. 2022. "Blue Planet, Black Lives: Matter, Memory, and the Temporalities of Political Geography." *Political Geography*, no. 96. https://doi.org/10.1016/j.polgeo.2021.102524.

Steinberg, Philip, Greta Ferloni, Claudio Aporta, et al. 2022. "Navigating the Structural Coherence of Sea Ice." In *Laws of the Sea*, edited by Irus Braverman. Routledge.

Steinberg, Philip, and Kimberley Peters. 2015. "Wet Ontologies, Fluid Spaces: Giving Depth to Volume Through Oceanic Thinking." *Environment and Planning D: Society & Space* 33 (2): 247–64.

Tinsley, Omise'eke Natasha. 2008. "Black Atlantic, Queer Atlantic: Queer Imaginings of the Middle Passage." *GLQ* 14 (2)–3: 191–215.

Tuan, Yi-Fu. 1997. *Space and Place: The Perspective of Experience*. University of Minnesota Press.

Walcott, Derek. 1986. "The Sea Is History." In *Derek Walcott, Collected Poems, 1948–1984*. Farrar, Straus & Giroux.

Walcott, Rinaldo. 2021. "The Black Aquatic." *Liquid Blackness* 5 (1): 67–73.
Wang, Jackie. 2016. "Oceanic Feeling and Communist Affect," Tumblr, December 3. https://loneberry.tumblr.com/post/153995404787/oceanic-feeling-and-communist-affect.
Winston, Celeste. 2021. "Maroon Geographies." *Annals of the Association of American Geographers* 111 (7): 2185–99.
Wright, Willie Jamaal. 2020. "The Morphology of Marronage." *Annals of the Association of American Geographers* 111 (4): 1134–49.

MO(U)RNING IN THE MEDITERRANEAN

Liquid Mortuaries and the Arts of Re-Membering

SUPRIYA M. NAIR

> This boat is your womb, a matrix, and yet it expels you. This boat: pregnant with as many dead as living under the sentence of death.
> —ÉDOUARD GLISSANT

> Death is the sanction of everything that the storyteller can tell.
> —WALTER BENJAMIN

Death around borders, indeed, literally *at* borders, is a transnational event that demands a scrupulous cross-cultural dialogue and alliance, even as the specific contexts must be kept in mind. Mass drownings in recent years in the Mediterranean resonate with the drownings of enslaved people during the Middle Passage and the later deaths at sea of Haitian migrants in the 1980s and 1990s, both tragedies reflected in the regions' literature. The moribund lines of the first epigraph from Édouard Glissant portend seaborne death and foster a poetics of relation between the older Black Atlantic context and my focus in this essay, the more mediatized contemporary scenes of fleeing migrants dying while crossing the

Mediterranean. The "pregnant" but abortive sea—an intrauterine "matrix" of death induced by imperialism, extractive capitalism, and racism—links both regions across vast, distant bodies of water despite the differences in histories, trajectories, and timelines. A growing number of global activist projects and transnational literary and cultural studies have paid attention to tallying, identifying, and commemorating the dead at various sites, and they frame my analysis of selected literary texts that resuscitate the drownings in the Mediterranean Sea. This essay is also inspired by the literature of loss and grief related to oceanic deaths, invoking a thanatic ethics which intersects with ecological imaginaries and thalassic materialities.[1]

The International Organization of Migration tabulates that in 2016, of 8,074 migrant fatalities recorded, 5,143 were in the Mediterranean.[2] The same website tracks deaths in 2021 as follows: of a total 2,083, 1,173 were in the Mediterranean,[3] with most of the dead notably of African origin. Alexandra Délano Alonso and Benjamin Nienass claim that the so-called crisis in the Mediterranean, where thousands have lost their lives in recent years and thousands more have disappeared in the perilous crossing, has corollaries in "Central America, Mexico, the United States, and Canada; in the Andaman Sea; [and] in the vast waters surrounding Australia" (2016, xxi). They argue that the epicenter of the catastrophe is not the migrants drowning en masse or "flooding" apprehensive countries but the stringent terrestrial border policies caused by the virtual abandonment of the Geneva conventions of 1951. The increasing reluctance to host refugees has only intensified their recourse to hazardous means of ingress. Many seeking sanctuary or new lives in countries are nervously, if not aggressively, confronted by armed border personnel who claim to be overwhelmed by the sheer numbers, as reinforced by the sensationalist media hype. Although the coverage has generated waves of international outrage, panic, or sentimentality, the circulation of photos of three-year-old Alan ("Aylan") Kurdi and the innumerable, related spectacles of overcrowded boats and desperate migrants are only too likely to lose their disruptive force and languish into business as usual.[4] While migrants dying in multitudes have merited lurid, if uneven, attention in popular media, tracking them more persistently, accounting for their lives as well as deaths, has involved a more assiduous global effort from various disciplinary perspectives, a couple of which I will mention here alongside my focus on the literary.

Some of the most poignant accounts of the first wave of COVID-19 deaths deal with the prohibitions against viewing the bodies of loved ones, the inability to conduct funerals and perform communal burial rituals that honor the dead across cultures under normal circumstances. One of the earliest signs of human civilization was the capacity to mark in place, mourn, and ritually consecrate the passing of a loved one, and the ungraven, anonymous deaths at sea trigger a primal horror for that reason. Gathering the remnants physically or revivifying them through narrative, restoring legibility—however shadowy—to their bodies and lives is one way of refusing the illegality and nonhumanity imposed on these migrant subjects who have been lost at sea. What Ewa Domanska calls the "archaeontology of the dead body" reads the materiality of the past through the corpse and their belongings, prompting the "contemplative approach" of scholars "engaged in reflection about death, the dead, and their remains" (2005, 391).

Not just scholars but writers have also dwelt on catastrophic death at sea and even inspired this archaeontological approach. "Illiterature," Hakim Abderrezak's neologism for francophone Moroccan literature of clandestine migration, undermines the conventional use of "illegal" in Spanish media through the insubordination of migrants who maneuver around the criminality imposed on them (2009). Although Abderrezak notes that the subgenre was dominated in the francophone field by male writers, I include other linguistic contexts for this growing literature, focusing in this essay on Margaret Mazzantini's novella *Morning Sea* (2010), translated into English from Italian (*Mare al mattino*), and Khaled Mattawa's collection of poems *Mare Nostrum* (2019), written in English despite the Latin title. Both texts depict the erosion of human rights in the Maghreb. Mazzantini, in particular, deals with the aftermath of the Arab Spring insurgency during Gaddafi's dictatorship. In contrast to the literature of migration and exile by the relatively more privileged descendants of those who migrated to colonial metropoles, the subgenre emphasizes the lives—and deaths—of those whose precarity is more patent. In a subversive trope, Abderrezak compares writers of illiterature to the *ḥarrāga* or *ḥarrāg* (from Arabic for "those who burn," denoting the clandestine North African and Arab migrants who survive the chancy sea crossing, burn their IDs to deter immigration authorities, and seek a fresh start in European nations).[5] The phoenix-like symbol of the enduring "burners" is in this case enabling, but, as we will see in Mazzantini's and Mattawa's works, the "burn" also invokes diesel fuel burns experienced on unstable, leaky seacraft, where the migrant bodies incorporate the wounds, smells, and inundations of the crossing, which extracts a high mortality in the dangerous transit. In countries such as Libya, the oil economy precipitated the conflicts compelling people to flee across water, so the spillages at sea (including bodily excreta) become even more portentous in their corrosive effects, aggravated by the salts and minerals in the waves. A significant characteristic of illiterature is that it tasks readers with "uncover[ing] and re-cover[ing] living and dead bodies between the pages" (Abderrezak 2009, 467). The hyphenated split in "re-cover" suggests both an exhumation of the dead who have been buried out of sight and a reverent assembly of their remains in an act of memorialization, rather than simply leaving their bodies exposed yet unknown or invisibly decomposing in the depths of the sea and in underequipped morgues.

Contrary to the sense of a gutted or irretrievably submerged history, the ocean amasses mute, mysterious, and yet intelligible bodies of evidence recording failed or deadly maritime voyages. To invoke a familiar trope in Caribbean literatures around the Middle Passage, the sea is a historical text, providing a scattered cargo space, even, to continue the conceit, a vast safe-deposit box, the contents of which can be withdrawn and accounted for as a living archive in a unique historiography. To quote from Derek Walcott's celebrated poem, "The Sea Is History":[6]

> Where are your monuments, your battles, martyrs?
> Where is your tribal memory? Sirs
> in that grey vault. The sea. The sea
> has locked them up. (1986, 364)

Teju Cole articulates the nexus that may have drawn Walcott to oscillate between the Caribbean and Mediterranean seas in the latter's poetic work. The chapter "Capri" in Cole's phototext volume *Blind Spot* undercuts the luminous epic spirit of the "shining fleet on the Mediterranean," a tourist frame familiar in Caribbean waters, by shadowing photogenic ships and sailboats in the adjacent print text with the prolonged and continuing history of war, empire, and migration. As Cole snaps the glossy scene, presumably from his hotel window, what he recollects is not just *The Iliad* but Edna O'Brien's unsettling words: "We know about these beautiful waters that have death in them" (qtd. in Cole 2017, 16).[7] I am particularly interested in the "mortiferous dynamics," as they link the art of forensics[8] with that of storytelling (elhariry and Talbayev 2018, 10). So striking have been the mediated spectacles of death in the Mediterranean waters that it is not surprising, as Laura

Sarnelli notes, that the region, once associated with the glories of classical civilization, has assumed Gothic characteristics in the persistent images of clandestine migration and smuggling, repeated collapse of friable vessels, mass drownings of innumerable refugees from parts of Africa and the Middle East, and the daunting infrastructure of walls, borders, gateposts, and centers amidst wars, famines, and other catastrophes. Sarnelli's categorization of the unwanted migrants on "ghostly" crafts as "zombies" ties the "thanatopolitics" and "necropolitics" of enforced oceanic migrations in the Caribbean to the fleeing refugees in the Mediterranean, here the *mare mortis*, which has a long history of death in its waters (2015, 149).

While chattel slavery is no longer what dictates the new passages, or charts contemporary cartographies, of forced migration, Black Africans, poorer and darker-skinned than Syrians, have faced racism at both ends of the border as they reach Libya from other parts of Africa and attempt to cross to Europe. Both Tunisia and Libya function as preliminary border controls for Europe, often detaining and deporting other African immigrants who arrive there in transit to Europe. In Mazzantini's novella, the imaginative fusion of temporally and regionally different coffles shows disparately motivated but inherited patterns of enforced movement. The sea is thus both a fluid conduit and what Abderrezak marks as a "hard line," where thousands of subjects are impeded from crossing and often do not make it (2018, 151). Even when they do, many stagnate in carceral regimes that harden the clandestine character of the passage. In *Morning Sea*, as young Farid flees with his mother, Jamila (whose husband, unknown to Farid, has been killed by the rebels), toward the Mediterranean Sea in the hopes of crossing to Italy, the third-person narrator describes the packed convoys of overcrowded trucks fleeing Libyan locals and immigrants, tellingly echoing an earlier traumatic passage into the Americas: "They will go towards the sea. The truck is full of packages and black men packed in like slaves. . . . Human beings deported like beasts" (Mazzantini 2015, 30). In the trash-strewn desert, empty oilcans, burnt cars, blown-out tires, colorful rags, and abandoned shoes build up to the final horror of heads, hair, jawbones, and hands sunk in the sand, transforming the desert into an "open-air cemetery." The narrator continues: "They are all black Africans. Dead for months already, from before the war" (31). The shocked gaze of the Libyans and other refugees fleeing the civil war raging between Gaddafi's regime and the various rebel groups is focalized: "Everyone on the truck knows they were migrants from Mali,

Ghana, Niger, abandoned in the desert after the colonel struck a deal with the Europeans to block the flow of desperate illegal immigrants" (31–32). The desert sand, then, precedes the seabed as a graveyard, although here parts of the dead are visible above the surface of sand and not buried deep in the sea.

While what I call liquid mortuaries demand specific modalities of retrieval and commemoration, the fatal outcome of many migratory crossings begins on land. By making the past visible through iterative events and retracing precarious routes, the author challenges any rigid distinction between topographies. *Morning Sea* dives below the superficially visible surfaces to excavate the deep time of slow evolutionary change while also emphasizing the dire, fast-tracked transformations wrought by the colonial Anthropocene. In the first of the three sections, titled "Farid and the Gazelle," young Farid, who has never seen the sea, imagines it in a geological memory: "He's looked for fossilized seashells buried millions of years ago when the sea extended into the desert. He's chased after fish lizards that swim beneath the sand. He's seen the salty lake and the bitter lake and silvery camels advancing like shabby pirate ships" (15). The familiar depiction of dromedaries as ships of the desert maps the landscape through centuries of rapacious trade along a "route used by merchants who cut across the desert from black Africa to the sea. They carried ivory, resin, precious stones and captives to sell as slaves in the ports of Cyrenaica and Tripolitania" (17). The pacification of the camels, however, is disrupted when the turbulent sea that Farid and Jamila navigate in a crowded, incapacitated vessel is likened to "an infinity of shaking humps, blue flesh spraying foam from its submerged mouth" (39).[9] While the oil gushing from the desert sand galvanizes multinational capital, modernizes the means of transportation, and makes Libya a wealthy petronation, the old man Aghib is unable to view "the black sea beneath the desert" sanguinely and blames it for the series of crises that convulse the country and force Libyans to flee to the other sea, the blue one. "*Oil is the devil's shit. Don't trust things that seem like blessings*," he warns Farid (42). Mazzantini maps the excesses of racism and capitalism from sand to water, the barrels of oil waste trailing in the wake of oil carriers and merging with the "human fertilizer" crammed into boats (136). The fact that the commodity fetish of oil has more value than the refugees whose land it has been extracted from is clear when a passing vessel sees Farid's boat in distress and does not stop. Both leaking oil and sinking bodies contaminate the water but are also fertilized as they interact with the dissolved salts and ions, hydrothermal fluids, and other life forms of the ocean and its floor.[10] Although similes are overworked in the text and the lyrical prose strains to bear the weight of the trauma, the haplessness of the migrants is emphasized, annulling colonial exertions (the oil fields, the urban settlements, the cultivated orchards) to reshape the environment in the desert, and subjecting the migrants to the formidable sovereignty of the sea.

But even on land, Farid's people, the Bedouins, have tenuous control. The nomadic communities once "possessed nothing, only footprints, which the sand covered over" (16). In a foreshadowing of what will happen to Farid, Jamila, and their fellow voyagers in the sea, the burying grounds shift with the Ghibli winds: "They disappeared in the dunes" (16). The constant equivalences between land- and seascapes, the pervasiveness of litter in both, and the disintegration of the human in the desert or when heaved from water onto sand—"remnants vomited up onto the beach that looks like a maritime rubbish dump" (52)—conjoin terrestrial and oceanic forms of life and decay and signpost the dead, however erratically. Farid's older parallel on the other shore, Vito, whose Italian mother, Angelina, was expelled as a child from Libya by Colonel Gaddafi on Revenge Day in 1970 along with thousands of other settlers, is forced to consider the annihilation of the Libyans now fleeing toward Italy. Vito "doesn't like to think about what the fish eat. He dreamt about it one night, the dark depths and a school of fish inside a human skull as if it were a cave full of fluttering sea anemones" (53). Unlike Walcott's sublime sense of the renewal of dead flesh and human bones into new forms in the fecund depths of the ocean, the image here is darkly Gothic, the human remains a prey to marine biota nibbling unconcerned at their once predatory food source.

In a continuation of the "open-air cemetery" that the desert becomes in the jarring disclosure of body parts in the sand, the sea converts to a "liquid tomb" that Sicilian fisherfolk avoid navigating because of the bodies, limbs, and meager personal possessions they capture in their nets. I borrow the phrase "liquid tomb" from Donald Carter, who cites Robert Harrison: "There are no gravestones on the sea. History and memory ground themselves on inscription, but this element is uninscribable. It closes over rather than keeps the place of its dead, while its unbounded grave remains humanly unmarked" (qtd. in Carter 2013, 62).[11] The unmarked seeps into the unremarkable, as thousands of deaths at sea are not even recorded and many of the bodies that wash ashore remain unidentified. While Harrison has a point, I want to argue that water alone is not the only uninscribable and shifting element in which human remains could disappear without a trace. In the novella, for instance, Angelina and her mother search fruitlessly for Vito's namesake's grave when they return to Libya. The pitiless Sonoran Desert of Arizona, where hundreds of Mexican and South American migrants perish, inspires Jason De León's epithet, or more pointedly his eponymous epitaph, for the region as "the land of open graves." The refusal to look away or to allow us to sidestep the decomposing corpses initiates a collective process of mourning that sanctifies every death, even the nameless and faceless who abandon water bottles, backpacks, sneakers and other apparel, precious identification papers, personal keepsakes, and photos. Salvaging their stories and retrieving their discards is De León's way of rejecting anti-immigrant rhetoric, which collapses the migrants—as "illegals," as "aliens"—with the "trash" they leave behind in the partly visible dispersed traces of their migrant routes through the desert (De León 2015, 198).

Amade M'charek embraces the word "waste" as precisely expressive of failed immigration policies more invested in security than hospitality, in preserving the sanctity of Fortress Europe rather than in raising the barriers. European border controls maintain an impressive surveillance system that generates large amounts of data on "arrival, interception, rescue, detention, and deportation of migrants," but are less forthcoming about information regarding the bodies recovered from beaches and dredged from the watery depths (M'charek 2018, 97).[12] M'charek notes that experts in such cases have to deal with the disfiguring effects of saltwater on the corpse, including the loss of skin that would provide fingerprints for identification. Claiming to be overwhelmed by living migrants, European border authorities find the dead less of a priority, adding to the thousands of missing people whose fate remains unknown. If interest in the fate of living migrants fades rapidly, in other words, dead ones draw even less sustained official and public attention.

While Judith Butler, in another context, considers "tarrying with grief" (2004, 30), M'charek asks us to tarry with waste, since its multiple manifestations operate as mute but active witnesses to a story that demands to be told. The components of waste at sea are different from those in the desert, but the bright orange of life jackets, the rotting planks of driftwood from boats that came apart, the gold or silvery sheen of foil from first-aid blankets discarded at the sea's edge, the putrefying smell of drowned bodies all form a companion narrative to body parts and artifacts unearthed from the desert sand. What M'charek at first bemoans as weak forensic infrastructure for identifying bodies from the sea bears the potential for creative knowledge production, since the "material traces that figure in forensic cases typically have a talent for joining desperate places and events and inviting scenarios around them so as to produce a possible story about what could have happened" (M'charek 2018, 106). In a telling phrase, she refers to forensics as the *"art of paying attention"* (96) to waste, litter, and impedimenta as vital elements of the people to whom they belonged and whose stories they help reconstitute.

Khaled Mattawa's collection of poems *Mare Nostrum* also pays homage to the "generations of rags" (Mazzantini 2015, 82) epitomizing native flight. The ongoing, drifting nature of their search for sanctuary and the exhausting relay from one country to another as each refuses permanent entry are evident in the poems' titles: "Season of Migration to the North/Northwest" (Mattawa 2019, 8; an intertextual reference to Tayeb Salih's also intertextual novel), "Psalm on the Road to Agadez" (10), and so on. The dizzyingly convoluted markings of the compass, "West to North/East to North/North to North/to North to North" ("Psalm on the Road to Agadez"; 10) involve other familiar sea and land signs, a series of hoops to jump through: "Wave, checkpoint and dune—" ("Constance Song"; 12), indicating the interrupted, circuitous, interminable process of migration from land to sea and perhaps back again. Like Farid and Jamila, the individual wanderers flee the "screech and roar of barrel bombs" ("Psalm Under Siege"; 15), from "the village drying up to sand, the town without jobs" ("Malouk's Ode"; 16).

The trail of flight begins from one's very home: "the courtyard littered, bottles, clothes, old photographs/like some carnival bacchanal the night before,/a town facing massacre just fled" ("Malouk's Ode"; Mattawa 2019, 16). The ironic contrast between the dissipations of revelry and one's possessions scattered by the impending threat of massacre identifies the panicked townspeople as pawns for international war games and corrupt national leaders. The helplessness of the migrants, who had displayed ingenuity and tenacity in making their way from land to the intractable sea, takes on a chillingly infantile rhyme like "Ring a Ring o' Roses," as "2 or 3 fall into the sea," followed by "mothers and babies," "I," and "us"—all easily "fall[ing] into the sea," one after the other from overpacked boats, while a hovering helicopter watches and finally throws one small inflatable dinghy ("Into the Sea"; 20). As in Mazzantini's novella, the vast and forbidding sea is an indomitable and vexatious foe for the voyagers. Infighting and the survival instinct tear them apart, and they bear not only the scratches and welts of onboard chaos but also the "burn" of "gasoline mix[ed] with water" ("Fuel Burns"; 26). Like the belongings they drop as they flee their homeland, the migrants themselves are discarded in the ocean, left to drown when refused rescue.[13] The cover page of *Morning Sea* bears the caption "When the Water Is Safer Than the Land" over the picture of a solitary figure on a boat adrift in the blue sea. Both authors overturn that perception.

Mazzantini and Mattawa reject easy closure for the unhealed trauma, lingering grief, and melancholia[14] in oceanic migration, where water has an ambivalent character as channel and chasm, life and death. The last lines of *Morning Sea* greet the news of Gaddafi's ignominious covert execution, in a hollow celebration that nevertheless underlines the art of forensics, the "memory" in the effaceable but potent trace:

Memory is chalk on bloody pavements.
We're free. Hurrah, hurrah. (143)

The chalk outline will not last, but "mourning remains," as David L. Eng and David Kazanjian insist (2003, 1–25). The grammar of "remains" as both a plural noun and the third-person present tense suggests that lingering over them is not defeatist but has a productive, historicist, even creative potential. Both the novella and the poems relate stories of failure in the conventional arc of the journey, since migration is not always completed but can end in death, deportation, or detention, confirming Abderrezak's concept of illiterature. But they also turn to a reparative art to avoid the paralysis of despair, marking the irreversible rupture that impels mourning, but also implying the possibility of the dawn of a new day, the paradoxical refusal to give up either melancholia or hope. Their ambivalent sense of mourning I see reflected in the homophone, the adjectivally ambiguous "mo[u]rning sea" of Mazzantini's title.[15] While the mythification of the ocean as an endless resource spanning vast stretches of the globe can be lethal in extractive capitalism, it is not simply a site of death, mourning, and lament. Vito's "art," as his mother, Angelina, views it, becomes an ethical one, as he repurposes the scattered belongings of the drowned on a panel he constructs at home and curates in a patchy archive. The irreparability of the past for Vito need not foreclose his deliberative act of memory-making, replicated in the authorial act of telling the story: "the reparative [as] an energy, a process, a specific set of narrative choices that propose to offer a conscious or unconscious strategy to a double process of recapturing and recovering" (Rosello 2010, 22). The past is not wholly exorcised and certainly not rehabilitated, as Vito notes, but his is nevertheless an anticipatory grieving practice that tries to influence a future ethics of migration and refugeeism.

The trace as an insignia of testamentary desire is implicitly recognized by Vito, who becomes amateur researcher, archivist, collector, and artist in response to the scenes he witnesses on the beach and in immigration centers. The yields of his beachcombing as a potential inheritance for posterity testify to Jacques Derrida's affirmation that something of one should remain behind, which may provide material, if fragmented, corpora for memory and mourning. As the third-person narrator in the novella observes,

> Vito has gathered memory. Of a blue gas tank, a shoe.
>   *Someone will need this someday. Someday, a black Italian man will want to look back at the sea of his ancestors and find something. A trace of their passage.* (139–40)

The words here, which acknowledge not just the collected forensic evidence of death by drowning but also a future of "black Italian" citizenship for the putative seeker, confirm that the sea belongs also to "his ancestors" and not just to Europe alone, anticipating a more accessible sense of the Mediterranean. The "big blue panel" (140) on which Vito has nailed all the scraps he forages from wrecks assumes the gravitas of a museum exhibit that, to return to Walcott, Vito has unlocked from the vault of the sea. When Angelina touches "those poor encrusted things, marine relics washed by salt," she believes that "it's like an intact archaeological site. A world saved" (140). But for Vito, there is "no tangible meaning," no coherent message in or link between "the page of a diary in Arabic. A shirtsleeve. A doll's arm" (138). The bedraggled, cryptic witnesses of aborted escapes like Farid and Jamila's are not for him the paradoxical posthumous-baptismal "art" that his mother thinks they are, but a cautionary reminder that his endeavor has not really "saved" the drowned. Vito's memory board of salvage from the sea functions, then, as not just the *khôra*, but "also a kairotic place," which, like the fragments of flotsam and jetsam nailed on it, paradoxically reminds us of the absent dead bodies and becomes "the final reference point of reflection upon the past as well as a departure point of hope for the future" (Domanska 2005, 406).

Melancholia, "mourning without end" (Eng and Kazanjian 2003, 3), is not absolutely pathologized, not even by Freud (1964), as scholars of the politics of mourning would argue. Vito's refusal to turn the page on the past keeps it animated through material practices such as the memory board, which displays the traces, if not the literal remains, of absent dead bodies. It reopens the wounds of history, lingers over the mourning, signals the losses, makes visible not just what is lost but what remains. While acknowledging that the *mare nostrum* is also "*mare mortum/mare monstrum*, a rotten sea of dead bodies adrift, a liquid cemetery," Sarnelli adds, "The Mediterranean today is a sea of monstrous melancholia not only because it is a site of ongoing mourning which has never been worked through, but also because it provides a possible basis for change. All that happened, and still happens, in the African deserts has now been forcibly brought to the attention of the international community. Migrant deaths not only take place, but also become visible, thus showing the need for transformation" (2015, 150). When the dead are regurgitated from the sea or swept ashore to be gathered, in a productive sense of the grotesque and the Gothic, the zombie figure resurrects "what was meant to be forgotten or lost" (150), whether through the lost objects that are found and displayed or in the stories that are told. It also manifests the repressed past of colonial violence, locating the deaths in a longer history than just Gaddafi's regime and the mixed blessings of petrowealth. The narrator's references in *Morning Sea* to Roman ruins in Libya suggest that the modern debris of civil war, petrochemicals, and sea wreckage are part of a long pattern of imperial settlement. But rather than the immobilized gaze of the Medusas at Leptis Magna (Mazzantini 2015, 71), the watchful, contemplative view of history is a forward-looking one (Domanska 2005, 392).[16] Although Farid, Jamila, and their unfortunate companions do not make it alive to tell their stories, the material artifacts testify to their lives, sensed by Vito and Angelina but related to the reader through the text in a more elaborate decoding of Vito's thalassic cryptograph. While the mnemonic potential of the wrecked boats and possessions from dead bodies could be generic and private, as against the captioned items in a public museum, they are still tangible and stimulate the imagination about what stories could lie behind them (one of which, Farid's, the reader is privy to).[17]

Following the initially toxic submergence of the migrants, the sea water literally "scours everything," and although the island where Vito finds the wreckage is referred to as a "cemetery," it is "without sorrow" (137). In a reversal of the anthropocentric damage to the sea-edge ecosystem, the fate of humans turns deadly in the treacherous waters, whereas the island becomes a refuge for human remains and nonhuman marine life when newborn turtles rush toward the safety of the sea (137–38). As Macarena Gómez-Barris notes, the ocean has been fetishized "not only [as] an object of voyeuristic pleasure, national entertainment, fascination, leisure, danger, and scrutiny, but especially [as] a geography of use-value" (Gómez-Barris 2019, 33). The brutal mortality of migrant history is not precisely healed but overwritten by the cyclical currents as the sea shifts once more from deadly matrix to vital agent, to invert the epigraph from Glissant.

Derrida's cautionary remarks on autoimmunity[18] reveal that he is aware of the more unpalatable consequences of visitation, just like Vito, who observes the stinking and overcrowded camps in his hometown, stops eating fish as dead bodies are trawled from the sea, and hears his neighbor scream as "a Tunisian slipped into her house to steal" (53). Unlike Angelina's occasionally whitewashed and victimized approach to Italy's colonial past in Libya, Vito is more conscious of just what "the dirty tail of a colonial history" brings in its wake (85). The significance of Oedipus's hidden crypt, his pledge to Theseus to bless the latter's kingdom in return for a safe harbor for his deteriorating body, and Antigone's need to honor her father's unknown grave frame Derrida's emphasis on hospitality rendered even to the dying and the dead. As he declares, "Let us say yes *to who or what turns up*, before any determination, before any anticipation, before any *identification*, whether or not it has to do with a foreigner, an immigrant, an invited guest, or an unexpected visitor, whether or not the new arrival is the citizen of another country, a human, animal, or divine creature, a living or dead thing, male or female" (Derrida 2000, 77). Such "pure and hyperbolic hospitality" (2005, 6), he characteristically adds, is an "impossible" gesture, but, also typically, he does not believe that it should prohibit setting up the conditions of possibility beyond what the laws of a nation intent on self-preservation allow. Vito likewise permits the remnants or revenants to cross his threshold and reside in his home, following Derrida's dictum to "say yes" even to inanimate things, especially as a way of honoring and remembering those who died together. The blue panel becomes a hospice for these artifacts of the dead, awaiting a descendant who might never show up to reclaim any of them or even know with any certainty to which subject they belonged. Against the tradition of dredging ancient relics or plunder from wrecks in the seas, the authors I have mentioned here offer a different set of tangible artifacts, those that bear witness to the grievable deaths, if not the livable lives, of the drowned.

NOTES

1. See "Thanatic Ethics: The Circulation of Bodies in Migratory Spaces—An Exploratory Workshop," April 1–2, 2021: https://www.thanaticethics.com/. The cover image on the poster is Ai Weiwei's 2015 *The Remains,* which lays out human bones replicated in porcelain in a neatly curated display. For a sense of how such displays are markedly controversial and political, see "Ai Weiwei: Bringing Human Remains to London": https://mikepitts.wordpress.com/2015/06/28/ai-weiwei-bringing-human-remains-to-london/. Although the bones in Weiwei's exhibit are not related to Mediterranean migration, I view Vito's memory board in Margaret Mazzantini's (2015) novella in a similar vein, here displaying remains from the sea to animate their histories. I thank Edwige Tamalet Talbayev for alerting me to this workshop, which I was unfortunately not able to attend. The workshop abstracts present an array of topics regarding death and the migrant body that speak to the contemporary interest in this topic from a range of disciplines, not just on the Mediterranean but connecting to other spaces, times, and populations. For an emphasis on sea as matter, see Talbayev 2021.
2. See https://missingmigrants.iom.int (accessed September 8, 2020).
3. See https://missingmigrants.iom.int (accessed August 3, 2021).
4. For an account of a controversial memorialization of Kurdi's tragic death, see https://www.cnn.com/style/article/ai-weiwei-alan-kurdi-syria/index.html. Weiwei's "in your face" politics demonstrates that remembering can be as troubling as forgetting.
5. As Hakim Abderrezak anticipates, the colonial histories of Spain, France, and Italy intersect with Maghrebi identities in the transnational literatures of migration that challenge the traditional canons, impersonating in print the unwelcome mobility of the clandestine migrants who "burn" national borders (2009, 468). The Maghreb, as Mireille Rosello, among other scholars, reminds us, is a confluence of East and West, and can be perceived as both an "Oriental" and Western denomination (2010, 31, 33). The Mediterranean is not simply of the "Occident": its sea edges touch multiple nations and facilitate this traffic.
6. When Epeli Hau'ofa cites this oft-quoted phrase of Walcott's, it is important to note that he speaks specifically from South Pacific and Oceania studies

perspectives that remain invisible to most of the world. He also insists on the granular difference of island- and shore-dwelling residents from those who are not immediately impacted by the nearness of water bodies. At the same time, he seems to share Glissant's anti-insular sense of the ocean as a global commons since the "water that washes and crashes on our shores is the water that washes and crashes on the coastlines of the whole Pacific Rim from Antarctica to New Zealand, Australia, Southeast and East Asia, and right around to the Americas. The Pacific Ocean also merges into the Atlantic and the Indian Oceans to encircle the entire planet" (Hau'ofa 2008, 54–55).

7. I thank Matthew Liberti and the other graduate students in the winter 2018 Diaspora Studies meetings for inspiring my thinking about this passage.

8. Although the current meaning of *forensics* is related to crime and evidence in which the body plays an important role, I would like to keep its other meanings, of forum or public discussion, in play, since the archaeontology of my sources involves making public or making visible that which has been repressed, unacknowledged, or forgotten.

9. Mazzantini's continuous desegregation of land and sea, flesh and foam, reminds us once again that intransigent borders between the elements of earth and water can be deceptive. Such infusions also signal contested "ownership" of water bodies, generally assumed to be more of a "commons" than terra firma, where borders can be more rigidly demarcated. The "legal status of ice," for instance, raises questions about its structure: liquid or solid; land, island, or float, since it is mobile in constitution (Steinberg et al. 2015, 47–48). With climate change, centuries of geological shifts are now accelerated, putting into question the stability and permanence of any space, whether of land or water. In an extraordinary image, Edwidge Danticat cites a passage from Haruki Murakami's short story "Thailand," which describes an earthquake: "We take it for granted that the earth beneath our feet is solid and stationary. We even talk about people being 'down to earth' or having their feet firmly planted on the ground. But suddenly one day we see that it isn't true. The earth, the boulders, that are supposed to be solid, all of a sudden turn as mushy as liquid" (qtd. in Danticat 2017, 52). Like Danticat, Mazzantini uses molten metaphors to connect disasters on a global scale. When Vito visits Tripoli with his anguished mother and grandmother, he remembers "9-11" in New York and "the burnt stink" of that Ground Zero: "Tripoli was their zero level, their memory razed to the ground, liquefied" (Mazzantini 2015, 108). His reassembly of the found objects from the wrecked boats and dinghies is an attempt to solidify memories and give them meaningful indexicality against the earth and sea that consume them or disgorge them as debris.

10. See Meyer 2010 and the "Theories and Methodologies Section" of the same issue of *PMLA* for another discussion of trash in the ocean.
11. M. NourbeSe Philip's insertion of names of dead enslaved persons thrown overboard at the bottom of the page is a deliberate marking of spectral gravestones in her poem *Zong!* In contrast to the earthy sense of exhume, she explains in her "Notanda," she turns to "exaqua" as a form of oceanic retrieval and remembrance (201). The etymological and semantic links between *obitus, obituary,* and *obiter* are implicit in this prose supplement to her poem. For a Caribbean context, see Valérie Loichot 2020 and Jenny Sharpe 2020.
12. My thanks to Alex Ramsey for drawing this chapter to my attention.
13. For an excellent account of what Charles Heller and Lorenzo Pezzani call the *Left-to-Die Boat* and the EU's "lethal policies of non-assistance" (2021, 216) after the termination of Operation Mare Nostrum, the humanitarian project of rescue at sea, see their chapter "The Other Boats: State and Nonstate Vessels at the EU's Maritime Frontier." In contrast to official accounts of the operation, such as Mare Nostrum, Mattawa's ironic poems and Heller and Pezzani's *Forensic Architecture* site (Heller and Pezzani 2021, 230nn7–8) focus on the wretched of the sea, explaining how nonassistance or inadequate rescue operations fostered "liquid violence" through the "geopower" of the sea, which enabled states to kill migrant subjects without direct intervention (216–20). The concept of "viapolitics," which riffs on Michel Foucault's biopolitics (Pezzani et al. 2021, 7) by emphasizing the infrastructure of migration (vehicles, routes, geophysical environments), is fundamental to this essay.
14. The parallel mourning in both families yearning toward the opposite coast in *Morning Sea* specifies not a universal grief but "migratory stress," which can lead to mental health problems so severe that they have created a new disorder in migrants who show chronic stress: the Ulysses syndrome (Achotegui 2019).
15. I prefer Mireille Rosello's choice of reparative over repentance narratives, although the latter is an important step in acknowledging and working through trauma (Rosello 2010). The stark divide between colonizers and colonized erases any shared sense of loss and collective mourning. Angelina's nostalgia in the novella (*mal d'Afrique*) runs the risk of being the "postcolonial melancholia" of the dominant who are no longer ascendant, but the abrupt collapse of the citizen into the refugee is a cautionary warning that any subject can become a prey to history, even colonizers. Rather than compete over the experience of whose loss was greater, Vito and Angelina grieve not just over a lost home but also over the atrocities that their colonial history uncovers.
16. For a compelling discussion of how disinterring dead bodies and reburying them matters for the future of grieving relatives and even for the nation in the

context of the *desaparecidos* in Argentina during the 1980s, see Domanska 2005, 399–402.

17. See Crooke 2019 for a discussion of found objects, mourning, and memorialization. The fact that Crooke discusses the blood-stained clothes of young men killed during the Troubles in Northern Ireland demonstrates that such a memorial practice (one form of thanatic ethics) is not restricted to Vito's commemoration of migrant deaths.

18. Derrida explains: "An autoimmunitary process is that strange behavior where a living being, in quasi-*suicidal* fashion, 'itself' works to destroy its own protection, to immunize itself *against* its own immunity" (2003, 94l).

WORKS CITED

Achotegui, Joseba. 2019. "Migrants Living in Very Hard Situations: Extreme Migratory Mourning (the Ulysses Syndrome)." *Psychoanalytic Dialogues* 29 (3): 252–68.

Abderrezak, Hakim. 2009. "Burning the Sea: Clandestine Migration Across the Strait of Gibraltar in Francophone Moroccan 'Illiterature.'" *Contemporary French and Francophone Studies: SITES* 13 (4): 461–69.

Abderrezak, Hakim. 2018. "The Mediterranean *Seametery* and *Cemetery* in Leïla Kilani's and Tariq Teguia's Filmic Works." In *Critically Mediterranean: Temporalities, Aesthetics, and Deployments of a Sea in Crisis*, edited by yasser elhariry and Edwige Tamalet Talbayev. Palgrave Macmillan.

Alonso, Alexandra Délano, and Benjamin Nienass. 2016. "Introduction: Borders and the Politics of Mourning." *Social Research: An International Quarterly* 83 (2): xix–xxxi.

Benjamin, Walter. 1968. "The Storyteller: Reflections on the Works of Nikolai Leskov." In *Illuminations: Essays and Reflections*, edited by Hannah Arendt, translated by Harry Zohn. Schocken.

Butler, Judith. 2004. *Precarious Life: The Powers of Mourning and Violence*. Verso.

Carter, Donald. 2013. "Navigating Diaspora: The Precarious Depths of the Italian Immigration Crisis." In *African Migrations: Patterns and Perspectives*, edited by Abdoulaye Kane and Todd H. Leedy. Indiana University Press.

Cole, Teju. 2017. *Blind Spot*. Random House.

Crooke, Elizabeth. 2019. "Memory Politics and Material Culture: Display in the Memorial Museum." *Memory Studies* 12 (6): 617–29.

Danticat, Edwidge. 2017. *The Art of Death: Writing the Final Story*. Graywolf Press.

De León, Jason. 2015. *The Land of Open Graves: Living and Dying on the Migrant Trail*. University of California Press.

Derrida, Jacques. 2000. *Of Hospitality: Anne Dufourmantelle Invites Jacques Derrida to Respond*. Translated by Rachel Bowlby. Stanford University Press.

Derrida, Jacques. 2003. "Autoimmunity: Real and Symbolic Suicides: A Dialogue with Jacques Derrida." Translated by Pascale-Anne Brault and Michael Naas. In *Philosophy in a Time of Terror: Dialogues with Jürgen Habermas and Jacques Derrida*, by Giovanna Borradori. University of Chicago Press.

Derrida, Jacques. 2005. "The Principle of Hospitality." *Parallax* 11 (1): 6–9.

Domanska, Ewa. 2005. "Towards the Archaeontology of the Dead Body." Translated by Magdalena Zapędowska. *Rethinking History* 9 (4): 389–413.

elhariry, yasser, and Edwige Tamalet Talbayev. 2018. "Critically Mediterranean: An Introduction." In *Critically Mediterranean: Temporalities, Aesthetics, and Deployments of a Sea in Crisis*, edited by elhariry and Talbayev. Palgrave Macmillan.

Eng, David L., and David Kazanjian. 2003. "Introduction: Mourning Remains." In *Loss: The Politics of Mourning*, edited by David L. Eng and David Kazanjian. University of California Press.

Freud, Sigmund. 1964. "Mourning and Melancholia." In *The Standard Edition of the Complete Psychological Works of Sigmund Freud, Volume XIV (1914–1916): On the History of the Psycho-Analytic Movement, Papers on Metapsychology and Other Works*, edited and translated by James Strachey. Hogarth Press.

Glissant, Édouard. 2000. *Poetics of Relation*. Translated by Betsy Wing. University of Michigan Press.

Gómez-Barris, Macarena. 2019. "Life Otherwise at the Sea's Edge." *Open Rivers*, no. 13, 27–47.

Hau'ofa, Epeli. 2008. *We Are the Ocean: Selected Works*. University of Hawai'i Press.

Heller, Charles, and Lorenzo Pezzani. 2021. "The Other Boats: State and Nonstate Vessels at the EU's Maritime Frontier." In *Viapolitics: Borders, Migration, and the Power of Locomotion*, edited by Lorenzo Pezzani, Charles Heller, and William Walters. Duke University Press.

Loichot, Valérie. 2020. *Water Graves: The Art of the Unritual in the Greater Caribbean*. University of Virginia Press.

Mattawa, Khaled. 2019. *Mare Nostrum*. Sarabande Books. Quarternote Chapbook Series 16. Kindle Cloud.

Mazzantini, Margaret. 2015. *Morning Sea*. Translated by Ann Gagliardi. One World.

M'charek, Amade. 2018. "'Dead-Bodies-at-the-Border': Distributed Evidence and Emerging Forensic Infrastructure for Identification." In *Bodies as Evidence: Security, Knowledge, and Power*, edited by Mark Maguire, Ursula Rao, and Nils Zurawski. Duke University Press.

Meyer, Patricia. 2010. "Editor's Column: Sea Trash, Dark Pools, and the Tragedy of the Commons." *PMLA* 125 (3): 523–45.

Pezzani, Lorenzo, Charles Heller, and William Walters. 2021. "Viapolitics: An Introduction." In *Viapolitics: Borders, Migration, and the Power of Locomotion*, edited by Lorenzo Pezzani, Charles Heller, and William Walters. Duke University Press.

Philip, M. NourbeSe. 2008. *Zong!* Mercury Press.

Rosello, Mireille. 2010. *The Reparative in Narratives: Works of Mourning in Progress*. Liverpool University Press.

Sarnelli, Laura. 2015. "The Gothic Mediterranean: Haunting Migrations and Critical Melancholia." *Journal of Mediterranean Studies* 24 (2): 147–65.

Sharpe, Jenny. 2020. *Immaterial Archives: An African Diaspora Poetics of Loss*. Northwestern University Press.

Steinberg, Philip E., Jeremy Tasch, and Hannes Gerhardt. 2015. *Contesting the Arctic: Politics and Imaginaries in the Circumpolar North*. I. B. Tauris.

Talbayev, Edwige Tamalet. 2021. "Seawater." *Contemporary French and Francophone Studies: SITES* 25 (2): 207–17.

Walcott, Derek. 1986. "The Sea Is History." In *Collected Poems, 1948–1984*. Farrar, Straus and Giroux.

WATER NECROPOLITICS

EDWIGE TAMALET TALBAYEV

This chapter seeks to answer one of the key questions explored in this collection: how to think the devastating relationship between the enforcement of borders on the outer edge of Europe and the submerged bodies of migrants who perish during their ill-fated journey across the watery expanse of the Mediterranean? Further, what role does water play in these dynamics?

Since the late 1980s, the unequal mobility regime between global North and global South has increasingly strengthened, marking out the Mediterranean Sea as a space of disparity between contrastive categories of migrants. Capitalizing on the systemic restrictions to mobility that were implemented during the colonial era of European expansion into Africa, attempts at controlling the southern border of the European Union have transformed the sea into a putatively impenetrable wall (Abderrezak 2018; Bensaâd 2006), a border zone aiming to deter the clandestine crossings of migrants from the south. Increased surveillance, the interception of rescue operations at sea, and the outsourcing of border enforcement to non-European states on the southern shore of the sea have all contributed to the illegalization of cross-border movement, with the corollary effect of bringing further precarity to the unstemmed flow of crossings by forcing migrants to adopt dangerous concealment strategies to avoid detection.

This securitization logic has turned the Mediterranean into a "hostile environment" (Pezzani 2020) where each year thousands of irregularized, undocumented men, women, and children come to meet an untimely, tragic end in capsized vessels on their way to supposedly more hospitable lands. As the odds of perishing at sea have risen from 1 in 42 in 2017 to 1 in 18 in 2018 (Human Rights Watch 2019), the Mediterranean has morphed into a space of death and disappearance where water has come to enforce the punitive purview of the European Union's security-based approach to migration. Whether in the guise of a "postmodern cemetery," for Iside Gjergji (2015, 21), or a "seametery," for Hakim Abderrezak (2018), the Mediterranean Sea abets the "creation of a dead zone, portals to the underworld" (Saunders 2016, 7).[1] Frances Saunders identifies in the maritime site of the drowning a "vanishing point, the point at which its human cargo simply dropped off the map. *Ne plus ultra*, nothing lies beyond" (7). In contrast, through a focus on seawater volume and on its corruptive power, the approach delineated in these pages wishes to restore the underwater dimensions of borders—their verticality and the biopolitical devastation they enact in the idiosyncratic, contested terrain of the sea. Intersecting Achille Mbembe's concepts of *necropolitics* and *borderization* with recent theoretical work in critical ocean studies and feminist new materialism, this chapter examines the kinds of readjustments a focus on water as corrosive agent imposes on the ways we read the biopolitical foreclosure of "illegalized" life, and on conceptions of the sea as a necropolitical space.

I probe the enmeshment of the violence performed by seawater with the regimes of borderization enacted across the space of the sea. Reading the Mediterranean as an aqueous frontier spotlights the fraught relationship between clandestine migrants (abjected, expendable bodies marooned on the edges of regimes of legality and deprived of legal protections) and the strictly enforced borders on which Europe's sovereignty rests. Yet, in this argument, seawater becomes more than the border *space* containing the fatal, fractal encounters between law and bodies; it is the very *substance* through which the deadly logic of borderization is enacted. Through seawater, irruptive migrant bodies, seeking agency, are reified and relegated to residuality, amalgamated into their maritime environments. They morph into what I call "residual migrants." By effecting the becoming-residue of drowned bodies on the site of the border, water brings to material, hyperbolic completion the logic of obliteration through which European sovereignty is enacted. Yet it concurrently calls into question the very notion of borderization enacted on, or even through, migrant bodies as the enduring residual forms of existence formed in the wake of the drownings reveal sites of resistance and alternative temporalities that escape the obliterating logic of borders.

ON BORDERIZATION

An idiosyncrasy of the contemporary border regime is that borders "may be found anywhere" (Guild 2003, 103). In the trenchant words of Étienne Balibar, "borders are no longer at the border" (Balibar 1998, 217–18), a pronouncement that should not be construed as indicating the disappearance of borders altogether but rather their broad dissemination. The "actual and heuristic disaggregating of the 'border'" brought about by globalization (Sassen 2005, 214) only makes them ubiquitous, inescapable—but also fractured and unstable. Suvendrini Perera adopted and expanded the concept of "borderscape" (Strüver 2005; Brambilla 2010) in the context of maritime liminal zones in the Pacific, to encompass "different temporalities and overlapping emplacements as well as emergent spatial organizations. A shifting and conflictual space, this Pacific borderscape is currently being reconstituted through technologies and discourses of securitization as well as through forms of new and ongoing spatial relations and practices that defy the categorizations of the border, and unsettle the univocity and stability of the 'proper'" (Perera 2007, 207). Through their dynamism and layered structure, borderscapes elude static representations and linearity. They are spaces of disjunction and strife, of layered time and conflicting emplacements. In other words, their very structure incites the proliferation of resistance and transgression.

As Mireille Rosello and Stephen F. Wolfe have argued, the very demarcation performed by borders is continuously challenged by human action. Through their clandestine mobility, illegal border-crossers recognize and reinforce regimes of bordering while concurrently subverting the exclusive spatial effects they enact (Rosello and Wolfe 2017, 7). Migrants' movement compounds the dispersion and fracturing of borders, their permeability and elasticity. Sabine Dullin and Étienne Forestier-Peyrat's concept of a "thick border" pinpoints the complex makeup of borders "on land and at sea, [which is] constituted by territories travelled by migrants and refugees, by networks organizing the crossings and by the many States that are involved in ever increased operational coordination between border police forces" (2015,

10). Each encounter at sea—with the regulatory forces of European sovereignty in the form of "rescue" operations or militarized boats intercepting migrants—maps out additional border interfaces, other negotiations of territoriality and agency, even though the border-crossers' agonistic struggle against the order of discrimination perpetrated against them often leads to a fatal outcome. Agency resulting in death, agency enacted through death—on the aqueous interface, processes of subjectivation and borderization go hand in hand.

Since the early 1990s, the Mediterranean basin has been incorporated into a fluid borderscape mediating a form of "liquid violence" (Heller and Pezzani 2018) exacted on transgressive migrant bodies whose very mobility undermines the power of exclusionary state policies. In other words, this precarious "liquid terrain" has been "enabling a form of killing without touching" (Heller and Pezzari 2018).[2] This form of aqueous violence shares significant semantic territory with Achille Mbembe's concept of "necropower," which the philosopher associates with "the ultimate expression of sovereignty[, which] largely resides in the power and capacity to dictate who is able to live and who must die. To kill or to let live thus constitutes sovereignty's limits, its principal attributes. To be sovereign is to exert one's control over mortality and to define life as the deployment and manifestation of power [necropower]" (2019, 66). How does this necropower intersect with the regimes of borderization enacted through the sea? Mbembe defines borderization as "the process by which world powers permanently transform certain spaces into impassable places for certain classes of populations . . . spaces of loss and mourning, where the lives of a multitude of people judged to be undesirable come to be shattered" (99). In this reading, borders come to mediate the order of violence born of capitalism writ large, whereby lives considered to lie in excess, to be superfluous, are designed to be eliminated: "no longer merely a line of demarcation separating distinct sovereign entities[, borders] are the name used to describe the organized violence that underpins both contemporary capitalism and our world order in general—the women, the men, and the unwanted children condemned to abandonment; the shipwrecks and drownings of hundreds, indeed thousands weekly; the endless waiting and humiliation in consulates, in limbo. . . . In short, an image of humanity on a road to ruin" (99).[3] Mbembe's conceptualization applies the paradigm of destruction to the "remote borderization" of liminal spaces, spaces of contact where the bodies of the undesirables (fugitive, errant, moved by the most primordial, intense push for survival) are reduced to their most dehumanized expression. In the case of the migrant drownings in focus here, this includes flesh—corrupted and dispersed—and disaggregating bone, chemical molecules released into the primordial soup of oceanic waters, awaiting re-formation and re-incorporation into other organic (or inorganic) structures. The victims of a logic of degradation, migrants turn into bodies, objects, targets of the "universal right of predation" (104) exerted by Europe.

The complex technostructure of the border applies the logic of securitization to the desire for mobility of those human bodies which it blends into one overarching, indeterminate category—an anonymized infrahumanity. The being-in-death afforded to the drowning migrants precludes their right to singularity. It marks the grotesque, hyperbolic extension of the denial of humanity perpetrated by necropolitical forces that have turned the Mediterranean into a grave. The transformation of the Mediterranean Sea into an "area of insecurity" ("région d'insécurité"; Mbembe 2020) holds significant consequences for the realization of subjecthood and citizenship across humankind. Carried out remotely through the mediation of geophysical forces (here water), necropower turns the sea into a space of surveillance, apartheid, and decimation. In this outlook, the maritime border becomes one of the most acute manifestations of the division laid out between classes of humanity on the basis of modernity's dual paradigm of productivity and waste. The differential logic underpinning capitalism and empire separates those within the purview of the law (the community, or *demos*, the political body producing sovereignty, a body composed of free, equal, and self-conscious subjects endowed with the full privileges of citizenship) from those *outside* the purview of the law:[4] those living in a "state of exception," the one bred by the "crisis" narrative, a temporary suspension of the state's law, which in the ongoing timeframe of crisis reaches long-term status. On shore, those subjects are commodified, divested of political autonomy; they dwell in the interstices of the state's welfare model as the target of policies that gear toward containment and partitioning. Some of them are kept in refugee detention camps outside Europe's confines, in keeping with the EU's externalization approach where the detention and management of migrants is outsourced to third countries, such as Morocco or Libya, often with well-known tragic consequences (detention in unsanitary, extremely precarious conditions; reports of violence; torture; rapes . . .). Caught in the web of "spatial violence, humanitarian strategies, and a peculiar biopolitics of punishment," these migrants fall prey to a "carceral" logic "in which people deemed surplus, unwanted, or illegal are governed through abdication of any responsibility for their lives and welfare" (Mbembe 2020, 97).

At sea, they are left without protection to brave the elements, sometimes at the price of their lives, attempting through their transgression to reclaim for themselves the agency underpinning subjective autonomy. The seacrossing mediates a desire to exceed the parameters of invisibility and dehumanization. It performs a form of "non-violent resistance that mobilize[s] vulnerability for the purposes of asserting existence" (Butler 2014, 17). For the crossing is intentional, the manifestation of what Fabienne Brugère and Guillaume Le Blanc have conceptualized as the contemporary incarnation of the *conatus* developed in Baruch Spinoza's *Ethics* (2017, 38)—the inherent inclination of a being to persevere in its existence and to further deploy its potentiality. Through migration, the derogated subjects oppose the obliterating violence of bordering regimes and reaffirm their right to the pursuit of life beyond bare survival. They set in motion a search for an externally validated form of existence endowed with the recognition of one's inalienable rights as a human subject—autonomy, protection, mastery over objects and nature. Yet the borderization logic enforced by the sea heralds the confiscation of universal human rights for migrants. In this respect, it is the corollary of the logic of "rescue, surveillance, and punishment" ("secourir, surveiller et punir"; Brugère and Le Blanc 2017, 122) reigning supreme in the migrant centers mushrooming on the edges of Europe. Even those who make it to the other shore are contained, enclosed in detention camps, many of which only provide scant necessities for a life reduced to its most limited expression. Kept in limbo, excluded from social time,[5] the incarcerated migrant teeters "on a threshold that belongs neither to the world of the living nor to the world of the dead: he is a living dead man" (Agamben 1998, 99). The humanitarian logic of the camp rests on what Brugère and Le Blanc have called the principle of "secours" (rescue), not that of "accueil" (welcoming but also giving the means to live a decent life). In other words, it is an aspiration to "let live" rather than to "make live" in any meaningful way that lies at the heart of this regimentation of humanity along racialized lines.

I would like to consider the dissolving bodies of drowned migrants through the lens of an extreme "baring" of bodies—and I am here referring to Giorgio Agamben's concept of "bare life" as the life of those who only have their body to exist (1998). I take this "baring" to indicate the ultimate implementation of a logic of disappropriation of migrant subjects—here, of their very physical integrity. Undoubtedly, these maritime forms of physical dissolution are not an anomaly nor a glitch in Europe's asylum-granting system. Nor are they the antithesis of a supposed politics of welcome that has taken root in the other shore of the sea. In fact, the amalgamation of bodies and borders (the sea in the transmaritime crossing, or the transit zone in camps) and the relegation of bodies to the boundaries imposed on them via borderization constitute the very essence of the supposed hospitality granted to refugees by European states. Baring migrants' bodies means to profoundly dehumanize them, to demote them from the realm of subjecthood to that of objecthood; to mark their humanity with the seal of conditionality inherent in the evidentiary regime of victimhood that Didier Fassin has identified at the core of the asylum-granting process.[6] Whether in the biopolitics of the camp ("the nomos of modernity" for Giorgio Agamben, and the most acute actualization of bare life) or in the violence perpetrated in the multiple border outposts out at sea (and in fact as far out as the Saharan Desert, which the migrants cross on their way to the Mediterranean), migrants are reduced to an indiscriminate multitude. This objectification pertains to the logic of invisibility and atomization inflicted on migrants. Either falling apart in their country of origin, dissolved in the maritime abyss, or succumbing to the invisibility of an inconspicuous life of clandestinity, migrants are always already on the verge of disaggregation (Brugère and Le Blanc 2017). The spectral lives they embark on when setting out on their nautical journey (Sarnelli 2015; Kovačević 2019) partake of the "creation of death-worlds," which, as Mbembe argues in an echo of Agamben, "purvey new and unique forms of social existence in which vast populations are subjected to living conditions that confer upon them the status of the *living dead*" (2019, 92). The haunting presence of death within life, their intermingling, throws in sharp contrast the rift inhabiting the conceptual category of *anthropos*, an unbridgeable gap segregating a denigrated subsection of humankind from the citizen class. Where sovereignty is denied, any aspiration to it is pathologized, in a move that pits the logic of national belonging and the planetary logic of mobility against each other, when a sober, rational assessment of international relations at this juncture unambiguously reveals their inescapable correlation and embedding. In the nonspace of the detention camp, on the outer limit of state-sponsored systems of recognition and accountability, migrants are derealized; they turn into specters. In the remaining pages, I would like to suggest another form of derealization, enacted not merely on the conceptual level but rather one affecting the very corporeal wholeness of the migrants, an actualization of the threat of disaggregation, here adjusted to encompass more than its usual social incarnations.

DISSOLUTIVE ONTOLOGIES: THINKING THE RESIDUAL BODY

This extreme form of dislocation takes the form of a merging of body and border. Marooned on the edge of regimes of lawfulness but also legal protection, illegalized migrants disintegrate into the border zone (the carceral dispositif containing them), becoming border themselves as their "bod[ies] become the threshold expelled from the nation" (Brugère and Le Blanc 2017, 142). They morph into what Mbembe dubs a *corps-frontière*—a border body, or even perhaps a body-border assemblage—which his recent essay *Brutalisme* identifies as "excess humanity . . . they partake of the realm of waste" (2020, 146). Devoid of surplus value, these subjects have no particular use for capitalism and no destiny to fulfill other than disappearance. This intermingling of bodies and borders features as a main characteristic of the European regime of hospitality granted to refugees in times of crisis. In this respect, these atomized bodies act as a bridge between the two incarnations of borders that are the camp and the sea's depth, as the disappearance of migrants at sea mirrors their virtualization during incarceration on the edge of Europe.

Of *corps-frontière* Mbembe writes, "divisible, dismemberable, and rememberable, decomposable, [it is] an assemblage ruled by the law of codes and spaces . . . a racialized body . . . it is fundamentally devoid of a protective membrane. Torn to pieces, this body is folded many times over, and it carries within its flesh the memory of all sorts of partitions and subdivisions" (144). The disfiguration hinted at spotlights forms of being that run afoul of social categories, or even in this case, of anthropological difference, as these mutilated, disjointed bodies are more proximate to their maritime environment than to the human category. Through drowning and dissolution into the maritime space of the border, *corps-frontières* fade out of the realm of representation. Unknown, unnamed, and destined to remain anonymous, they slide ever more deeply into collective oblivion, only to be resurrected as part of a multitude of sacrificed figures, always politically mobilized as a uniform, undistinguishable mass.

To situate *corps-frontières* both on land and at sea brings into view the resonance of this dynamics of fragmentation in the context of migrant drownings, enticing us to bring to light the underwater dimension of the process. For, below the surface, other understandings of emplacement and borderization prevail. Geographers Philip Steinberg and Kimberley Peters aver that "water is simultaneously encountered as a depth and as a surface, as a set of fixed locations but also as an ungraspable space that is continually being reproduced by mobile molecules" (2015, 252). Therefore, for Steinberg and Peters, the ocean is understood "not as a space of discrete points between which objects move but rather as a dynamic environment of flows and continual recomposition where, because there is no static background, 'place' can be understood only in the context of mobility" (257). What this means practically is that adding the consideration of volume to deployments of surface-level borderscapes brings out the dimension of verticality, which considerably muddles the disciplining power of border regimes, as verticality "complicates control" (253). As such, it tends to undo the very regime of domestication that borders implement. Water enforces border restrictions, but its volume and perpetual reformation also concurrently disperse them. Underwater, emplacement is subject to movement and drifting, to the churning and flowing of maritime currents. Reading the sea in terms of flatness amounts to privileging territoriality and securitization; spotlighting issues of depth and volume opens the door to other considerations. For subalterns, the sea's depths embody both peril and complexity, concealed beneath its seemingly tranquil surface. The seabed serves as a stark reminder, scattered with the remains of those who perished in its grasp, their bodies caught in eternal stillness—rooted in space yet removed from the progression of teleological time (Talbayev 2021, 210).[7]

Excluded from the usual social practices surrounding death and bereavement (e.g., the repatriation of bodies to the home country for a funeral, or rituals surrounding burial in a clearly circumscribed grave), the bodies of drowned migrants are anonymized and left to die at sea. They cannot even claim the fate of entombment in a maritime "cemetery" since such configuration would entail emplacement and spatial containment in a way that the restless flux of the sea does not allow. In fact, the very nature of water and its endless planetary circulation functions as a principle of dispersal and virtualization. Once deceased, these bodies are left to decompose in the elements, dissolved through the corrosive effect of seawater, dispersed and amalgamated into their submarine environments, disappeared from view and bereft of proper memorialization. Returning bodies to their most infinitesimal materiality, these Mediterranean drownings perform the exclusion of migrant subjects from the order of anthropological exceptionalism. Through the disintegration purveyed by submersion into seawater, radical forms of being-in-the-world develop that puncture representations of the natural world as being fundamentally other, incommensurable to the order of anthropological dominance. To intellectually commit to thinking the human through dissolution is to query the materiality of subjects, their co-constitution with the more-than-human world that includes them. It is to make room for what I call "dissolutive ontologies."

Below the ocean's surface, movements of degradation, corrosion, and *longue durée* stratification into geophysical cycles abound, paving the way for the construction of mixed human and more-than-human assemblages where bodily dissolutions into the liminal space of the border take on geophysical hues.[8] Rethinking the human through the aqueous opens up new vistas across the logic of bordering, both in spatial and biological terms. In the intimacy of submerged flesh, water reveals the intrinsic porousness of bodies: "Our bodies of water are neither stagnant, nor separate, nor zipped up in some kind of impermeable sac of skin. These bodies are rather deeply imbricated in the intricate movements of water that create and sustain life on our planet" (Neimanis 2017, 65). In this entanglement between flesh and water, the vulnerability of human bodies to their elemental environments can be descried. Humanness then becomes a product of the inescapable relationship between the anthropological and the geophysical, with water acting both as a connecting agent and a principle of disaggregation. "The human," Astrid Neimanis contends, "is always also more-than-human. Our wateriness verifies this, both materially and conceptually" (2017, 97). She continues, "water is that which interpermeates and connects beings. As such, it might teach us something about an expanded understanding of the ontological" (7). The fundamental wateriness of being seeps out of clear-cut demarcation lines. Human bodies are 60 percent water, born of water (in the evolutionary sense, the primordial ocean in which life appeared; on a human scale, the amniotic liquid sustaining us in our earliest moments of life), embedded in fluid exchanges with bodies of water, both intercorporeally and extracorporeally (through tears, perspiration, lactation, breath, etc.).

Admittedly, the porous, spongy interface between humans and water requires the prerequisite of a border, a biological threshold demarcating the biotic from the nonbiotic. Taking our cue from Neimanis, let us call it "membrane" (2012, 90). Reading membrane through Nancy Tuana's concept of "viscous porosity," Neimanis construes it as a biostructure enacting both permeability and separation. The human skin comes to mind. Connecting us to our environments and yet guaranteeing our integrity as differentiated subjects, membranes guard against the temptation of complete dissolution into a homogeneous, universal flow.[9] They mark out resistance and the forceful imposition of a human-scale temporality: If the migrants, born of water, may eventually return to water through submersion and dissolution, their physical incarnation temporarily defers their incorporation into planetary time. Biological borders, in this context, distinguish the human from the more-than-human, restricting the disaggregating violence of elemental forces and enacting connectivity between all bodies of water, human or more-than-human.

Yet "membrane" also pulses with intertextual echoes of Mbembe's prose. In his delineation of *corps-frontière*, Mbembe points out that border bodies are "fundamentally devoid of a protective membrane" ("membrane de sécurité"; 2020, 144). The semantic resonance between the French "membrane de sécurité" and the security logic of European maritime borderings traces the contours of a protective order of European modernity from which the migrants are excluded. It also delineates an ontological order of preservation predicated on bodily integrity, which remains forever out of migrants' reach. If we train our lens on the macabre encounters between migrants and the forces of nature, be they tides, marine life-forms, or simply corrosive saltwater, the extreme exposure suffered by human flesh transpires. "Bared" to their most elemental expression, these drowned, submerged bodies float at the mercy of currents. Through corrosion, water performs a material annihilation instigated by the disciplining forces of European sovereignty, a process that highlights the vulnerability of humans once they are unsheltered from a concept of anthropological difference resting on control and mastery over nature. Reduced to the trappings of their molecular morphology, these bodies are reduced to deformation in an endless cycle of decomposition and "compost" (Haraway 2016). In water, subjectivity is disintegrated. Subjects are awash in seawater, dissolved into elemental particles, dispersed into the hydrocommons before being ingested by various biological life-forms or stratified into the sea floor. These transmaterial ontologies (humans becoming more-than-human and the reverse dynamics of chemical molecules ultimately morphing back into human form) blur the boundaries between the human and the geophysical. They consummate humans' ultimate embedding and merging into the materiality of the natural world: "From one body surges another body, through dissolution, transmutation, and reformation, in a poignant reminder that being-in-water requires a morphology of becoming" (Talbayev 2023, 15).

Yet, beyond any eradicating logic, the intimate entanglement between irruptive bodies and watery environments sheds light on the persistence of the human—in other material forms. These dissolutive ontologies coalesce around the figure of the *residual migrant*—a watery disincarnation of the derogated migrant subject, whose blending into geophysical matter eschews necropolitical obliteration and disappearance. This water-based redefinition of humanity unfolds in timescales of the planetary order. Matter endures over *longue durée* timelines—incarnating, decomposing, reincorporating in an endless cycle of molecular becoming marked by mutations and re-formations. Human matter thus evolves throughout a lengthy afterlife, becoming part of other organisms, permeating the weft of life writ large. The pervasive recirculation and reincarnation of dissolved matter spotlights a new form of ontological *and* physical embeddedness between all life-forms across their biotic or nonbiotic incarnations. This remanence of the residual migrant, its becoming residue both within and beyond borders (biological, necropolitical), reveals new constellations of sovereignty and integration at the intersection between human and more-than-human: "we require each other in unexpected collaborations and combinations, in hot compost piles. We become-with each other or not at all" (Haraway 2016, 4). Through geophysical assimilation, discarded bodies evince a porosity to otherness that cuts across their membrane of self-protection. In this dense form of copresence to the natural world, another order of being emerges. Through assimilation into the geophysical, residuality morphs into a locus of resistance and contest, one where the power of biopolitical annihilation is interrupted. In this respect, it can be said to be capitalizing on water's own elusive ontology as an indomitable geopower that "we summon up rather than control"

(Grosz et al. 2017, 135). Through residuality, a new politics of matter can be devised across the human/more-than-human divide, in which agency is knotted around the "possibility of co-acting with living and abiotic matter" (Papadopoulos 2014, 76).

Contesting the attempted biopolitical suppression mediated by borders, residual ontologies of dissolution reassert the uncontainable persistence of derogated human life through novel entanglements with the geophysical—and through cycles of reformation, with new human life to come. The becoming-sea of drowned migrants figures a hyperbolic, materialist version of the social and ontological annihilation of migrants denied the right to existence beyond the threshold of the border—or in the case of encounters with the maritime border, the right to existence tout court. It puts a magnifying glass over the refusal to see migrants in their distinct humanity, as individual subjects, humans deserving of a full life, of life-making opportunities. Yet it has been this chapter's argument that a seawater perspective testifies not only to the ultimate power of borders to discriminate and disaggregate—water dissolves migrant bodies into a molecular mass, forever obliterating them as subjects—but *also* to their inability to survive the very process of dissolution that they set into motion. By tracing the mixed modes of existence born of exposure and dissolution, this outlook proffers an updated ontological model predicated on merging and relationality between the human and the geophysical. In the space of the border and in the space of the sea, the migrants undergo a becoming-border of the self, a dissolution into the border's space-time, into its regime of negativity. What these dynamics highlight is the migrants' condition as residue. They are the "waste" produced through labor-selection processes that duplicate the labor-selection processes put into place during the colonial period to furnish the European metropoles with a productive labor force. Migrants are residual insofar as they have failed to enter the space lying beyond the border. They are forever suspended, dwelling in this nonspace of disappropriation, in Mbembe's words, "these dead spaces of non-connection which deny the very idea of a shared humanity, of a planet, the only one we have, that we share together, and to which we are linked by the ephemerality of our common condition" (2020, 99). To conclude, I would like to propose that there is another meaning to this residuality, one stretching beyond disappearance, one perhaps more subversive and labile, much in line with water's own indomitable, shape-shifting character—the residual as that which exceeds the logic of obliteration itself, as what remains behind, what haunts it. Perhaps not merely the migrant disintegrating into the sea but the stubborn grain of sand thwarting the smooth running of the necropolitical machine. Maybe the residue that eventually stalls its progress.

NOTES

This essay was originally printed in slightly modified form in *Interventions: International Journal of Postcolonial Studies* under the title "The Residual Migrant: Water Necropolitics and Borderization" (April 2023; https://www.tandfonline.com/doi/full/10.1080/1369801X.2023.2190921). All translations are mine.

1. See also Álvarez 2022.
2. Desert spaces and rivers have been similarly weaponized. See, for instance, De León 2015; Duncan and Levidis 2020.
3. Likewise Étienne Balibar has recently argued that "in the Mediterranean or in the Bay of Bengal, it is not unreasonable to speak of genocidal tendencies against the wandering population, which finds itself confined between increasingly impassable hostile barriers: from rejection at the entrance and expulsion, we move to elimination, and from there to extermination, not proclaimed as a political objective, but organized de facto through the dismissal of responsibilities, the refusal of international obligations (including those of the law of the sea), and above all the systematic dismantling of rescue operations organized by NGOs" (2019).
4. "Hors du nomos" (outside the *nomos*), in Michel Agier's ascription, by which the anthropologist means the law ("la loi ordinaire des humains"; 2002, 55).
5. I am here referring to Melanie Griffiths's subdivision of the temporality specific to asylum-seeking into the discrete categories of sticky time, suspended time, frenzied time, and ruptured time (2014).
6. In *The Empire of Trauma*, Fassin ascribes the recognition of the right to asylum to "a regime of veridiction where . . . suffering, now uncontested, comes to attest to an experience that elicits sympathy and calls for reparations" (2011, 16).
7. In the Atlantic, enslaved Black bodies thrown overboard endured similar eradication under the corrosive influence of seawater. Christina Sharpe (2016) powerfully examines the endurance of the bodily matter they left in their wake. See also Gunkel 2021; Hameed 2021; Talbayev 2023.
8. In this respect, seawater's literal "baring" of these bodies spotlights the crucial impact of elemental geophysical forces that both reproduce and far exceed

power dynamics hinging on biopolitical life, such as the camp *nomos* discussed earlier. For an examination of the co-constitutive dynamics between biopower writ large and geopower, see Talbayev 2023.

9. See, for instance, Stacy Alaimo's provocation: "Contemplating your shell on acid dissolves individualist, consumerist subjectivity in which the world consists primarily of externalized entities, objects for human consumption. It means *dwelling in the dissolve,* a dangerous pleasure, a paradoxical ecodelic expansion and dissolution of the human, an aesthetic incitement to extend and connect with vulnerable creaturely life and with the inhuman, unfathomable expanses of the seas. It is to expose oneself as a political act, to shift toward a particularly feminist mode of ethical and political engagement" (2016, 168).

WORKS CITED

Abderrezak, Hakim. 2018. "The Mediterranean *Seametery* and *Cementery* in Leïla Kilani's and Tariq Teguia's Filmic Works." In *Critically Mediterranean: Temporalities, Aesthetics, and Deployments of a Sea in Crisis,* edited by yasser elhariry and Edwige Tamalet Talbayev. Palgrave MacMillan.

Agamben, Giorgio. 1998. *Homo Sacer: Sovereign Power and Bare Life.* Translated by Daniel Heller-Roazen. Stanford University Press.

Agier, Michel. 2002. *Au bord du monde, les réfugiés.* Flammarion.

Alaimo, Stacy. 2016. *Exposed: Environmental Politics: Pleasures in Posthuman Times.* University of Minnesota Press.

Álvarez, David. 2022. "Bridging Migratory Fault-Lines: Francis Alÿs's Performance at the Strait of Gibraltar." In *Figures of the Migrant: The Roles of Literatures and the Arts in Representing Migration,* edited by Siobhan Brownlie and Rédouane Abouddahab. Routledge.

Balibar, Étienne. 1998. "The Borders of Europe." In *Cosmopolitics: Thinking and Feeling Beyond the Nation,* edited by Pheng Cheah and Bruce Robbins, translated by J. Swenson. University of Minnesota Press.

Balibar, Étienne. 2019. "Sur la situation des migrants dans le capitalisme absolu." *Les Possibles,* no. 19. https://france.attac.org/nos-publications/les-possibles/numero-19-hiver-2019/dossier-des-migrations-et-discriminations-aux-gilets-jaunes/article/sur-la-situation-des-migrants-dans-le-capitalisme-absolu.

Bensaâd, Ali. 2006. "La Méditerranée, un mur en devenir?" In "De la richesse et de la pauvreté entre Europe et Méditerranée," edited by Thierry Fabre, special issue of *Rencontres d'Averroès,* no. 12, 99–112.

Brambilla, Cristina. 2010. "'Pluriversal' Citizenship and Borderscapes." In *Transient Spaces: The Berlin Syndrome*, edited by Marina Sorbello and Antje Weitzel. Argobooks.

Brugère, Fabienne, and Guillaume Le Blanc. 2017. *La Fin de l'hospitalité: Lampedusa, Lesbos, Calais . . . jusqu'où irons-nous?* Flammarion.

Butler, Judith. 2014. "Rethinking Vulnerability and Resistance." https://bibacc.org/wp-content/uploads/2016/07/Rethinking-Vulnerability-and-Resistance-Judith-Butler.pdf.

De León, Jason. 2015. *The Land of Open Graves: Living and Dying on the Migrant Trail*. University of California.

Dullin, Sabine, and Étienne Forestier-Peyrat. 2015. *Les Frontières mondialisées*. Presses Universitaires de France.

Duncan, Ifor, and Stefanos Levidis. 2020. "Weaponizing a River." *e-flux*, April. https://www.e-flux.com/architecture/at-the-border/325751/weaponizing-a-river/.

Fassin, Didier. 2011. *L'Empire du traumatisme. Enquête sur la condition de victime*. Flammarion.

Gjergji, Iside. 2015. "Lost in the Mediterranean: Theories, Discourses, Borders and Migration Policies in the 'Mare Nostrum.'" *RCCS Annual Review*, no. 7. https://journals.openedition.org/rccsar/628.

Griffiths, Melanie B. E. 2014. "Out of Time: The Temporal Uncertainties of Refused Asylum Seekers and Immigration Detainees." *Journal of Ethnic and Migration Studies* 40, no. 12: 1991–2009.

Grosz, Elizabeth, Kathryn Yusoff, and Nigel Clark. 2017. "An Interview with Elizabeth Grosz: Geopower, Inhumanism and the Biopolitical." *Theory, Culture & Society* 34 (2–3): 129–46.

Guild, Elspeth. 2003. "The Border Abroad: Visas and Border Controls." In *In Search of Europe's Borders*, edited by Kees Groenendijk, Elspeth Guild, and Paul Minderhoud. Kluwer Law International.

Gunkel, Henriette. 2021. "Alien Time: Being in Vertigo." In *Visual Cultures as Time Travel*, edited by Henriette Gunkel and Ayesha Hameed. Sternberg Press.

Hameed, Ayesha. 2021. "Sea Changes and Other Futurisms." In *Visual Cultures as Time Travel*, edited by Henriette Gunkel and Ayesha Hameed. Sternberg Press.

Haraway, Donna. 2016. *Staying with the Trouble: Making Kin in the Chthulucene*. Duke University Press.

Heller, Charles, and Lorenzo Pezzani. 2018. "The Mediterranean Mobility Conflict: Violence and Anti-Violence at the Borders of Europe." *Humanity Journal*. https://humanityjournal.org/blog/heller-and-pezzani/.

Human Rights Watch. 2019. "No Escape from Hell: EU Policies Contribute to Abuse of Migrants in Libya." January 21. https://www.hrw.org/report/2019/01/21/no-escape-hell/eu-policies-contribute-abuse-migrants-libya.

Kovačević, Nataša. 2019. "Dissolving into the Sea: Cinematic Migrants and the Problem of Agency." *Postcolonial Studies* 22 (4): 428–45.

Mbembe, Achille. 2019. *Necropolitics*. Translated by Steven Corcoran. Duke University Press.

Mbembe, Achille. 2020. *Brutalisme*. La Découverte.

Neimanis, Astrida. 2012. "Hydrofeminism: Or, On Becoming a Body of Water." In *Undutiful Daughters: New Directions in Feminist Thought and Practice,* edited by Henriette Gunkel, Chrysanthi Nigianni, and Fanny Söderbäch. Palgrave Macmillan.

Neimanis, Astrida. 2017. *Bodies of Water: Posthuman Feminist Phenomenology*. Bloomsbury.

Papadopoulos, Dimitris. 2014. "Politics of Matter: Justice and Organisation in Technoscience." *Social Epistemology* 18 (1): 70–85.

Perera, Suvendrini. 2007. "A Pacific Zone? (In)security, Sovereignty, and Stories of the Pacific Borderscape." In *Borderscapes: Hidden Geographies and Politics at Territory's Edge,* edited by Prem Kumar Rajaram and Carl Grundy-Warr. University of Minnesota Press, 201–28.

Pezzani, Lorenzo. 2020. "Hostile Environments." *eflux*, April. https://www.e-flux.com/architecture/at-the-border/325761/hostile-environments/.

Rosello, Mireille, and Stephen F. Wolfe. 2017. "Introduction." In *Border Aesthetics: Concepts and Intersections,* edited by Johan Schimanski and Stephen F. Wolfe. Berghahn.

Sarnelli, Laura. 2015. "The Gothic Mediterranean: Haunting Migrations and Critical Melancholia." *Journal of Mediterranean Studies* 24 (2): 147–65.

Sassen, Saskia. 2005. "When National Territory Is Home to the Global: Old Borders to Novel Borderings." *New Political Economy* 10 (4): 523–41.

Saunders, Frances Stoner. 2016. "Borders." *London Review of Books* 38 (5): 7–15.

Sharpe, Christina. 2016. *In the Wake: On Blackness and Being*. Duke University Press.

Steinberg, Philip, and Kimberley Peters. 2015. "Wet Ontologies, Fluid Spaces: Giving Depth to Volume Through Oceanic Thinking." *Environment and Planning D: Society & Space*, no. 33, 247–264.

Strüver, Anke. 2005. *Stories of the 'Boring Border': The Dutch-German Borderscape in People's Minds*. Lit Verlag.

Talbayev, Edwige Tamalet. 2021. "Seawater." *Contemporary French and Francophone Studies: SITES* 25 (2): 207–17.

Talbayev, Edwige Tamalet. 2023. "Hydropower: Residual Dwelling Between Life and Nonlife." *Angelaki: Journal of the Theoretical Humanities* 28 (1): 9–21.

FROM SURVEILLANCE TO CONTESTATION
—

The Ebb and Flow of the Mediterranean Frontier's Aesthetic Regime
AN INTERVIEW WITH CHARLES HELLER, BY
MARIE SANDOZ AND ANNE-KATRIN WEBER
TRANSLATED BY NICOLE HORNE

Aerial shots of an overloaded boat on which a group of racialized individuals attempt to cross the Mediterranean figure among the most regrettably emblematic vertical images of our time. The vastness of the sea, whose uniform surface stretches far beyond the outer edges of the photographs, contrasts with both the material finiteness of the makeshift watercrafts as well as the ontological finitude of the crossings, which often end up deadly. Omnipresent in a time marked by great migratory "crises," images of contemporary boat people also incarnate the West's indifferent and looming gaze over the ensuing tragedies. These pictures, taken from a distance at a vertical or oblique angle, additionally carry within them the risk of spectacularizing the violence of clandestine crossings (Blashke 2017, 161–64). The absence of spatial markers that characterizes them ultimately combines with a lack of contextualization that would otherwise enable a better grasp of the lived reality of the people they represent, their trajectories and their hopes: what remains illegible in them is the European Union's organizational responsibility for the drowning deaths of thousands of people.

The work of Charles Heller and Lorenzo Pezzani, founders of the Forensic Oceanography research project and more recently of the NGO Border Forensics, operates at the intersection of the hypervisibility of the images that circulate in the public sphere and the imperceptibility of those that would reveal other aspects of the conflicts unfolding in the Mediterranean. Their investigations build on a multiplicity of images—satellite, surveillance, photographic, thermal, cartographic, etcetera—brought together to renegotiate the (in)visibility structuring the maritime space and thus to contest border violence. In opposition to the quasi-total surveillance and control of the Mediterranean frontier and of the people looking to cross it, Heller and Pezzani disclose an alternative *sousveillance*, or under-surveillance, drawing from dominant technologies in order to overcome the secrecy surrounding security operations and denounce human rights violations perpetrated by governments. This appropriation of vertical images and their radical repurposing is a distinctive feature of the investigations led by the Forensic Architecture laboratories with which Heller and Pezzani are affiliated. It thus serves as the focal point of the interview we conducted with Charles Heller on August 20, 2021, in Neuchâtel.

Charles Heller, you are not only a researcher and filmmaker but also an expert on European migratory policies in the Mediterranean. In your work, you regularly bring together aerial and surveillance images and what we refer to in this context more generally as vertical images. Before opening up a discussion on these images, and on your work more broadly, let's begin with a brief digression into the history of Forensic Oceanography, the research group that you lead with Lorenzo Pezzani. In which context did you begin your investigations on the scopic regimes of migrations in the Mediterranean?

We introduced the Forensic Oceanography project around ten years ago while carrying out our doctoral research at Goldsmiths at the University of London. Within the framework of Forensic Architecture, we wished to conceive of a methodology that would support civil society actors looking to denounce human rights violations perpetrated by governments.

The investigation around the Mediterranean as a border space, with which Forensic Oceanography was first concerned, emerged in 2011 in the wake of the revolutionary uprisings taking place in the Arab world. The fall of authoritarian regimes, such as Ben Ali's in Tunisia, brought about a destabilization of borders, which were becoming less hermetic. This was compounded by the civil war taking place in Libya, and the number of migrations, specifically maritime migrations, increased. Crossings toward Europe took place under very precarious circumstances, and numerous cases of people drowning at sea were reported. These drowning deaths are occurring even as a surveillance system of an unprecedented scale is being deployed as part of NATO's military intervention in Libya. Yet in 2011 the Mediterranean is virtually unreachable for civil society. The conditions leading to these deaths remain in the shadows.

In order to denounce the gravity of such a situation and to gain a better understanding of it, the concept of "liquid violence" plays a key role in your approach. What do you mean by this expression?

Since the conditions of migrations across the Mediterranean and the modalities of their repression remain largely obscure for civil society, a methodological challenge arose for us as soon as we undertook our first investigation: How could we recover the traces of those who died at sea, while such a death, by its very definition, erases any trace? How could we document the violence that migrant people endure?

The more than forty thousand dead people in the Mediterranean have not, for the most part, died from direct violence, such as being shot to death by border guards. The majority of them die by drowning. Yet these deaths are not "accidents" but rather the outcome of the particular regime that governs the Mediterranean frontier: European policies that criminalize and thus make precarious the movements of populations from the global South. We coined the concept of "liquid violence" to account for such border violence, which most often operates indirectly. The concept enables us to both emphasize the material nature of this form of violence, and how it adapts and transforms over time.

"Liquid violence" refers to the ideologies, infrastructures, and practices responsible for the drowning deaths of tens of thousands of people. It seeks to draw attention to the mechanisms and multidimensional effects of European policies regarding the control of maritime borders. According to you, liquid violence is borne of an

aesthetic regime, the term aesthetic *here understood in the sense developed by Jacques Rancière: that which presents itself as sensorial experience. Can you tell us a little more about this?*

Lorenzo Pezzani and I have a dual outlook on the maritime frontier and the liquid violence deployed there. First of all, as members of an architectural research center, spatialization is central to our way of thinking about the world. But our gaze is also aesthetic: It includes a sensorial dimension, encompassing primarily sight and hearing, which are fundamental to understanding how maritime borders operate. The (in)visible and (in)audible structure the practices and policies of all the actors implicated in the control or transgression of these borders.[1]

By virtue of their situation of illegality, which is the direct result of European policies, people who try to cross the Mediterranean attempt to remain invisible so as to escape the eye of state actors. Thus, the majority of crossings take place at night, which makes them all the more dangerous. These clandestine practices—*clandestine* understood in the etymological sense as "hidden"—are imposed by the political border regime. But they also express the *agency* of the migrants, namely the migrants' calculated use of any room for maneuvering at their disposal in order to achieve their goals. As a matter of fact, migrant people maintain a certain obscurity around their crossings. Conversely, states attempt to make the bodies and vessels of migrants visible in order to better control them. This may be observed in the image taken by the Italian border police's surveillance plane of a migrant boat just before its interception (figure 1). The sensorial dimension is in this way inherent to the practices and policies governing the maritime frontier: In order to control, one must first perceive.

However, the aesthetic regime of the border cannot be summarized as a binary opposition between the visibility wished for by the State and the invisibility desired by migrant people. In situations of distress, the latter are going to call out for help and look to be both seen and heard. On the contrary, state actors can claim not to have noticed vessels in distress, in order to evade their obligation to rescue them. In this way they break maritime laws requiring that any ship made aware of a distress situation provide assistance.

What is the role of audiovisual technologies and aerial vision in this aesthetic regime, and in the control of borders more broadly?

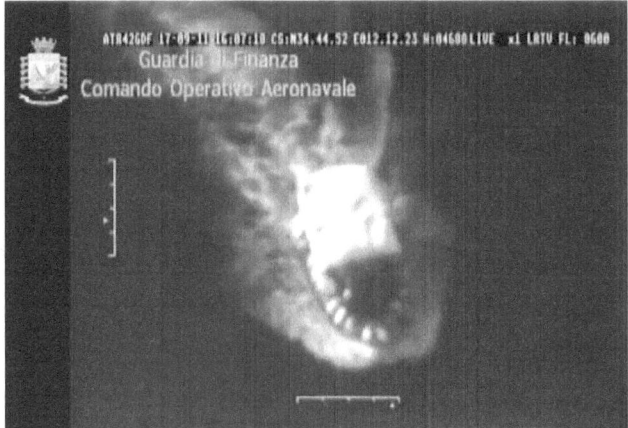

Fig. 1 "Lampedusa: Images inhérentes à l'activité de la Guardia di Finanza pour contraster l'immigration clandestine [Lampedusa: Images intrinsic to the work of Guardia di Finanza to fight clandestine immigration]," Lampedusa, September 17, 2011. (YouTube)

In their desire to render visible clandestine trajectories, states have recourse to a multiplicity of surveillance technologies. Within this arsenal, satellites, images captured by planes or by drones, etcetera, are just some of the tools, which also include radars or thermic cameras. According to the language they employ, states look to create an "integrated maritime picture." There is thus an assemblage at work, each tool having its own strengths and weaknesses (figure 2).

Let's take satellite imagery as an example. The sea is an extremely vast space that satellites allow us to visualize. There is a tension, however, between the geographical area that this visual technology is capable of capturing and the resolution of the final image. Within the assemblage, the relative importance of each instrument of control depends on the case and is modified over time, specifically according to the policies in effect and the parties involved. To put it more broadly, the practices that produce both liquid violence and the aesthetic border regime are in constant transformation.

This point is central to and resonates with the historical perspective of our line of questioning. Its contributions excavate the vertical image's multiple forms and practices, which vary according to the political context and the era. Could you tell

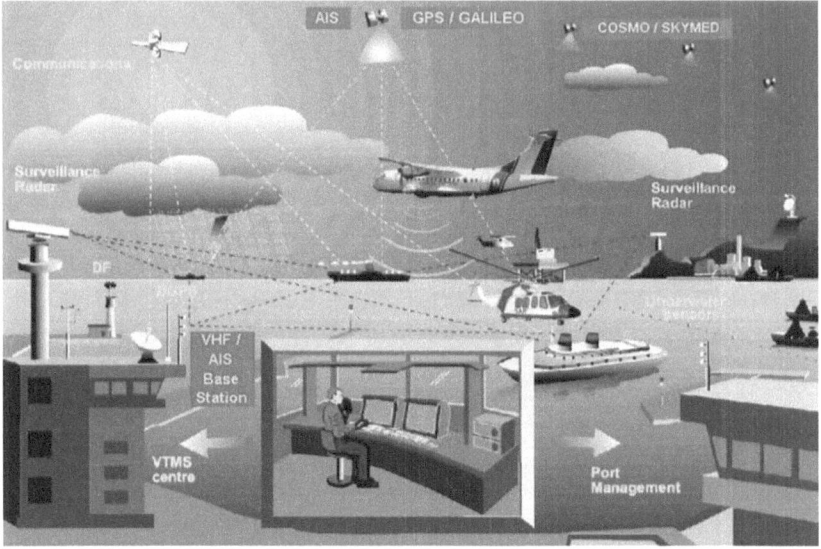

Fig. 2 Vessel traffic management information system (VTMIS), graphic pulled from the presentation "Dal VTS al VTMIS: Il sistema di controllo del traffico marittimo nell'ottica industriale," Rome, July 5, 2018. (Finmeccanica/Leonardo S.p.A.)

us more about the contemporary transformations of the fight for the Mediterranean and the role of images in this process?

The shipwreck that took place on October 3, 2013, one kilometer off the shore of the Italian island of Lampedusa, and its 360 victims constitute a moment of rupture in the representation of liquid violence. Before this event, the public was not very aware of the deaths occurring in the Mediterranean; they became visible as a result of this tragedy. In the days that followed, the airport hangar in Lampedusa was transformed into a mortuary space lined with coffins. At the same time, it also became an audiovisual production studio where journalists, photographers, and television cameras stood ready to capture European officials as they gathered together and proclaimed that these deaths were unacceptable. The phenomenon of spectacularizing drownings at sea is carried out in the context of what sociologist William Walters calls the "humanitarian border" (2010). This regime is characterized by a stated desire to want to "save lives," all the while maintaining the border's security function. Yet, beginning in 2013, this dimension became central to the Mediterranean's border-control regime. During a press conference in the wake of the Lampedusa tragedy, president of the European Commission Jose Manuel Barroso both expressed his grief and announced a budget increase for Frontex, the agency charged with securing Europe's maritime borders. Put otherwise, the spectacularization of liquid violence was exploited by the EU and European governments to justify an intensification of the security practices that were at the root of these shipwrecks.

Added on to the security piece, however, is a real "humanitarian impulse" that was incarnated primarily by Operation Mare Nostrum, led by the Italian marines and launched in the wake of the sinking at Lampedusa. Yet this operation, which was very much active in the rescue of migrant people, was accused by other European governments of being a pull factor and therefore the cause of an increased influx of people looking to get to Europe. In November 2014, one year after its launch, the Italian project had to cease operations because the European Union refused to offer any material and financial aid. Frontex took Mare Nostrum's place: In this way, the European Union knowingly left a vacuum in terms of emergency rescue services. This led to a new explosion in the death toll, which reached its shocking peak on April 18, 2015, when an overloaded vessel sank, resulting in over 950 dead and only 27 survivors. A veritable politics of nonassistance is at work here, operating throughout the Mediterranean and at the level of state planning.

Citizens and NGOs reacted to the consequences of the European Union's refusal to deploy rescue operations, by launching their own initiatives, like Sea-Watch. This new form of migrant assistance constituted a rupture in the border's aesthetic regime. These NGOs essentially break up the states' monopoly not only on available rescue services but also on the capacity to document these crossings. The maritime presence of NGOs thus changes the aesthetic regime, as what is and what is not visible is henceforth no longer exclusively controlled by the hegemonic power of states. Since 2016, these NGOs have also maintained their own aerial surveillance planes, allowing for both the detection of vessels in distress and the documentation of human rights violations. Yet, as of 2017, we are witnessing an attempt by states to criminalize NGOs, and the Mediterranean has once again become a more inaccessible space for civil society.

This opacity contrasts sharply with the observation that the space of the sea is currently surveilled more than ever, by means involving different visual technologies. The growing prominence of aerial surveillance within control systems is a new evolution. In recent years, the air has indeed become a central axis in European governments' strategies of repression. To avoid rescuing vessels in difficulty or being accused of not having done so, the European Union tends to move its ships out of the way of migrant paths. By contrast, planes and drones are being deployed off the Libyan coast with the aim of detecting clandestine vessels as rapidly as possible in order to inform the Libyan coast guard of their whereabouts so that they may intercept them. These aerial tools transmit images in real time to various coordination centers on European territory, such as Frontex, but such information remains inaccessible to civilians. This displacement of the border, and of its control from the air, in turn generates other forms of contestation: Civilian aerial missions document the presence of these planes and intercept the orders given to the Libyan coastguard via radio.

Ultimately, what we have here is an environment in flux, where we are observing ebbs and flows, as with the tide. The forms assumed by liquid violence and the aesthetic regime evolve based not only on the actors involved and their politics but also on the technologies they employ. If our desire is to contest the regimes of (in)visibility forged by states, we also need to take into account these transformations.

You talk about a "disobedient gaze" to describe your practice of contestation. How does this fit into your approach? Additionally, how do aerial images take part in the construction of this disobedient gaze?

The concept of "disobedient gaze" first and foremost conveys our positioning with regard to the technologies that we enlist, which are used "against the grain" of their intended purpose. Whereas states are trying to shed light on migrant crossings, all while obscuring border violence, our objective is symmetrically the reverse.

The concrete application of this concept is well exemplified by our initial investigation: the case of the Left-to-Die Boat. In March 2011, an inflatable boat with seventy-two people on board left the Libyan coast for Italy and drifted for two weeks on international waters surveilled by NATO as part of its intervention in Libya. No assistance was provided. Only eleven people were still alive when the vessel ran aground on the Libyan coast. This slow death became infamous following the publication of witness statements, most notably by *The Guardian*. The survivors reported, among other things, that a military helicopter flew over them and that a warship actually approached their vessel before setting off again. The French NGO GISTI (Groupe d'information et de soutien des immigrés) decided to focus on this case to draw attention to the deadly consequences of such nonassistance practices, of which the Left-to-Die Boat offers a flagrant example. According to GISTI, given the degree of surveillance of this area at the time, it is simply impossible that the military were not aware of its distress. They thus failed to uphold their legal obligation to rescue the boat. In June 2011, the NGO announced that it will be lodging a formal legal complaint, and we decided to support them in this process.

The question then arises as to which pieces of evidence we can bring forward to corroborate the testimonies. At first, there are few. We have access to only one image of the event: an aerial picture of the vessel taken by a French military surveillance plane on March 27, the day they set sail. However, other images do exist. The survivors report having shown the bodies of the deceased to the naval vessel's crew, which was positioned only ten meters away. But according to them, "All they did was take pictures." Moreover, the migrants' cellphones, which contained photographs of the interaction, were seized by the Libyan coastguard. The aesthetic regime is in this way not totally opaque, but the images and knowledge are generated by and/or placed in the hands of states who keep them secret. For us it is thus about giving them a new visibility.

Survivor testimony and distress signals relayed by the Italian coastguard enabled us first to estimate the location where the fuel-supply cutoff occurred. We then called upon an oceanographer to model the vessel's long drift based on sea-current data. We also knew that there were at least thirty-eight ships in the area in question. But where exactly were these ships, and did they neglect their duties? To answer this question, we brought together SAR (synthetic aperture radar) satellite imagery from the European Space Agency's Envisat-1 satellite (figures 3 and 4). This technology transmits microwave pulses towards Earth, which, after having reached Earth's surface, are scattered back to the satellite. The satellite then calculates the signals' time delay and forms an image. Calm sea surfaces appear black, while ships reflect all of the radar energy back to the sensor and are thus visible as small, bright dots. In our case, these images reveal that the closest ships were less than two hours from the dinghy in distress.

These satellite images are interesting for those looking to think about the concept of the disobedient gaze, largely because they are ambiguous. While

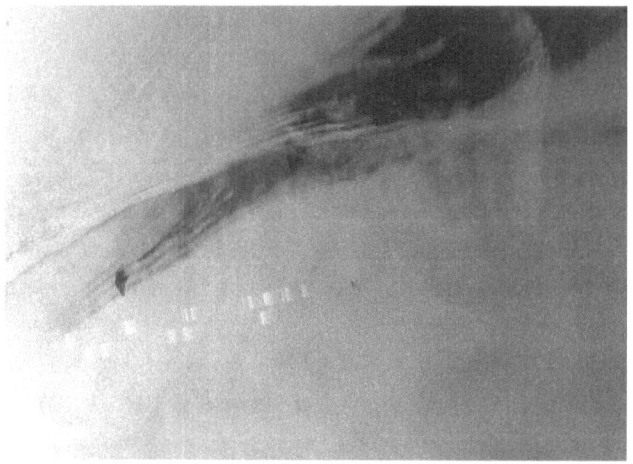

Fig. 3 SAR image taken on March 28, 2011, by the European Space Agency's Envisat-1 satellite. (Courtesy Forensic Architecture)

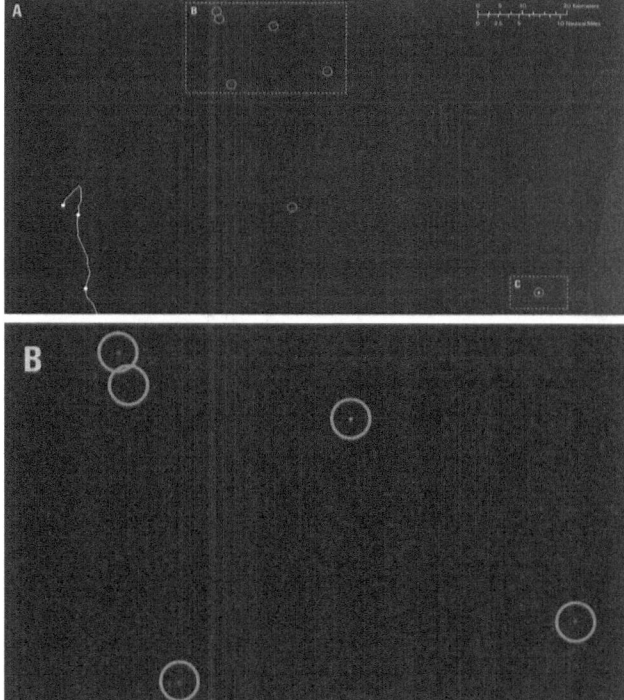

Fig. 4 Thumbnails and enlarged images of the naval vessels that were detected based on Envisat-1 satellite data from March 29. (Courtesy Forensic Architecture)

their broad coverage is useful for locating the ships over a vast area, the resolution of the images is relatively weak: 75 meters. In other words, any smaller vessel is simply not visible, whereas a 75- or 150-meter boat will correspond to one or two pixels. It is thus impossible to identify all of the boats that were present and, for those that can be seen, to say whether they are military or merchant ships. There is therefore an obvious political dimension to the resolution of the image, as it does not, in this instance, enable us to identify in great detail those state actors who neglected their duties. At the same time, this low resolution allows the presence of migrants who do not wish to be detected to remain hidden.

To adopt a disobedient gaze thus requires sophisticated knowledge of these technologies, to know their power and their limitations, in order to produce political results to counter those initially anticipated by the dominant gaze. Even though these technologies remain problematic, to appropriate them enables us in part to contest the "distribution of the sensible" as it has been established by governments. Here, SAR imagery proved that there were indeed boats that had forsaken their collective responsibility, without also disclosing the migratory paths of those who wish to remain in obscurity. The disobedient gaze therefore consists of making border violence visible, audible, and eventually knowable by attempting to forge a new regime of (in)visibility on behalf of the most vulnerable.

The aerial footage produced by the SAR satellite is totally illegible to the average person and highlights the need for specific skills in order to obtain information from them. In this respect, this image brings attention to one common feature of your probes: the mobilization of a range of sources and technologies that require varied expertise. How do you approach this interdisciplinary work, and in what way does this define the nature of the images that you produce?

Collective and interdisciplinary work is essential to critical forensic practice. Our objective is to bring back up to the surface traces of the events we investigate and to use them to build evidence. At the start of each investigation, we ask ourselves: "What happened?"; "At what moment in this chain of events was the law violated?"; "What traces might these occurrences have left behind?" Providing answers at the start of an investigation requires the exercise of imagination. It relies on the available, often meager, evidence, and on knowledge acquired via the study of similar cases that allow us to formulate initial hypotheses. After ten years of experience, we have devised a toolbox made up of the investigative strategies and technologies we regularly resort to. For us, it is important to have working knowledge of the available technical resources so that we are able to contact the relevant people or agencies. That being said, each technology requires sophisticated and detailed expertise, and it would be vain to want to master them all. We thus collaborate regularly with different specialists, such as the oceanographer for the Left-to-Die Boat, but also analysts who specialize in satellite remote-sensing data, graphic designers, etcetera. It is indeed all of these skills together that enable us to put together a body of evidence. Contrary to the widespread view in forensic science that a piece of evidence "speaks for itself," we find that the intelligibility of all evidence requires interpretation and thus entails a subjective dimension. There exists no "straightforward" image that is to be read like a document containing all the elements linked to an event. For example, the SAR satellite imagery that you mentioned not only needs to be processed and analyzed by a remote-sensing professional but also supplemented with other images and information, such as the model of the boat's drift path that was generated by the oceanographer. Interdisciplinarity is thus fundamental to our attempts to understand events, the reality of which states are trying to hide, and is reflected in the results we obtain. Our maps, models, and videos make up an assemblage of heterogenous data that complement and support each another (figure 5).

Another image you showed us highlights the multiplicity of technologies and infrastructures that come together to create images of the surveilled space. However, it also shows that surveillance is concentrated in aerial and maritime spaces but neglects the underwater space. In order to contest the effects of this surveillance, would it not be advantageous to "dig" underneath the flat surface of the Mediterranean, as it is represented in satellite images and aerial photography, in order to bring back up to the surface the drowned bodies and reveal the effects of liquid violence more broadly?

The question of volume is important. Maritime jurisdictions are, for that matter, three-dimensional and do take into account what is underwater. As far as documenting migrations is concerned, we have observed that very few underwater images exist. And this is for a relatively simple reason: They are

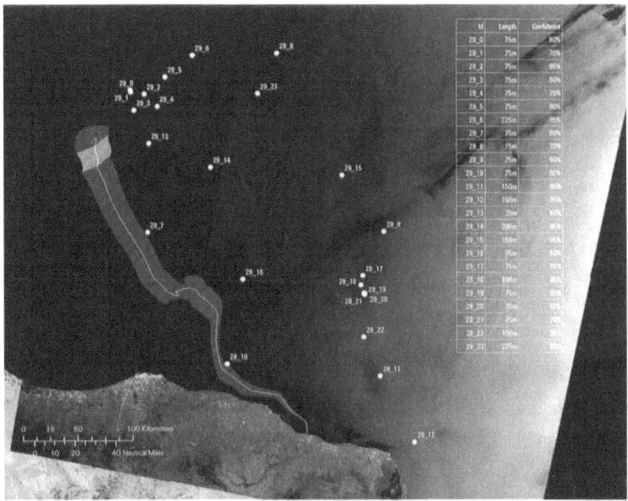

Fig. 5 Analysis of the Envisat-1 satellite image from March 29, 2011, indicating the modeled position of the *Left-to-Die* Boat (the diagonal section cross-hatched in yellow) and the nearby presence of several ships. To the right, the table indicates the ships' estimated lengths. (Courtesy Forensic Architecture)

not useful in intercepting migrants, hence the lack of state interest to produce any within the parameters of border control. Nevertheless, underwater photographs are occasionally taken by state actors, but they partake of the paradigm of spectacularizing migrant deaths. For example, some Italian agencies' images of the wreckage from Lampedusa in 2013 circulated. They performed the function of making visible the humanitarian response and the grief of the Italian nation, failing however to address the question of responsibility for these drownings, and to call into question the perpetuation, or even the reinforcement, of lethal policies.

Within the scope of our investigations, and with a view to knowing the real number of deaths at sea, we have explored tools that could enable the detection of wreckage. We began a dialogue with specialists in bathymetry, or the study of the topography of the seafloor. The data produced comes from sonar, as vision underwater is weak: Beyond a few meters, there is no longer any light. Unfortunately for us, no useful data could be produced. In fact, in order simply to calculate the natural reliefs of the ocean floor, the data that would reveal the presence of wreckages is altogether erased from the results.

Your investigations bear witness to a certain adaptability of surveillance technologies, whose impacts can vary—or even contradict one another—according to the political aim of the actors who take hold of them. However, these technologies and the images that they produce are never unambiguous. In your particular case, digital models and cartographic visualizations can have a tendency to diminish the sense of reality of the events they depict. Conversely, to represent migrants and their suffering can prove to be delicate in conditions that already tend towards their spectacularization. How do you manage these tensions?

Images always have a problematic dimension, in particular when they bear witness to a violent event, and our position in relation to them is never completely determined. I would say that our work on and with these images evolves across different forms, platforms, and temporalities, where the question of the relationship, and sometimes the tension, between technical reconstruction and lived experience is endlessly reformulated.

For example, during the publication of the report on the Left-to-Die Boat, which now serves as a basis for several legal complaints against the states involved in the 2011 military operations off the coast of Libya, Lorenzo and I were not satisfied: We found that there was too clear a separation between our technical and visual analyses on the one hand and the reconstruction of the migrants' lived experiences on the other. The report, of course, contains transcriptions of their statements, but these converse very little with the technical data. Such statements are nevertheless crucial to our investigations: They form the point of departure for our own reconstructions. But in 2014 we got the chance to make a seventeen-minute-long video, *Liquid Traces*, as part of Forensic Architecture's first major exhibition at the Haus der Kulturen der Welt in Berlin. This video allowed us to combine traces and lived experiences in a single form, and to make the objectivist vision of events that was generated through cartography and satellite imagery—the "view from above"—coexist with the audiovisual reconstitution of the passengers' testimony—what we call the "view from the boat" (see figures 6 and 7).

This particular example enables us to shed light on the different temporalities at play in our critical work on the image. The lengthy time frame is important in terms of what we mean by disobedience, which, in our view, distinguishes itself from the almost circumstantial dimension of refusal. For us, it is important to affirm that our work with these tools and images is

Fig. 6 Screenshot of the video of the interview of Charles Heller and Lorenzo Pezzani with a survivor, Milan, December 22, 2011. (Courtesy Forensic Architecture)

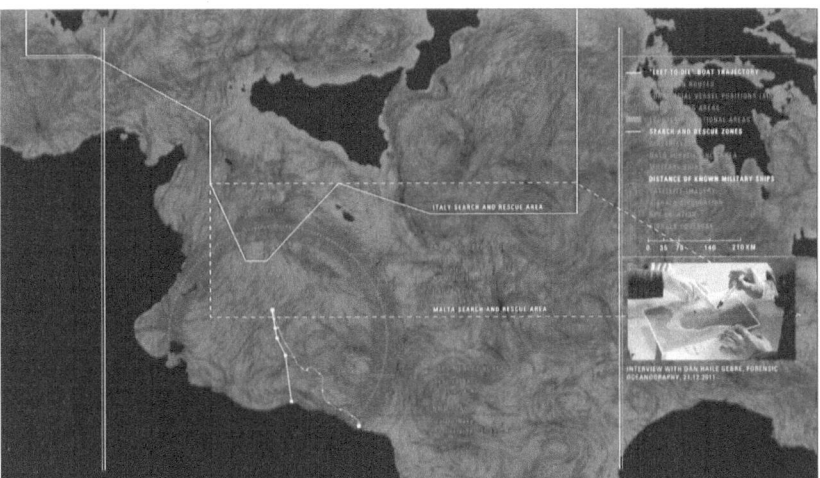

Fig. 7 Screenshot of the video *Liquid Traces: The Left-to-Die Boat Case*, by Charles Heller and Lorenzo Pezzani, video (17:00), 2014. (Courtesy Forensic Architecture)

carried out not only in different stages but also via different modes of communication, and intended for different platforms—not only legal but also artistic and academic.

As far as the representation of migrants in the images themselves is concerned, it would be interesting to take a look at a more recent case of liquid violence that we documented in a video made in partnership with the NGO Sea-Watch. The incident took place on November 6, 2017, at a few hours' sailing off the coast of Tripoli. A small vessel with between 130 and 150 people on board was in distress and was rescued simultaneously by a Libyan patrol ship and Sea-Watch. Yet it is the Libyan coastguard more than anything else that endangered these people, whose inflatable boat capsized. They also sought to prevent Sea-Watch volunteers from coming to their rescue, through intimidation. Twenty or so deaths could have been avoided, while those who were "saved" by the Libyan ship were probably imprisoned in camps, tortured, or even sold into slavery. This case provides evidence of a contemptuous mode of repression implemented by the European Union, which trains and finances the Libyan coastguard.

This incident took place at a very different moment from the Left-to-Die Boat case. While we had virtually no images directly documenting the latter, we have a plethora of images of the former provided by Sea-Watch, whose rescue workers wore GoPro cameras on their helmets during the intervention. It was also filmed by the surveillance cameras located on Sea-Watch's main ship. This constitutes a very different aesthetic regime.

These images became essential for us. They are the foundation of our reconstruction of the events, which also served as the basis of a legal complaint brought against Italy before the European Court of Human Rights. However, through them also arises a series of issues. For one, these are images produced automatedly within an apparatus defined by Sea-Watch, thus without the say of the people being filmed. Secondly, a hierarchy exists within the images themselves: between the white rescue workers and the non-white migrants being rescued. The photographs depict a group of calm and coherent volunteers retrieving from the water people from sub-Saharan Africa who are fighting for their lives. With such images, the risk is great of reproducing stereotypical representations marked by colonial hierarchies—representations, as it happens, that we are trying to contest. Thirdly, even though it was possible, through the collection of testimony, for us to impart a certain horizontality to the story of migrants being saved by Sea-Watch, and even though those whom we met did in fact want the images to circulate, these images still record the drowning deaths of several people whose consent we will never have. We can try to imagine what they might have wanted, but we will nevertheless remain haunted by the dead's lack of reply.

Ultimately, it seems not only important to us to show these images but just as necessary to underline the political and ethical problems linked to their production and circulation. It is, however, difficult to translate this ambivalent and contradictory stance into the language and institutions of law. Hence, we chose explicitly not to address this tension in our video reconstruction intended for the European Court of Human Rights. We have, on the contrary—and without offering a definitive response—discussed it in articles, presentations, and art installations.

The problems to which we have just alluded allow us to bring to light the fact that images produced in a context of either extreme distance or extreme proximity to a violent event are not more or less problematic in themselves. As Donna Haraway points out, all vision technologies involve power dynamics ([1988] 2007). Thus, any critical approach to the image must carefully attempt to position itself in relation to them. And this frequently involves inhabiting the border between competing imperatives.

NOTES

The original French interview "De la surveillance à la contestation: Flux et reflux du régime esthétique de la frontière en Méditerranée" was published in *L'Image verticale: Politiques de la vue aérienne*, edited by Marie Sandoz and Anne-Katrin Weber, special issue, *Transbordeur: Photographie, Histoire, Société*, no. 6 (2022): 88–97, https://journals.openedition.org/transbordeur/945. The interview appears with the kind permission of Éditions Macula / Association Transbordeur.

1. On the notion of "aesthetic regime," see also Heller and Pezzani 2020.

WORKS CITED

Blashke, Estelle. 2017. "The Boat Is Full." In *Lampedusa: Image Stories from the Edge of Europe*, edited by the Migrant Image Research Group. Spector Books.

Forensic Architecture. 2012. "The Left-to-Die Boat." https://forensic-architecture.org/investigation/the-left-to-die-boat.

GuardiadiFinanza, "September 17, 2011," posted September 19, 2011, YouTube, https://www.youtube.com/watch?v=E1eB--bK6w4.

Haraway, Donna. (1988) 2007. "Savoirs situés: Questions de la science dans le féminisme et privilège de la perspective partielle." In *Manifeste cyborg et autres essais: Science-fiction-féminisme,* edited by Laurence Allard, Delphine Gardey, and Nathalie Magnan. Exiles Editeurs.

Heller, Charles, and Lorenzo Pezzani. 2020. "Forensic Oceanography: Tracing Violence Within and Against the Mediterranean Frontier's Aesthetic Regime." In *Moving Images: Mediating Migration as Crisis,* edited by Krista Lynes, Tyler Morgenstern, and Ian Alan Paul. Transcript Verlag.

Heller, Charles, Lorenzo Pezzani, and Situ Studio. 2012. *Report on the "Left-to-Die Boat."* Forensic Oceanography. https://content.forensic-architecture.org/wp-content/uploads/2019/06/FO-report.pdf.

Walters, William. 2010. "Foucault and Frontiers: Notes on the Birth of the Humanitarian Border." In *Governmentality: Current Issues and Future Challenges,* edited by Ulrick Brockling, Susanne Krasmannet, and Thomas Lemke. Routledge.

CORALIZATION

Coral Materiality in Khal Torabully's Poetry

SHANAAZ MOHAMMED

Hester Blum's bold assertion that the "sea is not a metaphor" (2010, 670) engenders new oceanic readings that recognize the material significance of marine environments. It unearths a fundamental critical oversight that interprets the ocean's resolute fluidity from a cultural perspective to signify mobilities, interconnections, crossings, and interstitialities without paying attention to its complex multidimensional materiality. In rethinking the geophysicality of the ocean, scholars map a critical ocean studies that "turn[s] to ontologies of the sea and its multispecies engagements" (DeLoughrey 2017, 32). This shift, which repositions the sea from its conceptualization as a flat surface that stages human history and holds metaphorical value, engages the ocean's surface as much as it immerses into its depths to understand marine spaces as constitutive dynamic forces that simultaneously experience and are experienced. Guided by the critical invitations to pay more attention to the material components of maritime environments (Blum 2010; Steinberg 2013), this essay re-examines Khal Torabully's poetic and theoretical engagement with corals.

A critically acclaimed Mauritian poet, film director, and intellect, Khal Torabully plunges into the ocean's depths and engages corals in his poetic articulations that give voice to indentured diasporic histories and memories. Between 1849 and 1923, Mauritius received hundreds of thousands of indentured workers, also referred to as coolies, primarily from India but also China and Africa, at the immigration depot in Port Louis. These workers were hired as a cheap source of plantation labor in the post-abolition era and either stayed in Mauritius or left to work on sugarcane plantations in British, Dutch, and French colonies in the Caribbean. Torabully poeticizes their transoceanic journey in his *Cale d'étoiles: Coolitude* (1992) and *Chair corail: Fragments coolies* (1999), in which he develops a "Coolitude" or coralline poetics to circumnavigate cultural essentialisms and foreground not only the trauma of the indentured diasporic experience but also transcultural crossings that continue to inform indentured cultural identities. While critical explorations of Torabully's poetry tend to center on his depiction of corals as symbols of diversity and symbiotic relationships,[1] this essay shies away from these metaphorical interpretations and rereads Torabully's corals as agentic constitutive matter. It adopts a non-Western epistemological approach that disrupts knowledge systems of corals as inert, stable tourist destinations to be colonized and consumed, and passive mirrors of diasporic complexities. It prompts a material understanding of corals as actively and independently constituting their own agentic vibrancy that affects human and nonhuman life alike while also intertwining with the past, present, and future. Through critical analyses of Torabully's poetic texts, this essay studies their presentation of the materiality of corals, whose skeletons and skeletal structures compose visible submarine remnants of indentured history yet flourish into complex underwater multispecies ecosystems that create ontological symmetries and similarities between human and nonhuman coral life-forms. It uses material ecocriticism as its critical frame of reference and analyzes Torabully's coralline *architexture* and anthropomorphic representations of corals to suggest that corals are not mere metaphors but rather profound underwater networks of material relations, which, together with their oceanic environment, connect with the materiality of human lives in an indentured diasporic context. To express this material relational ontology reflected in Torabully's coral poetics, I use the term *coralization*, to emphasize corals' constitutive, prolific, and unpredictable form, which co-exists and co-acts with material histories and aesthetic expressions of indenture.

This essay's critical consideration of corals as matter unravels Western-based epistemologies that subordinate underwater perspectives. Historically, the underwater signified an enigmatic vacuity and exploratory frontier that aroused fear as "the earth's most mysterious and invisible domain" (Elias 2019, 1). Even in the early twentieth century, Western imaginations posited the deep sea and coral islands as "wilderness external to human beings and separate from technology, culture, and daily life" (15). These beliefs that construct coral reefs as a separate entity from human actors reaffirm social hierarchical divisions between human and nonhuman life-forms and dismiss their interdependencies. The inability to fully classify corals additionally added to their mystery. Perceived at times as mineral, plant, and animal, corals were considered as a "boundary object" that blurred the boundaries between the living and nonliving (Helmreich 2016, 49). By the 1920s, however, coral science resolved these classification ambiguities and dismissed corals' association with fear and bemusement. They were now reimagined as grandiose spectacles of wonder and beauty that nourished imaginations and engendered pleasurable modern experiences. As corals gained popularity through visual and popular media culture, the coral tourist industry proliferated. Considered a prime tourist destination, corals and coral reefs are socially constructed as an immobile, passive, and inert site to be conquered and consumed without any agency of its own or interconnectedness with humans in spite of the teeming life that comprises and surrounds them. Coral diving, for instance, promotes a neocolonial fantasy of corals and coral reefs as highly desired exotic precious stones that provide divers with a source of entertainment, Western-contrived paradise, and escape, disregarding it as a "traditional home for generations of peoples, marine animals, and plants" (Elias 2019, 231). It objectifies the deep sea and marine creatures, provokes voyeuristic gazes, and produces an ecological detachment that fails to recognize the impact of human agency on submarine life-forms.

But as Ann Elias contends, "corals are not a force of nature in which nature is conceived as something beyond the human but a powerful agent and participant in the creation of a 'political ecology' in which humans and nonhumans are today entangled not separate" (219). This recognition of mutual entanglement destabilizes Western binaries and galvanizes a broader non-Western epistemological understanding of the underwater world and its active correlation with humans and their particular histories. Indeed, in *Coral Lives: Literature, Labor, and the Making of America*, Michele Currie Navakas asserts that corals in nineteenth-century American thought were not only tied to labor systems and colonial exploitation and violence but also provided a framework for a racial, gender, and social class logic that justified these practices. Furthermore, Navakas highlights that corals' resistance to taxonomy allowed writers at the time to challenge the rigid boundaries of scientific racism (2023, 8). Her calls for a return to a time when corals "raised and re-shaped long-standing political ideas about identity, community, labor, race, belonging, and even time itself" (148) reveal corals' potential to disrupt and reshape dominant narratives that obscure their material significance.

Drawing from Navakas's insights on corals, the concept of coralization advances this understanding by considering Torabully's corals not as passive forms subject to human dominance but as vibrant, material entities with their own agency. Torabully's corals pulse with vitality, co-emerging and co-creating with human agents. This approach broadens critical inquiries into corals' complexities by reinterpreting them as vibrant physical and cultural forces that generate and constitute indentured historical narratives and theoretical conceptualizations.

SITUATING CORALIZATION

Coralization understands corals from a material ecocritical perspective. As a subtheory of New Materialism, material ecocriticism, developed by Serenella Iovino and Serpil Oppermann, proffers two main objectives. It first focuses on "the way matter's (or nature's) nonhuman agentic capacities are described and represented in narrative texts (literary, cultural, visual)" and second on "matter's 'narrative' power of creating configurations of meaning and substances, which enter with human lives into a field of co-emerging interactions. In this latter case, matter itself becomes a text where dynamics of 'diffuse' agency and non-linear causality are inscribed and produced" (Iovino and Oppermann 2012, 79–80). Moreover, material ecocriticism heeds the continuity of the human and nonhuman in "open and evolving dynamics" to attend to "the stories and the narrative potentialities that develop from matter's process of becoming" (83). Thus, *coralization* takes as its premise the idea of corals as matter replete with their own agency. More importantly, it considers corals not as matter that is fixed and immobile but, rather, productive, dynamic, ongoing, and generative. While corals, as they are articulated in Torabully's poetry, certainly hold symbolic weight, as he himself acknowledges on many occasions, metaphorizing them without recognizing their material significance as text and in text underplays and dismisses corals as agentic matter that constitutes untold postcolonial histories. Furthermore, it risks perpetuating Western epistemological perspectives that reduce corals to objects and flatten their multidimensional structural depth. In insisting on the materiality of corals, this essay does not attempt to overshadow metaphorical readings of Torabully's corals but complements them by producing new coralline knowledge structures that shed light on the significance of corals as matter. Coralization, therefore, offers a new conceptual framework of indentured ocean-based epistemology that puts indentured historical narratives in conversation with critical oceanic studies. As I discuss later in this essay, coralization is prompted by the relational and unpredictable characteristics that underpin both Édouard Glissant's *créolisation* theory and corals' material capacity to proliferate endlessly, constitute histories, and catalyze critical and aesthetic expressions. Coralization renders corals as an autonomous nonhuman entity, which intra-act with human forms to create a nonhierarchical coexisting material totality.

Torabully's conceptual and poetic engagement with corals accentuates the interplay between matter and meaning. He uses his Coolitude poetics to reconsider prevailing cultural identity paradigms (*Négritude, Antillanité,* and *Créolité*), rendering them more inclusive of indentured historical narratives, to counter imaginary returns to lost homelands (*Indianité*), and to promote a fluid relational indentured diasporic identity. Coolitude foregrounds the indentured diaspora's transoceanic journey and locates the ocean space as simultaneously traumatic and regenerative. This crossing not only constitutes a geophysical displacement from lost homelands, but it also signifies the merging of various cultural manifestations into a new, dynamic, and fluid diasporic identity that is celebrated in all its fractured complexity. Corals, as I contend, do not merely symbolize this human process but exist independently of it. Coralization shifts from an epistemology that objectifies corals, and envisions instead the confluence between human and nonhuman forms to emphasize their coexisting configurations and continual intra-actions.

Corals are part of complex multispecies ecosystems that engage with human and marine life-forms alike. They comprise a zoophyte form, which has a combination of animal, plant, and mineral characteristics. Corals themselves are constructed by and consist of thousands of tiny living plantlike animals called polyps, which can live individually or together in larger coral communities called colonies. These soft-bodied polyps, especially in stony corals, secrete and form a covering over limestone skeletons that protect the polyps and form the base of coral structures. They maintain a symbiotic relationship with zooxanthellae or algae that provides them not only with food but also their vivid colors, ranging from pink and blue to purple, orange, and green, suggesting that corals do not simply reflect diversity but actually constitute it materially. Furthermore, their symbiotic composition exemplifies, on a tangible level, animal, plant, and mineral elements coming together in a mutually beneficial relationship to create grandiose coral structures.

Corals additionally constitute openness and movement. They are open to the constant circulation of the ocean's flows and currents and their form is, therefore, always mutable. They are constantly subject to transformation, understood as both expansion and depletion, resulting from maritime currents and planetary changes. The submarine coral experience is thus always different depending on, for instance, "la profondeur des eaux, l'intensité de la lumière, [et] la densité de la vie marine" ("the depth of the water, the intensity of light, [and] the density of marine life";[2] *Creoleways* 2015). Corals are additionally ultramobile organisms located in an ultramobile space. They experience and display mobility on many levels. In addition to their individual movement as a polyp, pieces of coral can detach from the parent coral due to storm action, waves, or animal activity and reattach to a solid substratum such as other corals, rocks, concrete, plastic, rope, or line in an asexual reproduction process known as fragmentation or budding.[3] This coral fragmentation process, which involves connection and the possibility of thriving on and with other species in different spaces, creates material similarities and symmetries between corals and the diasporic experiences characterized not only by uprooting, dislocation, and relocation but also renewal, recreation, and relationality. Torabully considers corals' congealed connectivity as one of their distinctive material features:

> Le corail est dans la connectivité agglutinante, et non la connectivité errante du rhizome, seulement car le corail peut s'agglutiner à d'autres coraux, mais aussi à d'autres matières et supports tels des rochers, des coulées de lave, de[s] épaves de bateaux. . . . Donc, il quitte son espèce précise pour aller vers d'autres espèces. Cette caractéristique agglutinante lui a permis, dans ce lent travail de mise en contact, d'agglutination et d'étagement, de complexification patiente, par exemple, de constituer le plus grand organisme vivant sur terre, dans l'atoll du Grand Coral Bareer [sic], site naturel récemment classé par l'Unesco, et qui est la seule créature vivante visible depuis la lune. (*Creoleways* 2015)

> Coral exists in congealed connectivity, and not the rhizome's errant connectivity, because the coral can not only stick to other corals but also to

other materials and frames such as rocks, lava, wrecked boats.... Thus, it leaves its species to go towards other species. This feature of congealment allows it, in a slow process of contact, agglutination, terracing, and slow complexification, to constitute, for instance, the largest living organism on Earth, the Great Barrier Reef, a natural site recently inscribed by UNESCO, and the only living creature visible from the moon.

Torabully insists on the significance of the corals' congealed connectivity because, without it, corals may cease to exist. The corals' process of development, which involves sedimentation, agglutination, and eventual proliferation, materially illustrates Glissant's theory of créolisation, which is "un des modes de l'emmêlement—et non pas seulement une résultante linguistique—qui n'a d'exemplaire que *ses processus* et certainement pas les 'contenus' à partir desquels ils fonctionneraient" (Glissant 1990, 104; emphasis added; "one of the ways of forming a complex mix—and not merely a linguistic result—that is only exemplified by *its own processes* and certainly not by the 'contents' by which these operate" [Glissant 1997b, 89]). As corals multiply through a gradual formation process, the result, like Glissant's ongoing creolization process, is unpredictable, continuous, and infinite. Corals' complex materiality encompassing coralization forms part of and informs Torabully's poetry and poetics. Movement is moreover present from reef animals that are in constant motion as well as the surrounding mobile body of water, which itself is made up of moving molecules and forces that "push these molecules through space and time" (Steinberg 2013, 160).

Another symmetric entanglement that Torabully highlights between coralline matter and his discursive mediations on indentured diasporic cultural identity is the fact that corals are "ancré et mobile à la fois" ("both anchored and mobile"; *Creoleways* 2015). Existing on and constituted by hard limestone substances, corals evoke the concept of rootedness but without any predatory central root system. It must be noted, however, that the solidity implied by the anchored base is undermined by the high porosity and permeability of corals' limestone base, which allows for the free-flowing movement of matter on a micro level, thereby amplifying corals' fluidity and challenging perceptions of rigid boundaries and territoriality.

Coralline material entanglements with human life-forms persist even further through their skeletons and skeletal structures. Fossilized coral remnants, for instance, are mined and can take the form of dietary supplements such as coral calcium, which has been marketed as a treatment for numerous health conditions. Through their consumption, corals literally become part of human's material selves. Similarly, coral artwork, such as that created by Koral Kreations, rework dead corals artistically with the aim of "bringing the natural beauty back to coral skeletons after they moved on from their waterworld and finding them new homes looking over their descendants" (https://www.facebook.com/koralkreationsart/). Moreover, Jason deCaires Taylor embeds his submarine sculptures sunken off the coasts of Mexico, the Bahamas, and Grenada with coral fragments that would have otherwise died on the seafloor. Shards of corals additionally embellish jewelry and other accessories. Red coral, for instance, believed to possess vital powers and worn by Black women across African diaspora communities in the Atlantic world during the eighteenth and nineteenth centuries, became "unlikely sites of knowledge about the black diaspora" (Navakas 2023, 13), evoking "a shared African past" and contributing to "a diasporic identity and community that was forged by slavery yet not wholly defined by it" (126). In this sense, as Valérie Loichot points out, corals, with their exoskeleton secretions comprising calcium carbonate similar to bones, ally "beauty to the macabre" (Loichot 2020, 172). To this I would add that they also draw material connections between the liminalities of life and death, mortality and immortality, illness and health, immobility and transmigration, trauma and rehabilitation, decomposition and recomposition, destruction and reconstruction, knowledge and ignorance. Corals' seemingly infinite material capacity for creative endurance disrupts dualistic perspectives that hierarchize human and nonhuman life-forms, and instead creates meaning and gives rise to the notion of survival through transformation and preservation. Their irrefutable materiality, which empowers them to be their own forces with their particular trajectories and propensities, challenges conceptualizations that render corals as mere metaphors and passive objects onto which ideas are projected. Coralization offers a critical framework to reconsider corals as active matter and to be more perceptive about the inextricable comingling of human and nonhuman life-forms that inevitably supports and contributes to material-discursive agencies. It underscores a relational ontology, which, according to material ecocritics, aims to "enlarge the branches of our family tree, retracing broader genealogies, and therefore enriching our stories with more stories, namely with meanings emerging from the material forms that precede our existence or that are actual parts of our existence" (Iovino and Oppermann 2012, 87). Coralization promotes an epistemological understanding of Torabully's poetry and poetics as material articulations of indentured diasporic narratives that co-emerge with and from coral agencies.

CORALIZATION, COOLITUDE POETICS, AND KHAL TORABULLY'S POETRY

With all their visual appeal and agentic biological materiality, corals serve as catalysts for theoretical and aesthetic productions. Corals are a vital generative force that enables Torabully to create a material postcolonial theoretical palimpsest. In fact, they allow him to directly engage with his literary predecessors, namely Aimé Césaire and Édouard Glissant, to develop new critical and poetic articulations that recognize the indentured diaspora, often marginalized in dominant Francophone postcolonial discourses. Indeed, Torabully's poetics of Coolitude certainly recalls Césaire's Négritude, even though Torabully affirms that it is neither "Négritude à l'indienne" nor "a kind of Indian version of Négritude" (Carter and Torabully 2002, 144). Moreover, Torabully wrote his *Chair corail: Fragments coolies* after having met Césaire during his visit to the French Caribbean, and he makes several intertextual references to Césaire's *Cahier d'un retour au pays natal*, which I explore below. Furthermore, during an interview with historian Marina Carter, Torabully explains that he had been particularly inspired by the rhythm and poetic force of Césaire's writings and Glissant's rhizomatic perspectives. He states that in choosing corals to define Coolitude, he wanted to "underscore the symbolic importance of the 'rock' for Césaire, in the context of the struggle for the decolonization of minds. . . . Moreover, [the coral] brings to mind another metaphor, that of the rhizome, as used by Édouard Glissant" (Carter and Torabully 2002, 152). With their limestone base and multitudinous rhizome-like polyps, corals allow Torabully to locate his Coolitude poetics within and build upon prevailing discourses of Négritude and créolisation by drawing symmetries with corals' material specificities to conceptualize indentured diasporic identity not as fixed, immobile, and monolithic, but relational and always in progress.

In his *Chair corail: Fragments coolies*, corals' generative conceptual power is palpable. Book 3, "Chants du pays lumineux," makes an explicit material connection between Torabully's corals, Césaire's rock, and Glissant's rhizome, borrowed from Gilles Deleuze and Félix Guattari:

> D'abord corail car ma mémoire mûrit aux courants
> et folles traversées de phosphore
> Ensuite fragments pour déposer aux flancs sablonneux
> les gemmes de sa parole
> corail entre pierre et rhizome
> que l'oubli a couronné d'escaliers fossiles (Torabully 1999, 81)

> Firstly coral because my memory matures in the currents
> and crazy crossings of phosphorus
> Next fragments to deposit in the sandy sides
> gems of its speech
> coral between rock and rhizome
> that oblivion decorated with fossilized stairs

Torabully does not locate indentured memory in a lost homeland but rather in the fluid, mobile, and expansive depths of the sea. This reference to his memory ripening within the depths of the ocean recalls his first collection of poetry, *Cale d'étoiles,* which I analyze below, and in which corals with their phosphorus composition, similar to human bones, become an oceanic archive constitutive of indentured history. He renders the material and theoretical connection explicit through bold enlarged text that stands apart from the rest of the stanzas on the page. Corals' ambivalent materiality converges with Torabully's attempt to locate his Coolitude poetics within dominant Francophone postcolonial critical studies shaped by Césaire's and Glissant's writings, which often neglect to include the indentured diasporic presence. This conceptual and literary inattention is aptly connoted by the oxymoronic fossilized stairs, which, instead of being a gateway to new realms of conceptualization, are immobilized.

The poet continues and defines Coolitude, drawing intertextual inspiration from Césaire's poem *Cahier d'un retour au pays natal.* Torabully asserts:

> Dans ma mémoire sont des langues aussi
> Ma coolitude n'est pas une pierre non plus,
> elle est corail
> partage d'une terre de giboyeuse parole (82)

In my memory are languages too
My coolitude is not a rock either,
it is coral
fruit of an earth laden with speeches of birds and beasts

This passage directly evokes Césaire's *Cahier*, in which Césaire reveals:

Ma négritude n'est pas une pierre, sa surdité ruée
contre la clameur du jour (Césaire 2017, 124)

My negritude is not a stone, its deafness heaved
against the clamor of day (Césaire 2017, 125)

Torabully repeats the same Cesairean negative structure to describe his Coolitude poetics with the goal of establishing a textual interrelationship to generate related conceptual understandings before delineating his poetics and forcefully declaring that Coolitude *is* coral. If Coolitude memorializes indentured histories, this assertion suggests that indentured diasporic ontology emerges from the depths of the ocean. Coolitude is born out of the submerged indentured histories that are, as I explore later, calcified on the ocean's floor yet spring forth multicolored, free-floating coralline fragments that proliferate in a gradual process. Coolitude thus considers corals as submarine historical text that connects with and catalyzes material poetic text.

Coral matter continues to refine Torabully's Coolitude poetics and engenders intertextual connections:

Non plus l'homme hindou de Calcutta
Mais chair corail des Antilles
et des Amériques (Torabully 1999, 108)

No longer the Hindu man from Calcutta
But coral flesh from the Indies
and the Americas

By disassociating the indentured laborer from Césaire's "homme-hindou-de-Calcutta" ("hindu-man-from-Calcutta"; Césaire 2017, 92–93), Torabully undoes the sociocultural ostracism that estranged the Indo-Caribbean from

Antillean culture and brings the geocultural displacement from ancestral homelands into relief. He rewrites essentialist and static visions of an "Indian" indentured diasporic identity and instead locates the diaspora's sense of belonging as "chair corail des Antilles/et des Amériques" (coral flesh from the Indies/and the Americas). In contrast to the coral flesh from his *Cale d'étoiles: Coolitude*, which as I explain below constitutes human remnants, this anthropomorphic reference reveals similarities and symmetries between corals' material complex and ever-evolving multiplicity and the indentured diaspora whose cultural identity is open-ended, unpredictable, and perpetually multiple and mutable.

This evident interplay across material substances and discursive practices constitutes what Stacy Alaimo calls transcorporeality, which "traces the material interchanges across human bodies, animal bodies, and the wider material world" (Alaimo 2014, 187). By reinterpreting corals through the lens of coralization and emphasizing the biological and textual entanglements, corals no longer figure as objectified symbols but are rematerialized as active agents that engender meaning and co-create sociocultural and conceptual changes through human agency. With corals, Torabully expands territorial and botanical references by moving beyond the rhizome and returning to the ocean space, which once served as a conduit for the system of indenture, provoking trauma, loss, and nostalgia, to poetically reconceptualize cultural identity paradigms and render them inclusive of the indentured diasporic experience.

Moreover, Torabully's poetry actively engages coral materiality on textual and thematic levels. *Cale d'étoiles: Coolitude*, published in 1990, constitutes Torabully's founding poetic text on Coolitude. Receiving the Prix Jean Fanchette in 1993, it recounts the forgotten journey of the indentured diaspora. Torabully employs a coralline poetic architexture that complements his references to corals and coral reefs throughout the collection. *Cale d'étoiles: Coolitude* opens with a dedication that reads, "Pages d'un registre de bord absent," in which Torabully situates his Coolitude poetics as a necessary response to the historical, literary, and conceptual void that characterizes the indentured diasporic experience. The undulating margins of this poetic preamble mimic not only the ocean's ebbs and flows but also the jagged edges of coralline matter. Likewise, from the very first pages, large blocks of blank white spaces punctuate the text, indicative of the void in indentured historical narratives. His written text, as it floats in these empty white spaces, recalls coral buds that break off from the parent colony during the fragmentation process and cohere to underwater fragments to recreate new structures. Revealed in fragments, his text, with its regular and italicized forms, adding stylistic texture reminiscent of corals' variegated appearance, formally poeticizes and writes indentured historical memory into historical discourse and social consciousness. He delves into the collective memory of the past and commits to producing what Glissant calls "une vision prophétique du passé" ("a prophetic vision of the past"; Glissant 1997a, 227), in which both poet and literature work towards reconstructing the forgotten elements of the past to restore an imaginary plenitude. He gives poetic life to these buds of memories that latch on to the white spaces of the poetic text and become tangible material expressions of the history of indenture.

In this poetry collection, corals actively constitute indentured history, which is located within the ocean depths, submersed within crevices of corals. The opening poem, "A un coolie," reveals that the indentured subject suffers from "une mémoire perdue d'avance" (Torabully 1992, 15; "a memory lost in advance"; Torabully 2021, 13). Indentured memory is articulated as a painful silence, stuck in a state of suspension, and lost at sea in the crater of coral reefs. The poet indicates:

> ELLE est la voix de ton histoire de ton néant
> mémoirée murmurée pour le mélange des mers
> voix mangée par l'immense chaudière des brisants
> dont la dernière fois est un commencement de poèmes. (Torabully 1992, 15)

> SHE is the voice of your story, your life's void
> memoired murmured for mixing of seas
> voice consumed by the huge crater of reefs
> whose last sigh is a beginning of poems. (Torabully 2021, 15)

Torabully relays poetically this garbled and voided history dissipated within the coral crevices through the alliteration "mémoirée murmurée pour le mélange des mers" creating an audible muffle. Corals here are anthropomorphized as a devouring force, making them an underwater archive that actively subsumes indentured history. The image of the crater reinforces the void, which the poet fills through his poetic text:

C'est de ces horizons de sang de mots brouillés
que ta chaude parole fait chavirer la clarté
dans ma mémoire océanée (Torabully 1992, 15)

From these horizons of blood of garbled words
your heated word capsizes clearness
in my memory's ocean depths. (Torabully 2021, 14)

It is significant to note here, however, that Torabully's anthropomorphic representations do not minimize corals' agency. According to material ecocritics, anthropomorphism should not be regarded as "the sign of an anthropocentric and hierarchical vision but [as] a narrative expedient intended to stress the agentic power of matter and the horizontality of its elements" (Iovino and Oppermann 2012, 82).

In recollecting indentured memories from the ocean's depths, Torabully is also attentive to this space as a watery graveyard:

Coulé, le coolie, l'homme écorché,
écourté, écourté, écoutez!
Un homme tombé à la chair! (Torabully 1992, 18)

The sunken coolie, the skinned man,
cut short, cut short, listen!
A fallen man become flesh! (Torabully 2021, 16)

The rhyming scheme produced by the assonance in the first two verses replicates the slow sinking movement of the drowning coolie, which is abruptly halted by the resolute "écoutez!" The destiny of the sunken coolie, reinforced by the curt exclamatory verse that follows, is unambiguous. The coolie's body not only turns into carrion for underwater scavenging creatures, such as fish, crabs, and sea lice, but also eventually assimilates into the maritime environment to become "chairs de corail" (Torabully 1992, 51; "bodies of coral flesh"; Torabully 2021, 45). The sunken bones slowly transforming into marine silt become part of the seabed, amalgamating with coral's stony base to create layers of human and nonhuman history. In his poem "Récit du voyage," the poet references corpses that were piled up on the decks before being strewn into the ocean where they would try to flee "les pores," a possible reference to giant slit-pore sea rod coral:

Avant l'amorce d'une flamme
pour les morts avant l'aurore
les peaux s'amoncelaient sur les ponts
avant leur sort pour fuir les ports
avant le nord pour fuir les pores (Torabully 1992, 51)

Before the fire was lit
for the dead before dawn
dark-skinned corpses were poured onto decks
before their chance to flee the ports
before they headed north to flee the pores. (Torabully 2021, 44)

It is this coral flesh that constitutes history and memory for the poet:

et je disais chair plus que mémoire
syllabe plus qu'écriture
et mon absence même était migration
en d'autres chairs de corail (Torabully 1992, 51)

and I said flesh was more than memory
syllable more than writing
and my absence itself a migration
through other bodies of coral flesh. (Torabully 2021, 45)

By suggesting in this stanza that flesh is more significant than memory, the poet accentuates the tangibility of flesh constituted as coralline bodies that become visible and material remnants of the indentured laborers' bodies and, by extension, the indentured diasporic past. The corporeal intermingling between human and coral flesh underlines corals' agentic capacity to constitute untold indentured histories of death, loss, trauma, and suffering, rendering them a memorial reef or living watery gravesite. It additionally contrasts and undoes the Western-based tourist narratives that project corals and coral reefs as sites of marvel and desire devoid of historical agency.

This idea of coral reefs as an underwater gravesite for indentured history is additionally reinforced in "Aux naufragés du Ker Anna," which renders homage to the castaways of the *Ker Anna*, a French ship that sunk in 1894 off the coast of the island of Réunion. *Ker Anna* was used to transport sugar between Mayotte, Calcutta, Pondicherry, and Réunion. Stuck out at sea during a storm, the ship collided with a coral reef and was run aground. In contrast to the romanticized perception of them, corals in this incident present themselves as dangerous and a veritable existential threat to human lives on the ship. Of the fourteen persons on board, only six survived the shipwreck (Bohn 2018). In this poem, Torabully laments the loss and trauma suffered by the *Ker Anna* seamen:

> La mer flétrit pour les noyés.
> Et les sirènes font ablution
> au passage du camphre.
> O gloire au phosphore,
> sa légende a enseveli
> des étoiles en ma terre. (Torabully 1992, 72)

> The sea wilts for the drowned.
> And mermaids perform their ablutions
> when camphor wafts by.
> O praise be to phosphorus
> whose legend interred
> the stars in my native land. (Torabully 2021, 73)

In this passage, the sea loses its typical aggrandizement and mourns the deaths of the castaways through the poet's pathetic fallacy. Moreover, his invocation lauding phosphorus is significant. By referencing phosphorus, a mineral found in human bones and coral skeletal structures alike, Torabully weaves together human material history with the bony structural materiality of corals, proposing an alternative history-making narrative that renders corals constitutive of human history. Corals thus bridge the indentured past with the present and future. Torabully venerates the phosphorous because it becomes submarine debris of indentured memories that he ferries poetically to recount indentured histories that have been lost to the depths of the ocean. Yet phosphorus also brings the poet clarity. In one of his final poems, he says:

> Tu es partie d'un seul coup
> et les phosphores plus purs que l'azur
> jetèrent les copeaux aux lames de mes peaux
> qui te transperça d'un terrible écho? (Torabully 1992, 104)

You left all at once
and the phosphorus purer than azure
showered my skin with razor-sharp shavings: who ran you through
    with a ghastly echo? (Torabully 2021, 110)

Torabully seems to find poetic lucidity, reinforced by the internal rhyme ("purs" and "azur"), from the same mineral matter that constituted death, darkness, and trauma. The sharpness of the memories of suffering that launches against his skin is profound and revelatory, because they allow him to engage sunken untold histories and bring them to light. The corporeal connection between the razor-sharp shards and the poet's skin becomes a generative force that reverberates in and as his poetic body of text. In the same poem, Torabully reveals that "dans chaque grand corail les ombres s'égarent" (Torabully 1992, 104; "in each great coral reef, shadows lose their way"; Torabully 2021, 101). Shadows, evocative of blocked-off light, dissipate, allowing Torabully to carve out a space of clarity revealed through the coral spectacle. Although he fully recognizes the past traumas, sufferings, and setbacks inflicted by the system of indentureship on indentured laborers, the poet searches for a new beginning:

> Puisque le ciel gris tombera avec fracas
> je reviens à l'horizon avec mon corps.
> Avec le nombril pour quille d'aurore
> je saurai guider ma chair par cœur.
> Tais-toi nuage, tais-toi orage,
> Première voix pleurera dans la mer.
> Pour des êtres évanouis tais-toi,
> La fuite des êtres annonce LA NAISSANCE. (Torabully 1992, 104)

> Since the grey sky will come crashing down
> I return with my body, horizon-bound.
> With my navel as keel of dawn
> I'll know by heart how to steer my flesh.
> Hush up cloud, hush up storm,
> The first voice will weep in the sea.
> For beings who've disappeared, hush up:
> the flight of beings augurs BIRTH. (Torabully 2021, 101)

Torabully locates his return not to a terra firma but rather to the boundless celestial sphere, indicated by "l'horizon" and "l'aurore." His navel, a symbol not only of the center of life and rebirth but also connection to others and to the cosmos, floats in the mobile sea. His poetic course is figured as a coralline, submarine, transoceanic voyage, and the poet's hushed voice at the beginning of the poem now springs forth with a new confidence. The voice now calls for calmness, not to ignore the demise of the past but to underscore that it transforms materially through a sort of reincarnated poetic text.

CONCLUSION

Coralization articulates material readings of corals in Torabully's poetry, grossly overlooked in critical literature on Coolitude. This presents an opportunity to reconstruct coralline bodies of knowledge that tend to reduce corals to metaphorical spaces of diversity and connection. The concept of coralization disrupts the subject-object narratives that promote a hierarchical split between the human and nonhuman, and instead sheds light on their coexistence, interdependencies, and intra-actions. Viewed from this material ecocritical perspective, corals as they are engaged in Torabully's poetry and poetics are independent agentic matter that are constitutive and generative. Corals, with their material biological particularities, coemerge with and create theoretical configurations that connect indentured diasporic historico-cultural Coolitude projects with prevailing discourses of Négritude and créolisation. Moreover, corals' agentic powers and material vitality in Torabully's poetry transubstantiate the submarine: They are peculiarly alive through anthropomorphic representations that act as receptacles of indentured memories, and which the poet accesses to create his texts. The limestone structure of corals that co-constitutes human bones becomes an oceanic (though opaque, impenetrable) archive of indentured memories. These visible remnants of living history continue to be independent from, yet intertwined with, indentured narratives. By actively engaging with corals' materiality in his exploration of indentureship, Torabully's poetry and poetics emphasize the dynamic correlation between coralline matter and Coolitude ideologies that engender new understandings of indentured history and its place in Francophone postcolonial and oceanic studies.

NOTES

This essay was awarded the 2022 Northeast Modern Language Association (NeMLA) Postcolonial Essay Award.

1. In her "Transoceanic Echoes: Coolitude and the Work of the Mauritian Poet Khal Torabully," Véronique Bragard, for instance, interprets Torabully's image of the coral as an evocation of "fluidity and openness to relation" that echoes the "ramification, dynamism[,] and multiplicity" of the rhizome (2005, 229). Rainer Guldin contends similarly that "Torabully uses the coral as a metaphor for the hybrid world" (2020, 207) of indentured laborers, specifying that "the coral is a metaphor of the diversity of creolization" (208). Valérie Loichot also sees the "expanding, horizontal, multirelational coral provid[ing] a symbiotic metaphor for the 'coolie' Indian and/in the creolized world of Mauritius, instead of a model of cultural purity and hierarchies" (2020, 173). Ottmar Ette concentrates, however, on corals as symbiotic living creatures and indicates that Torabully "transforms the coral into a theorem of life, its properties as a living being also *embody* a knowledge of survival and living-together, allowing these communities of living creatures to grow to works of art of enormous proportions in their *sym-biotic* way of existence" (2017, 116).
2. Unattributed translations are mine.
3. In an effort to encourage coral growth, British artist Jason deCaires Taylor created submarine sculptures made from pH-neutral marine-grade concrete that are sunken off the coasts of Mexico, the Bahamas, and Grenada. These installations are intended to act as a stable base on which artificial reefs can form. They also promote algae growth, which helps to protect corals from bleaching. They are strategically placed to allow for the seeding of coral from one reef to another. For more information, see https://underwatersculpture.com.

WORKS CITED

Alaimo, Stacy. 2014. "Oceanic Origins, Plastic Activism, and New Materialism at Sea." In *Material Ecocriticism*, edited by Serenella Iovino and Serpil Oppermann. Indiana University Press.

Blum, Hester. 2010. "The Prospect of Oceanic Studies." *PMLA* 125 (3): 670–77.

Bohn, Éléonore. 2018. "1894: Naufrage du Keranna à La Réunion." *Le Télégramme*, February 5. https://www.letelegramme.fr/culture-loisirs/histoire/1894-naufrage-du-keranna-a-la-reunion-78499.php.

Bragard, Véronique. 2005. "Transoceanic Echoes: Coolitude and the Work of the Mauritian Poet Khal Torabully." *International Journal of Francophone Studies* 8 (2): 219–33.

Carter, Marina, and Khal Torabully. 2002. *Coolitude: An Anthology of the Indian Labour Diaspora*. Anthem Press.

Césaire, Aimé. 2017. *Journal of a Homecoming / Cahier d'un retour au pays natal*. Translated by N. Gregson Davis. Duke University Press.

Creoleways. 2015. "Khal Torabully: 'La Coolitude n'est ni un pavé ni une pierre, mais un corail.'" Accessed 2 June 2, 2020. https://creoleways.com/2015/04/28/khal-torabully-la-coolitude-nest-ni-un-pave-ni-une-pierre-mais-un-corail.

DeLoughrey, Elizabeth. 2017. "Submarine Futures of the Anthropocene." *Comparative Literature* 69 (1): 32–44.

Elias, Ann. 2019. *Coral Empire: Underwater Oceans, Colonial Tropics, Visual Modernity*. Duke University Press.

Glissant, Édouard. 1990. *Poétique de la relation*. Gallimard.

Glissant, Édouard. 1997a. *Le Discours antillais*. Gallimard,

Glissant, Édouard. 1997b. *Poetics of Relation*. Translated by Betsy Wing. University of Michigan Press.

Guldin, Rainer. 2020. *Metaphors of Multilingualism: Changing Attitudes Towards Language Diversity in Literature, Linguistics and Philosophy*. Taylor and Francis Group.

Helmreich, Stefan. 2016. *Sounding the Limits of Life: Essays in the Anthropology of Biology and Beyond*. Princeton University Press.

Iovino, Serenella, and Serpil Oppermann. 2012. "Material Ecocriticism: Materiality, Agency, and Models of Narrativity." *Ecozona* 3 (1): 75–91.

Loichot, Valérie. 2020. *Water Graves: The Art of the Unritual in the Greater Caribbean*. University of Virginia Press.

Navakas, Michele Currie. 2023. *Coral Lives: Literature, Labor, and the Making of America*. Princeton University Press.

Ottmar, Ette. 2017. "Khal Torabully: 'Coolies' and Corals, or Living in Transarchipelagic Worlds." Translated by Mark Minnes. *Journal of the African Literature Association* 11 (1): 112–19.

Steinberg, Philip E. 2013. "Of Other Seas: Metaphors and Materialities in Maritime Regions." *Atlantic Studies* 10 (2): 156–69.

Torabully, Khal. 1992. *Cale d'étoiles: Coolitude*. Azalées Éditions.

Torabully, Khal. 1999. *Chair corail: Fragments coolies* [Coral flesh, coolie fragments]. Ibis Rouge Éditions.

Torabully, Khal. 2021. *Cargo Hold of Stars: Coolitude*. Translated by Nancy Naomi Carlson. Seagull Books.

IS THE SEA HISTORY?

The Marine Life of Recent Haitian Fiction

MARTIN MUNRO

> Where are your monuments, your battles, martyrs?
> Where is your tribal memory? Sirs,
> in that grey vault. The sea. The sea
> has locked them up. The sea is history
> —DEREK WALCOTT

> We islanders aren't familiar with that vertigo of the earth. We bind vertigo to its greatest tension, we must contract our space in order to live there. Our field is of the sea that limits and opens. The island presumes other islands. Antilles.
> —ÉDOUARD GLISSANT

> Rule, Britannia, rule the waves:
> Britons never will be slaves.
> —JAMES THOMSON

The rather odious sentiment expressed in James Thomson's poem—and, stunningly, still sung every year at the Last Night of the Proms in London—that imperial Britain must control the seas and that by doing so its white subjects will never be enslaved, even as they enslave millions of others, says much about the importance of maritime domination to the nation's wealth and its very idea of itself: Rule the sea and you can rule the land, and the people.

Derek Walcott's poem contrasts sea- and land-based European notions of history with the marine, or submarine, history of the Caribbean. For the European, in Walcott's reading, history is something to be dragged from the seas, memorialized and concretized on the land in statues and books. For the Caribbean, by contrast, the land is marked by historical absence—there are few memorials or monuments that attest to the trials and triumphs of the past. Instead, Walcott insists, it is in the sea that historical memory is located, in the depths and shadows that are in a sense timeless. This history is "all subtle and submarine," characterized by death—of the men "with eyes heavy as anchors who sank without tombs"—but which also contains in it the seed of the new future that the poem writes of, the sense "of History, really beginning" in the "salt chuckle of rocks, with their sea pools" (1986, 365–66). Walcott's idea of the sea as not just a metaphor of history, but its only possible embodiment is echoed in Kamau Brathwaite's equally famous statement, that across the Caribbean, "the unity is submarine" (1975, 1), an idea taken up by Édouard Glissant, who cites both Walcott and Brathwaite in the epigraphs to his *Poétique de la relation* (1990). Glissant's view of Caribbean history is clearly influenced by this image of submarine convergence, of underwater roots "floating free, not fixed in one position in some primordial spot, but extending in all directions in our world through its network of branches" (1989, 67). Therefore, the sea in Caribbean literature and thought is often the means by which connections are made, physically, culturally, and historically. Indeed, over the last thirty years or so, broader Caribbean theoretical discourse has been characterized by notions of marine or submarine "ungroundedness, relationality and mobility," rather than the "fixity, stability and definition" that are more commonly associated with land-centered ideas of identity and culture (McCusker 2011, 42). The growth of Atlantic studies has only further intensified the theoretical interest in the sea as a metaphor and vehicle for forms of identitary, historical, and cultural fluidity and movement.

Reading Caribbean literature is also a matter of, to use Mary Gallagher's term, "sounding," a word that denotes primarily the measuring of the depth of a body of water, as if the critic has to gauge the writing through using echoes to know its deepest recesses. For Gallagher, sounding is a particular way of reading and knowing that responds to the "fluid, volatile space/time" of the Caribbean (2022, 3). Fluidity is thus a vital element in the writing: Nothing is solid or at the surface, all is liquid and abyssal. In addition, the term is used "to register respect for the integrity or resistance of the writing" (3). Importantly, Gallagher evokes Walter Ong's idea that "hearing can register interiority without violating it. I can rap a box to find whether it is empty or full or a wall to find whether it is hollow or solid inside'" (3). These are helpful metaphors for the work of Caribbean literary criticism: rapping the work, striking it to hear its echoes, what it holds inside, its emptiness and plenitudes. Indeed, Gallagher's further citation from Ong, "the field of sound is not spread out before me but is all around me," is all the more helpful in that it can be applied directly to much of Caribbean writing: One sounds the writing as a means of understanding history, and the past that for many Caribbean authors is all around them, unfinished, ongoing, unending, liquid. If, as Ong says, sound also has that quality of being past, present, and future, then sound must be one of the primary means of understanding, knowing, sensing, sounding this liquid past. Sounding, as such, is a question of depths, layers, resonances, and echoes, and should, Gallagher says, "counteract the temptation to remain safely at the surface" (4).

This fluid, marine-like quality in Caribbean writing has also to do with the complicated relationship with the land, especially for those whose ancestors were transported to the islands to be either enslaved or indentured. One cannot understand the importance of the sea to Caribbean writing without registering that of the land. As Helen Tiffin writes, the legacies of history are still relevant for people's notions of land and belonging: "Unlike indigenous peoples, such relative 'newcomers' bring with them the values, cultural memories, knowledge, and traditions of their former environments, a prior 'natural' history of being-in-the-world that, consciously or unconsciously, implicitly or explicitly, influences (through expectation, comparison, and contrast) their perceptions of the new" (2005, 199). It follows that the representation of the land and the landscape is not straightforward, "imbricated as it is in crucial ways with histories of transplantation, slavery, and colonialism and with imported European traditions of land and landscape perception and representation" (200).

For Édouard Glissant, such a complicated relationship with the land leads to a conception of the islands as an "antispace" (1989, 160). The land is unloved, abandoned, and the formerly enslaved prefer to live marginalized in the urban areas than take possession of the land, for the land has historically been associated with the white other and with alienating, forced work. This history has created a distorted relationship with the land, and a poetics of excess, the scream, the cry, where all "is exhausted immediately" (160). The land becomes a site upon which the various kinds of historically inherited madness and neuroses—the impossibility of belonging, the compensatory urge for excess and exhaustion—are projected. Crucially, this drive for excess and exhaustion, Glissant says, denaturalizes the connection with the land in the sense that it interrupts and wears out the "rhythms of the land" (1989, 160).

This rather obscure idea of an arrhythmic, out-of-step relationship with Martinican space perhaps becomes clearer in relation to Glissant's idea of a distorted Antillean experience of time. The loss of collective memory and the careful erasure of the past have made of time and history little more than a series of natural disasters, so that Martinicans have no real sense of a linear progression through time, which instead "keeps turning around in us" (1989, 161). The rhythms of time and history, like those of the land, have therefore been ruptured and denaturalized by the effects of slavery, colonialism, and departmentalization. Time turns in cycles, not in any kind of salutary, natural way, but in a way that perpetuates the neuroses and alienation. This idea is developed when Glissant considers the virtually unchanging pattern of the seasons in the Tropics, what he calls the "rhythmic plainsong" that denies to the Martinican the pattern of seasonal changes that influence and shape to some degree Western consciousness. Glissant says that the absence of such a shifting pattern of seasons allows Martinicans to live according to "another rhythm . . . another notion of time" (1989, 161).

Perhaps the most succinct Caribbean way of expressing such a complicated attachment to the land is in the Haitian proverb "Ayiti se tè glise" (Haiti is a slippery land). For the white populations of the islands, however, the relationship with the land was markedly less slippery, and mirrored to some degree their relation to non-white populations: The land, like the people (and indeed the sea), could be regulated, surveyed, and controlled. Not only could people be classified, judged, and ranked—in primarily visual terms—but the land itself could be represented visually in maps, charts, and other ocular means, including painting. The colonization of the Caribbean land through harnessing the full optical power of the planters demonstrates the prevalence and importance of what Mary Louise Pratt calls the "imperial gaze," which in her study of early travel writing is the means by which "the seeing-man" comes to possess the world (1992, 9). By harnessing the power of the visual, white European travelers developed their ability to catalog and classify the world, which is considered to be primarily visual in nature, and could thereby be controlled and exploited.

Theorists of the Anthropocene are beginning to address the contemporary ramifications of such a colonial relationship to the Caribbean land. Elizabeth DeLoughrey, for instance, writes of the Caribbean islands as "originary spaces of the Anthropocene," given the long history there of "transatlantic empire and slavery, the radical dislocation of humans from their ancestral soil, and a violent irruption of modernity that predates the industrialization of nineteenth-century Europe" (2019, 35). Arguing that capitalism was "constituted by transatlantic slavery and the plantation system," DeLoughrey points out that the term "Plantationocene" has recently been used "to further specify the ways in which an economic and political system of empire is exacted on the earth" (2019, 35). DeLoughrey's concerns are echoed in the work of Malcom Ferdinand, who writes of the "modern tempest" and the need to address the "double fracture [that] separates the colonial history of the world from its environmental history" (2022, 3). In Ferdinand's terms, as the "eye of modernity's hurricane, the Caribbean is that center where the sunny lull was wrongly confused for paradise, the fixed point of a global acceleration sucking up African villages, Amerindian societies, and European sails" (2022, 12). For Valérie Loichot, the sea is a site of "unritual," which in the context of Caribbean history is "a state more absolute than desecration or defilement" in the memorialization of the unremembered dead of the Middle Passage. Unritual, she writes, "is the obstruction of the sacred in the first place" (2020, 7). Drawing on Glissant, she argues that "ecological solidarity, the relational sacred, and artistic compositeness appear as the modes of healing and dealing with the unritual" (2020, 24). One vital way of understanding these processes and crises and the ongoing effects they have had on the imagination of Caribbean people, especially in regard to the land, the sea, and the environment, DeLoughrey insists (and Ferdinand and

Loichot implicitly agree), is through a "critical engagement with narrative" and, specifically, as she emphasizes in her recent work, the uses of allegory, which was "integral to representing the colonial violence of transatlantic empire and the plantation" (35).

Taking up DeLoughrey's insistence on the importance of narrative, the rest of this chapter analyzes several recent Haitian works of fiction in which the sea is a prominent feature and seeks to understand why there is a marked shift toward the littoral and the marine in these works. For sure, since at least the nineteenth century and through the indigenist period of the mid-twentieth century, the land was evoked as a marker of national (and often racial) authenticity—think of Manuel in Jacques Roumain's *Gouverneurs de la rosée* (1944) or Hilarion Hilarius in Jacques-Stephen Alexis's *Compère Général Soleil* (1955) as two obvious examples of characters drawn, and fatally attached, to the land. This chapter discusses more recent examples of novels situated by the sea and argues that the movement away from indigenist-inspired romantic notions of the land has accelerated following the earthquake of 2010, an event that literally and metaphorically shattered the notion of the land as a marker of solidity and security.

In a paper entitled "L'Ancrage à la terre chez quelques auteurs de la littérature haïtienne," Gary Victor (2013) writes on the theme of the land in Haitian writing. For an author, he writes, the land is more than a material entity; it is a site of memory, closely related to the imaginary, a place of feelings and myths. Most fundamentally, he writes, the land is related to identity, it is the "place of the desire to be. Site of the emergence of its true self."[1] The land can also be a site of conflict, "a mixture of fascination and repulsion, a forced clinch between love and hate, tradition and modernity, between proper attachment and flight." Similarly, the attachment to the land can become a form of imprisonment for the individual and the literary imagination, "being captured by myths with as a corollary the impossibility to see and question reality."

The shifting, often contradictory meanings ascribed by Victor to the land appear at various points in Haitian literary history. The nineteenth-century imperative to defend the romanticized land gave way in the mid-twentieth century to more skeptical visions of the land and the nationalist meanings associated with it. This shift was signaled in the movement from the mystical, allusive, grounded poetry of indigenists like Léon Laleau and Carl Brouard to novels of exile and the concomitant uncertainty over ideas of identity and its relation to the land. A paradoxical period of forced exile and literary liberation, the post-1946 movement of many of Haiti's intellectuals into exile was the point at which the Haitian novel began to turn away from the indigenist imperative to write of nation, race, and the essential connection to the land. As J. Michael Dash says, the period from 1946 to the fall of the Duvaliers in 1986 instigated a "rethinking of the discourse of authenticity and a reevaluation of the fixed ideas of otherness, elsewhere, and exile" (1994, 455).

Exile and dictatorship ruptured the apparently natural connection between authors and the land. The apogee of Marxist-indigenist writing and of the literary veneration of the land as a maternal guarantor of identity comes at the end of Alexis's *Compère Général Soleil*, when the hero Hilarion returns from the Dominican Republic and lies dying on the Haitian side of the river that separates the two nations. Falling to the "cool ground of the native land" (Alexis 1955, 283) and seeing "Old Brother Sun" rise over Haiti (288), Hilarion reconnects with the natural elements and in particular the land, which are closely connected with Alexis's vision of Haitian authenticity. Echoing the death of Manuel in Roumain's *Gouverneurs de la rosée*, Hilarion dies slowly under a century-old mahogany tree (289). The final scene's exhilarating mix of natural imagery, the political symbolism of the rising red sun, and the dying exile's regret that he will never see again the "towns, villages, and fields of Haiti, the domain of Ayiti Tomas" (350), are one of the most memorable statements of the apparently unbreakable bond between Haitian identity and the land. The passage also marked more or less the death of the messianic trope in Marxist-indigenist writing, and with it the end of the close connection between nature, nation, and identity.

Noirisme was a form of political and cultural ideology that grew out of indigenism, which in turn was a reaction to the American occupation of 1915–34.[2] During the occupation, Haitian intellectual culture was re-energized in diverse and often contradictory ways, constructing a discourse of resistance that would finally imprison the nation in a rigid idea of cultural and racial authenticity that served also as the ideological justification for the worst excesses of the Duvalier regime. Africanity and racial authenticity became the tenets of the political ideology of the rising black middle class, who saw in this ideology "the rationale for a black cultural dictatorship" (Dash 1981, 101). Noirisme was fundamentally anti-liberal and promoted an authoritarian and exclusive state, which would be realized in the presidency of François Duvalier (1957–71). As Jean Price-Mars, the great idol of the Griots had cautioned, the social divisions created by the movement undermined indigenism's aim of national unity. And, as he prophetically warned, "a politically radical black consciousness could ultimately lead to despotism" (Smith 2009, 27). Indeed, Duvalierism resulted in the "deterioration of social cohesion and the complete dehumanization of a people" (Chancy 1997, 143). In addition, it "brought the manipulation and violation of cultural norms to new levels" (Caple James 2010, 57) and led to the "near annihilation of a rich culture," the creolizing way of life that had evolved during and after slavery, and which was predicated less on an understanding of cultures as absolutely different from each other than on a proto-Glissantian model of relation, contact, and unpredictable evolution (Chancy 1997, 143).

The Duvalier dictatorships and the subsequent exile of many prominent authors led inevitably to reconsiderations of the relationship between the land and identity. The land seems to bear the effects of the broader repressive, life-sapping regime. In Émile Ollivier's 1991 novel *Passages*, the land is a restrictive, unhomely space, marked by decay and decline, "deserted" by water (17). Ollivier's novel echoes the opening scenes from *Gouverneurs de la rosée*, in which are presented the life-sapping effects of drought on the land and the people: "We will all die . . . and she thrusts her hand into the dust . . . the dust runs between her fingers. The same dust that the dry breath of the wind blows over the devastated field" (13). However, in contrast to predecessors like Roumain and Alexis, Ollivier presents no comforting myth of the land, no solution to the ecological devastation of Haiti other than to leave the land. In Ollivier's novel, as in other works of exile, the alienated and impoverished people are inevitably drawn to the sea, which is not presented positively as a sign of freedom or escape, but as the site of historical return, as one of Ollivier's characters suggests: "Christopher Columbus had come by sea; all the ills of this people had always come from the sea: the slave ships, the freebooters, General Leclerc's armada, the American occupation, hurricanes, smallpox, syphilis, AIDS . . . Did the ghost of the Genoese still, after five centuries haunt the unconsciousness of this people? The conquest is at the root of all their suffering" (220). The sea, as Walcott suggests, is indeed history, though in this case it is a source of historical suffering, which returns over time in waves, and which somewhat paradoxically draws the people back to it, in desperation to escape that seaborne history. A similar idea is suggested in Yanick Lahens's 2000 novel *Dans la maison du père*, in which the narrator says that Haitians have "never much liked the sea, thinking that it has brought all of our misfortunes" (73). She is, however, drawn to it, and liked to walk along the shore feeling it lapping on her feet, saying that she liked the sea as she liked dance: "I liked its mysteries of foam, salt, and water. My eyes wide open, I dreamt of its fantastical and violent disorder so far away. Of its violent poetry . . . The idea of life and death in this watery womb of the world became a salutary dream that enchanted me" (73).

This idea of the sea as a source at once of dread and enchantment reappears in certain prominent works written since the 2010 earthquake. As the critic Mark Anderson writes, nothing shakes one's worldview as much as a natural disaster, and disaster is essentially a "rupture or inversion of the normal order of things" (2011, 1). An earthquake in particular destabilizes the notion of the solidity of the land, and with it is apparently ruptured the "natural" connection between the land and identity, for such an event "sweep[s] the ground from beneath our feet and reduc[es] to rubble our literal and conceptual edifices" (1). One senses in some post-earthquake works a similar feeling, of the idea of the land as a solid guarantor of identity being further weakened, and a consequent relocation to the coast, the littoral, and the sea.

For example, in Makenzy Orcel's *Les Immortelles* (2010), the young prostitute says that all she ever wanted was to be on a bus on an "endless highway . . . with the sea rolling endlessly before my eyes" (118). Marvin Victor's *Corps mêlés* (2011) begins with the narrator's birth scene, which takes place in the sea: Her grandfather is "taken by an excess of trance or drunkenness" and insists that the mother be taken to the shore, for "only the sea could deliver that which it had started" (16). The land is implicitly sterile and unable to give new life, while the people's origins are related to the sea, particularly in the case of the godmother. She traces their origins to the seas off the African coastline, which explains for her "our hatred of the sea, that secular hatred that leads us all to turn our backs on its turbulent immensity, another way perhaps of letting ourselves be all the more consumed by it" (18). At the end of Kettly Mars and Leslie Péan's *Le Prince noir de Lillian Russell*, the protagonist Henri takes to the sea again, leaving behind the various attempts to tie him down and categorize him on the land. It seems significant too that in the context of post-earthquake writing from Haiti, Henri should end the novel at sea, unable to return to Haiti. The sea offers to him a source of solidity and reassurance that he does not find on the land. He finds in the sea's depths "the answers to all the questions that I ask myself" (329). The sea is a maternal entity, related to time. "In its breast," he says, "sleep my past lives and those to come" (329).

Gary Victor's *Le Sang et la mer* (2011) opens with the protagonist's dream of an apocalyptic surge of water, whereby the sea invades the coastal village where she and her brother were born. She then boards a large truck that reminds her of the container she and her brother took to the city, and which then takes the form of a shark that is shocked by the misery it sees in the slums of Port-au-Prince. In the dream, the protagonist persuades the sea not to destroy the slum, and the movement of the sea echoes the rhythm of the blood that flows from her internal wound (11). As such, the dream asserts in cryptic form the themes of the novel: the great and tragic migration of country people to the city, and the resultant susceptibility of the urban poor to the effects of nature, which is itself, as in for example Victor's previous novel *À l'angle des rues parallèles* (2003 [2000]), a potentially deathly, vengeful entity. As the protagonist reflects, the journey to the city inside a container was like that inside the "hold of a slave ship, where human bodies amalgamate, cemented together by sweat and excrement" (43), in other words, another traumatic crossing, a repetition of the people's history of exile and forced transportation. The destination is itself a deathly place—the mountainsides covered with a "grey carpet" of buildings that resembles a cemetery (44).

A journey is undertaken in the opposite direction—from city to the sea—in Kettly Mars's *Aux frontières de la soif* (2013), during which the author figure, Fito, realizes that he had been "obsessed by Port-au-Prince and its despondency" and considers the trip to be like "escaping from prison" (105). The journey is a reaffirmation of place, and a reconnection with nature. The blue sea guides the travelers to their destination; and coconut and banana trees, oaks, and flowers line the route, while the dense vegetation of the hillsides "seemed to open up to let them pass" (106). The visual images of nature are accompanied by the "song of the sea," a rhythmic sound that rises and falls with the movements of the waves and the wind (107). Their destination is Abricots, the small town at the end of the southwestern peninsula of the country, and a kind of hidden haven—"the secret," as the narrator describes it (106).

The destination is in fact the same as that of the narrator of Dany Laferrière's 2009 work, *L'Énigme du retour*. In Laferrière's book, the narrator travels to Abricots as part of his process of mourning for his dead father. To Laferrière's narrator, Abricots is also something of a secret, the place thought of as "paradise" by the Arawaks (297). As in Mars's novel, Abricots is a place to which the protagonist escapes the city, and where he renews his connection with a forgotten Haiti and the natural world, the trees touching the sea, the red fish wriggling in the fishermen's boats, the children devouring sweet mangoes, the "languorous life of the time before Columbus" (297). In both cases, too, Abricots seems to exist in another time. Mars's narrator describes the colonial cemetery, and the "sense of peaceful eternity" that existed there (108). Significantly, the precise recording of time that occurs when writing of the city is replaced by more vague, impressionistic mentions of time that draw on the position of the sun and the changing effects of the light (as in Edwidge Danticat below). For instance, when they arrive at Abricots, the narrator writes of the sun tilting already toward the horizon, and how it was a "moment of warm and golden light" that signaled the "first quivers of the shadows" (109). Unsure of whether he is in a "real time" in Abricots, Laferrière's narrator steps into this world he has long dreamed of, reposing in this pre-Columbian haven for three months to cure himself of the rhythms of urban life, to no longer think of his existence as a constant alternation between polar opposites, winter and summer, north and south, and to discover at last "spherical life," as he puts it (297, 298). Cradled by the "old Caribbean wind," he sleeps with a smile on his face, like he did when he was a child living with his grandmother, a time that "has finally come back" (299, 300). In this sense, Laferrière's narrator becomes "truly contemporary" in Giorgio Agamben's terms, one who truly belongs to his time by neither perfectly coinciding with it nor adjusting to its exigences. As such, he becomes "irrelevant" in the way suggested by Agamben, that is, paradoxically present through "disconnection" and "anachronism" and able to "grasp" his own time (Agamben 2009, 40). This is also the kind of "jerky, fragmented, unsynchronized temporality" referred to by yasser elhariry and Edwige Tamalet Talbayev, a present that is "deeply attuned to subjective temporal experiences, to internalized past moments of crisis—those reverberating traumas that modernity has occasioned and whose ripple effects can be perceived in multiple contemporary presents" (2018, 4). This jerkiness, these ripple effects of time, have also perhaps to do with the temporality of the seas: The "old

Caribbean wind" that Laferriere's narrator refers to as blowing in from the sea is what allows him to feel finally that he is present, contemporary in the ways suggested above.

The association of the sea with notions of timeless culture and being—and a paradoxical sense of ever-presence—also features in Lyonel Trouillot's *La Belle amour humaine* (2011), which opens with a scene of fishermen returning from a day's work to their village homes, where there is a collective "obsession" or "illness" related to the sea. The men take to the sea every morning and return in the evening with "stories of the sea in their mouths, the smell of the sea on their clothes, images of the sea in their eyes, and their footsteps, when they walk, sway to the rhythm of the sea" (60). The sea figures in the folktales and the proverbs that reflect the community's intimate bond with it. The sea is more than a site of work and identification; it is also associated with danger, and potential death, as it is in Edwidge Danticat's *Claire of the Sea Light* (2013), which is also the first of Danticat's full-length works to be situated away from the city, and specifically on the coast.

In this way, Danticat reflects the tendency evident in Laferrière's *L'Énigme du retour* and Trouillot's *La Belle amour humaine* to turn away from the city and revisit the small coastal communities, a move that also involves a certain revision of the idea of the land as the primary marker of national(ist) identity, and a reconsideration of the sea and the people's particular relation with it.[3] In the acknowledgments section of the book, Danticat thanks her family in Léogâne, "those gone and those still there, for introducing me and reintroducing me to the sea" (2013, 241). Léogâne was at the epicenter of the earthquake, though it has been relatively neglected in terms of media attention and relief support. With the memory of the destructive potential of the land so raw, one imagines that she revisits the sea as a natural element with which the people have an ancient and, in many ways, unchanging relationship, and around which lives and identities have long been shaped. In many ways, Danticat's novel is about light: the effects of the sea light in particular on the life of a community and an individual; light as a natural agent that is ever-changing yet permanent and predictable (again, as opposed to the degraded land); bringing light to problems and enlightenment; and lightness and clarity, implied in the very name Claire. One senses too that through the narrative, Danticat is also returning to the sea and the light, that perhaps like Virginia Woolf in *To the Lighthouse* she is seeking to rediscover what one critic calls "the lost light of early summers and the lost rhythms of the sea"

(Dunmore 2011). That light and those rhythms persist and have a durable quality that Claire apparently senses as she runs from the false security of the land back to the sea and the light, a movement that the author herself undergoes, and which appears to echo her post-earthquake conviction that life, and any worthwhile creative work, are risky, uncertain, and ultimately "dangerous" endeavors.

To turn to the sea in a time of crisis is, then, as Walcott suggests, to return to the marine, oceanic beginnings of modern Caribbean history and being. In the contemporary Haitian context, it is also, I would ultimately argue, an anti-apocalyptic move, a means of resisting notions that these are the end times for Haiti. In this way, the various moves toward the sea in recent Haitian fiction recall Antonio Benítez-Rojo's claim that the culture of the apocalypse is a culture of the land, of Europeans for whom the sea is a "forgotten memory" (1997, 11). The culture of the Caribbean, in contrast, is, Benítez-Rojo says, not terrestrial but "aquatic": "a sinuous culture where time unfolds irregularly and resists being captured by the cycles of clock and calendar . . . a chaos that returns, a detour without a purpose" (11). The Caribbean is, finally, for Benítez-Rojo, as for so many of the region's authors, "the natural and indispensable realm of marine currents, of waves, of folds and double folds, of fluidity and sinuosity . . . a culture of the meta-archipelago: a chaos that returns, a detour without a purpose, a continual flow of paradoxes" (11). In these regards, the turn to the sea in recent Haitian fiction in particular is a return to a sort of historical home, the past that is also always the source of the new; perhaps—and this is admittedly an optimistic interpretation—in these marine narratives there is the seed of something new, a faint sense amid the uncertainty of History, as Walcott said, "really beginning" (or re-beginning) (1986, 365–66).

The sea is also the site of renewal, reconfiguration, and re-beginning in Glissant's later works, notably *Une nouvelle région du monde,* in which he meditates at length on the Diamant Rock, the uninhabited island that sits about three kilometers off the south coast of Martinique. The island is not land but rock, and yet it is a site of memory for Glissant, who writes of "these centuries that cling to the Diamant Rock," as if history and time grow there, sprayed by the sea foam and the strong currents that make the place "one swirling chaos-opera" (2006, 11). Glissant describes obliquely a visit to the rock, the "gateway to the sea," where he sees a "vivid alliance of light and darkness," the light that "thrusts in turns like the weft of a text" (11). The sea, the rock, and the light are elemental to the place, to history, and to writing, the very "weft" of the author's craft. Glissant's great originality is to read the seascape as a text, to see in the play between light, water, and rock forms of narrative that are not so much readable as writerly, *scriptible* in the sense intended by Roland Barthes, for whom "the writerly text is a perpetual present, upon which no *consequent* language (which would inevitably make it past) can be superimposed; the writerly text is *ourselves writing*, before the infinite play of the world (the world as function) is traversed, intersected, stopped, plasticized by some singular system (Ideology, Genus, Criticism) which reduces the plurality of entrances, the opening of networks, the infinity of languages" (2002, 5).

Barthes's idea of the scriptible text bears close comparison to Glissant's reading of the sea as a writerly entity, a perpetual present in which one can read, or indeed reread, and reframe the past, as part of what Barthes calls "the infinite play of the world," which is endlessly plural, an opening—a gateway, as Glissant terms the sea and the rock—and a form of language in itself. Accordingly, Glissant's further descriptions of the sea and the coastline employ metaphors of language and writing: One would find "almost anywhere," he says, "on the tormented or flat coasts of seas and oceans these same signs of exclamation or interrogation, made of tangled cliffs and cut out in chalky laces" (2006, 12). Such signs are part of the language of the archipelago, the writerly text that Glissant at once reads and writes: It is already there in the "curve barely glimpsed under the water, the terrain of the collapse of a long time ago . . . which is in itself an old archipelago," but it is also of the present and the future, so that it "seizes you, like a rolling tide" where "everything is clear and legible" (13). As the reader-writer of the seas, Glissant feels himself "sinking . . . into the chaos of signs, before slowly finding [him]self in the clarity or density of a meaning" (13). In all of this sinking, reappearing, ending, re-beginning of the language of the archipelago, it is, Glissant insists, in a way that again echoes Walcott and many of the other Caribbean authors evoked in this chapter, the ocean that embodies time, history, being, and narrative. The world may have been shaped by "all the powers of the winds and the waters and the friable heat and the brittle cold," but from Brazil to Brittany and Tierra del Fuego to Norway, it is the "blue randomness" that persists and relates, so that everywhere, as the swirling sea foam around the Diamant Rock constantly reminds him, it is always "the sea that matters" (14).

NOTES

1. Unattributed translations are mine.
2. Valerie Kaussen writes that *noirisme* was a response not only to the failure of liberal politics to make a lasting impression in Haiti "but also to the failures of the U.S.'s liberal colonial project in Haiti (based on the free market, individualism, and the promise of social mobility) and to the ways it reinforced as well as negatively transformed traditional Haitian hierarchies of racial difference" (2008, 71).
3. See Elizabeth DeLoughrey's argument that the rise of "ocean studies" marks out a "route away from the territorialism of the nation-state" (2010, 705).

WORKS CITED

Agamben, Giorgio. 2009. *"What Is an Apparatus?" and Other Essays*. Translated by David Kishki and Stefan Pedatella. Stanford University Press.

Alexis, Jacques-Stephen. 1955. *Compère Général Soleil*. Gallimard.

Anderson, Mark D. 2011. *Disaster Writing: The Cultural Politics of Catastrophe in Latin America*. University of Virginia Press.

Barthes, Roland. 2002. *S/Z*. Translated by Richard Miller. Blackwell.

Benítez-Rojo, Antonio. 1997. *The Repeating Island: The Caribbean and the Postmodern Perspective*. Translated by James Maraniss. Duke University Press.

Brathwaite, Kamau. 1975. "Caribbean Man in Space and Time." *Savacou*, nos. 11–12, 1–11.

Caple James, Erica. 2010. *Democratic Insecurities: Violence, Trauma, and Intervention in Haiti*. University of California Press.

Chancy, Myriam J. A. 1997. *Framing Silence: Revolutionary Novels by Haitian Women*. New Rutgers University Press.

Danticat, Edwidge. 2013. *Claire of the Sea Light*. Knopf.

Dash, J. Michael. 1981. *Literature and Ideology in Haiti, 1915–1961*. Macmillan.

Dash, J. Michael. 1994. "Exile and Recent Literature." In *A History of Literature in the Caribbean*, edited by A. James Arnold, vol. 1. John Benjamins.

DeLoughrey, Elizabeth. 2010. "Heavy Waters: Waste and Atlantic Modernity." *PMLA* 125 (3): 703–12.
DeLoughrey, Elizabeth. 2019. *Allegories of the Anthropocene*. Duke University Press.
Dunmore, Helen. 2011. "To the Lighthouse." *Granta*. May 11. https://www.granta.com/New-Writing/To-the-Lighthouse.
elhariry, yasser, and Edwige Tamalet Talbayev. 2018. "Critically Mediterranean: An Introduction." In *Critically Mediterranean: Temporalities, Aesthetics, and Deployments of a Sea in Crisis*, edited by yasser elhariry and Edwige Tamalet Talbayev. Palgrave MacMillan.
Ferdinand, Malcom. *Decolonial Ecology: Thinking from the Caribbean World*. Translated by Anthony Paul Smith. Polity Press, 2022.
Gallagher, Mary. 2002. *Soundings in French Caribbean Writing Since 1950: The Shock of Space and Time*. Oxford University Press.
Glissant, Édouard. 1989. *Caribbean Discourse: Selected Essays*. Translated by J. Michael Dash. University of Virginia Press.
Glissant, Édouard. 1990. *Poétique de la relation*. Gallimard.
Glissant, Édouard. 2006. *Une nouvelle région du monde*. Gallimard.
Glissant, Édouard. 2010. *Poetic Intention*. Translated by Nathanaël. Nightboat Books.
Kaussen, Valerie. 2008. *Migrant Revolutions: Haitian Literature, Globalization, and U.S. Imperialism*. Lexington Books.
Laferrière, Dany. 2009. *L'Énigme du retour*. Grasset.
Lahens, Yanick. 2000. *Dans la maison du père*. Le Serpent à Plumes.
Loichot, Valérie. 2020. *Water Graves: The Art of the Unritual in the Greater Caribbean*. University of Virginia Press.
Mallet, David, James Thomson, and Thomas Augustine Arne. (1740) 1773. *The Songs, Chorusses, &c. in "The Masque of Alfred," as It Is Now Revived at the Theatre-Royal, Drury-Lane*. T. Becket.
Mars, Kettly. 2013. *Aux frontières de la soif*. Mercure de France.
Mars, Kettly, and Leslie Péan. 2011. *Le Prince noir de Lillian Russell*. Mercure de France.
McCusker, Maeve. 2011. "Writing Against the Tide? Patrick Chamoiseau's (Is)Land Imaginary." In *Islanded Identities: Constructions of Postcolonial Cultural Insularity*, edited by Maeve McCusker and Anthony Soares. Brill.
Ollivier, Émile. 1991. *Passages*. L'Hexagone.
Orcel, Makenzy. 2011. *Les Immortelles*. Mémoire d'encrier.
Pratt, Mary Louise. 1992. *Imperial Eyes: Travel Writing and Transculturation*. Routledge.
Roumain, Jacques. 1944. *Gouverneurs de la rosée*. Imprimerie de l'état.
Smith, Matthew J. 2009. *Red and Black in Haiti: Radicalism, Conflict, and Political Change, 1934–57*. University of North Carolina Press.

Tiffin, Helen. 2005. "'Man Fitting the Landscape': Nature, Culture, and Colonialism." In *Caribbean Literature and the Environment: Between Nature and Culture*, edited by Elizabeth M. DeLoughrey, Reneé K. Gosson, and George B. Handley. University of Virginia Press.

Trouillot, Lyonel. 2011. *La Belle amour humaine*. Actes Sud.

Victor, Gary. 2003. *À l'angle des rues parallèles*. Vents d'ailleurs.

Victor, Gary. 2011. *Le Sang et la mer*. Vents d'ailleurs.

Victor, Gary. 2013. "L'Ancrage à la terre chez quelques auteurs de la littérature haïtienne." Public lecture. Florida State University. October 30.

Victor, Marvin. 2011. *Corps mêlés*. Gallimard.

Walcott, Derek. 1986. "The Sea Is History." In *Collected Poems: 1948–1984*. Farrar, Straus and Giroux.

LIQUID LANGUAGE

AARON PINNIX

On October 13, 2016, I had the pleasure of observing poet Bob Perelman read aloud his poem "Before Water" at Columbia University as part of the Long Poem Conference. This reading, which was recorded and can be viewed online, was the nascent start for this chapter (Perelman 2017b). Perelman's poem was inspired by the experience of standing on a beach and watching waves come in. Recirculating a set number of words among its 395 lines, each line functioned like both a wave and a sentence. As the words recirculated into different configurations, I was struck with how this recirculation emphasized the poem's wavelike qualities. As an audience member, I could barely catch a line's meaning before it had disappeared, replaced with the next line. I was reminded of how water molecules circulate within waves, transferring their energy from molecule to molecule, and I felt that here the words were doing something similar. Perelman himself describes the poem as "trying to gesture toward making that impossible connection of word and thing" (Perelman 2017b, 0:47–0:52), and I have taken seriously this idea of what might come out of interconnecting word and water. As the chapter title "Liquid Language" indicates, I explore here the similarities between how language and water function. As I show, both water molecules and words function within a global matrix of shifting relationships with other water molecules or words, each gaining their meaning within this larger web of shifting intensities. Similarly, waves and sentences in turn organize water molecules and words into larger structures. As I have found, considering the similarities between water and language offers us ocean-inspired insights into how language functions.

Considering the question of how language functions like water, in this chapter, I explore a lineage of poetic works drawn from the last 120 years that use the movement of water as a model for understanding the interplay between meaning and uncertainty within language. These poems express this fluid inspiration in both form and content as they explore how words depend on other words for meaning, as well as how meaning transfers among words much like energy transfers among water molecules within waves. Considering Stéphane Mallarmé's *Un coup de dés jamais n'abolira le hasard* (A Roll of the Dice Will Never Abolish Chance [1897]; hereafter, *A Roll of the Dice*), Bob Perelman's "Before Water" (1977), and Nick Montfort and Stephanie Strickland's *Sea and Spar Between* (2010), I show how these poets find a fecund model for understanding language in the movement of water. This fluid inspiration is realized in these poems through the spatial arrangement of words across the page or screen, as well as by repeating words in different configurations that alter words' meanings. In presenting words whose meaning changes over the course of the poem, these texts reveal the iterability of signs, or how language refuses to ossify or solidify into any singular meaning. Ultimately, these poems show how both language and the ocean are dynamic spaces of persistent change that function through an interplay of fluid convergence and deliquescence, locating meaning within ever-shifting networks of molecules that are in constant motion.

Water is a productive model for discussing language's inherent ambiguity, since every water molecule is affected by, and exists in relation to, all the molecules that surround it, which are in turn affected by other molecules, each affecting the other in a spatial web of effects as vast as the ocean itself (consider, for instance, semidiurnal global tidal shifts). It is the water molecule's structure of two hydrogen atoms and one oxygen atom that enables larger ocean phenomena like waves. Oxygen is sixteen times heavier than hydrogen and pulls on the hydrogen's electrons, creating a covalent bond that also gives the hydrogen atoms a positive charge. These positively charged hydrogen atoms are weakly attracted to the oxygen of other water molecules, creating hydrogen bonds that are constantly forming and breaking among water molecules (Chaplin 2019). This weak attraction of hydrogen bonds creates water's cohesion, which can be seen firsthand in water's surface tension and in water's viscosity, its internal friction. Water's viscosity, or the ways in which water molecules interact with each other at a large scale, in turn enables ocean phenomena to appear in forms we are familiar with, since if this viscosity were different, phenomena like waves would look different

(Curriculum Research and Development Group 2019). This original rupture between individual water molecules also allows for effects at a distance, which Jen McWeeny strikingly describes:

> I had the good fortune of swimming with a whale shark that was about nine meters in length off the coast of Western Australia. Although I was at least twenty feet away from the whale shark in the water, I would get sucked in toward the animal and then pushed out somewhat violently every time that it moved its tail. In my experience, the water played the role of a connective tissue, linking my experience of my own body to the movements of my enormous swimming companion even though we never touched. (2011, 157)

Water's role as a connective tissue depends on the transfer of energy from molecule to molecule. This transferal of energy can organize individual water molecules into larger fluid structures such as tides, currents, upwellings, and downwellings. Perhaps the most familiar example of these fluid structures are waves. Waves are formed from the friction created by wind blowing over the surface of water. This energy accumulates in the crest of the wave, while individual water molecules within the wave move in circles, transferring energy from molecule to molecule (National Oceanic and Atmospheric Administration 2021). Water's molecular structure lies at the heart of its viscosity, which in turn organizes and structures waves. We can think of this as comparable to how words enter into diverse and changing relationships with other words, each semantic change affecting the larger web of linguistic meaning, much like energy affects and organizes water molecules.

I argue in this chapter that words function similarly to water molecules and sentences function similarly to waves. As the three poems discussed in this chapter show, every word, like every water molecule, gets the energy of its meaning from its relations to the words and blank spaces that surround it in a constant interplay of jostling differences. In turn, these words function together in the larger structure of sentences, which in turn derive their meaning from the various words contained within them. By repeatedly placing words within different arrangements, these poems reveal how words are in constant interplay with other words, much like water molecules are in constant interplay with other water molecules. Similarly, much like water molecules self-organize to express the transferal of energy found in a wave, words arrange into sentences that express the transferal of meaning among words. We see here a growth in complexity between words and sentences that functions like the growth in complexity between water molecules and waves.

While looking to water as a central reference for understanding language, I also consider Jacques Derrida's concept of iterability, *différance*, and the ways that signs always refer to more signs without solidity or final signification. Derrida argues that all signs are constituted through différance, and that meaning is a process of a continual deferral, explaining that "it is because of différance that the movement of signification is possible only if each so-called 'present' element, each element appearing on the scene of presence, is related to something other than itself" (Derrida 1982, 13). Depending on a necessary rupture that distinguishes individual signs from each other, this différance gives rise to semantic meaning. Similarly, the interplay of signs and différance leads to a sign's iterability, or the possibility for a sign to both maintain and change its meaning over time, since at its core a word's meaning depends on a constant interplay of differences among signifiers. Derrida designates the persistent churning between signification and nonsignification that enables meaning to rise to the level of signification as "arche-writing" (14). By appending this Derridean-influenced understanding of how language functions to our understanding of how water functions, we can see how both operate through a constant interplay of individual units within a surrounding matrix of other individual units. As such, there is an important similarity between the functioning of water and words that depends on both rupture and an underlying churn that enables differentiation.

In looking to the ocean as a means of recontextualizing our understanding of language, this chapter takes up the calls of thinkers such as Astrida Neimanis, Philip Steinberg, and Stefan Helmreich to theorize *with* seawater and attend to the ocean's real materiality in our considerations. In "feminist subjectivity, watered," Neimanis argues that "a deep and detailed attention to the material capacities, or the specific logics, of water can inspire us to reimagine how we emerge as subjects" (2013, 29). Similarly, Steinberg argues that the ocean's physical properties are important for understanding the human-ocean assemblage, and that the ocean, "rather than being a neutral surface ... has been socially constructed through history" (2001, 18). Finally, Helmreich proposes that as a theory machine, seawater provides us with concepts for understanding human life, and that we should treat seawater and theory as simultaneously abstractions and real, since our understanding of both operates off of human comprehension, yet retains real-world effects (2011, 132, 138). As Neimanis, Steinberg, and Helmreich show, humanity's considerations of the ocean are socially constructed, and by extension dependent on the very words we use in describing the ocean. This chapter follows these theorists' calls to look to the ocean's materiality as a means of discovering new conceptual insights.

The three works I discuss here interrelate the movements of water with the movements of language. I first consider French Symbolist Stéphane Mallarmé's 1897 *A Roll of the Dice* as inaugurating a poetic lineage that engages with, and is guided by, the ocean as a means of exploring ambiguity in language.[1] I then discuss Language poet Bob Perelman's poem "Before Water," first performed in 1977, as presenting lines in which words recirculate, evoking waves crashing on a beach. Turning to the digital age, I conclude with a consideration of Nick Montfort and Stephanie Strickland's digital poetry generator *Sea and Spar Between*, released online in 2010. By repeating a set of words drawn from the poems of Emily Dickinson and Herman Melville's *Moby-Dick* to create 225 trillion stanzas, none of which repeat, *Sea and Spar Between* uses linguistic repetition to evoke the ocean's vastness. Taking as their central inspiration the movement of water molecules and waves, these poems reveal how water and words share a fluidity that enables the arrival of structure out of an underlying churn of deliquescence. As Bob Perelman points out in his gloss on "Before Water,"

> The ocean is not available to the senses
> You can't see it
> You can say you do
> You can look (2017a, 112)

As the poems discussed in this chapter show, the same is true of language. Conjoining language and the ocean refuses the possibility of reducing either to something solid, since persistent change lies at the heart of both. Neither the ocean nor language cohere, but rather they operate within constantly shifting webs of intensities, giving rise to iterations that we interpret as meaningful against a broader fluid background that escapes circumscription.

STÉPHANE MALLARMÉ'S
A ROLL OF THE DICE

> the page layout ... is where all the effect is to be found
> —STÉPHANE MALLARMÉ

With *A Roll of the Dice*, Mallarmé inaugurated using the ocean as a means of better understanding language (figure 1). Written in 1896, the poem was published in the journal *Cosmopolis* on May 17, 1897. Nervous about the poem's difficulty, the journal's editors included a preface written by Mallarmé, as well as an explanatory "Editorial Note," while also reducing the spacing of words across the page (Mallarmé 2006, 262–63). Unhappy with this version, Mallarmé began working on a luxury edition arranged to his specifications. However, Mallarmé died in 1898 before this revised version was finalized. Drawing on galley proof notes, the text was published in 1914 as Mallarmé intended, particularly regarding spacing and typeface variations (Bowie 1978; Meillassoux 2012).

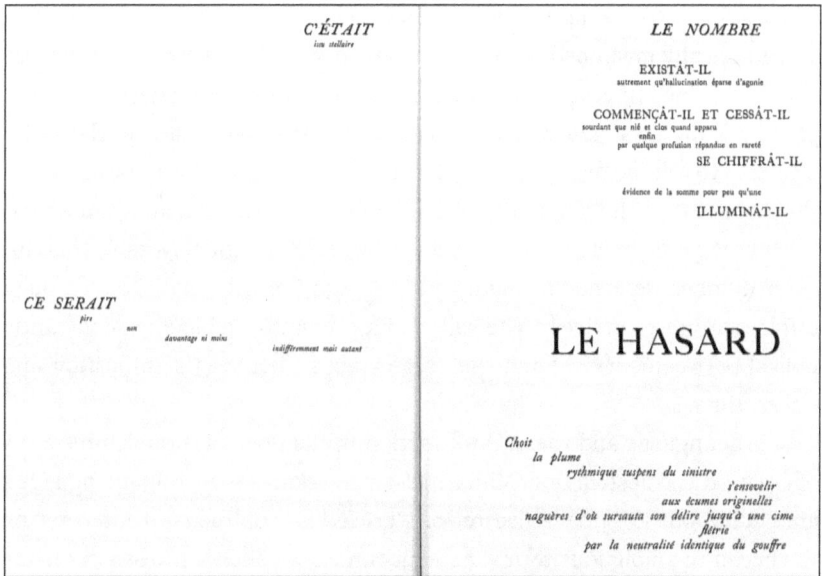

Fig. 1 Excerpt from the 1914 publication of *A Roll of the Dice*. Note that lines are to be read across the page break (the gutter), activating the page's blank space as meaningful. (*La Nouvelle Revue Française*)

With its attention to, and usage of, the page's surface, *A Roll of the Dice* functioned as a sea change in poetry, particularly after its publication in book form. Refusing punctuation or normative syntax, *A Roll of the Dice* disrupts the expected operations of reading practices by spatially arranging the text across the page in a manner that activates the page's white spaces as meaningful. As Johanna Drucker points out, "The textual elements forge links of meaning in their visual and verbal relations but those relations function as their own gestalt," a dynamic approach that "has no pre-existing referent and is not contained within the signifying structures of ordinary language" (1994, 55, 59; see Badiou 2005 and Hibri 2002). Space is utilized in original ways that affect the work's meanings. As Mallarmé writes in a letter to his friend André Gide, "the page layout . . . is where all the effect is to be found" (qtd. in Millan 1994, 313).

Conjointly with this inauguration of a spatially attentive poetics, the narrative, to the degree that there is one, follows a sailor's attempt to avoid shipwreck and sinking into the "neutrality of the abyss" (Mallarmé 2015, 19). The poem begins "A ROLL OF THE DICE WILL NEVER EVEN WHEN THROWN UNDER ETERNAL CIRCUMSTANCES FROM THE DEPTHS OF A SHIP-WRECK THOUGH the Abyss whitened spreads furious beneath the flat tilt disparagingly of a wing its own fallen in advance" (3–7) and continues in a syntactically enjambed (though spatially dispersed) manner that refuses the organizing impetus of grammar in favor of constructing meaning out of paratactically arranged words. Rocked by a tempestuous storm, the sailor attempts to roll the dice and find "the unique Number unable to be an other" (8–9) that offers the possibility of controlling the situation, an ultimate signifier that would control the ocean and bring him salvation. Notably this singular number, detached from any other (a signifier *not* constituted through différance) never arrives.[2] The sailor's fate remains ambiguous, constantly poised between survival and the oceanic abyss, between signification and uncertainty.

Both language and the ocean function in the poem as double presences of creation and destruction. Mallarmé's innovation is to highlight language's ambiguity, but the poem also reflects preceding traditions of interpreting the ocean in ambiguous terms. As Malcolm Bowie shows, the sea in fin-de-siècle French literature inhabited a double position as "both the source of all form and the threatened loss of all form," since the sea is "a storehouse of species, a living monument to the diversity of the world, the unfathomable, generative force from which the welter of life-forms springs," as well as "sinister and threatening, not just liquid but deliquescent, offering an unintelligible, non-construable surplus of possible worlds and threatening at every turn the human drive for clarity, order and coherence" (2000, 90). Poised between this dual possibility of creation and deliquescence, *A Roll of the Dice* applies this double vision of the ocean to language, postulating within language both order and chaos akin to the ocean.[3] This conjoining of linguistic and oceanic ambiguity is significant, since if the sailor futilely seeks the ultimate signifier that will save him from the abyss, then the abyss also makes this ultimate signification impossible because the abyss remains ever-present. Erratically navigating between this abyssal nonmeaning and the singular meaning of THE NUMBER, the text refuses to settle into any one position. While Mallarmé's usage of white space has been misinterpreted as silence (Mittenthal 2012, 69), it is more accurate to consider the text's white space as the location of a dispersed abyssal circulation, or arche-writing, out of which meaningful words arise and into which they sink in a constant interplay that refuses to ever settle. Taken together, we can see here how Mallarmé has constructed a robust model for understanding language as functioning similarly to the ocean.

We can see an example of this interplay between meaning and deliquescence in the text's interplay between "la vague" (wave) and "le vague" (uncertainty).[4] About midway through the poem, the sailor's "callow shadow" is "caressée et polie et rendue et lavée/assouplie par la vague et soustraite" (caressed and polished and worn and washed/softened by the wave and freed) (Mallarmé 2015, 10). The wave, "la vague," softens and frees the shadow, displaying a moment of meaningful interaction between the two transient instantiations of shadow and water. Later, the poem describes "ces parages/du vague/en quoi toute réalité se dissout" (these regions/of the uncertainty/in which all reality is dissolved) (21). Uncertainty ("du vague") here dissolves reality, and thus meaning. The two instances of "vague" are differently gendered ("la vague," "le vague"), a gendered distinction that extends to the indefinite article that appears in the second example ("un vague"). While "the wave" ("la vague") points to a definite wave, "an uncertainty" ("un vague") points to an indefinite uncertainty. Embedded in these gendered and linguistic distinctions is the possibility of both structure and deliquescence: a singular wave, as well as the disappearance of structure into deliquescence and uncertainty.[5] Both possibilities are activated through the visually similar "vague," though the particular meaning of the term depends on the words that surround "vague," highlighting how a word's meaning depends on the words that surround it.

BOB PERELMAN'S "BEFORE WATER"

> My big simple thought was: sentence = wave.
> —BOB PERELMAN

Language writer Bob Perelman has a long history of exploring new forms of poetry.[6] His poem "Before Water," a long poem of 395 lines, was first performed in 1977, and has subsequently been published in various journals and books (figure 2). As noted earlier, I was introduced to "Before Water" via Perelman reading it at the Long Poem Conference. During this reading, I was struck by how words that were repeated in different lines evoked the poem's inspiration of waves, an effect that was heightened by my inability as a listener to return to previous lines. This circulation of words acoustically enacted how words develop through repetition and différance, as well as how sentences organize and transfer meaning among words.

"Before Water" began as a collaboration between Perelman and his wife, Francie Shaw. As Shaw describes it, "I had this idea in my head of filming ocean waves coming in again and again and again.... My movie of the ocean was one position of the camera, just straight shots, and I can't think of it as a particularly interesting film" (Shaw and Perelman 2010). The original performance involved Shaw projecting film of waves onto a long roll of paper previously prepared with blue, green, and charcoal washes. As Perelman read the poem, Shaw painted blue paint over the projected waves before moving the roll down, constantly refreshing the painted screen and creating paper waves on the floor.

Perelman's inspiration was the goal of imitating ocean waves in poetry, along with the challenges such a project entails. "For me," he notes, "the question was how long can I keep it up? Can I write non-identical, similar permutations on this notion of a wave coming in? The infinity of the ocean and the finite wave. It was a powerful, open-ended notion" (Shaw and

I think this through or the water stays
Each complete sentence says time will end
I see it as it falls away
Noisy water again
One is a loop
A complete sentence invites the world to be outside
No sound inside shape
I read my mind
Water said to be water once
I extend the line between water and its shape
Thought has no choice between water and thought
The world occurs against what the sense of it enables the sentence to say
I fall is the edge
A sentence is here and over
No blue, no green, no water, itself complete
A separated noise clears the way to blue
A sentence threw all the water away
Say it through it
Clever noise across the clear world
Once a noise is a thought it's all I hear
It took here to think more sound
See blue where blue was
Think once in and edge
Tied itself across what was said
Goes dry extends to water
I think a sentence while it starts
Blue water makes a noise in green water
Inside the uncovered sounds
Leave the water at birth
Edge to sense noise around itself
I see it until it's water
Once in a line in order ponderous noise to nowhere before
I can't think again
Tell the water where to start
To make sense the middle disappears
One separate from itself nowhere but here
I see around the sound
Sense makes noise ready to make sense
The thought was uncovered by the end of the sentence
I'll hear this noise end
Sound in the same sense as birth makes noise
In it to say again one
The sentence goes back to where it came from
Green through itself

Fig. 2 Excerpt from Bob Perelman's "Before Water." Present here are just 44 of the 395 total lines, or 11 percent. Note, too, the lack of punctuation beyond apostrophes. (*Dibur*)

Perelman 2010). Perelman's translation of the infinite ocean and finite wave into language interconnects the ambiguity inherent within language, archewriting's persistent churn, with the arrival of new meaning in each new line. Similarly, Perelman interconnects the organizing structure of the wave with the sentence. As Perelman describes it: "My big simple thought was: sentence = wave" (2017a, 115). Much as waves organize water through a transferal of energy, sentences organize words through a transferal of meaning.

The repetition of words throughout "Before Water" develops our understanding of language's materiality by recirculating words that describe both language and waves. In keeping with the poem's interests, the words repeated the most include *water* (repeated 117 times), *noise* (96), *sentence* (78), *sound* (55), and *blue* (50).[7] In looking at a few lines, we can see language's variability as "water" takes on very different characteristics in the following examples:

> To the end of noise the mind occurs once falls water (104)
> Every sentence is water (104)
> The water read my mind before my birth (106)

Faced with these diverse possibilities, the reader must decide what characteristics water holds. Is it a silence that occurs after noise? Or analogous to language? Is water clairvoyant and precognizant? These examples reveal différance at play, since each instance of water is meaningfully different due to the words that surround and engage with "water." This range of meaning is fluid and cannot be settled. Perelman's poem makes arche-writing's subaqueous circulation appear by showing how each iteration of a word occurs at the shifting nexus between a word's meaning and the matrix of words and blank spaces that surround it.

Spatiality is a key aspect of this poem, and one can begin at any line, or skip around, without any real loss of meaning, since themes circulate but do not build in a narrative or linear manner. Evoking the perspective of someone watching waves breaking on the shore, the repetition of words means that readers encounter a constant deferral of meaning from line to line; the poem's readers are themselves constantly "Before Water." This repetition also evokes repeated time, since much as "before" is a spatial preposition, it is a temporal one too. Each line embodies its own moment and then is refreshed.[8] Eschewing punctuation, the delineating task of grammar has been replaced with the poem's spatial arrangement, traits also shared with

A *Roll of the Dice* and *Sea and Spar Between*. The emphasis on spatiality in these poems helps reveal how words derive their meaning from the matrix of words and spaces that surround them. Subtracting the organizing structure of grammar means words are more easily able to be identified by the reader as circulating throughout the text, along with the changes in meaning such circulation entails. Similarly, the brief irregular lines clearly evoke the waves that inspired them. In (re)organizing the words, these lines reveal how meaning transfers among words like water molecules get (re)organized into waves.

NICK MONTFORT AND STEPHANIE STRICKLAND'S *SEA AND SPAR BETWEEN*

> In this poetry generator, we leave the Atlantic shore and become lost at sea, crushed beneath the weight of water and superfluity of output. The reader is deprived of any horizon, or shore.
> —STEPHANIE STRICKLAND

On December 16, 2010, Nick Montfort and Stephanie Strickland released their massive digital poetry generator *Sea and Spar Between* on the online journal *Dear Navigator* (figure 3).[9] The work is a poetry generator, rather than a poem, since the text is constructed by a JavaScript computer code that gets generated anew every time a user activates the program. The program is also open source, so anyone can download and alter the JavaScript code, in turn altering the text that the code outputs.

After creating sets of words drawn from Herman Melville's *Moby-Dick* and the collected poems of Emily Dickinson, Montfort and Strickland created code that merged these words into 225 trillion stanzas, an amount Montfort and Strickland describe as "comparable to the number of fish in the sea," though this number is actually 64 times larger than the 3.5 trillion fish estimated to live in the ocean (Montfort and Strickland 2010a; Chepkemoi 2017). None of the word arrangements repeat, and if you allotted 30 seconds to reading each stanza, it would take 421,232,877 years to read the text as a whole (Flores 2013). The poem is navigated by moving one's mouse, which in turn migrates the program among x and y axes, each of which range from

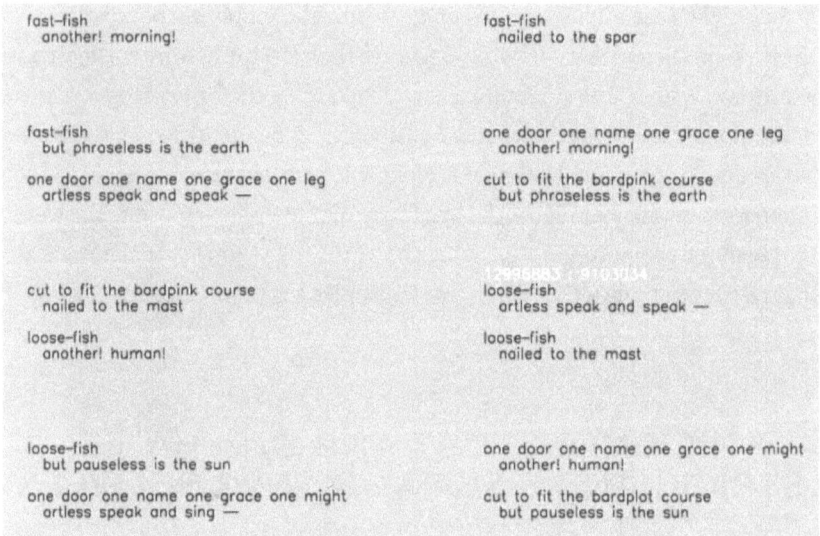

Fig. 3 Screenshot of *Sea and Spar Between*. Please note that this is an *extremely* small amount of the entire text. (Screenshot by the author)

0 to 14,992,383. The lattice of stanzas is stable, but the reader is placed at a random location each time *Sea and Spar Between* is launched, meaning readers' experiences of the text will necessarily differ. Similarly, readers can read across the stanzas both horizontally and vertically since, much like in "Before Water," the text does not progress in a linear narrative manner. Montfort and Strickland describe the reader as "deposited 'at sea,' located in a poem which surrounds or environs him or her, affording the view of a sailor, yet not in Pound's sense of a sailor's view of the shore—here, now, in this poem the shore has disappeared" (Montfort and Strickland 2010a).[10] This oceanic effect is heightened by the notable blueness of the text, with words a darker blue against a lighter blue background. The placement of stanzas as two lines conjoined by a central empty space also suggests an internal rupture, a differentiation that enables each stanza to exist alone and to function in relation to all other stanzas. The attention to the circulation of words and their relationships with the spaces and words that surround them inaugurated with Mallarmé's *A Roll of the Dice* has been developed here to a massive scale. With its digital vastness evoking the ocean's own vastness, *Sea and Spar Between* is a striking example of the similarities between language and water.

With its *x* and *y* axes functioning like latitude and longitude, one might consider *Sea and Spar Between* as emulating a map's flat depiction of the ocean, though the program actually constructs the poem as a torus projected onto a flat surface. Challenging visions of the ocean (and, by extension, language) as flat, here the words are tumultuous; the words texture the poem by recirculating through numerous arrangements and carrying their various meanings along with them. As Strickland notes, not only is the reader "deprived of any horizon, or shore," they are also "crushed beneath the weight of water and superfluity of output" (Strickland 2019, 265). The sheer vastness of the text makes reading *Sea and Spar Between* in any straightforward manner impossible. If "Before Water" models the breaking of waves as seen from the perspective of a human on a beach, then *Sea and Spar Between* completely overwhelms the human scale.

The human presence, while important for the creation, activation, and reception of *Sea and Spar Between*, is far less controlling than the program's own JavaScript logic. This computer code merges the iterability of language, or the possibility for words to mean different things within different contexts, with the technological possibilities of digital repetition in order to emulate the ocean's vastness through language. At the same time, the program's usage of a closed set of words makes the human task of interpretation even more apparent, since any synergy of meaning found within the lines is the result of readers' own engagement with the text.[11] The computer code does not intend for a line or stanza to be especially meaningful in a cohesive or singular way. We also discover arche-writing's subaqueous circulation in *Sea and Spar*'s construction of kennings, in which multiple nouns are conjoined as a substitute for a single noun. Kennings have their roots in Old Norse and Old Germanic poetry and can be found, for instance, in the Old English poem *The Seafarer*, in which *hwælweg*, or "the whale-way," stands in for "the sea" (Cammarota 2018, 45; Lindow 2012, 768). In replacing a noun with a conjoined noun phrase, kennings realize through ancient poetic practice the underlying mutability of language. The program's gloss describes how the poetry generator conjoins single-syllable words from *Moby-Dick* and Emily Dickinson's poems in such a way that either source could be the sole contributor, or either could contribute the first or second syllable (Montfort and Strickland 2010a). Kennings occur in every other stanza, and we can see two examples in figure 3: "bardpink" and "bardplot."

When I first wrote on *Sea and Spar Between*, I discovered that there were *no* words from the Melville word set in any of the kennings. All of the kennings in *Sea and Spar Between* were constructed from the Dickinson set alone. Melville's absence from the kennings, and this difference between the intent described in the gloss and the text itself, had thus far remained undiscussed in all critical discussions of *Sea and Spar Between*, revealing a fascinating insight into how the oceanic inspiration of massive spatiality and repetition created such a vastness of form and content that the absence of words from *Moby-Dick* in the kennings had escaped authors' and readers' discovery.[12]

Considering the similarities between how water and language function offers us new possibilities for understanding how meaning-making occurs in language, as well as a new way of understanding how something as vast as the ocean functions via the interplay of individual water molecules. As the poems discussed in this chapter show, a poetics that attends to the liquidity of language demonstrates how rupture and interconnection lie at the heart of language's meaning-making activities. These ocean-focused poems, with their warping and bending of language, are particularly well suited for making these connections by using the movements of water molecules and waves to show how language is ever-changing. *A Roll of the Dice*, "Before Water," and *Sea and Spar Between* draw on this generative pairing of language and liquidity to reveal how the shifting relationships between individual units within language and the ocean give rise to both meaning and deliquescence.

NOTES

1. Briefly, we might consider here the distinction between an open text, which includes diverse possibilities for interpretation, and a closed text, which leads toward a singular reading interpretation. Breaking with the Romantics, it is Mallarmé's *A Roll of the Dice* that inaugurates this open, as opposed to closed, poetics, and all of the texts discussed in this chapter follow in this lineage of open texts. Though she doesn't mention Mallarmé directly, see Hejinian 2009.
2. Quentin Meillassoux argues that this number is 707 (2012, 67).

3. My reading here both draws on and importantly detours from Derrida's analysis of Mallarmé's work. In *Of Grammatology*, Derrida cites Mallarmé as enacting "the first break" between sign and meaning (1997, 68). In "The Double Session," Derrida explores the interplay of meaning and nonmeaning in Mallarmé's *A Roll of the Dice* in a robust manner. However, rather than utilizing the oceanic and abyssal presences found within the text as theory machines, as I do here, Derrida evokes a problematically sexualized biological reference for representing the arrival of signification in the poem (1981, 285). I refuse his invocation and present fluidity itself as a better explanatory model. See Wahl Rabine (1990) for further critique.
4. The relationship between these two terms has been commented upon in Bowie 2000 and Allar 2017.
5. As Neal Allar points out, "each wave (vague) rising completely unique yet inevitably falling into the vagueness (vague) of the ocean. This marine vagueness, both ancient and new, is the very image of Mallarméan poetics" (2017, 244–45).
6. Language poetry largely refers to a group of writers that emerged in America and Canada in the early 1970s who emphasized how a reader's experience of a text affects the text's meaning. See, for instance, the anthologies by Andrews and Bernstein 1984, and Silliman 2001, as well as Perelman 1996. Of Bob Perelman, Steve Evans notes that "in the three decades since his first magazine publication in 1969 Bob Perelman has played a significant role in defining a formally adventurous, politically explicit poetic practice in the United States. . . . Availing himself of a variety of forms . . . Perelman has pressed toward a poetry of radical deconcealment, searching for the deep structure of social experience beyond the epiphenomenal shell game of postmodernity" (Evans [1998] 2010).
7. I used *WriteWords* to count word frequency: https://www.writewords.org.uk/word_count.asp.
8. As Kit Robinson describes the poem, "One line recedes before the next. There is no consistent prosody, no stanzas, each line is self-contained, in paratactic relation, like waves, one after the other" (2010).
9. *Dear Navigator* 1, no. 3 (2010). The journal is now defunct, though the poem can be found elsewhere online. Nick Montfort, a professor at MIT, has published numerous books on digital media, as well as computer-generated novels and poetry. Stephanie Strickland has published numerous books of poetry, as well as digital works with a variety of collaborators. Strickland has a strong interest in fluidity that manifests in her larger oeuvre. Critical responses to *Sea and Spar Between* include Aquilinia 2018 and Hayles 2018.
10. In conversation with Stephanie Strickland, she pointed out that this quote is referring to Ezra Pound's notion of *periplum*, or voyage or journey.

11. Much like the other poems discussed in this chapter, *Sea and Spar Between* is an example of an open text.
12. After I noted the absence of words from *Moby-Dick* and discussed this absence with Strickland, Montfort and Strickland updated the poetry generator's digital code to include Melville's set of words in the kennings, while also publishing a note detailing my contributions and the changes that were made. In all, only eleven characters were added to the code, but this in turn created thousands of new kennings. See Montfort 2020.

WORKS CITED

Allar, Neal. 2017. "Creolizing Mallarmé." *Nineteenth-Century French Studies* 45 (3–4): 236–53.

Andrews, Bruce, and Charles Bernstein, eds. 1984. *The L=A=N=G=U=A=G=E Book*. Southern Illinois University Press.

Aquilinia, Mario. 2018. "Electronic Literature and the Poetics of Contiguity." In *The Bloomsbury Handbook of Electronic Literature*, edited by Joseph Tabbi. New York: Bloomsbury.

Badiou, Alain. 2005. *Handbook of Inaesthetics*. Translated by Alberto Toscano. Stanford University Press.

Bowie, Malcolm. 1978. *Mallarmé and the Art of Being Difficult*. Cambridge University Press.

Bowie, Malcolm. 2000. "Sea and Structure in Fin-de-Siècle France: Mallarmé and Debussy." *European Review* 8 (1): 87–94.

Cammarota, Maria Grazia. 2018. "Translating Medieval Texts: Common Issues and Specific Challenges." In *Tradurre: Un viaggio nel tempo*, edited by Maria Grazia Cammarota. Edizioni Ca' Foscari.

Chaplin, Martin. 2019. "Hydrogen Bonding in Water." *Water Structure and Science*, March 29. https://water.lsbu.ac.uk/water/water_hydrogen_bonding.html.

Chepkemoi, Joyce. 2017. "How Many Fish Live in the Ocean?" *WorldAtlas*, April 25. https://www.worldatlas.com/articles/how-many-fish-are-there-in-the-ocean.html.

Curriculum Research and Development Group. 2019. "Hydrogen Bonds Make Water Sticky." *Exploring Our Fluid Earth*. https://manoa.hawaii.edu/exploringourfluidearth/chemical/properties-water/hydrogen-bonds-make-water-sticky.

Derrida, Jacques. 1981. "The Double Session." In *Dissemination*, translated by Barbara Johnson, 173–286. University of Chicago Press.

Derrida, Jacques. 1982. "Différance." In *Margins of Philosophy*, translated by Alan Bass. University of Chicago Press.

Derrida, Jacques. 1988. "Signature Event Context." In *Limited Inc*, translated by Samuel Weber and Jeffrey Mehlman. Northwestern University Press.

Derrida, Jacques. 1997. *Of Grammatology*. Translated by Gayatri Spivak. Johns Hopkins University Press.

Drucker, Johanna. 1994. *The Visible Word: Experimental Typography and Modern Art*. University of Chicago Press.

Evans, Steve. (1998) 2010. "Bob Perelman." *Third Factory: Notes to Poetry*. Originally published in vol. 193 of the *Dictionary of Literary Biography*. https://www.thirdfactory.net/perelman.html.

Flores, Leonardo. 2013. "'Sea and Spar Between' by Nick Montfort and Stephanie Strickland." January 2. https://iloveepoetry.org/?p=117. Accessed May 28, 2022.

Hayles, N. Katherine. 2018. "Literary Texts as Cognitive Assemblages: The Case of Electronic Literature." *Electronic Book Review*. https://electronicbookreview.com/essay/literary-texts-as-cognitive-assemblages-the-case-of-electronic-literature/.

Hejinian, Lyn. 2009. "The Rejection of Closure." *Poetry Foundation*. October 13. Originally a lecture given in San Francisco, CA, April 17, 1983. https://www.poetryfoundation.org/articles/69401/the-rejection-of-closure.

Helmreich, Stefan. 2011. "Nature/Culture/Seawater." *American Anthropologist* 113 (1): 132–44.

Hibri, May. 2002. "The Mallarmé of Alain Badiou." In *Alain Badiou: Penser le multiple*, edited by Charles Ramond. Paris: L'Harmattan.

Lindow, John. 2012. "Kenning." In *The Princeton Encyclopedia of Poetry and Poetics*, edited by Roland Greene. 4th edition. Princeton University Press.

Mallarmé, Stéphane. 1914. *Un coup de dés jamais n'abolira le hasard*. La Nouvelle Revue Française.

Mallarmé, Stéphane. 2006. *Stéphane Mallarmé: Collected Poems and Other Verse*. Translated by E. H. Blackmore and A. M. Blackmore. Oxford University Press.

Mallarmé, Stéphane. 2015. *A Roll of the Dice*. Translated by Robert Bononno and Jeff Clark. Wave Books.

McWeeny, Jen. 2011. "Sounding Depth with the North Atlantic Right Whale and Merleau Ponty: An Exercise in Comparative Phenomenology." *Journal for Critical Animal Studies* 9 (1–2): 144–66.

Meillassoux, Quentin. 2012. *The Number and the Siren*. Orchard Press.

Millan, Gordon. 1994. *A Throw of the Dice: The Life of Stéphane Mallarmé*. Farrar, Straus and Giroux.

Mittenthal, Robert. 2012. "An Ecology of Vispo: A Blindfold Test." In *The Last Vispo Anthology: Visual Poetry, 1998–2008*, edited by Crag Hill and Nico Vassilakis. Fantagraphics Books.

Montfort, Nick. 2020. "Sea and Spar Between. 1.0.1." *Post Position* (blog), January 30. https://nickm.com/post/2020/01/sea-and-spar-between-1-0-1/.

Montfort, Nick, and Stephanie Strickland. 2010a. "Cut to Fit the Toolspun Course: Discussing Creative Code in Comments" (blog). https://nickm.com/montfort_strickland/sea_and_spar_between/sea_spar.js.

Montfort, Nick, and Stephanie Strickland. 2010b. *Sea and Spar Between*. https://nickm.com/montfort_strickland/sea_and_spar_between/.

National Oceanic and Atmospheric Administration. 2021. "Why Does the Ocean Have Waves?" February 26. https://oceanservice.noaa.gov/facts/wavesinocean.html.

Neimanis, Astrida. 2013. "feminist subjectivity, watered." In "Water," special issue of *Feminist Review*, no. 103, 23–41.

Perelman, Bob. 1996. *The Marginalization of Poetry: Language Writing and Literary History*. Princeton, NJ: Princeton University Press.

Perelman, Bob. 2017a. "Before Water." In "The Long Poem," ed. Uri S. Cohen, Michael Golston, and Vered K. Shemtov, special issue of *Dibur*, no. 4, 103–15. https://arcade.stanford.edu/dibur_issue/long-poem.

Perelman, Bob. 2017b. "Prof. Bob Perelman Reads from Before Water—a Long Poem." From October 13, 2016, as part of The Long Poem Conference at Columbia University, *YouTube*, 22:43, June 23. https://www.youtube.com/watch?v=3uHXv7h90KI.

Robinson, Kit. 2010. "'Before Water,' After Years: Bob Perelman and the Turn to History." *Jacket*, no. 39. https://jacketmagazine.com/39/perelman-robinson.shtml.

Shaw, Francie, and Bob Perelman. 2010. "Francie Shaw and Bob Perelman in Conversation with Kristen Gallagher and Chris Alexander." *Jacket*, no. 39. https://jacketmagazine.com/39/perelman-shaw-iv-kg-ca.shtml.

Silliman, Ron, ed. 2001. *In the American Tree*. 1986. Orono: National Poetry Foundation.

Steinberg, Philip. 2001. *The Social Construction of the Ocean*. Cambridge: Cambridge University Press.

Strickland, Stephanie. 2019. *How the Universe Is Made: Poems New and Selected, 1985–2019*. Boise, ID: Ahsahta Press.

Wahl Rabine, Leslie. 1990. "The Unhappy Hymen Between Feminism and Deconstruction." In *The Other Perspective in Gender and Culture: Rewriting Women and the Symbolic*, edited by Juliet Flower MacCannell. New York: Columbia University Press.

BETWEEN THE MOUNTAINS AND THE SEA

―

*Currents and Currency of Terrestrial Waters
and Aqueous Idioms in Morocco*

MATTHEW BRAUER

I n the Moroccan capital of Rabat, just beyond the old city, a pedestrian pier extends hundreds of meters into the Atlantic Ocean. A distinct arc of reclaimed land built on jagged boulders, the pier presents a sharp physical manifestation of the boundary between land and water when facing the sea. Turning toward the shore, however, the pier appears as a mediator of the elements. It affords corners of shadow under its irregular stones, where people gather to cast their gaze and their fishing lines out to sea. It calms the Atlantic waters, allowing for casual surfing in windier months while sheltering the municipal beach and its characteristic rhythms: in and out of the water, up and down the sand with the tides. The Wadi Sala estuary of the Bou Regreg River divides the beach, coming to the sea through the city awash with humid summer breezes or cold winter rains. These terrestrial waters, swelling with tides or rain, overflowing or restrained by the Sidi Mohammed Ben Abdellah Dam reservoir, shrinking with the seasons or drought, say that water does not end at their banks any more than at the shore.

This essay follows Moroccan hydrology inland from the sea to the mountains to theorize terrestrial waters alongside oceans in literary and cultural studies. How do terrestrial waters serve as mediums, in the senses of connectivity and materiality, of human history and culture, just as the oceanic turn in the humanities and social sciences has shown regarding seas? I begin in the first section with a material and theoretical reflection on terrestrial waters as an omnipresent gradation of wetness that varies over time and place in the water cycle. Amid a recent profusion of hydro-affixed neologisms, I focus on the mutual interactions of water and society as what political ecology calls the hydrosocial cycle (Swyngedouw 2009; Linton and Budds 2014).

In the second section, I present a summary of Morocco's colonial history that attends to changing ways of knowing and managing the water cycle from the nineteenth century to the present, spanning the periods before, during, and after the French and Spanish Protectorates (1912–56 and 1912–58, respectively).

These nineteenth-century ecological, financial, and political crises in Morocco are the setting of Ahmed Toufiq's 1998 novel *Shujayrat hinna wa-qamar* (*Moon and Henna Tree*). In the third section, I read Toufiq's novel from the vantage point of the Anthropocene and the contemporary climate crisis–driven focus on water, analyzing how literature may infuse language with the spatial and temporal dynamics of terrestrial waters and the hydrosocial cycle. I call this hydropoetics, meaning language whose history, content, and form expresses fluid dynamics. Toufiq, a professional historian, fills his novel with historical literary forms and language that have disappeared, submerged, as Morocco is figuratively flooded by foreign capital invested in engineering ports, canals, dams, and irrigation works that literally redirect the flow of water. *Moon and Henna Tree* churns up the sedimented bed of Moroccan poetics, disrupting the flow of the aqueous languages that characterize imperialist pretension and capitalist development. I conclude in the fourth section with a meditation on the dam, which concretizes the imperialist and capitalist displacement of waters, lands, peoples, and languages to make room for capital investment. The dam embodies a future sold off ahead of time. Toufiq's novel draws on the variable temporalities of terrestrial waters to resurface a drowned hydropoetics and restore futurity to an alienated water logic (Talbayev 2018, 266–67) while offering an eerie anticipation of a present drained of its futurity and an uncanny iteration of what is yet to come (Nuttall 2020, 469–70).

TERRESTRIAL WATERS AND THE WATER CYCLE

We first move from the sea inland toward the mountains. As humanities scholarship has given increasing account of water, the focus has been on oceans. Oceanic studies has unbound human history and culture from the land alone to the planetary space of the "terraqueous globe" (Blum 2015; Cohen 2010). Recent works on coasts, beaches, and ports emphasize human and elemental comingling across land and water (Allen et al. 2017; Freed-Thall and Cadieu 2021; Gillis 2012). From the transitional space of the shore, we turn to the variegated liminal forms of water found inland. Attending to terrestrial waters enables a reconceptualization of land as a wetness, both materially and socially produced. "Terrestrial" thus means not merely "land-bound" but the omnipresent interaction of land and water whose wetness is measured in degrees. The question is as follows: If wetness is everywhere, to paraphrase Anuradha Mathur and Dilip da Cunha (2020, 139), why do we not see water inland?

Becoming sensitive to this omnipresent wetness requires thinking with the materiality of the water cycle. Wetness is variably distributed over time in many forms, many of them not even liquid, at altitude or depth, free or in suspension. Such forms and transformations may seem ethereal or abstract, rather than concrete, to human perception. The water cycle has temporalities that do not translate into human time, like the "pluvial time" of rain (Nuttall 2020) and the polyrhythms of tides, monsoons, hurricanes, and floods (Mathur and da Cunha 2001, 2–5; 2009, 3–4). Consequently, every human perspective on the water cycle implies a representational logic that concretizes specific moments of the water cycle.

The modernist "eye" on the water cycle, as da Cunha has shown with "Alexander's eye" in the Indian context—naming a way of seeing the subcontinent's terrestrial waters, used since Alexander the Great up to the contemporary Indian technocratic bureaucracy—conceives of hydrology in discrete features, like rivers, lakes, and seas, between which there are ephemeral passages. This "eye" sees the Ganges River, for example, as a continuous line on a map, whereas the word "Ganga" originally names rain, a moment in the water cycle when water moves in "complex, field-like ways" (2019, 10–11). When and what an "eye" sees makes water actionable in different forms and times.

The "eye" on the water cycle may be connected to the political ecological concept of the hydrosocial cycle, which "envisions the circulation of water as a combined physical and social process, as a hybridized socionatural flow that fuses together nature and society" (Swyngedouw 2009, 56). The hydrosocial cycle reproduces the variable time and wetness of the water cycle in terms of the social experience and management of water. As such, a constitutive process of the hydrosocial cycle is the attempt to resolve the temporal and material complexity of the water cycle with the timescales of human societies. The hydrosocial cycle is therefore not constituted by definitive human control of otherwise natural processes but rather by the socioenvironmental turbulence that forms when water is in a place, time, or form not prescribed by technical interventions in water management or expected by one of the many experiential and theoretical understandings of the water cycle. The differential flows of the water and hydrosocial cycles create powerful, churning currents. These can take destructive forms, as when water overflows human prediction or infrastructure in storms, floods, or other disasters. Conceptually, they also drive thinking about a world shaped by water and its uses, as the recent profusion of hydro-prefixed neologisms testifies.

I discern two principal currents among these hydro-concepts. The first consists of understandings of hydropower (Talbayev 2023). I gloss hydropower as encompassing the geophysical forces that water exerts and the ways water becomes a material and ideological component of power relations. I include under this heading other concepts that designate the polyvalent power of water in specific contexts, such as hydrocolonialism, hydroimperialism, and hydrocapitalism (Bystrom and Hofmeyr 2017; Hofmeyr 2019b; Hofmeyr 2020; Pritchard 2012). These concepts share a sensitivity to the "political and agentive power of water" as an actant in hydrosocial interactions (Hofmeyr 2019a, 3). Water is a force whose action, however conceived in human terms, shapes and is shaped by law, social practice, and hydrological infrastructure. In the intimacy between terrestrial waters, land territories, and human settlement, the agentive capacity of water comes into a contingent, ambivalent relationship with projects that seek to channel water to particular ends, such as those of empire or development in Morocco across the twentieth century. Terrestrial waters, even when managed by irrigation works, dams, and reservoirs, shape settlement and colonization practices. Freshwater supply, from the seasonal variations of watersheds fed by snowmelt or monsoon climates to the exceptional years of flood or drought, affects land tenure and class formation, deciding the fate of political projects and social actors (Pascon 1986).

The second conceptual current is that of hydropoetics, which I use to designate the aesthetic, critical, and material relationship of literary language (construed in the broadest possible sense) to water. I associate with this heading the diverse aesthetic possibilities afforded to language by different ideas of and relations to water (Bystrom and Hofmeyr 2017, 3–4), the critical means of reading for modernist, extractivist approaches to water as a resource in hydrofiction, on the model of petrofiction (Boast 2020, 3), and imagining hydronarratives of alternative, more just water futures (Henry 2022, 6). Hydropoetics may describe or evoke water, take on aqueous forms, but most of all it is language suffused in material wetness. Neither abstract nor metaphorical, hydropoetics is infused with water's agentive power, such that water "inhabits our sense of memory and time, and itself generates forms of feeling, knowing" (Nuttall 2021, 19). I understand the nonmetaphorical nature of the aqueous infusion of language through Marxian theories of language materiality, which consider that language exists only in the moments and mediums when it is used, neither as a universal nor purely inner mental construct. Rather, the production, transmission, and interpretation of language are embedded in the material political-economic conditions of their contexts (Cavanaugh and Shankar 2017, 6–14). Hydropoetics is language embedded in the socionatural political ecology of the hydrosocial cycle. Hydropoetics thus also names what Thangam Ravindranathan describes as "the story-work by which literature has always processed the earthly, whereby metaphor has been the cover, the irreducible encryption code, for matter to enter our stories at all" (2019, 27–28). Attention to hydropoetics can show how novels let in the waters that would otherwise be abstracted by hydropower, bringing out the ways that water and human hydraulic knowledge and practice reveal and reproduce unequal power relations (Pritchard 2012, 592). Language ripples with the material changes worked on hydrology, which in places like Morocco range from customary arrangements of water use among small farmers and herders to state-sponsored, capitalized dam building and irrigation works, reforms of land and water rights, agricultural development, and the public and private financing schemes that accompany them. In Morocco, when a reservoir floods villages behind a dam, the deluge changes when, where, and how the villagers speak, sing, or write of themselves and their town, as radically as the erasure of the village itself. When governments, imperial or postcolonial, consolidate collectively owned lands into tribal reservations before developing irrigation on former tribal lands opened up to favored outside groups, then the oral register of tribal water rights is amended, as is the social role of the register. Hydropoetics, from its surface to its submerged idioms, forms, and genres, allows us to critically read the confluence of language suffused with the time of the water cycle and the aqueous idiom of capital flows.

IMPERIALISM AND HYDROSOCIAL CRISIS IN MOROCCO

This section briefly summarizes Morocco's historical location amid oceanic and terrestrial waters. I introduce the crises that spring from imperialist and capitalist infiltrations into the Moroccan hydrosocial cycle from the late nineteenth century into the Protectorate period (1912–56), arguing that terrestrial waters are key to unlocking precolonial and decolonial water logics.

Despite sitting at the juncture of the Atlantic Ocean and the Mediterranean Sea—two bodies of water with long-standing disciplines dedicated to studying their environmental, historical, and political dynamics (Boelhower 2008; Horden and Purcell 2000)—Morocco has long been seen as island-like in its relative geographic and social insulation. The name that Arab geographers gave to the region following Islamic conquest in the eighth century, Jazirat al-Maghrib, "the Island of the West," still resonates with historians (Burke 1976, 1). While North Africa might resemble other regions in Fernand Braudel's formative history of the Mediterranean, where it is one of five isomorphic "peninsulas" (1966, 21–22), early modern Moroccan interactions with Europeans and Americans remained essentially maritime, with inland ventures largely limited to ransoming captives taken at sea (Lévi-Provençal 1922, 1–2).

The seas ceased insulating terrestrial Morocco in the early nineteenth century, when repeated bombardments of North African ports by European and United States ships put an end to state-sponsored privateering. Under immense foreign pressure, the Moroccan Sultan Sulayman (r. 1793–1822) disbanded his navy in 1820 (Miller 2013, 11). Morocco embarked on an isolationist policy, turning landward within its "island" of mountains and desert (Miège 1961, 2:22-23). Yet Sulayman's isolationist policies and the return to engagement with Europe undertaken by his successors were not only reactions to Western imperial aggression on the seas and in Moroccan ports. Their approaches were based on a confluent hydrosocial construction, following routes along oases that stretch outward from the imperial capital of Fez. These chains of fertile, watered outposts were a material expression of the sovereign extent of the Moroccan empire, employed by even the most far-flung regions to call for the Sultan's help in the face of English and French infiltration (Laroui 1977, 60-64). Such aid was increasingly needed, as the sea became a supply line for European imperialism, and the frontier, displaced onto the shore, brought Moroccan terrestrial waters into foreign view.

As Moroccan-European interactions shifted inland across the nineteenth century, foreign travelers took careful notice of Moroccan hydrology. European accounts focus especially on the military and industrial potential of rivers as potable water, transportation networks, and irrigation sources. With an eye for hydropower, they envision a colonial future already inscribed in the landscape, seeing Moroccan terrestrial waters as channels for imperial foreign investment.

Charles de Foucauld's *Reconnaissance au Maroc* (1888) set the standard for the genre, earning recognition from the Geography Society of Paris for its strategic knowledge of a country bordering French Algeria (Peters 2009, 116-18). *Reconnaissance* provides detailed descriptions of the breadth, depth, current, and seasonal variation of every river crossing on Foucauld's voyage. These narrative descriptions are synthesized into an encyclopedic account of Morocco's river basins, including lists of tribes, towns, markets, shrines, and, most tellingly, the number of rifles, soldiers, and cavalry each region can muster. Rivers map a strategic organization of space according to the needs of a future imperial conquest.

European accounts also frequently invoke what I call the "fertile but fallow" trope, positing a latent potential in natural features otherwise perceived as poor in quality and poorly managed (Davis 2007, 1-2). Colonial engineers echo these laments, presenting North African hydrology, from its physical waters to its arid drylands, as problems to be remedied by imperial infrastructure (Davis 2016, 2-8; Pritchard 2012, 594-96). A British journalist based in Tangier issues a characteristic judgment on Moroccan rivers: "though probably under a European government . . . these rivers would be utilized for navigation, at least with barges, no use is made of them now, and the lack of bridges renders them a serious obstacle, instead of an aid to internal communication" (Meakin 1901, 12). These scouting missions chart military and engineering interventions intended to optimize Morocco's productive potential by acting on its waters. European hydropower follows this course with an influx of capital, credit, and influence managed by diplomatic, military, political, and financial agents. The result is a hydrosocial crisis.

HYDROPOETICS OF CRISIS: WRITING PRE- AND POSTCOLONIAL MOROCCO IN *MOON AND HENNA TREE*

I read Moroccan hydrosocial crisis in precolonial, postcolonial, and anthropocenic triplicate. As looming crises of rising seas and drying aquifers draw our urgent attention to the water cycle in the present, how may we apprehend the story-work of letting the waters into language in previous periods of crisis, to recall Ravindranathan's formulation (2019, 27–28)? It is in this sense that I examine the role that water played in European imperialism in Morocco through the novel *Moon and Henna Tree* by contemporary Moroccan writer and historian Ahmed Toufiq. Set amid the High Atlas foothills and mountains southeast of Marrakesh in the late 1800s, the novel draws extensively on Toufiq's academic history of that region, *Moroccan Society in the Nineteenth Century: Inoultan, 1850–1912* (1983). Toufiq's novel, first published in Arabic in 1998, appeared at the end of decades of political and civil society repression under King Hassan II (r. 1961–99), commonly known as the Years of Lead. This was an ambivalent moment in Moroccan history, when the experience of living under an oppressive regime had called into question the liberatory ambitions of colonial independence and postcolonial culture and governance.

Moon and Henna Tree confronts the intellectual and cultural crisis of its time of publication with a hydropoetic representation of the genesis of crisis in precolonial Morocco. The text's construction and narrative demonstrate its engagement with the hydrosocial, linking pre- and postcolonial crises hydropoetically in an indictment of the Moroccan government's wholesale adoption of capitalist hydropower. Now, more than twenty years later, we may also read the novel as speaking to an era of environmental crisis.

THE HYDROSOCIAL CRISIS DEPICTED IN *MOON AND HENNA TREE*

I begin by showing how Toufiq's novel uses hydropoetics to recover past forms of the hydrosocial cycle, drawing on his own historical study of the lived experience of crisis in nineteenth-century Morocco, as recorded in the historical archive and as collective memory tied to the landscape and transmitted orally. Afterward, I analyze how three hydropoetic forms integrated into the novel channel the terrestrial waters of precolonial Morocco.

To both contemporaneous and later observers, the precolonial period in Morocco (ca. 1820–1912) was marked by instability across social strata. The Moroccan historian Ahmad ibn Khalid al-Nasiri concludes his 1895 account of his homeland with a striking summation of his sense of radical social changes in authority, economy, and morality that occurred within his lifetime: "The habits of the people are completely reversed, the behavior of merchants and craftspeople is unlike what it used to be in regard to money, price and the conduct of affairs, to the point where people are in dire straits" ([1895] 2001, 8:221; qtd. in Miller 2013, 55). The opening pages of *Moon and Henna Tree* echo al-Nasiri: "The way of life had undergone a significant change. There was more money around, and its value had diminished. People's moral character had taken a turn for the worse, and blessings were few and far between" (Toufiq 1998, 3; hereafter *MHT*). A range of internal and external forces were indeed driving social and economic change in Morocco at a rapid pace, eliciting a generalized sense of disorientation and anxiety about the disintegration of social norms and bonds, tied to worsening economic conditions.

Toufiq's historical study emphasizes the impact of changes in Morocco's internal hydrosocial structure, linking the social and environmental variability of water access to periods of conflict in Moroccan mountain communities, whether among themselves, with neighbors in more fertile regions, or with the state. In much of Morocco, access to water is much more valuable than land by itself. By the nineteenth century, water rights became increasingly fragmented. The resulting conflicts prompted sultans to assert their control by dispatching family members or military officers as governors to replace local leaders in restive regions (Toufiq 1983, 70–80). This was a period of administrative and military reform, much of which was financed and executed with the support of European advisors and capital. Morocco's social structure was being reworked from without as well as within. Fluctuations in the hydrosocial cycle emanated as much from issues of water rights and governance as from the upstream flow of foreigners and foreign capital infiltrating deeper into Morocco, beyond the court and the ports to which they had largely been contained under previous regimes. Al-Nasiri attributes social change precisely to Europeans "mixing with us . . . so that their ways and customs have overtaken ours and absorbed them completely" ([1895] 2001, 8:221; qtd. in Miller 2013, 55). Material factors bolstered the ascendancy of European social norms. Morocco incurred a series of diplomatic and military setbacks that increased foreign leverage over the state and opened the door to the exploitation of other Moroccan notables and landholders through indebtment. Following the French capture of Algiers in 1830, French troops frequently violated Moroccan territory. A Moroccan army raised in 1844 by Sultan Abd al-Rahman (r .1822–59) to stop French incursions suffered a catastrophic defeat in the Battle of Isly in northeastern Morocco. French ships then bombarded the ports of Tangier and Essaouira, forcing the Sultan to recognize French rule in Algeria. In 1859, a brief but even more disastrous war broke out with Spain, which held the northern city of Tétouan and demanded a massive indemnity payment from Morocco for its return. Morocco plunged into a series of debts from which it would never emerge, first ceding control of its customs revenue before accepting the imposition of French and Spanish protectorate regimes.

HYDROPOETICS IN *MOON AND HENNA TREE*

Out of the hydrosocial turbulence caused by cultural contact and economic upheaval, *Moon and Henna Tree* weaves a story about Hmmu, an impulsive, acquisitive regional governor whose violent ambitions exceed the backwater status of his territory. His disruptions of the hydrosocial order open him up to infiltration through flows of credit from foreign agents, creating a channel where European hydropower flows forcefully. Hmmu's rise and fall thus foretells in miniature the fate that befell Morocco: its economy indebted to European capital; its natural resources seized to secure credit or as payment for debt; its government converted into a revenue-collecting body for creditors, like a dam collects waters; and the dams that France and later the French contractors of the Moroccan government will build all over the country.

Moon draws its plot from the hydropoetics of historical literary forms that were submerged in the cultural sea change wrought by European imperial action on Moroccan terrestrial waters and, later, the postcolonial Moroccan state's embrace of capitalist hydropower. In this way, Toufiq's fiction draws on the methodology of the field interviews conducted for his study of nineteenth-century Morocco. There, Toufiq examines collective memory of the precolonial era through conversations with twentieth-century subjects about physical sites of the land- and waterscape, whose material qualities shape and inform human social memory in a predominantly oral culture. Toufiq reports that discussing "tangible historical sites and extant remnants" elicits specific linguistic forms: "whenever an event or a fact was tied to an aphoristic saying, it was able to survive oblivion" (1983, 41). Literary forms like aphorisms, proverbs, and poetry are able to preserve the "depths" of social structures over time, lending themselves readily to the novelist's and historian's task of recovering a submerged history, in contrast to the "superficiality" of European travelers' remarks on Morocco (1983, 38, 41). This hydropoetics of surface and depth responds both to the European hydrocolonial eye, which skimmed the surface of Moroccan terrestrial waters, and the poetics of the dam, which, literally, drowned many of the places that spark memory and, figuratively, represents the submersion of oral culture under the currents of capital investment driving modern hydropower.

Consequently, the voices of Toufiq's fictional characters and historical interlocutors, as well as the narrative and authorial language of his writing, are suffused with the Moroccan hydrosocial cycle. Water, whether flowing from snowmelt and rainfall down mountains over fields to the sea or held in reserve in aquifers and oases, provides the material support for Moroccan social structures, and the medium for language to describe the flow of authority from the sultan to his governors to the people, the balance of power between regions and tribes, the circulation of resources and wealth, and the moral order of society. This language is not just metaphorical. It emerges from a lived relationship to changing land- and waterscapes. Toufiq's novel resurfaces linguistic usages and literary genres that had been transformed, especially regarding the Arabicization of Amazigh languages, by changes in land tenure and political economy over the intervening century (Hoffman 2007, 24).

THREE SUBMERGED GENRES

The Moroccan hydrosocial cycle manifests in *Moon and Henna Tree* in proverbs, poetry, and devotional literature. These three submerged genres of Arabic and Amazigh expression depict, with their aqueous language, a territory suffused with wetness, watered by rains and irrigation, and possessed of deep aquifers. These material elements of the water cycle infuse oral and written literary language with wet forms of expression, whose hydropoetic currents will be co-opted by flows of capital and credit that infiltrate Moroccan terrestrial waters.

Terrestrial Wetness: Proverb

In *Moroccan Society in the Nineteenth Century,* Toufiq reports a proverb often repeated by his interviewees in the field, exemplifying the role of aphorisms in the formation of historical memory. "Field to field until the sea" (Toufiq 1983, 41) was the way a well-respected historical governor declined to use his position to acquire property, disclaiming a possessive desire that could not be sated even if he owned all the fields down to the sea.

Toufiq borrows this historical proverb to characterize the fictional Hmmu's father, 'Ulla, in *Moon and Henna Tree*. 'Ulla is rewarded with the governorship for his service in the Sultan's army. Although 'Ulla arrives as an outsider, he wins his new subjects' confidence through his restrained approach to governing. Notably, he refuses to acquire property beyond a small field for his cow, invoking "a saying of his that had become a proverb in his homeland: 'Taghult s taghult ar aman,' which in the Amazigh tongue means: 'From field to field until I reach the sea'" (*MHT* 4; translation modified). The proverb channels multiple messages: on the surface, the proverb deals in the landed logic of private property. 'Ulla, like his historical model, disavows the desire to possess. Yet the image is not so dry as it might appear: The contiguity of fields up to the sea follows the flow of water from mountain watersheds in rivers and runoff to the coast. This sense is echoed in oral forms documented by other researchers, like this song recited in the Anti-Atlas to the south of Toufiq's region: "We are one, you and me, we share walls/Our fields share boundaries and springs/and from our channels we water yours" (Hoffman 2007, 6). 'Ulla's good governance is about maintaining the hydrosocial order that depends on the flow of water as a shared resource.

A slight difference in the proverbial forms recorded in Toufiq's history and recreated in his novel reflects the transformation of the Moroccan hydrosocial cycle. The historical form that Toufiq reports from his interviewees borrows the Arabic word for "sea," *baḥr*, whereas the fictional 'Ulla uses the Amazigh word *aman*, meaning "water," which could refer to a spring, lake, river, or, by extension, the sea.[1] Restoring a usage lost in the Arabicization of Amazigh languages introduces a more nuanced sense of wetness into the proverb, as the word *aman* scales between local and distant waters across the many forms of the water cycle.

Rains and Irrigation: Song and Poetry

Maintaining the flow of terrestrial waters fed by the water cycle sparks the novel's conflict when Hmmu ascends to the governorship upon his father's death. Hmmu is the antithesis of the historical proverb that characterized his father. Acquisitive in all matters, Hmmu schemes to extend his influence via marriage to al-Salima, the daughter of a neighboring governor who rules the plains adjacent to Hmmu's mountain territory. Al-Salima's family perceives Hmmu's aggressive disposition as a normal difference between plains and mountain peoples. This difference is expressed in improvised poetry sung at the celebration of al-Salima's engagement to Hmmu.

The song begins with a line offered by al-Salima's father: "The plains are watered by the mountains/And here beauty wins out." A professional singer reprises this couplet, then adds another: "The lovely gazelle bats its eyelashes/Just like a warrior's sword." Al-Salima whispers another line to the singer, who then intones it aloud: "So, beloved of my heart,/How is it we are selling you for money?" (*MHT* 26–27).

As with 'Ulla's proverb, this improvised song draws on the hydrosocial cycle. It naturalizes an image of the water cycle, where precipitation, snowmelt, and spring waters gather in upland catchments to flow downward to the plains, supporting settlements, herds, and farmlands, as well as the social hierarchy between plains dwellers and mountain folk: It is in the plains that water yields its greatest agricultural and cultural benefits. The second line reinforces the plains' cultural refinement by connecting its advantageous hydrological situation with established poetic tropes of the beloved as gazelle and warrior (Bürgel 1989). In this sense, the water refers to al-Salima too, since by bringing the bounty of the plains to the mountain, her tribe remains the ultimate beneficiary of the marriage. Al-Salima's final riposte, however, brutally reveals the transactional character of this hydropoetic expression: Her marriage is essentially a trade deal that alienates a part of the plains' beauty to the unrefined mountains. She foreshadows the way that foreign financial transactions will disrupt the Moroccan hydrosocial cycle.

The Reservoir: Devotional Literature

Whereas 'Ulla's proverb and al-Salima's song follow the flow of water from the mountains to the sea to understand the relationship between the different ethnic, linguistic, and social components of Moroccan society, a third social group and literary form in the novel is watered by oases and reservoirs, granting them a degree of independence from the more flow-dependent aspects of the water cycle.

In the novel, the Nayit Ibrahim mountain tribe represent what Toufiq and others have called the "human reservoirs" of the Atlas population, a human counterpart to the region's water resources (Toufiq 1983, 101; Burke 1976, 2). Although nominally falling within Hmmu's governorate, the Nayit Ibrahim are materially independent, thanks to an impenetrable fortress and a jealously guarded oasis. Hmmu desires nothing more than to make them submit, which he achieves only through environmental sabotage, cutting down the mature trees of their orchards.

Although Hmmu annexes the Nayit Ibrahim, he does not control them. He forces marriage with the chief's daughter Kima, hoping to instigate a rivalry between his wives, but the two women become close, discovering more of their world through each other's family, language, and cultural practices. The Nayit Ibrahim's material and symbolic reservoir manifests in al-Salima and Kima's friendship. When Kima invites al-Salima to visit her family, the latter is deeply impressed by the women's Friday prayer gathering, where they "read portions of a book in Tamazight that women memorize and recite as a kind of worship.... First she [the *shaykha*] would read out a phrase, then the women would repeat it, swaying as they did so out of sheer emotion" (*MHT* 159; translation modified). The novel refers here to *The Sea of Tears*, by Muhammad bin 'Ali Awzal (d. 1749), a major work of the Tashelhit Amazigh language that has long played an important role in women's religious education and devotional practice (Boogert 1996, 127–34, 151–64; Rausch 2006, 180–83, 187–88). In the novel, Awzal's titular sea is constituted as a terrestrial body of water formed by women's tears of devotion and the iterative temporality of their collective "bathing" (*MHT* 159) every Friday since childhood. This figurative inland sea enables al-Salima's "plunge" (*MHT* 159) into her deepening relationship with Kima. In another evening of chanting and dancing at Kima's home, al-Salima dives into the movements that unite the dancing women, whose steps and voices respond to the drums and calls of men in the adjoining room. The men's sung poetry melts into liquid forms that sustain Kima and al-Salima's dance as they desire to "dissolve" into the melody and "in the river waters below" (*MHT* 158). When the song ends, al-Salima and Kima embrace, forming their own sea of "copious tears" (*MHT* 158).

Later, al-Salima has the Tashelhit chants translated and discovers that she and Kima subverted a ceremony not unlike her own engagement. The song begins with men singing, "O rose, o Veronica flower," and women responding, "Happy is the one who waters you!" (*MHT* 157; translation modified). Al-Salima ignores the implicit reference in these verses to Hmmu—the one who waters the two flowers—and thinks instead of her relationship with Kima, wondering which flower each would be. Al-Salima and Kima draw new relational potentials from this reservoir of cultural practices.

These proverbs, poems, songs, and devotional literature draw on Morocco's hydrology to articulate political relations between subjects, spouses, tribes, and governors. They give expression to a social order meant to contain disruptions caused by the likes of Hmmu, even as he flouts norms to capitalize on his authority—but that will not be the only cause of Hmmu's downfall.

One More Hydropoetic Form: Debt

Throughout the novel, another liquid logic is infiltrating the Moroccan hydrosocial system. Hmmu's construction projects, military campaigns, and luxury goods are all financed on credit, largely from foreign merchants, who flooded Morocco after an 1856 treaty granted diplomatic protections to foreigners and their agents (Miège 1961, 2:401, 477). Hmmu becomes an investment opportunity for European creditors, to whom he grants access to his territory's natural resources in return for loans. Because Moroccan legal frameworks did not account for the situation of a governor like Hmmu with large, unsecured debts to foreign *protégés* (Moroccan subjects granted legal protections by European governments for whom they served as local agents),

European creditors, merchants, and diplomats took advantage of this lacuna to pressure Morocco into allowing consular courts and mixed commercial courts to decide cases involving *protégés* and Europeans, eroding the legitimacy of Moroccan legal institutions and the Sultan's authority (Laroui 1977, 258–60).

Ultimately, Hmmu contracts a debt he can never repay, in a futile attempt to acquire a Circassian concubine, leading to Kima's death and his own demise. By connecting Hmmu's manipulation of the hydrosocial cycle to debt, the novel's plot foreshadows the fall of the Moroccan state. Morocco's public foreign debt will foreclose its independent political future, conjuring colonization into the precolonial present, just as European travelers had envisioned. European governments claimed oversight of Moroccan state activities by leveraging indemnities, loans, and reform projects, beginning with the indemnity demanded by Spain after the Hispano-Moroccan War (1859–60). Great Britain mediated a loan with London banks that allowed Morocco to make an initial payment, while the rest of the indemnity and the British loan were secured on customs revenues. For the next twenty-five years, foreign agents collected all customs duties, only forwarding revenues to the Moroccan treasury after servicing debt. At the same time, the Suez Canal opened, flooding the Moroccan market with cheap goods, shifting the balance of trade unfavorably, and contributing to the devaluation of Moroccan currency. Successive sultans undertook promising but costly administrative, military, and tax reforms, all hampered by competing interests within Moroccan society and among European powers. Great Britain and France deepened their influence over Morocco by arranging more loans, inspired by the success of such practices in Egypt and Tunisia. The French foreign ministry facilitated several loans in the early 1900s, which justified French oversight of customs revenues and, eventually, a protectorate regime.

HYDROPOETICS OF THE DAM

Imperial capital channels hydropower through the credit extended to the fictional Hmmu and the historical Moroccan state in the same way that it invests in durable infrastructure like railways, electrical grids, and dams. Infrastructure projects drive investment by selling shares in the present based on the speculative value of future profits promised by the material durability of the construction. So too did indebted public and private Moroccan entities promise long-term returns in the colonial future manifested in the debts that would justify foreign seizure of control. Thus, the dam offers a conceptual, poetic, and material figure for thinking this transformation, as well as human interactions with the water cycle more generally (Byrnes 2018, 20–22). Dams modulate and concentrate the flow of terrestrial waters in different states at different moments (Shokr 2009, 11), unfurling a repertory of language, techniques, and effects in relation to different actors and at different scales (Mitchell 2002, 35–39). Dams embody the proximity of an aqueous lexicon of flow, openness, and indeterminacy with capital's language of liquidity, surplus, and scarcity.

The dam has other historical poetics in Arabic literature, too. The Sabaean kingdom in pre-Islamic Yemen maintained a dam for irrigation and flood protection at Ma'rib for more than two thousand years (Nicholson 1907, 14–16). Its collapse caused a mass emigration that is referenced in the Qur'an (34.15–16), poetry, and an erudite poetic expression for scattering, *dhahabū aydī sabā*, "*they went away* in a state of dispersion, *in the ways of Seba*" (Lane 1872, 1287). Eric Calderwood shows that this phrase was current among an educated elite in nineteenth-century Morocco. The historian al-Nasiri used it to evoke the disorder of the Moroccan army in the face of disciplined Spanish troops in 1859–60. Al-Nasiri's reflections combine classical Arabic poetic tropes with a call for reform after the defeat (Calderwood 2012, 404, 408), such that the collapse of a dam—or an army—enables the imagination of a renewed future.

Thinking the dam alongside *Moon and Henna Tree*, however, suggests that reform was infiltrated by flows of European capital that co-opt Moroccan hydrosocial structures. Hydropower flows through the Moroccan state just like the Suez Canal or the Aswan Dam in Egypt, using the language of development to justify new colonial cartographic and engineering perspectives (Derr 2011, 140–46; Mitchell 2002, 81–82) and drive capitalization projects for European financiers (Piquet 2004, 111–12). The durable infrastructure of the Moroccan state, like a canal or dam, provides a channel for debt to manifest a colonial future in a precolonial present (Mitchell 2014, 479–81, 484–85). Bonds of Moroccan debt were floated on Parisian markets, to the profit of the crediting banking consortium and individual investors (Guillen 1973, 150). The financiers of Moroccan loans went on to invest in massive holding companies like Génaroc and Compagnie marocaine, which funded and managed state-private cooperative enterprises like the power company and railroads (Hatton 2009, 258; Saul 2016, 481).

Today, Morocco pursues its own capitalist hydropower, harnessing forces first unleashed by imperialism. European and Middle Eastern investors have pumped hundreds of millions of dollars into Moroccan dams. In agriculture, which employs some 45 percent of the Moroccan labor force but faces a 10–20 percent decrease in water availability due to climate change (Schilling et al. 2012, 14–19), foreign direct investment initiatives like greenhouse farming have stressed groundwater resources beyond sustainable limits (Van Cauwenbergh and Idllalene 2013, 495–99). State-led development of the tourist industry also strains water availability (Tekken et al. 2013, 379–80).

These looming crises of modernity manifest a future that has already been sold off, capitalized in a past debt. Rereading Toufiq's novel in the Anthropocene shows that the temporality of crisis precedes our contemporary moment. Restoring futurity to alienated water logics must consider futures foreclosed in the past, as *Moon and Henna Tree* does in the physical and imaginative depths of Moroccan terrestrial waters, unleashing the currents of past temporalities and the cultural forms that embody them. Standing downstream, before any noncolonial future was sold off in Morocco, the precolonial period emerges, not as a stage of history progressing from the colonial to the postcolonial, but rather as the moment when debt manifested imperial future into the present.

NOTE

1. I am grateful to Brahim El Guabli for his insight into Amazigh language terms.

WORKS CITED

Allen, Nicholas, Nick Groom, and Jos Smith, eds. 2017. *Coastal Works: Cultures of the Atlantic Edge*. Oxford University Press.

Al-Nasiri, Aḥmad ibn Khālid. (1895) 2001. *Kitab al-istiqsa li-akhbar duwal al-maghrib al-aqsa*. 8 vols. Edited by Muhammad Hajji, Ibrahim Bu Talib, and Ahmed Toufiq. Matbaʿat al-Najah al-Jadida.

Blum, Hester. 2015. "Terraqueous Planet: The Case for Oceanic Studies." In *The Planetary Turn: Relationality and Geoaesthetics in the Twenty-First Century*, edited by Amy J. Elias and Christian Moraru. Northwestern University Press.

Boast, Hannah. 2020. *Hydrofictions: Water, Power and Politics in Israeli and Palestinian Literature*. Edinburgh University Press.

Boelhower, William. 2008. "The Rise of the New Atlantic Studies Matrix." *American Literary History* 20 (1–2): 93–101.

Boogert, Nico van den. 1997. *The Berber Literary Tradition of the Sous: With an Edition and Translation of "The Ocean of Tears" by Muhammad Awzal*. Netherlands Institute for the Near East.

Braudel, Fernand. 1966. *La Méditerranée et le monde méditerranéen à l'époque de Philippe II*. Vol. 1. 2nd ed. A. Colin.

Bürgel, J. C. 1989. "The Lady Gazelle and Her Murderous Glances." *Journal of Arabic Literature* 20 (1): 1–11.

Burke, Edmund. 1976. *Prelude to Protectorate in Morocco: Precolonial Protest and Resistance, 1860–1912*. University of Chicago Press.

Byrnes, Corey. 2018. *Fixing Landscape: A Techno-Poetic History of China's Three Gorges*. Columbia University Press.

Bystrom, Kerry, and Isabel Hofmeyr. 2017. "Oceanic Routes: (Post-It) Notes on Hydro-Colonialism." *Comparative Literature* 69 (1): 1–6.

Calderwood, Eric. 2012. "The Beginning (or End) of Moroccan History: Historiography, Translation, and Modernity in Ahmad b. Khalid al-Nasiri and Clemente Cerdeira." *International Journal of Middle East Studies* 44 (3): 399–420.

Cavanaugh, Jillian R., and Shalini Shankar, eds. 2017. *Language and Materiality: Ethnographic and Theoretical Explorations*. Cambridge University Press.

Cohen, Margaret. 2010. "Literary Studies on the Terraqueous Globe." *PMLA* 125 (3): 657–62.

Da Cunha, Dilip. 2019. *The Invention of Rivers: Alexander's Eye and Ganga's Descent*. University of Pennsylvania Press.

Davis, Diana K. 2007. *Resurrecting the Granary of Rome: Environmental History and French Colonial Expansion in North Africa*. Ohio University Press.

Davis, Diana K. 2016. *The Arid Lands: History, Power, Knowledge*. 2016. MIT Press.

Derr, Jennifer L. 2011. "Drafting a Map of Colonial Egypt: The 1902 Aswan Dam, Historical Imagination, and the Production of Agricultural Geography." In *Environmental Imaginaries of the Middle East and North Africa*, edited by Diana K. Davis and Edmund Burke. Ohio University Press.

Foucauld, Charles de. 1888 *Reconnaissance au Maroc, 1883–1884*. Challamel.
Freed-Thall, Hannah, and Morgane Cadieu, eds. 2021. "Beaches and Ports," special issue of *Comparative Literature* 73 (2).
Gillis, John R. 2012. *The Human Shore: Seacoasts in History*. University of Chicago Press.
Guillen, Pierre. 1973. *Les emprunts marocains, 1902–1904*. Richelieu.
Hatton, Georges. 2009. *Les enjeux financiers et économiques du Protectorat marocain (1936–1956): Politique publique et investisseurs privés*. Société française d'Histoire d'outre-mer.
Henry, Matthew S. 2022. *Hydronarratives: Water, Environmental Justice, and a Just Transition*. University of Nebraska Press.
Hoffman, Katherine E. 2007. *We Share Walls: Language, Land, and Gender in Berber Morocco*. Blackwell.
Hofmeyr, Isabel. 2019a. "Literary Ecologies of the Indian Ocean." *English Studies in Africa* 62 (1): 1–7.
Hofmeyr, Isabel. 2019b. "Provisional Notes on Hydrocolonialism." *English Language Notes* 57 (1): 11–20.
Hofmeyr, Isabel. 2020. "Imperialism Above and Below the Water Line: Making Space Up (and Down) in a Colonial Port City." *Interventions* 22 (8): 1032–44.
Horden, Peregrine, and Nicholas Purcell. 2000. *The Corrupting Sea: A Study of Mediterranean History*. Blackwell.
Lane, Edward William. 1872. *Arabic-English Lexicon*. Vol. 1. Williams and Norgate.
Laroui, Abdallah. 1977. *Les Origines sociales et culturelles du nationalisme marocain (1830–1912)*. François Maspéro.
Lévi-Provençal, Evariste. 1922. *Les historiens des Chorfa: Essai sur la littérature historique et biographique au Maroc du XVIe au XXe siècle*. Emile Larose.
Linton, Jamie, and Jessica Budds. 2014. "The Hydrosocial Cycle: Defining and Mobilizing a Relational-Dialectical Approach to Water." *Geoforum*, no. 57, 170–80.
Mathur, Anuradha, and Dilip da Cunha. 2001. *Mississippi Floods: Designing a Shifting Landscape*. Yale University Press.
Mathur, Anuradha, and Dilip da Cunha. 2009. *Soak: Mumbai in an Estuary*. Rupa and Co.
Mathur, Anuradha, and Dilip da Cunha. 2020. "Wetness Is Everywhere. Why Do We See Water Somewhere?" *Journal of Architectural Education* 74 (1): 139–40.
Meakin, Budgett. 1901. *The Land of the Moors: A Comprehensive Description*. Swan Sonnenschein.
Miège, Jean-Louis. 1961. *Le Maroc et l'Europe*. 4 vols. Presses universitaires de France.
Miller, Susan Gilson. 2013. *A History of Modern Morocco*. Cambridge University Press.

Mitchell, Timothy. 2002. *Rule of Experts: Egypt, Techno-Politics, Modernity.* University of California Press.
Mitchell, Timothy. 2014. "Economentality: How the Future Entered Government." *Critical Inquiry* 40 (4): 479–507.
Nicholson, Reynold Alleyne. 1907. *A Literary History of the Arabs.* T. Fisher Unwin.
Nuttall, Sarah. 2020. "Pluvial Time / Wet Form." *New Literary History,* no. 51, 455–72.
Nuttall, Sarah. 2021. "The Time Sea." *Wasafiri* 36 (2): 13–21.
Pascon, Paul. 1986. *Capitalism and Agriculture in the Haouz of Marrakesh.* Edited by John R. Hall. Translated by Edwin Vaughan and Véronique Ingman. KPI.
Peters, Rosemary A. 2009 "Mapping the Desert: Arthur Rimbaud, Charles de Foucauld, and the Société de Géographie, 1884–85." *Journal of Historical Geography,* no. 35, 104–27.
Piquet, Caroline. 2004. "The Suez Company's Concession in Egypt, 1854–1956: Modern Infrastructure and Local Economic Development." *Enterprise and Society* 5 (1): 107–27.
Pritchard, Sara B. 2012. "From Hydroimperialism to Hydrocapitalism: 'French' Hydraulics in France, North Africa, and Beyond." *Social Studies of Science* 42 (4): 591–615.
Rausch, Margaret. 2006. "Ishelhin Women Transmitters of Islamic Knowledge and Culture in Southwestern Morocco." *Journal of North African Studies* 11 (2): 173–92.
Ravindranathan, Thangam. 2019. "The Rise of the Sea and the Novel." *Differences* 50 (5): 1–33.
Saul, Samir. 2016. *Intérêts économiques français et décolonisation de l'Afrique du Nord (1945–1962).* Geneva: Droz.
Schilling, Janpeter, Freier P. Korbinian, Elke Hertig, and Jürgen Scheffran. 2012. "Climate Change, Vulnerability and Adaptation in North Africa with Focus on Morocco." *Agriculture, Ecosystems and Environment,* no. 156, 12–26.
Shokr, Ahmad. 2009. "Hydropolitics, Economy, and the Aswan High Dam in Mid-Century Egypt." *Arab Studies Journal* 17 (1): 9–31.
Swyngedouw, Erik. 2009. "The Political Economy and Political Ecology of the Hydro-Social Cycle." *Journal of Contemporary Water Research and Education,* no. 142, 56–60.
Talbayev, Edwige Tamalet. 2018. "Afterward: Critical Mediterranean Times." In *Critically Mediterranean: Temporalities, Aesthetics, and Deployments of a Sea in Crisis,* edited by yasser elhariry and Edwige Tamalet Talbayev. Palgrave Macmillan.
Talbayev, Edwige Tamalet. 2023. "Hydropower: Residual Dwelling Between Life and Nonlife." *Angelaki* 28 (1): 9–21.

Toufiq, Ahmed [Ahmad al-Tawfiq]. 1983. *Al-Mujtamaʿ al-maghribi fi al-qarn al-tasi ʿashar (Inulatan, 1850–1912)*. Kulliyat al-Adab wa-l-ʿUlum al-Insaniyya.

Toufiq, Ahmed [Ahmad al-Tawfiq]. 1998. *Shujayrat hinna wa-qamar*. Dar al-Qubba al-Zarqaʾ li-l-Nashr wa-l-Khadamat al-Thaqafiyya.

Toufiq, Ahmed [Ahmad al-Tawfiq]. 2013. *Moon and Henna Tree*. Translated by Roger Allen. Center for Middle Eastern Studies at The University of Texas at Austin.

Tekken, Vera, Luis Costa, and Juergen P. Kropp. 2013. "Increasing Pressure, Declining Water and Climate Change in North-Eastern Morocco." *Journal of Coastal Conservation*, no. 17, 379–88.

Van Cauwenbergh, Nora, and Samira Idllalene. 2013. "Tapping into Al-Andaluz Resources: Opportunities and Challenges for Investment in Morocco." In *Handbook of Land and Water Grabs in Africa: Foreign Direct Investment and Food and Water Security*, edited by Tony Allan, Martin Keulertz, Suvi Sojamo, and Jeroen Warner. Routledge.

TOWARDS A ROMANTIC HYDROCOMMONS

—

Victor Hugo, Humanity, and Hydrology
BRADLEY STEPHENS

John Keats is not the only Romantic poet whose epitaph might proclaim a name that is "writ in water."[1] As European modernity quickened its pace in the late eighteenth and nineteenth centuries, water's elemental force offered an auspicious and deeply symbolic means of engaging with the free flow of natural creation, of time and history, and of human consciousness. Immanuel Kant's topography of the sublime in 1790 as "the boundless ocean set into a rage [and] a lofty waterfall on a mighty river" (2000, 144) marked a wellspring for the Romantic exaltation of nature. The world's overwhelming vitality was to be channeled so as to break through the neoclassical levees of stylized magnificence and to free up more extemporaneous modes of self-awareness and self-expression. The Roman poet Horace's description of Pindar's lyricism as "a mountain stream, swollen with snowmelt, a turbulent cataract roaring along" (2014, 157) anticipated how Romanticism would conceive of artistic creation as what William Wordsworth famously called "the spontaneous overflow of powerful feelings" in his 1800 preface to *Lyrical Ballads* (Wordsworth and Coleridge 2005, 291). Such excess depended on the individual opening themselves up to nature's sublime wonders. A heightened state of astonishment would result, allowing for a less cerebral, more palpable awareness of reality, as Edmund Burke had concluded over four decades earlier (1998, 53) and as Jean-Jacques Rousseau had intimated in the late 1770s when he cast off burdensome reflections by walking around, and floating atop, Lake Bienne (2011, 49–58). The line "water, water everywhere" from Samuel Taylor Coleridge's 1798 "Rime of the Ancient Mariner" (Wordsworth and Coleridge 2005, 56) could serve as a fitting subtitle to any Romantic anthology, whether national or continental.

Water's widespread Romantic appeal as the universal solvent tends to be qualified in terms of its metaphoricity "as a primarily natural structure with which to represent a worldview that reconciles the user to mutability," and which "embodies a faith in continuity or permanence-in-change" (Farnsworth 2001, 14). Its allegorical capacity is often located at its most celebrated sites, such as Wordsworth's Lake District, Alphonse de Lamartine's Lac du Bourget, and Friedrich Hölderlin's Danube. Martin Heidegger's 1942 readings of the latter, however, point to how water might be thought of as a less ornate and less localized feature of Romantic production. The river's indomitable flow reconnects humankind to its shared prodigious imminence with the material world, and furnished Heidegger with another opportunity to use Hölderlin "as a kind of 'mouthpiece' (*Sprachrohr*) for a new and radical form of thinking, a poetic-philosophical attempt to devise a language that would be able to 'turn back,' 'get over,' or 'recover from' (*verwinden*) the language of Western metaphysics" (Bambach 2017, 40). Instead of the abstractions and totalizations of being that Heidegger warns against, Hölderlin's river resists emblematic or reflective meaning. It leaves the reader to reckon with their own incalculable immediacy, even if Heidegger's lectures reveal "a political vision that often undermines this Hölderlinian openness" and the poet's drive towards alterity (Bambach 2017, 57). In this encounter with water, the humanist mind-body dualism gives way to a more fundamental interrelationship between cognizance and materiality, and between self and other.

When made to resonate through this phenomenological tenor, the Romantic dialogue with water speaks to the twenty-first century's discourses of posthumanism and ecocriticism in ways that have yet to be fully registered or articulated. The human exceptionalism of modern history's anthropocentric slant has ultimately spurred geopolitical crises and accelerated climate change, amplifying the need to rethink how we interact with one another and with our environment. Since the 1990s, the New Materialist defiance of individualist metaphysics has come to understand all phenomena through what Karen Barad terms an "agential realism." This theory of knowing and being at once cuts apart and cuts together the somatic and the discursive by conceiving of agency as relational rather than individualistic: "as an enactment, not something that someone or something has" (Barad 2007, 235). Because the human and the nonhuman are always already entangled with one another, "we don't obtain knowledge by standing outside the world; we know because we are of the world. We are part of the world in its differential becoming" (185). This "intra-action" that posthuman thought foregrounds in human knowledge and behavior dispenses a relatively fresh paradigm in which to analyze the creative and concrete power that water holds for the Romantic imagination. "If it is true," writes Donna Haraway, "that neither biology nor philosophy any longer supports the notion of independent organisms in environments, that is, interacting units plus contexts/rules, then sympoiesis is the name of the game in spades. . . . Barad's agential realism and intra-action become common sense" (2016, 33). This "intra-action" lends new depths to Romantic thinking, the vigor of which remains too easily siphoned into reservoirs of clichés about individual genius, nostalgic sentimentalism, and patriarchal certainty. Over the past decade, a number of those truisms have been questioned by Kate Rigby and other ecocritics who have re-evaluated the "bio-inclusive" and decolonizing potential of Romanticism "for its probing of the category of the human, and of humankind's relations with otherkinds and our shared earthly environs" (Rigby 2020, 11). Since "aesthetics can become a decisive force for or against environmental change" (Buell 1995, 3), Romanticism promisingly extends key lines of current enquiry in posthuman and ecocritical thinking by providing less hierarchical and more generous figurations of being.

As I argue in this chapter, a Romantic poetics of water—in its espousal of materiality and circulation rather than just form and flux—can energize the epistemological, ontological, and ethical objectives of the posthuman critical turn. An especially illustrative and compelling example from French literature models how the Romantic fascination with water can itself be divulged and intensified by the confluence between the human and nonhuman. The need for the environmental humanities to step beyond the Anglo-American corpuses analyzed by Rigby and to develop a more transnational (and multilingual) stance has been reiterated by numerous recent studies, including biocultural analyses of watercourses in African American memory (Wardi

2011), of Pacific Oceanic writing (Shewry 2015), and of rivers in Latin American literature (Murphy and Rivero 2018). French ecocriticism has accordingly diversified its historical, geographical, and theoretical range (Finch-Race and Posthumus 2017, 9–13), and French Romanticism has no shortage of possible cases to survey, whether they pertain to François-René de Chateaubriand's (1964) elegiac musings on the waterways of North America in 1791, Charles Baudelaire's mid-century pairing of man and the sea as "implacable brothers" (1993, 33), or Marceline Desbordes-Valmore's embrace of the closeness between the poetic subject and water (1860, 21–23).

Notwithstanding the rich possibilities carried by such affluents into the mass of European Romantic writing and art, it is the largest crest of French Romanticism's second wave that will be the focus of my analysis. The writer and statesman Victor Hugo has already been recognized for the "proto-environmentalism" of his poetry and fiction (Quandt 2017, 78), but Hugo's work suggests that his ecosensibility towards nature and horticulture owed more to a curiosity in the life-giving powers of water than has previously been highlighted. He was beguiled by Earth's "terrestrial gestation," believing it to be "an alembic distilling forests, rivers, the Blue Nile Falls, the Rhine Falls, glaciers, roses, rubies, deserts of sand and snow, steppes, savannas, prairies, lakes, and streams" (1904–52, 10:317–23). This "centric vitality" made water synonymous with life, from extensive natural and agricultural growth to the microorganisms of marine foraminifera and freshwater infusoria (1904–52, 10:360–62).[2] In his narrative digression on the Parisian sewage system in his magnum opus, *Les Misérables* (1862), he therefore concluded that the city needed a new two-channel arrangement with adequate drainage to maximize the water cycle's benefits for public health and agriculture (2008, 1030–45).

Water's essential role in making life possible gives it both sublimity and substance as at once a literary trope and an intrinsic element. More than a metaphor in Hugo's eyes, it became a hermeneutic tool for understanding how human beings are congruent with the world entire. Water's transient properties and permeation with all living things revealed to Hugo a universal condition of being that is both endlessly evanescent and fundamentally nebulous. Its representative potential cannot be pulled away from its environmental power, since its materiality is integral to a protean world and, by extension, to all human activity within that same sphere. Hugo felt himself to be part of this natural vibrancy rather than just a conduit for it as a poet, and he resisted the discrete classification of human and nonhuman that would imagine humankind as being extractable from (and superior to) the world in which it lived. His work can therefore be characterized by what Georges Piroué has hinted is the writer's empathetic rather than just sympathetic relationship to nature (1968, xxii), which problematizes reductive notions of Romantic individualism and its typically gendered differentiations between subjectivity and objectivity. Since water is both dilutable and diluting, transformative and tenacious, the agency it energizes is qualified as porous and absorbent rather than self-contained. Such an interrelationship likewise recalls Lowell Duckert's method of "hydrography" (2017): textual modalities of the human and nonhuman in early modern travel writing and literature that broke down ideas of singularity and human sovereignty through the writers' physical encounters with bodies of water. By qualifying Hugo's attraction to water and then tracing both its instrumental and interventional presence in a necessarily select sample of his critical writing, poetry, and fiction, my argument rethinks the assemblages of human and indeed gendered identity that appear within his work.

The Canadian feminist Astrida Neimanis's posthuman phenomenology and her idea of a "hydrocommons" help to conceptualize the transformative power of Hugo's empathetic relationship to water and its implications for his colossal oeuvre's predictable (if not lazy) association with patriarchal autonomy. Neimanis departs from metaphorical uses of water, such as Zygmunt Bauman's characterization of modernity as "liquid," and instead she advocates a more tangible affiliation with liquidity. Such a link connects to the multivalent cycles of water that bind life on Earth together. These are the circulations in which water is distributed, absorbed, and flushed on a planet whose surface alone is around 71 percent water, in addition to the specific kinds of bodies that water comprises, transforms, and dissolves (including the human body, which in its adult form is comprised of around 60 percent water). This constant redistribution is defined by Neimanis as "an always emergent planetary hydrocommons" (2017, 39). The continuum that the water cycle enacts between organic and environmental waters reveals a kinship between biotic and abiotic bodies, between the biological and the physical, whether it be the journey of bodily urine through wastewater discharges or dissipating sweat within a humid climate (2017, 55). Neimanis insists that "our bodies of water are neither stagnant, nor separate, nor zipped up in some kind of impermeable sac of skin. These bodies are rather deeply imbricated in the intricate movements of water that create and sustain life on our planet" (2017, 65). These traversals are diverse in their movements and so cannot be reduced to fluidity or flow alone. They also take myriad forms and interrelated guises: bodily spinal fluid, the succulent fruit on the vine, the early-morning frost atop a lawn, and so on.

In its expression of commonality among difference, this hydrocommons promotes an embodied ethics of coexistence that feminists like Barad and Haraway have espoused as a challenge to the patriarchal credo of itemization, exchange, purchase, and possession. Being cannot be bound within self-sufficient sovereign bodies and flattened states, since it is a dynamic and generative condition, as underlined by Neimanis's references to Maurice Merleau-Ponty's phenomenology of the human body as something we inescapably are rather than something we own. The shared aqueous corporeality of Earth's vast ecosystem disputes any restrictive conception of embodiment, and "water, as that which interpermeates and connects beings, might [therefore] teach us something about an expanded understanding of the ontological" (2017, 97). Neimanis substantiates the ethical import of this hydrocommons by utilizing Luce Irigaray's psychoanalytic critique of how the female body's ebb and flow prompts a male anxiety about self-loss, and how masculinist systems of language and logic favor solidity over liquidity, as well as unity over plurality. As Irigaray notes, a specular economy of representation reduces any play of meaning and phallically requires man to "erect himself [and his world] as a solid entity out of an undifferentiated subjectum" (2002, 233). The absolutism of the masculine *logos* can be thwarted by the fluidity of the female body, in both the literal sense as a menstruating form and in the figurative sense as man's other. Neimanis therefore extends what Irigaray presented as a "mechanics of fluids" to her own departure from the ontological hierarchies of human and nonhuman and to her call for "proxy stories" from the creative economy of art. These narrative encounters activate and augment "the lived experience of water as undertow, as stronger than my own measly self" (Neimanis 2017, 55–56), especially in light of Jamie Linton's argument that society cannot continue to think of water abstractly as a simple resource when the "hydrological colonial present" has dragged the planet into an ecological emergency (2010, 72). Such stories deploy what Haraway labels "material-semiotic actors": figures that enact rather than just represent or elucidate different relationships between human and nonhuman ways of being. Neimanis cites video installations as one example, but the objective of taking an audience beyond "the usual spatio-temporal proximities" to decenter the human is open to other media as well, including the written word.

To borrow the terminology that Neimanis takes from Irigaray, Hugo's work stands as an interface with a world that it experiences in "gestational" rather than perfectible terms, as a space of constant becoming rather than consummate or perennial being. It would be tempting to take Gaston Bachelard's well-known 1942 essay *Water and Dreams* as a complementary theoretical approach towards the deliquescence of Hugo's work, and certainly there are parallels to draw between Bachelard's material imagination and Hugo's insistence on poetry capturing "all that is intimate in everything" (1904–52, 24:5).[3] Bachelard's essay is, however, prone to patriarchal undercurrents since water conspicuously risks being subjugated to a reasoned masculine knowledge rather than utilized for "the deconstructive potential of a seductive, fluid, and unmasterable feminine force" (O'Shea-Meddour 2003, 81). A more constructive integration of Hugo's Romanticism with Neimanis's hydrocommons comes from Theodor Schwenk's anthroposophical studies of water. Schwenk was indebted to Rudolf Steiner, whose own anthroposophy formed part of a nineteenth-century esotericism in which Hugo himself would not be out of place. Schwenk was also interested in the German Romantic Novalis, who spoke of nature stirring "those primaeval waters in us" and of the world having been shaped in an embryo of "primal fluidity" (2005, 103–5). Schwenk argues for water's eminence in resisting the binary of human and nonhuman, since "every organ in the human organism is originally born of water: the forms of the joints, of the limbs with their convoluted bones, of heart and blood vessels, of ears, brain and sense-organs—the forms, in short, of all the functional systems" (1989, 153). His argument corroborates Neimanis's stipulation that humanity must expand its comprehension of what it means to be. By perceiving water as the planet's essential "sense organ," Schwenk demands that human knowledge engage with organic relationships of an enlarged order beyond anthropocentric hierarchies of being so as to preserve the planet and to emulsify the elemental with the sociocultural.

Such a hydrocommons, in which the phenomena of water and humankind are synchronous, allows Hugo's hydrological sensibility to be understood more ambitiously than before, given that scholarship on water's importance to him has yet to probe this subject as deeply as possible. This oversight is on the one hand the result of assumptions about Romanticism's supposedly unified sense of self, as typified by Rodney Farnsworth's portrayal of the water-cycle metaphor as a "coping mechanism" for a Romantic voice whose integrity is besieged by sweeping industrial, political, and spiritual change (2001, 325). On the other, it is due to the ultimately limited topographical moniker of the "ocean man" or *homme océan* that Hugo coined to describe genius and that has often mapped and demarcated his oeuvre as a result, such as for the Bibliothèque nationale de France's exhibition for the 2002 bicentenary of his birth. Yet water for Hugo fashions what M. H. Abrams described as "a complex subjective event" in his influential reading of wind as both metaphorical inspiration and literal respiration or breath in English Romantic poetry (1957, 113). The Romantic iconography of rivers confirms that bodies of water can be more than a stand-in for something else. Wordsworth's *Prelude*, for example, evidenced a psychology in which sensation cannot be separated from reflection, and water's mutability suggests "the substantial character of thought" (MacLean 1948, 388). Similarly, the river in Goethe's *Song for Mohammed* can be read as "a visible expression of nature's laws and forces" with the verse taking on its "free-flowing rhythms and associative rush of images" (Jolle 2004, 434). "The problems of ontology, being, and becoming [are] palpably rendered" so as to deliver "a measure of self-knowledge otherwise inaccessible" (Colwell 1989, 4–5), although this epistemology need not be confined to Romantic rivers or to the seas they feed. In Hugo's work, water in all its guises allows the poetic self to disperse and more knowingly integrate with the surrounding world. That world in turn becomes less of an object to behold than a condition to be actuated, even if the Romantic ideal of "a controlled violence, a self-ordering impetus of passion" (Abrams 1957, 129) does not automatically prove more desirable for Hugo than the less marshaled reality that water reveals.

In a series of essays he wrote in the early 1860s (some of which form part of an abandoned preface for *Les Misérables*), Hugo advocated for a freer, more passionate appreciation of reality than either dogmatic faith or scientific knowledge alone could provide. Humankind could not simply be cast within some archaic religious script or anchored by the patterns of biological and sociological behavior that were becoming increasingly prevalent in the wake of the Enlightenment. In effect, "man wants to be running water. What a wonderful thing it is that freedom is our very constitution. Streaming, thrumming, dipping, coursing, leading, knowing—there is no life without that" (1904–52, 35:615).[4] In this heaving statement, Hugo argued that the transitory character of water was the condition for all existence, as demonstrated by nature's manifold cycles, which themselves could never be distilled into refined and permanently objectified forms. All life was never-ending creation: creation on tap, forever forming and dissolving in what he saw as a "dizzying regeneration" or "multiplication vertigineuse" (1904–52, 10:346).

Hugo's statement is telling in two overlooked respects, each of which brings belated nuance to the much-cited image of the homme océan. The lack of simile makes his observation dependent not on a comparison between human life and water or on a desire to be like water, but on an irresistible instinct to *be* water. Just as water is autotelic and manifests its own freedom of movement, so too does humanity embody an indeterminacy of being. Freedom is not presented in abstract terms but instead as a physical condition: as *santé*, which can also be translated in English as "bodily aptitude" or "state of health." The human and the hydrological are interchangeable rather than discontinuous since they are both part of a limitless—and thus immeasurable—cycle of creation. Together, they establish a physical basis for humankind's status as a part of the natural world, amalgamating proclivity, corporeality, and milieu in a typically Romantic conviction. It is that belief which obliges the symbolic activities of literature to do more with a natural element like water than extol it as an archetypal image or constrain it within a particular space.

The second noteworthy aspect of Hugo's declaration that *l'homme veut être eau courante* ("man wants to be running water") is his choice of nouns. Unlike the distinct, if enormous, body of the ocean, water is not localized. It is universal rather than particular; everywhere rather than just somewhere. The French feminine noun *eau* feminizes the phrase's masculine subject and lubricates the slippage between their supposed difference. The incongruous moniker of "ocean man" is consequently not as totalizing or patriarchal an appellative as its masculine pairing at first suggests. Homme océan is Hugo's most indelible condensed metaphor, characteristically taking two nouns that are not usually paired, so that they may modify one another's meaning, and the epithet's assonance in French allows for a melodic memorability in his formulation of the idea in his 1864 essay on William Shakespeare. "There are indeed ocean men," he wrote as he looked out upon the English Channel during his second decade of exile in the Channel Islands from Napoleon III's imperial regime: "These waves, this flux and reflux, this terrible coming and going, the noise of all this wind, these darknesses and these transparencies . . . this infinite, this unfathomable, all of it can be in a mind—and this mind calls itself genius" (1904–52, 35:5).[5] He focused on Shakespeare and predecessors like Aeschylus and Dante who all moved with the universe's infinite ebb and flow without bringing it to rest, thus evoking the despair and the delight of a fathomless existence. Encountering their work was akin to confronting the ocean itself, in which thoughts peak and trough, swell and dissolve. This maritime signature follows the same rationale of liberation that Hugo used for his poetics, which is why the commonplace protagonists of his fiction and theatre (both male and female) could demonstrate its verve in their actions. The dynasty of genius he inaugurated is conspicuously lacking in women and betrays how easily Hugo could gravitate towards idealized gender differences and essentialism, but as I have argued elsewhere, "[his] own poiesis calls for a less presumptuous, more conceptual scrutiny of gender in his thinking" (Stephens 2019, 4), not least given his admiration for female peers like George Sand. The homme océan is a deceptively subversive aspiration when contextualized in this way, compounding a new identity of indistinct fluidity and discrete flesh that is at once unconventional and unrestrained. Such context further teases out the effect of the unusual plurals for darkness and transparency, which disclose his typical penchant for pluralizing rather than solidifying the singular.

The importance of nonthalassic water for Hugo's poetics must therefore not be overlooked, and his own travels point to how water's dissolving and deontologizing effects within his work warrant more sustained attention than the sea alone. Readers such as Piroué (1968) and Marie Blain-Pinel (2003) subscribe to the conventional view that Hugo's more profound deliberations about water surface when he comes into contact with seawater in the mid-1830s and recognizes a symbol for allegorizing an amorphous universe. The first eighteen months of his life had been spent on his father's military postings in Marseille, Corsica, and Elba, and he had also enjoyed a brief stay in Bayonne close to the Atlantic coast before he was ten, but it was not until his holiday in Brittany with his mistress Juliette Drouet in 1834 that the adult Hugo laid eyes on the sea. Subsequent vacations with Juliette in Brittany, Normandy, and back to the Bay of Biscay acquainted him with the Atlantic and the English Channel before his exile in Jersey and Guernsey, while their later trips to Belgium also introduced him to the North Sea. But Hugo also spent much of his childhood in Paris, where the River Seine imprinted itself upon his imagination, and his inland vacations were not spent solely treading across hardened surfaces either. His annual family holidays from the late

1820s to the late 1830s took him to Louis-François Bertin's estate Le Château des Roches, where the River Bièvre flows into the Seine. Travels through the Alps in 1825 and the late 1830s as part of his Rhineland expeditions, as well as his vacation to the Pyrenees in the early 1840s, all included visits to mountainous lakes and spas in addition to the mighty Rhône and Rhine rivers, bringing moments of personal and professional restoration.

The hydrology of Hugo's work hence invites the kind of reach associated with the sea's open horizons but exceeds even those vistas. His teenage idol Chateaubriand's rhythmic prose and travelogues loom over his 1826 preface to *Odes and Ballads*, in which he promoted artistic freedom by juxtaposing the symmetrical order of the Gardens at Versailles with the self-directing order of a New World forest. The world's natural condition was one of spontaneity and diversity, not neoclassicism's regularity and uniformity. The comparison of Versailles's petrified statues and transplanted trees with the forest's free spirit and unspoiled habitat was essential to the Romantic notions of art as unbridled creativity, and he specifically contrasted "the captive or languishing waters" of the Versailles fountains with the forest's great rivers and huge waterfalls (1904–52, 24:25).[6] In spite of being recounted secondhand, North America's natural waterways were essential to making this argument for democratized literature. One year later, in his influential preface to *Cromwell* (1827), Hugo committed himself to the egalitarian aesthetics of Romantic drama by comparing history to three different bodies of water, in a generalized model similar to Lucretius's three-age approach. The primitive, antique, and modern eras were likened to a lake, river, and ocean respectively to reflect their lyrical, epic, and dramatic modes (1904–52, 23:22–23). Later references underscore the continuity between these water formations. In 1846, Hugo likened the ever-growing dimensions of his body of work to an oceanic swirl—"a build-up of drifting works into which my mind throws itself without knowing if it will re-emerge" (1972, 1:368)[7]—and he considered whether "ocean" would be appropriate as its title. The totalizing drive that this choice of word betrays is disrupted, however, by a striking parallel in his recollection of the Rhine Falls four years earlier: "Ideas and images haphazardly build up together ... I have the Rhine Falls inside my head" (1904–52, 4:397).[8] This similar impression of marvel confirms that his mind's ability to liquefy and disband did not rely on seascapes alone and found itself instinctively pulled towards movement rather than delimitation. The "immense horizon" of 1846 and its heap of ideas can be foreseen in the "immense ferment" and confused pile-up of thoughts he senses at the Rheinfall.

It follows that Hugo was interested not simply in the aquatic, as that which relates to water, but also in the aqueous, that which is itself watery. This distinction draws attention to the Romantic blending of the metaphorical with the literal, as emphasized by two poems from *Autumn Leaves* (1831). In "Reverie's Slope," he recounts how his mind slides from the imminent conscious world to an immaterial, unconscious plane as he gazes out from his window on a luminous spring day following a rainstorm. All of Paris begins to float before his eyes, and human faces blend into an indistinguishable mass, like a stream merging into a lake. The explicit naming of the Seine implies that it is the river that takes him into "the double sea of time and space" (1904–52, 17:86).[9] An earlier poem confirms this proximity he sensed between his own being and water. The Ovidian citation at the start ("causa tangor ab omni," or "am touched by everything") marks what follows as evidence of the poet's recognition of a shared but initially imperceptible motion with the mountain glacier before him.[10] Written in the present tense to lend immediacy to what in reality is a prolonged transformation, the poem hails the process through which the poet's imagination merges with water's proliferation into a new understanding of being. The poetic subject metamorphoses into droplets of dew lifting towards the skies, where it wanders with the clouds and regains density as snow before compacting into a glacier and being sent on its way once more by the sun's heat:

> Often, when my richly metamorphic mind
> Slumbers and floats across the ocean of things,
> God . . . strikes it with a beam and, like a drop of dew,
> Gathers it up and carries it to the skies.
> My lofty poetry, become an errant cloud,
> Waywardly flies with no clear path . . .
> And is finally broken by a jealous wind atop the Alpine snow
> Of an old mountain, a grey-haired colossus . . .
> It falls cascading back into the world's ocean . . .
> My thoughts thereby obey a divine breath,
> Forever propelled in an eternal circle. (1904–52, 17:30)[11]

Through the poem's irregular caesuras, its rolling internal rhymes, and its drifting assonance, an affinity is established between the text's composition and the water cycle's displacing, distributive effects. The poet presents neither the glacier nor his own sense of self as spatially or physically centered.

The visualization of the melting glacier being hollowed out into an empty crater at the poem's midpoint opens up a productive void at the heart of this transformation. Dematerialization becomes constitutive of being and dependent on successive contact with natural stimuli, from the burning sun and the brisk night to the windbreaks of the mountaintops.

Through its rehabilitative processes of evaporation, condensation, precipitation, collection, and flow, the hydrological cycle's unremitting loop tirelessly primes and propels the poet's consciousness, as it does life itself. Crucially, the material world yields its zest through such imbrications. Sliding into reverie and accessing a vision of life that could see beyond the limitations of mortality, Hugo saw the peripatetic and the buoyant in all things: "In everything there is drift and glide. Form, billowing, is unbound and infused with sense" (1904–52, 35:302).[12] His poetic vision or *voyance* mimics time-lapse photography in these poems, by which processes that are usually too subtle for the human eye become prominent. Remembering a visit to the Paris Observatory in 1834, Hugo elsewhere chronicled how the moon's mountains became granite waves and the lunar surface spilled into a rolling tide, since these landscapes were not unchanging when seen across the infinite expanse of time (297–302).

A notable consequence of this vantage point was that humankind was wrong to believe that it could definitively master the world or center itself as the source of all knowledge, since it could only ever be subject to natural force. Subjectivity is sustained but humbled. "Each of us holds the drop of water, but no one holds the ocean entire" (1904–52, 10:394),[13] giving rise to Hugo's questioning of the many personifications of nature's divine dominion in man's own recognizable image:

> This theatre in which the wind blows against the receding
>   downpours,
> This is what a single atom of rain has put together.
> So what need do you have of a Vishnu, an Allah,
> a Buddha, a horned Amun, to comprehend it all?
> Why withdraw from the circle in which the real closes in on you?
> What good comes from dethroning the elemental and the
>   embryonic? (1904–52, 21:367)[14]

Welcoming this commonality with all life—and realizing that solidarity did not mean solidity—was essential to a prosperous future, so Hugo intuitively turned to ways of thinking and behaving that were looser and less figurative than a methodical mindset would allow for. His work's mélange of genres insists in its stylistic mix on the interchangeability of opposites like the sublime and the grotesque, themselves as intimately connected as day and night. This holistic view of existence slipped through the tight grip of categorical thinking, in which everything has a firm outline and permanent anchor, and it exhibited an insurmountable moral force in its ability to disestablish forms and types: "That which to us is bronze or granite ultimately throngs, dissolves, and floats away. Is the shark a despot . . . is the monster an actual monster? We do not know for certain" (1904–52, 11:559).[15] In sociopolitical terms, this intrinsically fluid order required the liberties enshrined in the democratic ideals of the French Revolution, lest daily reality would stagnate and putrefy. As a result, humankind needed freedom of expression, along with a social equality based on the shared responsibilities of inclusive rather than divisive politics.

Hugo's most famous novel throws this Romantic hydrocommons into sharper relief by exemplifying its associated range of formal properties and thematic concerns. The "laws of constructive decomposition" that Victor Brombert identifies in *Les Misérables* become more emphatic when understood with regard to Hugo's intra-action with water. The novel's swelling prose cascades and retracts as it flows from a variable universe in which "disintegration is part of the dynamic process of transformation" (Brombert 1984, 93–94), as is most apparent in the notorious digressions: his drifting asides on a miscellany of subjects such as the inventiveness of Parisian slang and the history of convents, which each collapse any neat distinction between the narrative's main arcs and its many margins, and between the focalizing processes of contraction and dilation. Similarly, the novel uses a fluid symbolism to evoke the rush of human history, such as the river of Parisians spilling outwards in the early moments of the June 1832 insurrection (Hugo 2008, 931–32). But water's material impacts on this sociohistorical odyssey cannot be flushed from these readings, as Brombert's perceptive argument implies (but does not fully develop) when he discusses the digression on the Battle of Waterloo. Brombert notes the importance of water imagery to Hugo's descriptions of an undulating landscape and of how the battle itself "becomes a metaphor for the endless toiling of the sea," but he also observes that "the reign of water" signals a historical turning point in its undoing of the Napoleonic Empire. Overnight rainfall leaves the ground too sodden for the French artillery to move swiftly enough into position (1984, 92–93). What remains under the surface of Brombert's reading is the conspicuously interventionist character of this downpour, which the narrator specifies was unseasonal and which starts falling all the harder when Napoleon arrogantly brags of his superiority over his opponents (Hugo 2008, 261–65). Imperial authority—and its militarized masculinity—is overpowered by a sublime but natural flow, through which the alliance that Brombert identifies between water, disintegration, and reconstruction is as material as it is metaphorical.

This symbiosis of water and human destiny is at work across the novel's reasoning, its plotting, and its use of character. Water repeatedly appears as essential both to natural prosperity and to the well-being of individuals, such as the riverside flowerbeds that sooth Georges Pontmercy's estrangement from his son Marius, the moist verdant gardens of the Petit-Picpus convent where Jean Valjean takes refuge, and the humidity of the Rue Plumet garden where Cosette and Marius fall in love in a space "full of sap and euphoria" (826). Rainfall brings the urchin Gavroche and his two lost brothers together; it hydrates the lush Luxembourg Gardens (where those two boys retreat) while causing subsidence in the Parisian sewers during the June insurrection; and it shifts the temper of Cosette's wedding day away from sunny visuals to a less idealized, more affective mode of celebration. In particular, the cycle of creation that water powers—at once destructive and propagative—is indispensable to the development of the novel's hero, Jean Valjean. Valjean's imbrication with water allows him to embody a connective order of freedom in which his humanity greatly deepens and the masculine traits of strength and independence interflow with feminine sensitivity and devotion. His ability to cry is a crucial measure of his moral worth, in that his nineteen-year incarceration left his soul "dried up" and unable to shed a tear: "Dry heart, dry eye" (80). Bishop Myriel's clemency revives this well of emotion and reveals Valjean's ability to connect with others rather than close in on himself, such as the teardrop that builds in his eye when Cosette returns to his side: "one of those big tears, which are the somber pearls of the soul" (1189). Not by coincidence, his diet intimates a strongly alimentary liquid intake. One of the first observations made about him is that he stops twice to rehydrate as he enters Digne (52). The first two components of the supper that Bishop Myriel's housekeeper gives him are listed as water and oil (66), and the reader learns that Valjean ate soup every night when living with his sister but reserved any hearty contents for her children (71), while he favors water over a solid meal when mourning his departure from Cosette's life (1169). The versatile pruner-turned-convict-turned-mayor-turned-fugitive—who also blends the roles of parent, sibling, child, and companion to Cosette (968)—continuously exhibits an ability to "be" with water successfully. The watercress beds and ponds of Montreuil-sur-Mer make for a fertile environment in which he can share his agricultural secrets as mayor, for example, and his substitution of turpentine as a natural solvent for the human-made one of distilled spirit is key to the bead-manufacturing process that he introduces to the town's factory.

Furthermore, Valjean is twice able to rise from a watery grave. When he plunges into the sea from the warship *Orion* as part of his escape from the galleys after coming to a fellow convict's rescue, his precise entry and total immersion into the waves convey a natural reconciliation of sorts: "he had disappeared into the sea without so much as a ripple, as though he had fallen into a vat of oil" (312). Later, when fleeing through the sewers of Paris, he raises the wounded Marius above his head as he sinks ever deeper, like the mother carrying her child through the Flood, and his perseverance is rewarded (1061). In both cases, Valjean's self-sacrifice and adaptability, as seen in his philanthropy and his many changes of identity, are connected to water's interrelated ontology. In stark contrast, his single-minded pursuer, Inspector Javert, cannot cope with the shock of an unsettled world in which opposites like vice and virtue are not mutually exclusive, and in which "authority is ambiguous and can vacillate" (1084). Perched above a turbulent junction of the River Seine, which has been swelled by the overnight rainfall, his thoughts spin and unspool like the rapid beneath him. His suicidal leap and muted splash are at once a tangible illustration and symbolic reminder of how his steadfast paternalistic logic of right and wrong is consumed by nature's indefatigable currents in Hugo's eyes. Such flux unsurprisingly closes the novel and lays unending claim to its everyman hero. Rain and wind have erased the unpretentious epitaph that had been chalked upon Valjean's gravestone, which now lies in a flagrantly damp and wetted milieu. It is covered in mold, lichen, and bird droppings in a deserted corner of the Père-Lachaise cemetery where no one treads due to the long grass and soggy ground. The quatrain remembered by the narrator condenses hundreds of pages of story into four unsentimental lines about Valjean's "truly odd" destiny: the fact that he now sleeps and that "The thing just happened of its own accord,/As night comes on when day is done" (1194). Unlike the lost text, the implication is clear: Human words and deeds lack the permanence of the relentless natural forces of which we are a part, and which forcibly displace any sui generis understanding of agency and power.

Alongside Valjean's androgynous, asexual character, this displacement raises as yet unanswered questions about the constitution and dissolution of gender identity that such poetics make possible. Since Hugo's enormous state funeral in Paris in 1885, the so-called "great man" or *grand homme* of French letters has been monumentalized as an enduring patriarchal icon of both moral authority and national virility. But Hugo insisted that this "genre of great men dissolves in the face of progress" (1904–52, 35:216),[16] as emphasized by the juxtaposition of Valjean's overtly self-effacing resting place with "all those fantastic tombs that show off death's ghastly fashions in the face of eternity" (2008, 1194). Hugo's interest in the commensurability of the hydrological and the human marks out a fresh approach to the Romantic relationship between grandeur and masculinity. That connection remains prone to stereotypes such as Napoleonic greatness and Byronic desire, through which historical male figures can be neatly framed as exemplars of gender normativity and its assumptions about human embodiment. Urgent questions must be asked, however, about how the "great" men of the Romantic canon might wade into the waters that Hugo stirs in his work and how they fashion or frustrate gender fluidity as a result. The vast dimensions of Hugo's body of writing and graphic art tantalizingly invite further exploration of its aqueous potential in this respect.

For the moment, however, this chapter has established the ways in which Hugo's hydrocommons confirms the significance of Romantic perspectives to ecocriticism's biocultural analyses. "How humans engage with water is as cultural as it is natural" (Strang 2015, 8–9), so understanding Romanticism within the biosphere enables its challenging conceptions of individual subjectivity to take on new weight. In the ongoing effort to facilitate a relational apprehension of humankind's place within the world and to imagine a more sustainable future, Romantic bodies of water like Hugo's can be revisited to explore alternative ontologies and recontextualize different cultural heritages. The potency of literature and art for these revisionist critiques cannot be underestimated, nor does the consideration of how to figure human being beyond ontology need to limit itself to particular bodies of water. Romain Rolland's idea of an "oceanic feeling" may expedite the Freudian ego's dispossession and spur timely questions about "what affinities, responsibilities, and solidarities emerge from the watery depths," as Erika Balsom's scintillating study of film and the sea has shown (2018, 11), but the resultant sense of unboundedness and relationality is not exclusive to screen media or maritime waters. The multiplicity of media used by Romantic artists—from the literary to the visual and the aural—is a reminder of the miscellaneous ways in which audiences can be drawn into new experiences of depletion and belonging through the intra-action with water.

NOTES

1. "Here Lies One Whose Name was writ in Water" is the epitaph that Keats requested for his gravestone, as recorded by his friend Joseph Severn (1821).
2. When providing my own English translations, I will include the French original in the notes. "La gestation terrestre . . . la vitalité centrique, alambic qui distille des forêts, des fleuves, des chutes du Nil, des cataractes du Rhin, des glaciers, des roses, des rubis, des déserts de sable, des déserts de neige, des steppes, des savanes, des prairies, des lacs, des torrents."
3. "La poésie est ce qu'il y a d'intime dans tout."
4. "L'homme veut être eau courante. Chose merveilleuse, la liberté, c'est la santé. Un ruissellement, un murmure, une pente, un parcours, un but, une volonté, pas de vie sans cela."
5. "Il y a des hommes océans en effet. Ces ondes, ce flux et ce reflux, ce va-et-vient terrible, ce bruit de tous les souffles, ces noirceurs et ces transparences . . . cet infini, cet insondable, tout cela peut être dans un esprit, et alors cet esprit s'appelle génie."
6. "Des eaux captives ou détournées de leur cours."
7. "Entassement d'œuvres flottantes où ma pensée s'enfonce sans savoir si elle en reviendra."
8. "Les idées et les images s'y entassent pêle-mêle . . . j'ai la chute du Rhin dans le cerveau."
9. "Cette double mer du temps et de l'espace. . . . Mon esprit plongea donc sous ce flot inconnu,/Au profond de l'abîme il nagea seul et nu."
10. This poem proves that Hugo sometimes rearranged his dates of composition to suit his mood (while his memory could be prone to haste). The poem could not have been written next to Switzerland's Rhône Glacier, as the title claims, since Hugo was in Paris on the stated date of May 1, 1829. Nor could he have been recalling his 1825 trip to the Alps, during which he visited the Chamonix region and could only have seen glaciers like the Mer de Glace that feeds into one of

the Rhône's tributaries. Irrespective of which glacier Hugo was looking at, it is the effect upon him that is noteworthy.
11. "Souvent, quand mon esprit riche en métamorphoses/Flotte et roule endormi sur l'océan des choses,/Dieu . . . Le frappe d'un rayon, et, comme une rosée,/Le ramasse et l'enlève aux cieux./Alors, nuage errant, ma haute poésie / Vole capricieuse et sans route choisie . . ./Enfin sur un vieux mont, colosse à tête grise,/Sur des Alpes de neige un vent jaloux la brise . . ./Il retombe en torrent dans l'océan du monde . . ./Au gré du divin souffle ainsi vont mes pensées,/Dans un cercle éternel incessamment poussées."
12. "Il y a dans tout de l'errant et du flottant. La forme dénouée ondule mêlée à l'idée."
13. "Chacun a la goutte d'eau; personne n'a l'océan."
14. "Ce théâtre où le vent combat la trombe enfuie,/Voilà ce qu'a construit un atome de pluie./Quel besoin as-tu donc d'un Vishnou, d'un Allah,/D'un Bouddha, d'un Ammon cornu, pour tout cela?/Pourquoi sortir du cercle où le réel t'enferme?/À quoi bon détrôner l'élément et le germe?"
15. "Ce qui est pour nous bronze et granit devient là nuée, et se dissout, et flotte; le requin est-il un despote . . . le monstre est-il un monstre ? nous l'ignorons."
16. "Ce genre de grands hommes est soluble au progrès."

WORKS CITED

Abrams, M. H. 1957. "The Correspondent Breeze: A Romantic Metaphor." *Kenyon Review* 19 (1): 113–30.
Balsom, Erika. 2018. *An Oceanic Feeling: Cinema and the Sea*. Govett-Brewster Gallery.
Bambach, Charles. 2017. "Who Is Heidegger's Hölderlin?" *Research in Phenomenology*, no. 47, 35–59.
Barad, Karen. 2007. *Meeting the Universe Halfway: Quantum Physics and the Entanglement of Matter and Meaning*. Duke University Press.
Baudelaire, Charles. 1993. *The Flowers of Evil*. Translated by James McGowan. Oxford University Press.
Blain-Pinel, Marie. 2003. *La Mer, miroir de l'infini: La Métaphore marine dans la poésie romantique*. Presses universitaires de Rennes.
Brombert, Victor. 1984. *Victor Hugo and the Visionary Novel*. Harvard University Press.
Buell, Lawrence. 1995. *The Environmental Imagination: Thoreau, Nature Writing, and the Formation of American Culture*. Harvard University Press.

Burke, Edmund. 1998. *A Philosophical Enquiry into the Sublime and Beautiful*. Oxford University Press.

Chateaubriand, François-René de. 1964. *Voyage en Amérique*. 2 vols. Didier.

Colwell, Frederic S. 1989. *Rivermen: A Romantic Iconography of the River and the Source*. McGill-Queen's University Press.

Desbordes-Valmore, Marceline. 1860. *Poésies inédites*. Jules Pick.

Duckert, Lowell. 2017. *For All Waters: Finding Ourselves in Early Modern Wetscapes*. University of Minnesota Press.

Farnsworth, Rodney. 2001. *Mediating Order and Chaos: The Water Cycle in the Complex Adaptive Systems of Romantic Culture*. Rodopi.

Finch-Race, Daniel A., and Stephanie Posthumus. 2017. *French Ecocriticism: From the Early Modern Period to the Twenty-First Century*. Peter Lang.

Haraway, Donna J. 2016. *Staying with the Trouble: Making Kin in the Chthulucene*. Duke University Press.

Horace. 2014. *Odes*. Translated by David R. Slavitt. University of Wisconsin Press.

Hugo, Victor. 1904–52. *Œuvres complètes*. 45 vols. Edited by Paul Meurice, Gustav Simon, and Cécile Daubray. Paul Ollendorff and Albin Michel.

Hugo, Victor. 1972. *Choses vues*. 2 vols. Edited by Hubert Juin. Gallimard.

Hugo, Victor. 2008. *Les Misérables*. Translated by Julie Rose. Vintage Classics.

Irigaray, Luce. 2002. *To Speak Is Never Neutral*. Translated by Gail Schwab. Continuum.

Jolle, Jonas. 2004. "The River and Its Metaphors: Goethe's *Mahomets Gesang*." *MLN* 119 (3): 431–50.

Kant, Immanuel. 2000. *Critique of the Power of Judgement*. Translated by Paul Guyer and Eric Matthews. Cambridge University Press.

Linton, Jamie. 2010. *What Is Water? The History of a Modern Abstraction*. University of British Columbia Press.

MacLean, Kenneth. 1948. "The Water Symbol in *The Prelude* (1805–6)." *University of Toronto Quarterly* 17 (4): 372–89.

Murphy, Jeanie, and Elizabeth G. Rivero, eds. 2018. *The Image of the River in Latin American Literature: Written in the Water*. Lexington.

Neimanis, Astrida. 2017. *Bodies of Water: Posthuman Feminist Phenomenology*. Bloomsbury.

Novalis. 2005. *The Novices of Sais*. Translated by Ralph Mannheim. Archipelago.

O'Shea-Meddour, Wendy. 2003. "Gaston Bachelard's *L'Eau et les rêves*: Conquering the Feminine Element." *French Cultural Studies* 14 (1): 81–99.

Piroué, Georges. 1968. "Victor Hugo et la mer." In Victor Hugo, *Œuvres complètes*, vol. 9, edited by Jean Massin. Club Français du Livre.

Quandt, Karen. 2017. "Victor Hugo and the Politics of Ecopoetics." In *French Ecocriticism: From the Early Modern Period to the Twenty-First Century*, edited by Daniel A. Finch-Race and Stephanie Posthumus, 61–79. Peter Lang.

Rigby, Kate. 2020. *Reclaiming Romanticism: Towards an Ecopoetics of Decolonization*. Bloomsbury.

Rousseau, Jean-Jacques. 2011. *Reveries of the Solitary Walker*. Translated by Russell Goulbourne. Oxford University Press.

Schwenk, Theodor. 1989. *Water: The Element of Life*. Translated by Marjorie Spock. Anthroposophy Press.

Severn, Joseph. 1821. "Letter About John Keats's Last Illness, 14 February." https://wordsworth.org.uk/blog/2021/02/23/writ-in-water-the-gravestone-of-john-keats/.

Shewry, Teresa. 2015. *Hope at Sea: Possible Ecologies in Oceanic Literature*. University of Minnesota Press.

Stephens, Bradley. 2019. "How Do You Solve a Problem Like Cosette? Femininity and the Changing Face of Victor Hugo's *Alouette*." *Modern Languages Open* 5 (1): 1–28.

Strang, Veronica. 2015. *Water: Nature and Culture*. Reaktion.

Wardi, Anissa Janine. 2011. *Water and African-American Memory: An Ecocritical Perspective*. University Press of Florida.

Wordsworth, William, and Samuel Taylor Coleridge. 2005. *Lyrical Ballads*. Routledge.

"FOREVER FOLDING AND UNFOLDING"

The Critical Depths of David Gascoyne's Poetics
ISABELLE KELLER-PRIVAT

David Gascoyne, a poet engaged in the politics of his time, and critical of the spiritual crisis that characterized, from the 1930s onwards, the cultural and social life of Europe, was also a diarist, a historical witness, a literary critic, an actor, and a translator. Deeply versed in Greek and German philosophy, he wrote with similar ease in English and in French—prompting the Surrealist French poet Philippe Soupault to assert: "David is not an English poet, he is a French poet writing in English" (Gascoyne 1998, 15). He kept traveling between languages and continents, constantly hankering after foreign shores, as he confessed in an interview: "I found something in American poetry that was more exciting than English poetry" (Gascoyne 1998, 50). The French Surrealists, Rilke, Hölderlin, Hart Crane, Emily Dickinson, Robert Frost, e. e. cummings, Wallace Stevens, Allen Ginsberg, García Lorca were amongst those that inspired him.[1]

Crossing frontiers and bodies of water as he journeyed through Europe and the US,[2] David Gascoyne also turned his experience with the sea into a meditative and ontological enquiry. His beginnings as a Surrealist poet mark him as one of those for whom, according to Walter Benjamin, "life was only meaningful at the point where the threshold between wake and sleep was furrowed . . . by the ebb and flow of a sweeping flood of images" (Benjamin 2019, 81–82). These dreams, recorded in his early poems and revisited in the later ones, long after Gascoyne ceased to see himself as a Surrealist, are repeatedly pitted against the undertow of persistent sea-inspired metaphors, structures, and rhythms that build up a significant symbolic, formal, and critical pattern throughout his poetic work.

This is why I contend that the sea in Gascoyne's writing, far from being a stylistic ploy, operates as a hermeneutic metaphor that displaces and challenges our viewpoint. Gascoyne's sea ushers in a new reading of the signs in and of the world, considerably altering our relation to a space that can no longer be envisaged through the paradigm of what Elizabeth DeLoughrey calls "the blue or oceanic humanities" (DeLoughrey 2019, 22). Instead, it forces us to reconsider our environment along new, shifty, unmoored lines, as defined by Gilles Deleuze and Félix Guattari's concept of "a smooth space ... an open space with a vortical movement that can rise up at any point" (Deleuze and Guattari 2002, 363). Such a shift in perspective implies the acceptance of risk-taking, of what Margaret Cohen calls "experimentation at the limits" (Cohen 2010, 660). Joining for a time the British Communist party and going to Spain, like W. H. Auden, during the Civil War, to support the Republic, Gascoyne, throughout these years and those that followed, kept publishing poems that were written, as George Orwell has expressed, "directly, or indirectly, against totalitarianism" (Orwell 1982, 28). The early Surrealist poems, as well as the later ones, such as *Night Thoughts,* summon bodies of water that call into question the striated world of Western political and economic hegemony that has always relied on the domestication and taming of space, especially maritime space, as Deleuze and Guattari have explained: "the sea is also, of all smooth spaces, the first one attempts were made to striate, to transform into a dependency of the land, with its fixed routes, constant directions, relative movements, a whole counterhydraulic of channels and conduits" (Deleuze and Guattari 2002, 387). Gascoyne challenges such a "counterhydraulic" paradigm most forcefully in his early poems from 1932 to the 1940s by transforming what DeLoughrey calls the "anthropocentric and colonial 'aqua nullius' [and] inert backdrop" (DeLoughrey 2019, 22) into a Deleuzian fold: the sea can no longer be considered as a place of domination, a site for crossings, or the mere locus of "a *marine* habitat" (DeLoughrey 2019, 23), but as a trope in the etymological sense of the word—a turning point in our relation to the world. We shall see how this transformation of the object of our gaze ushers in a "correlative transformation of the subject" (Deleuze 2006, 27) and provides us with what Iain Chambers calls "ontological criteria with which to reconfigure our theoretical prison house" (Chambers 2010, 679).

I shall first explore how the sea provides us with what Chambers calls "both a passage and a bridge" (Chambers 2010, 681), a place of perpetual movement that reverses the paradigm of distance and proximity. Metaphorizing our ontological experience of dissolution and alienation, Gascoyne's sea places his readers "in the sharp brink" (2014, "Roman Ghosts" [1932], 9) and invites them to embrace their own finitude and to go beyond the reaches of the visible. The sea in Gascoyne's poetry functions both as a surface and as an inner depth, precluding univocal directions and fixed dimensions, whether spatial or temporal. Foregrounding an unshackled temporality that conjoins the material and the spiritual, it stands out as a locus of resistance opposing the hydrologic of "absolute movement" (Deleuze and Guattari 2002, 387) to the chartered, territorial logic. As a result, Gascoyne's sea is to be considered as an empowered agent, what Jane Bennett defines as an "actant," "a Thing-Power Power [endowed with] the curious ability of inanimate things to animate, to act, to produce effects dramatic and subtle" (Bennett 2010, 6). It is the agent of a new form of awareness that forces man to revisit long-established scales and reinvigorates poetry as an act of foundation that upsets the rules of common language and provides us with a perpetually labile point of view in "between the dark land and tomorrow's sea" (2014, "Chorus" [1936–38], 98). The spatial and temporal motion subsumed in this line corroborates Kimberley Peters and Philip Steinberg's analysis of the properties of the ocean, which they see "not as a space of discrete points between which objects move but rather as a dynamic environment of flows and continual recomposition where . . . 'place' can be understood only in the context of mobility" (Steinberg and Peters 2015, 257). We shall see in the course of this chapter to what extent this specific property is central to our understanding of water logics in Gascoyne's poetry.

SEA VIEW: DIFFRACTIVE AND SHIFTING PERSPECTIVES

The various bodies of water that span Gascoyne's early poems collected in *Roman Balcony* (1932) initially seem to connote the passage into a dismal beyond. In "The Bridge," river water is associated with the "bodies of the suicides" (2014, 12). Water stands still ("steely water") and is "soaked with the sins of the City," reminding the reader of the sinister caveat in T. S. Eliot's *The Waste Land*: "Fear death by water" (2002, 54). Sea water is equally threatening, echoing the waters of the flood and of the Last Judgment. In "The roots of evil" (2014, 38), "the silently boiling sea dissolves the rocks," ushering in an unearthly element that metamorphoses solid matter into an indeterminate aqueous entity redolent of primal chaos: "the swollen landscape" (38) gives birth to "foaming monsters" (2014, 38). The earth turns into "succulent mire" (2014, 38) that exposes the depraved taste of humanity and corrupts the fount of life: "Poison the source of the sources and springs" (2014, 38).

In the collection *Man's Life Is This Meat* (1936), the poem "The Chariot" pictures the sea simultaneously as a watery and a fiery element: "The sea envisages huge wheels of flames" (2014, 45). The ambiguity of the verb "envisage," which can be understood as "conceive" (placing the sea as the font of the world) and as "contemplate," "confront," or "refract," dramatizes the hesitation that characterizes the image of the sea in the poem as both a locus and as an agent. The destruction of the chariot that "crashes on between the waves" (2014, 45) enhances this hesitation: should the waves be read as the place or the agent of destruction, or both? In that case, is it not both a weapon of destruction ("Its orbs disintegrate" [45]) and of redemption ("The chariot grinds their debris into dust/And rides into the infinite once more" [45])? Such equivocal meaning forecloses any direct interpretation and points to the hermeneutic polyvalence of the sea, which cannot be framed within a unique symbolical equation. This hermeneutic polyvalence is enhanced by the biblical echoes that lend the poem a timeless aura, since, in the Bible, the waters of the flood are the same that serve to announce Christ's second coming and are agents of both destruction and redemption.[3]

In order to fully understand the complex structural role played by the sea in Gascoyne's poetry, one must turn to an early poem that gives the sea a central role, "Seaside Tragedy." Originally published in the collection *Roman Balcony* (1932), it stages the sea as the threshold between life and death, an in-between zone where man experiences the porous boundaries between the material and the immaterial spheres. Using as an enunciative threshold the epigraph of the newspaper clipping that inspired Gascoyne, the poem initially pictures the sea as the setting for an ordinary drama: "A Verdict of

Suicide ... on Mrs X, a widow, at Bournemouth" (2014, 14). Paradoxically, the sea triggers the reminiscence of factual details that set the stage for a hardly noticeable or memorable disappearance. It would seem that the hydrologic of "absolute movement" (Deleuze and Guattari 2002, 387) threatens the logic of writerly inscription:

> 'Long, long ago it was remembered
> on the seashore
> (by one of those who find it possible to remember),
> it was remembered that
> black is never white
> and that the snow
> will fall into the sea
> and at once become part of the sea;
> and that a door will open
> and let fall upon the linoleum
> a square of light,
> white against the black of the shadow.' (14)[4]

The welding of the voice in the epigraph with that of the anonymous speaker inserted between quotation marks in the poem, along with the presence of parentheses, underlines the hypothetical nature of the remembered event and evokes the overlapping and disjointed film sequences of surrealist cinema.[5] Only retrospectively do the readers visualize the body falling from the open window, the shaft of white light reverberated by the sea and reflected on the black linoleum. And only then can they fully grasp the symbolic correlations between black and white, light and shadow. As a consequence, the sea does not so much function as a place of anchoring where the reader can find his bearings but rather as an element of confusion meant to throw him into an opaque, oneiric vision where indistinction rules and where unidirectional interpretative schemes no longer apply:

> It has become impossible to distinguish
> between the sea and linoleum.
> I shall think of black and white
> until I see them mingle in the sea
> and intertwine and die. (14)

The terrestrial and aqueous surfaces are no longer distinct, leading the poet to explore further contradictory associations, like fire and water, or water and earth. Such an unreliable, moving setting paves the way for the mutability of language: color adjectives veer into nouns in the chiasmatic construction "How the light is white!/And how the green is in the sea!" (2014, 15). The poem simultaneously plays on the interpolation of the poet's contending voices and of the suicidal widow, who is alternately referred to using first- and third-person pronouns, reverberating the constant shifts in focus that contribute to the reader's disorientation. The dotted lines separating and highlighting fragmented utterances, the multiple parentheses and quotation marks, the unaccounted-for enunciative shifts suggest that we are entering a death dream where the deceased, anonymous widow is given a voice at last. The hydrologic is a transversal logic that shatters the lines between the living and the dead, the here and the beyond. In that regard, the sea truly functions as a Surrealist image, as defined by Gascoyne in his *Short Survey of Surrealism*, published in 1935, one year before the London International Surrealist Exhibition: "an image which brings about the union of two mutually distant realities upon a plane equally unrelated to either of them" (Gascoyne 2000, 59). Gascoyne's sea therefore functions as the crucible of an ontological uncertainty, inviting the reader to penetrate the circumvoluted folds of a Surrealist dream and to realize, as Walter Benjamin expressed, that "the language of the dream is not in the words but beneath them" (Benjamin 2019, 73). Offering us what Gascoyne describes as "a new way of knowing the world [that] incessantly opposed all the old pragmatisms" (Gascoyne 2000, 93), Gascoyne's sea opens up new ways of unknowing the present world, so that we may not feel too surprised when the barely distinguishable sea of the early lines suddenly resurfaces and displays, in the second half of the poem, a world turned upside down, a world envisaged from the point of view of its depths:

> She saw the sea.
> She heard the barrel-organs
> Playing eternally
> At the bottom of the sea. (17)

The crossing has been mysteriously enacted "beneath the words" to reveal what the newspaper clipping in the epigraph could not apprehend, what the mundane world of the widow's defunct life concealed behind its trite materiality: "playing bridge," "removing her teeth," "buying chrysanthemums/For her husband's grave" (16). And yet the return and accumulation of the mundane in spasmodic memories ("She remembered,/(As she approached the sea),/The linoleum,/And the artichokes, And the geyser" [17]; "She remembered her husband./She remembered the chrysanthemums" [18]) is combined with the recurring spiritual symbols ("Candles must rise out of the waves" [17]; "Wandering among Paul's serpents" [18]) that progressively contaminate material reality. Thus, "the barrel-organ/playing in the street outside my window" (15) that appears "at the bottom of the sea" (17) is endowed with candles "reflected in the mirrors" (17) and accompanies the widow's funeral march. The banal and the unearthly are brought into contact: watertight distinctions no longer hold, and the familiar world acquires an unsuspected depth that cannot be traced back to a phenomenological origin. Hydrologic is a rhizomatic logic that connects but does not bind, following the "principle of asignifying rupture" (Deleuze and Guattari 2002, 9), as exemplified in the following excerpt where the alliterations and assonances hint at submerged and fragile connections:

> 'Immeasurably wan
> the grace of women,
> ...distant,...distant;...
> and rose-petals lying fading on the grass;
> and the hush and the sway of the sea,
> which seems like dew dying the fruit
> with ermine and jasmine.' (16)

This stanza signals the beginning of the widow's visionary apprehension of the material reality, her acceptance of the harmonious symbiosis between the human and the natural, the tangible and the intangible worlds that keep merging into one another: "Sad wraith,/Thy hair (white,...white),/Flowing out like towel" (17).

Eventually the widow's suicide is resemanticized as a new mode of sharing, a final communion with the momentum of the sea that is to carry her into the beyond and that the cyclic flow of the final stanza's forward moving lines materializes:

> 'Unending, unending,
> Beyond the veil

there is no death,'
(The waves cover her),
'linoleum, artichokes, the geyser
   so damp, so distant,
      rose-petals and skeletons
         unending, unending,
            unending.' (19)

Entering the dreamlike substance of the sea is construed as the ultimate trial—"The sea shall give up its dead" (18)—whereby man undergoes the decisive journey that takes him not further away but closer to the rhythm of life, bringing the distant within the scope of the familiar. The hydrorhythm of Gascoyne's poetics showcases the ruptures and dissolutions that preclude man's hold on life, space, or time and forbid definite interpretative associations that would congeal meaning. Heralding man's encounter with death, Gascoyne's sea is akin to the sea of the Old Testament that simultaneously offers a right of passage and submerges; it is both lethal and liberating and constantly points to a further shore.

If the sea can be read in "Seaside Tragedy" as the source of an individual form of trial, it is also construed in later poems as the harbinger of man's communal trial. In "Phantasmagoria" (2014, 107–11), dated 1938 and concluding the collection *Surrealist and Other Poems* (1936–38), the sea slowly evolves from a symptomatic locus of doom into the agent of rebirth. It is first pictured as the anchoring of a "little black town" that cannot be placed on a map but that is only located in reference to a changing, dark-colored, and ominous sea. The earthly location is, fundamentally, an in-between place, standing on the brink between water and land, between night and day. The entire poem reads as a message of dread and hope in the wake of the oncoming world war and as a bitter comment upon the slow drowning of European culture, whose remaining fragments (Homer's "violet sea" or Faust) testify to the overpowering hegemony of "the scorpions of the darkness" (108) and the "barbaric corteges" (110).

The "green" sea of "Seaside Tragedy" (15) becomes a hellish landscape suffused with deep, fiery colors ("preserved in wine," "as black as a burnt cake," "a charred bun," "a vein-coloured sea," 108) in "Phantasmagoria," where individuals walk like shadows ("the passers-by turn pale") in a death-ridden universe lit only by "the dust of poisoned stars" (108). If the sea appears to turn deathly, it is because it stands for an immaterial entity, alien to the striated world of "window-bars," "cell" (108), and "cage-like haunts" (109). As the tide changes, the sea progressively takes on life and becomes the harbinger of light—"a heliotrope sea" (110) that reorients our gaze towards the light to reveal, beyond the death-ridden "inland" (110) world, the poet's invisible sacrifice as he bears testimony to a dying world in "blackberry-juice ink" (108). This is how David Gascoyne warns man of his forlorn state, confined as he is in a darkness of his own making. "The thoroughfares of Evening" belong to the malevolent city of capitalist consumerism peopled by "sickly faces weak as greasy smudges left by flies," where "the last birds" have been hypnotized by death, and where electricity only enhances darkness: "the lamps of lust and terror" (109). The sea that surges is indeed the flood of the Apocalypse, the sea of despair—no longer a natural element but a trope that exposes man's fall. And yet, it is simultaneously a "heliotrope" reminiscent of Audisio's *Héliotrope*: a sea that becomes a source of insight and poetic intimations.[6]

Significantly, the source of light lies at the bottom of the sea in the shape of a supernatural being, half-man, half-bird, and his apparition marks the beginning of the anticlimax: "the great water-spouts of midnight have subsided out at sea" (110). The sea is no longer a menacing chaotic force. This is the point when the wind that "has stopped" (107) earlier on now becomes "the livid wind [that] once more begins to lift" (111). Just like the sea, the wind is clearly not a mere physical element but the anima that breathes life into the world and that brings both change and peace. The "little black town on the edge of a violet sea" (107) is no longer an isolated, dark locus but "the radius" (111), the rhizomatic impetus wherefrom the whole perspective springs back into motion. The inhabitants that used to flee ("invisible slippers," "invisible blood" [110]) and "to hurry home" (108) reappear as a welded community ("swarms," "sealed") attuned to the silence of the night. They dwell under the "spell of dream" that marks them like the seal of a new covenant between man and the universe, and their progress opens up the perspective to "the East" (110) and upwards, leading our eyes towards a regenerated world bathed in the soft sibilants of the final lines:

> swarms of somnambulistic barefoot children creep
> by slow degrees, still sealed by spell of the dream,
> towards where soon the spume be-silvered waves shall shine and
>   seethe
> as a new Sun soars like song out of the silence of the sea. (111)

After a time of confusion and chaos, Man is reunited with himself and with others in a harmonious, balanced universe: the "new Sun" has shed the trappings of the material, earthbound world and is bathed in a paradoxically silent song that can only be conveyed by the soft undertone of the alliterative pattern. The perfect poise between "Sun soars" and "silence of the sea" is heightened by the central place of the word "song" that conveys the logic-defeating purpose of poetry embedded in the hydrologic of the poem: chaos ebbs out into harmony, estrangement into solidarity.

Therefore, the sea is not just the metaphor for a journey into the other world but the very medium through which our contemporary world is recast into a new perspective. The poet's struggle with the language of the sea, as evinced in the pattern of sibilants, liquid consonants, and assonances in /i:/, or the almost perfect rhyme scheme, testifies to the powerful influence of hydrologic, which reverses the classical paradigm opposing the realms of things and beings, and redefines our conception of our environment as a "place where thought is experienced in space, calling into question the distinction between the *res cogitans* and the *res extensa*" (Collot 2014, 188). As the Cartesian dichotomy between the subject and its environment founders, poetic matter incorporates the water-logic of its subject to convey the unimpeded flow of life that connects man to his world despite the rifts of history. As a trope, and as a linguistic and prosodic device, Gascoyne's seawaters also qualify as a symbol answering to his own definition of symbolism: "The symbol is a bridge between subjective reality of personal experience and the objective reality of the Spirit" (Gascoyne 1998, 77). The specificity of David Gascoyne's symbol lies in the foregrounding of a sensual relationship to the world, as poet Kathleen Raine points out: "the poet does not observe with camera-eye's detachment, but senses the imaginative import of each image; he reads the signs like words in some human record" (Raine 2017, 80). Seawaters can be read as a hermeneutic device mapping out a new reading of the world that encompasses the impending arrival of what lies beyond—the unknowable and uncontrollable that defeats the logics of appropriation and domination—and which, through the sheer power of the word, is brought closer.

One of the most striking specificities of Gascoyne's seawaters is the weaving of the invisible and the remote that they articulate, reversing the paradigm of distance/proximity upon which our apprehension of reality relies from a very early age. This reversal of scale has already been pinpointed by Iain Chambers, who argues that "when we travel on a ship in the open sea, home and the familiar ground beneath our feet slip away, reduced to a distant shore" (Chambers 2010, 680). Water logics implies a very specific type of displacement that does not just entail distance but also instability and movement; as "our feet slip away" we are also deprived of our hold upon our surroundings. It is a displacement that combines estrangement and dispossession and turns the subject into the passive recipient of motion. The defamiliarization of the familiar is particularly explicit in the first poem of the collection *Other Early Poems* (1932–35), "By the Sea" (2014, 25), where Gascoyne deploys an epistemological crossing from what he calls the "Traditional Form" to the "Modernist Poem," jeopardizing our formal bearings and certainties. The poem is divided into two poems, where the first one, following the pattern of the sesta rima,[7] conjures up a very recognizable English poetic form that makes way for the deployment of a sensuous landscape in the lingering rhyme of the final couplet. However, Gascoyne chooses to alter the rhyme scheme that links up a series of three couplets, offering multiple forms of expansion of the poetic soundscape.[8] Gascoyne anchors his poem within a familiar and markedly lyrical tradition that has been haunting our "ear-eye"[9] since Wordsworth's "I wandered lonely as a cloud" (1807), while taking his distance from the fixed form. Readers are brought to experience the dissonance of the familiar as they are simultaneously brought back and tugged away from a recognizable pattern, feeling their "feet slip away" too.

The second poem, the "Modernist Poem," further experiments with the decomposition of formal patterns. It is divided into six numbered stanzas—as if to parody the sesta rima—and echoes the tone and form of Edith Sitwell's or e. e. cummings's works. Lines, words, and syntactic units are broken; rhymes, meter, and punctuation are wiped out; the soundscape is characterized by multiple alliterations, repetitions, and onomatopoeias. The disruption of lexical units from the third to the fifth stanzas conjures up baffling blanks within the prosodic structure, as if the words were casting off their moorings: "Lettuces are grow/ing in the blue c/averns/little f/ish sw/ish in/and out of them." Finally, semantic structures are progressively reintegrated in stanzas 5 and 6, which appear to recapture the theme and lines of stanza 1 in a final attempt to bring back narrative coherence. Here are the first and sixth stanzas:

(1)
the whiskey windwhite
        waves spit in my
face they are so grey so stony cold the

```
                waves
           are grey stone walls the
       sea is an old washerwoman's wh
    O (ooo)spitsand flings grey stones atm
    E (eee) (25)
    . . . . . . . . . . .
```

```
(6)
the sea is an old washerwoman
forever folding and unfolding
her blue with cold enormous
arms
forever rolling and unrolling
her white froth with enormous
eyes. (26)
```

The reader is brought back to the beginning of the poem in a "forever folding and unfolding" (26) reading that is metonymic of the movement of the sea. The twofold process of distancing and dispossession characteristic of water logics is made more complex in this second poem where estrangement paradoxically triggers recognition. The ebb and the flow of words disassembling and reassembling prompt the readers to build up unstable lexical, syntactic, and semantic identifications that are simultaneously denied and reasserted. This is characteristic of the oceanic logic defined by Peters and Steinberg as "a dynamic pattern of repetition and reformation that provides stability and texture in an environment of underlying instability" (Steinberg and Peters 2015, 248). Broken structures acquire meaning not through a formal reconstruction but precisely as dismantled forms that have grown familiar yet remain beyond repair. Gascoyne seems here to be putting into practice not only e. e. cummings's disjunctive arrangements but also his conviction that

```
since feeling is first
who pays any attention
to the syntax of things
will never wholly kiss you; (1977, "since feeling is first" [1926], 23)
```

Teaching his readers to distrust any form of fixed combination, Gascoyne takes them further away from what Chambers calls our "familiar ground"

(Chambers 2010, 680) and bestows upon them a new vantage point. The sea is therefore no longer the mere object of poetic vision but becomes an active cleaving and binding principle that connects the human and the nonhuman worlds while raising our awareness about the gap that divides both. The comparison object (the sea) is progressively endowed with the qualities of the compared one (the washerwoman) as the verb "folding" is followed by "rolling," substituting the image of the waves for the washerwoman's laundry sheets. This metaphorical projection ushers in an allegory whereby the sea becomes a figure of gigantic, mythical proportions endowed with arms and eyes. The sea as we know it, or thought we knew it, has "slipped away" (Chambers 2010, 680), and becomes an unfamiliar yet close presence that watches us "with enormous/eyes," demanding from us a new vision and consequently displacing our own position as subjects. Gascoyne construes maritime space not as a distant, threatening other to be tamed but as what DeLoughrey calls an "embodied ocean [that] foregrounds mergers between the human and a planetary nonhuman other that are naturalized" (DeLoughrey 2019, 27). Such a device accounts for the progressive systematic erasure of geographic references as the sea takes up the entire picture and becomes the indefinite, all-expanding element against which other natural elements are defined. Gascoyne's poetry significantly merges the sea and the ocean, taking the sea in its first acceptation as "the continuous body of salt water that covers the greater part of the earth's surface and surrounds its land masses" (*New Shorter Oxford English Dictionary*), which also corresponds to the definition of the ocean, the Greek *ōkeanos* (*potamos*), "the great river encompassing the earth, the great sea" (*NSOED*). Gascoyne's poetic exploration of the sea-ocean displays an unexpected, disquieting consequence of water logics: the geographic, peripheral body of sea waters covering the surface of the earth and surrounding its land masses is remapped as an all-encompassing body—the eye of the universe refracting man's mortal essence.

Significantly, the "enormous/eyes" concluding "By the Sea" lead us to follow in the subsequent poem, "Seaside Souvenir" (27), the progress of death from "the pattern the jelly-fish left behind," to "a pocketful of sand" and, eventually, "a dead, pressed leaf." These isolated items, about to be washed away, can be read both as distinct elements and as the successive metamorphoses of the same object: "the pattern of the jelly-fish." The eyes of the sea, then, not only reverberate the process of dissolution but also draw our attention to a new system of signs that renders the negligible and the invisible

visible and meaningful. Such a reversal, which highlights the "wide boulders" instead of "the cliff," or the "beam" instead of "the lighthouse," brings back "traces, faded, indistinct" into existence. Hydrologic invites readers to a deeper contemplation of the traces that human and natural subjects leave behind them. Etymologically the word *trace* derives from the Latin *trahere*, to "pull" or "draw": it is what, in the very process of its disappearance, draws us into its quest, what we follow or track. But it is also the mark we leave behind, the sign of our passage, of the scriptural marks intended to trace back what is gone. Such is the import of "the pattern of the jelly-fish": it is the presence of a movement of erasure, the visible sign of an ongoing disappearance of which the waves, forever forming and vanishing, are the perfect epitome. "The pattern of the jelly-fish" is emblematic of the water logics of Gascoyne's poetry, which aims to guide its readers from indistinction to distinction and to turn their gaze towards the invisible.

In the second stanza, the petrified landscape is converted into an active one as we move from a horizontal to a vertical perspective that embraces "The cliff's wide boulders, the immense/*rocking* of ocean through the bay,/the lighthouse beam *stabbing the rainy night*" (my emphasis). The syntactic expansion from one element to the next combines with the run-on lines to mimic the indomitable, wild forces of the marine element. The ternary sequence ("cliff's boulders"/"immense rocking of ocean"/"lighthouse beam") comes to replace the three traces in stanza 1. These are as huge and overpowering as the three previous ones were tiny and indistinguishable, and function, oddly, not so much as "memories," or remembered objects, but as active subjects, revealing another paradoxical inversion. Indeed, the poem moves at the end of the first stanza from the "faded, indistinct" to the "not separate, but one—and quite distinct" at the end of the second one. Both contradicting and echoing one another, the last lines of each stanza echo the cyclic movement of the sea and its paradoxical logic. Annihilating discursive coherence, the poem ushers in an epistemological rift that metamorphoses the "indistinct" and inert flotsam of life into a perpetual onrush of energy and light that binds the landscape in its "woven rhythms."

The circular structure of the poem is therefore not only mimetic of the movement of the sea: it is, fundamentally, prophetic. The hydrologics embedded in the poem, carving its rhythm, images, and structure, turns the text into an agent that profoundly modifies our relation to the world by making visible and closer what is distant and indistinct.

LOOKING DEEPER

Reconfiguring our definition and apprehension of the sea, Gascoyne turns the sea into a new tool of exploration of the real, implementing "a reorientation of critical perception . . . that rhymes with . . . perspectival and methodological shifts" (Blum 2020, 671). He envisages the sea not only as a surface but, quintessentially, as a depth, a volume, a three-dimensional reality that encapsulates a fourth one—an unfettered temporality. The sea offers a markedly different type of volume from the one we know on land: constantly moving and reforming, significantly affected by time and tide, it is an uncontrollable and unfathomable "surface-depth," "a dynamic, voluminous materiality" (Steinberg and Peters 2015, 252). And, as Peters and Steinberg have argued, oceanic time is also quite distinct from land time, since the constant process of dissolution and recomposition of oceanic matter necessarily takes place within a cyclic, "nonlinear and fluctuating" time, "a process of ongoing reformation" (Steinberg and Peters 2015, 256). Oceanic time can be defined as anti-teleological time, the opposite of earthly, accountable time. This might be one of the reasons for poets' endless fascination with the sea, for their desire to converge with a space that is indistinguishable from its temporality, where time and being are at one with each other.

The epistemological depths induced by Gascoyne's poetic reconfiguration of the sea are particularly perceptible in the prose poem "The World of de Chirico" (30), where the sea becomes prophetic of the impending destruction of the world: "the sea lies waiting for the hour when it shall rise to overwhelm this dead and empty city" (30). The sea is "waiting" in a timeless vacuum where "we cannot tell the hour" (30): time like the tide is constantly dissolving and reforming. The beginning of the poem conjures up a very recognizable painting, *The Departure of the Poet* (1914), while hinting at elements from various works by de Chirico,[10] reproducing the hallucinatory compositions favored by the painter himself, who was prone to produce several copies of the same work or to reuse various elements from previous works, which he kept rearranging. Poetic and pictorial time partake of the same hydrologics in which the sea, just as "the infinity of the horizon," functions as a blank space, as an invisible line inviting the viewer to see beyond the materiality of objects, to cross the implicit divide between the real and the imaginary, the factual and the symbolic, between time and space.

Just like de Chirico, Gascoyne resists the poetry of abstraction and delineates the contours of the real world in strong, harsh lines, while distorting Euclidian perspective and superimposing conflicting planes in order to transform outer reality into the sign of a deeper symbolic pattern. "The Euclidian conception of space as a stable surface" (Steinberg and Peters 2015, 248) has been discarded both by poet and painter and replaced by a fluctuating space-time. As a result, free associations, disconnected images, and sensations herald a form of revelation that was also at the heart of the painter's quest: "Revelation always plays an essential role. A painting reveals itself to us without our seeing anything, even without our thinking at all, and, seeing *something* may also reveal a painting to us but in that case the painting will not be the faithful reproduction of what has triggered its revelation but will only resemble it faintly, like someone's face seen in a dream and *the reality* of this person's face" (De Chirico's manuscripts, qtd. in Lista 2009, 239; my translation). What the prose poem reveals is the dream image of the painting's revelation, as processed by the poet and reflected in a disjointed, blurred composition that plunges the reader-viewer into an ongoing oneiric projection. The sea lying in wait acquires a metaphysical meaning: the hardly visible yet tenuous presence of the physical body of water threatening to overflow the peaceful, lyrical atmosphere of this "dead and empty city" may also be interpreted as the faint sign of the ever-present immanence of the world that takes possession of the artist's mind and allows him to become aware of his inner Stimmung—what Gascoyne calls in his journals "a different plane": "I shall always believe that there is another plane. I also know that in order to be able to reach it and to speak of it, one must lose everything, and be destroyed" (Gascoyne 1991, 150, 155).

The sea that "lies waiting" (30) materializes this plane of dissolution and recomposition and signals the shift from the vision of the "dead and empty city" to the living one peopled by extraordinary figures and objects ("Roman soldiers," "terrific horses," "plaster casts of heads," "strangely-marked wands"), until the final revelation of the artist's "abnormally tall figure" (30). This other plane throws us out of our depths: by enlarging the infinitesimal and the mundane, the poet gives movement and impetus to the inert representation of matter and endows separate fragments with a dynamic pattern. The sea is far more than a placid horizontal line: it is "a world of immanence and becoming . . . open, porous, mobile, and changing . . . that can stabilize temporarily . . . its territory can be anything" (Steinberg and Peters 2015, 255).

Borrowing Deleuze and Guattari's concept of assemblage and following their analysis of "a land that is eccentric, immemorial, or yet to come" (Deleuze and Guattari 2002, 505), Peters and Steinberg define the ocean as a "territory... of emergence" (2015, 255). The oceanic paradigm of "immanence and becoming" is both at the heart of the poem and of Gascoyne's lifelong poetic endeavor as evinced in his journals, where he expresses his longing for "a perpetual explosion [that] would be my ideal mode of life," or for "a (special) sense of existence," or his desire to "communicate on the *inhuman* plane" (Gascoyne 1991, 20, 81, 94). The hydrologics of Gascoyne's poetry convey the poet's quest for the "inner *Stimmung*," which Martin Heidegger defined as the advent of Being in language that opens up the subject to an attentive mode of reception of the *Stimme*, or voice. Listening to the *Stimme* of Being implies an effort of contemplation and, as Heidegger explains in his comments upon Hölderlin, the best expression of this voice is poetry because "it is first poetry that makes language possible" (Heidegger 1973, 55; my translation). In that regard, we may say that sea logics and poetic logics coalesce in Gascoyne's opus: both rely on the principle of the adventive moment, the principle of becoming, defined by Deleuze and Guattari as an assemblage that "produces nothing other than itself" (Deleuze and Guattari 2002, 238).

It is no wonder that "The World of De Chirico" should end on the dismantled "abnormally tall figure" that displays the fragments of de Chirico's compositions, as if waiting to be reassembled. De Chirico's world revisited by Gascoyne is an oceanic volume on the move whose various items do not offer us an actual painting or series of paintings as much as the potentialities of an invisible material. The hydrologics of the poem foreground Gascoyne's epistemological shift from invisibility to visibility. The unstable reconfiguration of de Chirico's brushstrokes in Gascoyne's lines supplements the visible by hinting at another plane of perception—a metaphysical one that develops into a critical perspective showcasing the frailty of language.

THE FOUNDING SPEECH ACT OF POETRY

If we are to agree with Heidegger that "it is first poetry that makes language possible" (Heidegger 1973, 55), then we are forced to admit that such a language, relying on an experimental relation with syntactic, prosodic, and semantic systems, is highly precarious. Gascoyne's relation to the sea, just like his relation to the politics of his time that transpires in his writing, is first and foremost an artistic relation that, according to Chambers, brings us "into the presence of a contingent, temporal relation and into the multiplicity of the present, which is irreducible to its representation" (Chambers 2010, 682). Embracing oceanic logic in his poetry, Gascoyne summons "a zone of feeling, a resonance, a vibration" (Chambers 2010, 682), what Peters and Steinberg call a "*frisson* of matter and meaning" (2015, 256) that exists beyond language. Aware that poetry can neither encompass nor represent oceanic immanence, Gascoyne offers his readers sea images "*as* life, a life already imagined, activated, and sustained in the image" (Chambers 2010, 682).

The poem "Unspoken" (2014, 54–55), from the Surrealist collection *Man's Life Is This Meat*, offers an illuminating insight into the complex relation between language and its object. The title of the poem underlines a fundamental paradox since poetry is quintessentially a speech act. Such is Heidegger's analysis of "Dichtung," based on his reading of Hölderlin, a poet to whom David Gascoyne felt particularly close: "Poetry is foundation through and in speech. . . . The poet names the gods and all the things as they are. This nomination does not consist in endowing with a name something that would already have been well-known; but the poet having uttered the essential word, Being is, through this naming, called to what it is, and, as such, becomes known *as* Being. Poetry is the foundation of Being through speech" (Heidegger 1973, 57; my translation). "Unspoken" explores the obverse side of language by dismantling the common language of communication to probe into a deeper, unfathomed reality. Poetry is opposed to Hamlet's misleading "Words, words, words" (*Hamlet* II.2), which Gascoyne ironically alludes to in the "buried speech/Drowning the words and words" (55). "Unspoken" is the art of poetry that brings back to the fore language not as the tool of communication and deceit but as a threshold opening onto the very foundations of our being. As Heidegger goes on to explain: "Poetry ushers in the revelation of the unreal and the dream to confront the palpable and noisy reality where we believe ourselves to be at home" (Heidegger 1973, 57; my translation).

The negative prefix of the title combines with multiple negations scattered throughout the poem: "Words spoken leave no time for regret" (54), "No two roads the same/Nor ever the same names to places," "unspeaking mountains," "deafened valleys" (55). They convey an image that unfolds like a black-and-white photographic negative, showing a discolored, inverted representation, what *is* not. Such is the true object of Gascoyne's poetry, and of the art of poetry, as W. H. Auden powerfully states in his elegy "In Memory of W. B. Yeats" (1939): "For poetry makes nothing happen: it survives/In the valley of its making . . ./. . . it survives/A way of happening, a mouth" (Auden 1994, 248). As poet Matthew Zappruder explains, "negation creates possibility . . . the emergence of the presence of something strange and unsaid behind what is familiar" (2017, 204).

Gascoyne's modern exploration of the negative capability of poetry is quite telling of his own humble posture. Following the curves of the hydrologics that sustain his poetic imagery, his poetic voice is resolutely nonassertive and nondidactic, as if already dispossessed of its own agency. It is a voice that "does not represent, but rather proposes" (Chambers 2010, 682), aware that the desired convergence with its object entails its own dispossession, not unlike the surfers and swimmers evoked by Peters and Steinberg, who "become one with the waves as the waves become one with them, in a blend of complementarity and opposition" (2015, 250). Such is the prerequisite for the emergence of "the unreal and the dream" (Heidegger 1973, 57) that unveils the relentless ebb and flow of the poetic imagination at work. Gascoyne draws us closer to the hydrologics of his poetic art through the overlapping images that summon a disembodied poetic utterance subsumed in the "voiceless cry/Spinning helpless between sleep and waking" (55). Standing on an impossible threshold, he devises a poetic space answering to oceanic logics, "a space of churning, where . . . place is provisional and forever being (re)produced" (Steinberg and Peters 2015, 258):

> Speech flowing away like water
> With its undertow of violence and darkness
> Carrying with it forever
> All those formless vessels
> Abandoned palaces
> Tottering under the strain of being (54)

The simile likening language to the dark flows transforms the thinking subjects into "formless vessels" and reveals a hitherto unheeded perspective: man is no longer a conscious, willful agent, but an object buffeted by the sea. Significantly, the aqueous simile is then displaced onto sleep that metaphorically floods the scene: "In sleep there are places places/Places overlap/. . ./Shadow as shallow as water" (54). Veering from the common uses of language, speech comes to be identified as the language of dreams, the language of an unshackled space-time:

> Slipping between the cracks
> With the face of memory and the sound of its voice
> More intimate than sweat at the roots of the hair
> . . . .
> Swifter than air between the lips
> . . . .
> Travelling through man's enormous continent (54–55)

The poet reshapes the land as an oceanic assemblage, an "enormous continent" forever unchartered where man is perpetually drifting, always bordering nothingness:

> Migrating towns and fluid boundaries
> There are no settlers here there are
> No solid stones (55)

The confrontation of "there are no" and its contrary "there are" on the same line highlights the paradoxical nature of the poetic image that "does not represent, but rather proposes" (Chambers 2010, 682), summoning a receding vision. By foregrounding the adverb "No," the last line creates another puzzling effect for the reader, who feels tempted to read its palindrome hidden in the final word, "stones." Negative forms abound and refract one another in dizzying combinations until the final lines of the poem that bring us to "navigate our daylight vessels/Following certain routes to uncertain lands." With no final period, the poem suggests that there is no end to the doing and undoing enacted in the precarious poise between "certain" and "uncertain." The relentless flow of assertions counterbalanced by negations paves the way for the unknown, the ultimate withdrawal of meaning and of self that is the course chosen by the poet.

The route sketched out through "words/Slipping between the cracks" (54) is a nondirectional impetus, rather than an oriented trajectory, that only promises "uncertain lands" (55) and expands rhizomatically through the intertextual echoes to Conrad's *Heart of Darkness*: "Clear waves of soundless sight/Lapping out of the heart of darkness." The route leads outward as well as inward, into the mysteries of the poetic self, following the relentless watery rhythm of the lines, "Beginning again and beginning/Again" (55), like the stubborn return of the waves. Gascoyne's words ebb and flow, making room for the mysterious otherness of the sea in the blank space that foregrounds the run-on line linking the last final stanzas:

> Beginning again and beginning
> Again
> Till unspoken is unseen
> Until unknown
> Descending from knowledge to knowledge (55)

The suspense that both binds and holds apart the end and the beginning of the two stanzas foreshadows the final descent into the depths of the "unspoken," the "unseen," the "unknown." The uncircumscribed depths of poetic creation can only be matched by the unfathomable oceanic depths materialized in the "breaking / . . . shifting slanting turning," the "wheel of fortune" and "the circling seas" (55), which entail both temporal and spatial dissolution and absolute dispossession: that of the "voiceless cry," the "motionless wind," "the bodiless body" (55).

Gascoyne's poetics not only borrows from the sea its imagery and watery rhythms: it adopts oceanic logics as its operating principle and turns it into a critical prism through which man's position in the world is reassessed and reframed. Encapsulating life's momentum in "the cycle of return and change" (55), it brings to the fore the frailty of our "daylight vessels" (55) and calls for a wider awareness and acknowledgment of the "foaming oceans of disintegration" (55) as the thrust of life.

As always in David Gascoyne's poetry, man's growing awareness is only fully achieved when it expresses itself through a communal spirit. The poem "Antennae" (61–63), taken from the same collection, foregrounds the sea as a shared locus, a poetic and symbolic common ground that expands well beyond its geophysical boundaries:

> The sea is a bubble in a cup of salt
> The earth is a grain of sand in a nutshell
> The earth is blue. (62)

Readers cannot fail to recognize here Blake's line—"To see a world in a grain of sand" (1979, "Auguries of Innocence" [1866])—and Éluard's poem "La terre est bleue comme une orange" (The earth is blue as an orange). From these universal and timeless poetic resonances, David Gascoyne moves to the particular, reactivating the physical tension that fosters our fascination for the ocean as our gaze is caught between the infinity of the boundless expanse and the close observation of wave formation. We move from "The earth is a grain of sand" to:

> The tongue between the teeth
> The river between the sands
> Love in my hand like lace
> Your hand enlaced with mine. (62)

The sea stands out both as a threshold onto the limitless potentialities of poetic ramifications and as the crucible of a newly founded harmony.

Indeed, the absence of punctuation marks highlights the Blakean "fearful symmetry" (1979, "The Tyger" [1794]) of Gascoyne's image and its timeless echoes within the broader poetic tradition. Simultaneously, the parallelism between the tongue and the river, the teeth and the sands, finds its climax in the reconstruction of a self-contained, perfect universe in the following couplet. The alliterations in /l/, highlighted by the prevailing use of monosyllabic words, combine with the chiasmus linking "my"/"mine" and "lace"/"enlaced" to suggest the completion of a new world reborn in love, and whose flawless circularity summons the words of Solomon's Song: "A garden inclosed is my sister, my spouse" (4.12).

From that point onwards, the lovers are at one with each other: the repetition of "between our eyes" suggests that they see eye to eye, while their final dissolution as a physical body ("When gone the body's warmth") paves the way for a plural pronoun: "For now we are suspended above life." In the final line, the use of the preposition "in" ("Held in both hands"), combined with the elision of the possessive adjective, materializes the perfect unity of the "bubble in a cup of salt." Just as human love can be held "in both hands," the sea can be held "in a cup" and this "cup of salt" blends the human and nonhuman spheres in a single metonymy that encapsulates both the boundless ocean and all those endowed with a visionary perspective who are, after Matthew's words, "the salt of the earth" (Matthew 5.13).

This newly founded community anchored in true love expands beyond the dual image of the couple, which is another metonymy for Man's unity with the world.

I have shown how Gascoyne's poetics construes the sea as a "focus," a "point of view" that raises aesthetic and epistemological issues foregrounding a radically different sensorial and conceptual approach of reality from the prevailing one that rules modern capitalist society. The sea is, indeed, as early as the Hebrews' time in Exodus, the place of a harrowing passage dramatizing man's personal and collective ordeal. But it is also the point wherefrom our old paradigms are revisited, inviting us to a critical reassessment of our position and relation to the self and to others. The sea functions as a conceptual tool ushering in a deeper awareness. Through his use of intermedial and intertextual references, Gascoyne supplements the visible and welds oceanic logic into the very matter of his own poetics. He probes the depths of creation by expanding the realm of the sensible and foregrounds poetry as the place of foundation, the place of our constantly shifting, common ground.

NOTES

The quoted phrase in the title is from Gascoyne 2014, 25–26. All further quotations are from Gascoyne 2014.

1. See Roger Scott, "David Gascoyne and American Poets and Poetry," (unpublished paper).
2. See Fraser 2012, 243–52.
3. "For as in the days that were before the flood they were eating and drinking, marrying and giving in marriage, until the day that Noe entered into the Ark, and knew not until the flood came, and took them all away; so shall also the coming of the Son of man be" (Matthew 24.38–39).
4. This poem plays with echoing dialogic voices singled out by quotation marks, which have been faithfully reproduced as they stand in the text edited by Roger Scott.
5. We may remember here that Luis Buñuel's *Un chien andalou*, with its mesmerizing fade-in and fade-out and baffling narrative disconnections, was released only three years before the publication of *Roman Balcony*.

6. We may remember here Gabriel Audisio's apostrophe to the Mediterranean Sea: "Quand ma vie, la coque à l'air, traînera sa décrépitude dans les formes de radoub, tu me rendras toutes les images, toutes les odeurs, toutes les aventures du monde dans le frissonnement des algues et la musique des conques marines" (Audisio 1928, 13).
7. The sesta rima (six lines divided into a cross-rhymed quatrain and a couplet rhyming a-b-a-b-c-c) was used by George Herbert, Christina Rossetti, and Matthew Arnold, up to John Clare in the twentieth century, and all poets display various arrangements in line lengths, feet, and rhymes.
8. The notion of the soundscape has been explored by R. Murray Schafer in his seminal essay *The Soundscape: Our Sonic Environment and the Tuning of the World* (1977).
9. See Roubaud 1995, 126.
10. We may mention, amongst other oils on canvas, *The Delights of the Poet*, 1913 (69.5 × 86.3 cm; Basel: Private collection), and *Ariane*, 1913 (135.6 × 180.5 cm; New York, The Metropolitan Museum of Modern Art).

WORKS CITED

Auden, W. H. 1994. *Collected Poems*. Faber and Faber.
Audisio, Gabriel. 1928. *Héliotrope*. Gallimard.
Benjamin, Walter. 2019. *Dream*. Bierke Verlag.
Bennett, Jane. 2010. *Vibrant Matter. A Political Ecology of Things*. Duke University Press.
Blake, William. 1979. *Blake's Poetry and Design*. Norton.
Blum, Hester. 2010. "The Prospect of Oceanic Studies." *PMLA* 125 (3): 670–77.
Chambers, Iain. 2010. "Maritime Criticism and Theoretical Shipwrecks." *PMLA* 125 (3): 678–84.
Cohen, Margaret. 2010. "Literary Studies on the Terraqueous Globe." *PMLA* 125 (3): 657–62.
Collot, Michel. 2014. *Pour une géographie littéraire*. Corti.
Conrad, Joseph. 1979. *Heart of Darkness*. Penguin.
cummings, e. e. 1977. *Selected Poems, 1923–1958*. Faber and Faber.
Deleuze, Gilles. 2006. *The Fold*. Translated by Tom Conley. Bloomsbury.
Deleuze, Gilles, and Félix Guattari. 2002. *A Thousand Plateaus*. Translated by Brian Massumi. Continuum.
DeLoughrey, Elizabeth. 2019. "Toward a Critical Ocean Studies for the Anthropocene." *English Language Notes* 57 (1): 21–36.

Eliot, T. S. 2002. *Collected Poems, 1909–1962*. Faber.
Fraser, Robert. 2012. *Night Thoughts: The Surreal Life of the Poet David Gascoyne*. Oxford University Press.
Gascoyne, David. 1991. *Collected Journals, 1936–42*. Skoob Books Publishing.
Gascoyne, David. 1998. *Selected Prose, 1934–1996*. Enitharmon Press.
Gascoyne, David. 2000. *A Short Survey of Surrealism*. Enitharmon Press.
Gascoyne, David. 2014. *New Collected Poems, 1929–1995*. Enitharmon Press.
Heidegger, Martin. 1973. *Approches de Hölderlin*. Translated by Henri Corbin, Michel Deguy, François Fédier, and Jean Launay. Gallimard.
Lista, Giovanni. 2009. *Giorgio de Chirico suivi de l'Art de la Métaphysique*. Hazan.
Orwell, George. 1982. *The Collected Essays*. Vol 1. Penguin.
Raine, Kathleen. 2017. *David Gascoyne et la fonction prophétique / David Gascoyne and the Prophetic Role*. Black Herald Press.
Roubaud, Jacques. 1995. *Poésie, etcetera: Ménage*. Stock.
Schafer, R. Murray. 1977. *The Soundscape: Our Sonic Environment and the Tuning of the World*. Knopf.
Steinberg, Philip, and Kimberley Peters. 2015. "Wet Ontologies, Fluid Spaces: Giving Depth to Volume Through Oceanic Thinking." *Environment and Planning D: Society & Space* 33 (2): 247–64.
The New Shorter Oxford English Dictionary. 1993. Clarendon Press.
Zappruder, Matthew. 2017. *Why Poetry*. HarperCollins.

AFTERWORD

Logics of Port Cities

BRIAN T. EDWARDS

I am fascinated by port cities, their lives as multivalent trading centers, the vestiges left behind and inscribed within them, the experience of living alongside water as ever-present threat and fraught source of inspiration.

I sit in Dakar, on the back side of the *presqu'île* du Cap-Vert, watching waves lap against smooth black rocks; teenagers play shoeless soccer on wet sand. "Presqu'île" denotes a special kind of peninsula, a word we don't have in English: almost an island, but not quite. Dakar juts out into the Atlantic, surrounded by water, the westernmost point in Africa. The ocean on the east side of the almost-island, looking down the coast toward the tip of the plateau, is calmer than on the west. The water is light blue, the color of postcards. Yet the idyllic beach scene belies what has been called an "ecological disaster" just north of here in Hann Bay, on the other side of the port, where wastewater and industrial discharge have created a crisis over the decades that Dakar multiplied in size (Lewis 2016).[1]

The previous month, I was in Tangier, nearly 3,000 km north of here, and looked out from Cap Spartel, the northwestern point of Africa, the place where the Atlantic Ocean meets the Mediterranean Sea. The Strait of Gibraltar is a magical and treacherous confluence of waters. The mythical city of Atlantis, it has long been rumored, may have lain here just off the present coastline, swallowed by the waters. Fifteen kilometers to the east of Cap Spartel, the city is undergoing a transformation. The old railway station near the port has been closed, replaced by a modern terminal three kilometers away, where a TGV connects Tangier to Casablanca in just over two hours, a ride that used to take triple that time. Forty-five kilometers to the east, the massive new port Tanger Med opened in 2007 and has since grown to the largest trading hub on the southern side of the Mediterranean, reorienting Morocco's center of gravity and transforming the local economy dramatically. In central Tangier, massive renovation projects have been completed in the past decade and a half: A ring road along the coast now connects the old port to Merkala Beach, a new luxury marina hosts yachts and sailing vessels, and an extravagant shopping and entertainment mall juts into the sea.

A month before that, I was in Havana, nearly 7,000 km to the west, where I met with architects and urbanists and artists in another great old port city. Havana was suffering from a lack of drinking water, the city's crumbling infrastructure forcing shutdowns during the excessive midsummer heat. The lack of running water for days at a time compounded the lack of fresh food and restricted access to commodities. During the summer of 2023, the city struggled under the weight of U.S. sanctions, low levels of tourism that had not returned since restrictions from the first Trump administration, and what many called a pandemic hangover.[2] The unobstructed vista across open waters enhanced the sense of isolation. Havana looks out on the Strait of Florida, which separates the island nation from the plenitude of the U.S., barely 170 km across a treacherous sea to Key West.

From Dakar, I'll head home soon to New Orleans, just as we enter the heart of hurricane season—August and September—when the warm waters of the Gulf of Mexico accelerate storms that make their way from the Atlantic past Cuba and turn left. When I ask someone in Dakar if people worry about hurricanes, she tells me that the fuel for the storms we receive in New Orleans comes from the west coast of Africa. Whether or not a major storm lands this year (it seems almost inevitable), water organizes everything in my home city, an "unnatural metropolis" built between the Mississippi River and the estuary Lake Pontchartrain (Colten 2006). A city that lives with water in excess, a city marked by "overflow," as Olivia Durand puts it in her contribution to this collection. In the past three years, the cost of my homeowner's insurance has risen more than 250 percent despite having made no claims and living in a no-flood zone, ever so slightly above sea level. Andy Horowitz, author of *Katrina: A History, 1915–2015* (2020), quipped a few years ago that it wouldn't be the hurricanes that kill New Orleans but the insurance companies; as my premiums rose sharply again this year, his comment struck home.[3]

I am not able to see the river from my home—nor are most people who live in New Orleans, the levee blocking sight of it—but as I try to make my way across the Crescent City, everything is dictated by its course. The city is built in a long bend in the river, plotted on a series of isosceles triangles that all start at the river: the plotting of old plantations, their bases stretching along the river's bank and converging at a point in Mid-City. The campus of my university, for example, is built on one such triangle and gets narrower as it heads toward Lake Pontchartrain. This grid of triangles makes for difficult navigation for the uninitiated. We don't say "north" and "south" in New Orleans but "lakeside" and "riverside," "uptown" and "downtown." It took me months to figure out that the fastest way across town was not to follow the major boulevards, which echo the curve of the river, but to head away from the river toward the center, then follow a different axis down.

THE EDGE

At one of the high points of Tangier sits the Café Hafa, a legendary place as famous for its relationship to literary history as it is for its stunning location. On a clear day, you can see the white buildings of the town of Tarifa across the Strait of Gibraltar, on the southern coast of Spain. If you arrive at Tangier from the sea, on a ferry from Spain or perhaps on a cruise ship or even a yacht, the picturesque view presents itself, a hilly city facing out toward the port. But from the Café Hafa, the gaze is reversed. For the price of a glass of mint tea, you can sit for as long as you like. The view is taunting to those who aspire to make their way to Europe. Remember the opening lines of the 1942 film *Casablanca?* Those hoping to obtain exit visas to get to Lisbon and from there to America, wait in Casablanca, ". . . and wait . . . and wait . . . and wait." Even in 1942, that line described a Hollywood fantasy city and was more suited to wartime Tangier, an international zone and a den of spies, smugglers, and diplomats (Edwards 2005). It still describes Tangier for the many hopeful migrants who make their way from sub-Saharan Africa to the port city, and for Moroccans who wait for a chance to "burn," as they say in Moroccan Arabic (*h'rig* [حريق]), a word that signifies illicit migration, as in burning your papers). There is something about the temporality of port cities, where the repetition of undulating water evokes waiting and hoping (*espérance*).

Situated atop the cliffs in the neighborhood called the Marshan, the Café Hafa is a short stroll from a set of prehistoric tombs believed to have been created by the Phoenicians as many as seven centuries before the Common Era. The tombs are rectangular openings in smooth rock, the size of large coffins, and the effect is a smooth face of stone pockmarked with deathly openings. Contemporary Tanjawis come here to enjoy themselves; there are carts selling popcorn and small snacks. Children play and lovers sit on the edges of tombs and look out across the treacherous Strait. What Edwige Tamalet Talbayev calls "water necropolitics" is starkly visible here; the ancient death of the tombs, the danger of migration, what Hakim Abderrezak darkly calls the "seametery" of the waters (Abderrezak 2019).

The word *ḥāfa* (حافة) means "edge," an evocative concept for those who think in terms of continents and nations, and this café is on the northwestern edge of Africa, the brink of a continent, the edge where land and water meet, a rim and a border. The café itself is terraced. To make your way down the six or seven levels of this vertically oriented establishment is to feel gravity pulling you toward the sea. The café is nestled into the hill, its back against the land mass. The Café Hafa is in this sense the consummate port city café, as I have come to think about the special status of port cities: one's back to the land and one's face to the sea, the edge of land and water. But here, too, one feels the land mass reaching out under the water, the depth of the sea visible until it disappears. The edge, that is, reaches out farther than the line between blue and brown on the map.

What is the logic of the edge? In a brilliant 1951 essay, "East Side: North Africa," Jane Bowles, who lived in Tangier, equates various edges, both physical and psychological and national: "The highest street in this blue Arab town skirted the edge of a cliff. I walked to the thick protecting wall and looked down" (Bowles 2017, 347). Bowles published the piece as nonfiction in *Mademoiselle*, but the essay had not yet found its form; it still skirted its edge as a piece of writing. She rewrote it as a short story, now entitled "Everything Is Nice," an expression I have argued that she translated from a colloquial Tanjawi expression. In "Everything Is Nice," Bowles uses the elusive English word "nice" to end conversation, to place a limit at understanding between people, an edge separating American and Moroccan conversation. Edges are like that, as are port cities. Sixty years later, the Tangier director Lëila Kilani's 2011 film على الحافة (*'Alā-l-ḥāfa* [*On the Edge*]) is another such port city fiction, a noirish cinematic narrative that evokes the rough aspect of Tangier's edginess, centered around girls who work in a factory shelling shrimp by day and steal and hustle by night. To be "on edge" in English is a state of anxiety. Port cities are, in this sense, anxious places, their marginal status and their exceptional status overlaid.

PORT CITY DYNAMICS

What are the dynamics of port cities? And what might they tell us about water logics more generally? Port cities are not like other cities, or rather they are like other cities but in excess. They contain the immensity of other worlds in their complexity. Water threatens them but also makes them; it is the dialectic of their being. Water connects ports to other ports, nodes across a global network of trade and travel. But water also is their limit, with their backs to the land behind them.

One of these days water will submerge us, they say in New Orleans, and when the rain comes down hard at noon on July days, those incredible downpours that punctuate the summer, the streets and sidewalks pool up. People know where not to park, and the so-called neutral ground in the center of the broad boulevards fills up with cars as a storm approaches. The city feels always as if it is sinking; new potholes emerge overnight and grow bigger and deeper. They are treacherous and they are celebrated at once.[4] We live in a saucer floating inside a basin of water, people explained to me when I moved to the Big Easy.

What is it about port cities that makes them compelling? These are places that share characteristics that go beyond their specific national contexts. Like Tangier, like New Orleans, like Dakar and Naples, they often are exceptional to or pushed out from or forgotten by their capitals. In her essay on New Orleans and Odessa, two port cities at the heart of her contribution to this collection, Olivia Durand understands them both as "edge zones" to emphasize their place "on the peripheries of empires."

As Durand shows, New Orleans relied too much on its river, and what was once the third-largest city in the United States in the 1840s quickly receded in importance. This was not only because of the end of the Civil War and the slave economy, within which New Orleans was a major capital. It was also because of the lack of diversification of transportation networks. Durand points to the railroad here and the ways in which the major route bypassed New Orleans for Houston, leaving New Orleans isolated. Richard Campanella has argued elsewhere that the failure to invest in other industries beyond a mercantile economy led to New Orleans's gradual and then rapid decline within the growing U.S. (Campanella 2022).[5]

Port cities changed again profoundly after the arrival of the standardized intermodal container in 1956, a massive structural change in global trade (Levinson 2016). Now in places like Tangier, New Orleans, and Dakar, even while trade by water has increased in terms of tonnage, the dominance of intermodal containers has dramatically lessened the human aspect of trade in port cities, as robotic cranes have replaced stevedores. What vestiges of the human aspect of global trade do we live with in port cities in the age of containers? What palimpsest of features and memories do port cities share?

Port cities, it must be repeated, have certain features in common, both negative and positive.[6] And this is what fascinates me about them, why they may have their potential embedded in them, even while they struggle with their precarity. They struggle, commonly, with environmental crisis, with forms of criminality and poverty and corruption that follow in the wake of places of smuggling and trade. But higher levels of multilingualism and multinationalism are also inscribed within them and continue to distinguish them. Perhaps this is why a sense of relationality—a kind of gritty cosmopolitanism—pervades them, as if the fact of so many peoples and languages coming together was woven into their social fabric. Pidgin versions of English or French or Arabic or Spanish, Creole tongues, emerge, and distinct ways of saying things in them can prove elusive to national tongues. These are accented cities, where speaking with an accent, one of many, is the norm.

There is a relationship between water and multilingualism, as land that opened itself up to trade among peoples leads to a proliferation of languages. Before the French followed a man named Jean-Baptiste Le Moyne de Bienville, then governor of the French colony of Louisiana, to an area up the Mississippi River that he thought was safe from storm floods and hurricanes because of its position at a turn in the river, the native peoples had identified it as a trading port. The Biloxi, Choctaw, Chitimacha, Houma, and Tunica called this place Bulbancha, a Choctaw and Chickasaw word alternatively translated as "place of many tongues" or "place of other tongues." Here, before the French settlement, what's been called Mobilian jargon emerged as a trade language between Indigenous tribes.

The multilingual aspect of port cities, then, is inherent and connected to confluences of waters and peoples. Today in Dakar, the number of languages—Wolof, predominant among them, but also Pulaar (Fulani), Serer, Mandinka (Bambara), Joola, Soninke, and at least fifteen other African languages—marks its complexity. Tangier too is a city in which moving between the multiple languages in use there (Arabic, Tamazight, French, Spanish, and English) is done fluidly; monolingual residents are rare. A palimpsest of street signs and markers indexes the internationalism of the city. This was, after all, an International Zone for several decades in the twentieth century (1925-56), during which multiple postal systems, currencies, and legal codes were simultaneously in use while a committee of nations oversaw governance.

NO ONE LIVES IN DAKAR

The Senegalese philosopher Babacar Mbaye Diop teaches me the Wolof expression "Kèn dëkut Dakar," which he translates for me as "personne n'habite à Dakar." No one lives in Dakar, but of course everyone seems to live in this complex and overcrowded city, the presqu'île more and more crowded with every year, as rural Senegalese flee drought and climate change in the interior to come to the peninsula. In this construction, it is the Lebou, the fishermen of Dakar, who are understood to be the primary people of the peninsular city, the "only ones" to truly live here. I am interested in Lebou thinking about the water. Another philosopher, Hady Ba, helps teach me. He points me to Moustapha Sall and Et Oumy Mbaye's work on Lebou thinking, which identifies the two kinds of water that are part of the cosmography, a feminine water with vegetation and a masculine water without vegetation, the sea of the Yoff (Sall and Mbaye 2017).[7] Understanding these two "waters," a word that has only one gender in the languages I know, opens up my understanding of the port city.

Kèn dëkut Dakar. The plentitude that is Dakar and its languages and people is countered by lack. No one lives in Dakar means of course that everyone lives in Dakar. And that recalls the moments elsewhere in the network of port cities where the absence of water accompanies the surfeit of it. In New Orleans, floods lead to boil alerts, during which the infrastructure is taxed to the point where the drinking water is not safe unless boiled. Or the infrastructure of Havana, where the water is shut off in neighborhoods for a week at a time. In Havana, I see water tanks on the tops of residences, in which the tap is left on so as to be ready to fill those tanks the next moment the supply is opened again. One hopes that one's personal tank will gather enough until the next shutdown.

WATER AND DISCIPLINES

In their provocative introduction to this collection, yasser elhariry and Edwige Tamalet Talbayev suggest that literary studies comes at the "tail ends of creative and generative processes." I am intrigued by this observation from the standpoint of the disciplines themselves, the movements and products of culture that flow or meander eventually into a range of areas of inquiry. As this inspiring collection reminds us in new ways, there are many tributaries that academics live alongside; scholars based in multiple disciplines learn from and expose for us their logics.

Water is undisciplined. Water teaches us that we cannot contain it, just as we cannot contain thinking and human expression within the academic disciplines that have formed to organize our thinking. Water and ports thus connect the disciplines and overwhelm them at the same time. They require an interdisciplinarity—perhaps even an "indisciplinarity."

In his *Les Sentiers de l'indiscipline* (2021), novelist and playwright Driss Ksikes connects the oceanic with such an approach. In a section of that plentiful book, entitled "La grille et l'océan," Ksikes opposes the ocean to the grid. He opposes the measurable (*la grille*) which is rational, limiting, and the expansive oceanic, connected for him to literary inspiration itself. *La grille* is associated with measurement, the grid of graph paper, and also the grid of the prison and fences. Ksikes starts his mediation with the Portuguese poet Fernando Pessoa's meditation on the slave ship, where the tension between the oceanic and imagination and imprisonment is abrupt and clear. Ksikes also compares in his indisciplined way Gilles Deleuze and Félix Guattari's opposition between the smooth (*lisse*) and the striated (*strié*). Something that is oceanic, Ksikes tells me, is something that you cannot categorize as you can science. This sense of immensity, this oceanic feeling, recalls for me Gaston Bachelard, but also the Moroccan philosopher and poet

Abdelkébir Khatibi, who thought frequently about water and the plurality of the Maghreb. Khatibi's narrator in his great novel *Amour bilingue* [*Love in Two Languages*] merges with and masturbates in the sea. And I think too of Mohammed Mrabet, the analphabetic Tanjawi fisherman whose thirteen books, composed in an indisciplined way with Paul Bowles, emerge from the water, from a speaking fish, from life in a port city.

My own comments here are indisciplined in a way analogous to what Ksikes means. I am jumping between academic disciplines, forms of responding to and living with the ocean and the river and the port.

These are, after all, port city dynamics, creative and complex and dangerous and inspiring. Water logics run through them and continue to flow.

NOTES

1. See the following for one example of projects to depollute the bay and accounts of the impact of the influx of waste water into the sea: https://www.afd.fr/en/actualites/hann-bay-senegal-partnership-depollution-and-restoration.
2. "Havana Suffers Water Shortages as Cracks Show in Aging Cuban Infrastructure," *Reuters*, July 4, 2023, https://www.reuters.com/world/americas/havana-suffers-water-shortages-cracks-show-aging-cuban-infrastructure-2023-07-04/.
3. Travis Lux featured Horowitz on an NPR program, "Life Raft: Could Flood Insurance Sink Us Before the Water Does?" February 23, 2021, https://www.wwno.org/coastal-desk/2021-02-23/life-raft-could-flood-insurance-sink-us-before-the-water-does.
4. For exuberant examples of the latter, follow @lookatthisfuckinstreet on *Instagram*. You're welcome.
5. See also Campanella 2020.
6. See Brian T. Edwards and Driss Ksikes, "Port Cities, Creative Cities" (2024), for an elaboration on these points. The present essay was written after that one, and incorporates observations on Dakar and Havana subsequent to the observations and theorization in the "interim report."
7. For Souleymane Bachir Diagne, the Senegalese philosopher Assane Sylla, in *La philosophie morale des Wolofs*, "a pensé à la frontière de la philosophie et de l'anthropologie."

WORKS CITED

Abderrezak, Hakim. 2019. "The Mediterranean Sieve, Spring and Seametery." In *Refugee Imaginaries: Research Across the Humanities,* edited by Emma Cox, Sam Durrant, David Farrier, Lyndsey Stonebridge, and Agnes Woolley. Edinburgh University Press.

Bowles, Jane. 2017. "East Side, North Africa." 1951. In *Jane Bowles: Collected Writings,* edited by Millicent Dillon. Library of America.

Campanella, Richard. 2020. *The West Bank of Greater New Orleans: A Historical Geography.* Louisiana State University Press.

Campanella, Richard. 2022. "Missed Opportunities: History's Stinging Lesson on Economic Diversification in New Orleans." *New Orleans Advocate / Times Picayune,* 7 July. https://www.nola.com/news/business/missed-opportunities-historys-stinging-lesson-on-economic-diversification-in-new-orleans/article_8797759e-f70a-11ec-a546-832ac108619c.html.

Colten, Craig. 2006. *An Unnatural Metropolis: Wresting New Orleans from Nature.* Louisiana State University Press.

Edwards, Brian T. 2005. *Morocco Bound: Disorienting America's Maghreb, from Casablanca to the Marrakech Express.* Duke University Press.

Edwards, Brian T., and Driss Ksikes. 2024. "Port Cities, Creative Cities." *Public Culture* 36 (3): 313–28. https://doi.org/10.1215/08992363-11593027.

Ksikes, Driss. 2021. *Les Sentiers de l'indiscipline.* En toutes lettres.

Levinson, Marc. 2016. *The Box: How the Shipping Container Made the World Smaller and the World Economy Bigger.* 2nd ed. Princeton University Press.

Lewis, Joris. 2016. "Cleaning Up Muddy Waters: The Fight to Revive Senegal's Hann Bay." *Environmental Health Perspectives* 124 (5): A92–A97. https://www.ncbi.nlm.nih.gov/pmc/articles/PMC4858393/.

Sall, Moustapha, and Et Oumy Mbaye. 2017. "Le Patrimoine cultuel et culturel Lebou en mileu urbain Dakarois (Cap-Vert, Sénégal)." *O Ideário Patrimonial,* no. 8, 6–20.

CONTRIBUTORS

MATTHEW BRAUER is assistant professor of French and Francophone Studies at the University of Tennessee, Knoxville. Brauer studies writing in Arabic and French from historical, material, and aesthetic perspectives, with a focus on situating the postcolonial cultures of North Africa and France in transnational frames from the nineteenth century to the present. Examining how developments to literary languages and forms implicate environmental, economic, legal, and political change, Brauer is preparing a monograph on the rise of the novel in North Africa and has published research in journals such as *PMLA, International Journal of Middle East Studies,* and *Tamazgha Studies Journal.*

OLIVIA DURAND is a historian specializing in global history, with expertise in the politics of history and memory, settler colonialism, and colonial port cities. Her research also spans nineteenth-century Russia, Ukraine, and America. Durand has held positions at the University of Oxford, Freie Universität Berlin, and the Institute of Historical Justice and Reconciliation in The Hague, and she is currently a fellow at the Institute of Historical Research (SOAS) in London. Alongside her academic work, Olivia is dedicated to public history and fostering engagement with research through her involvement in public-facing projects.

BRIAN T. EDWARDS is the Herb Weil, PhD Professor of the Humanities and dean of the School of Liberal Arts at Tulane University. He is the author of *After the American Century: The Ends of U.S. Culture in the Middle East* and *Morocco Bound: Disorienting America's Maghreb,* and coeditor of *Globalizing American Studies,* which emerged from a project based at Northwestern, where he was on the faculty for nearly two decades. His essays have appeared in *Public Culture, PMLA, American Literary History, NOVEL, Sewanee Review, The Believer, McSweeney's,* and many others.

YASSER ELHARIRY is associate professor of French Studies at Dartmouth College. He is the author of *This Book Is Full of Holes: Literary Bodies and the Invention of an Idiom* and *Pacifist Invasions: Arabic, Translation, and the Postfrancophone Lyric*, as well as editor and coeditor of several essay collections, including *Re-Membering Hospitality in the Mediterranean; Abdelkébir Khatibi: Literature and Theory; Literature as Sound Studies; The Postlingual Turn;* and *Sounds Senses*. His essays appear in *Yale French Studies, Oxford Research Encyclopedia of Literature, New Literary History, L'Esprit Créateur, Contemporary French Civilization, Contemporary French and Francophone Studies: SITES, Francosphères, French Forum, Parade sauvage: Revue d'études rimbaldiennes*, and several edited volumes.

STEFAN HELMREICH is Elting E. Morison Professor of Anthropology at MIT. He is author of *Alien Ocean: Anthropological Voyages in Microbial Seas, Sounding the Limits of Life: Essays in the Anthropology of Biology and Beyond*, and *A Book of Waves*. His essays have appeared in *Critical Inquiry, Representations, American Anthropologist, The Wire, Cabinet, Public Culture,* and *BOMB*.

CHARLES HELLER is SNF Professor at the Department of Social Anthropology of the University of Bern, where he is Director of Research of the Border Forensics Investigation Agency, and leads the Circumference of Violence Research project (2024–28). Prior to founding the Border Forensics agency, Heller codirected the *Forensic Oceanography* project with Lorenzo Pezzani (2011–21). As a researcher, filmmaker, and human rights activist, his work has a long-standing focus on the politics of migration, borders, mediation, and the law within and at the borders of Europe.

NICOLE HORNE is a teacher, writer, and translator from New Orleans, Louisiana. She has a doctorate in French Studies from Tulane University, where her research focused primarily on francophone migrant and postcolonial literatures. She currently teaches French at an arts conservatory high school in New Orleans and serves as editorial assistant for the bilingual academic journal *Expressions maghrébines*.

ISABELLE KELLER-PRIVAT is professor of English at the University Toulouse Jean Jaurès, where she teaches British literature, travel writing, poetry, and translation. She is chief editor of *Caliban, French Journal of English Studies*. She has published the first book-length study of Lawrence Durrell's poetry collections—*Lawrence Durrell's Poetry: A Rift in the Fabric of the World*. With yasser elhariry and Edwige Tamalet Talbayev, she is coeditor of the forthcoming *Re-Membering Hospitality in the*

Mediterranean. Her current research focuses on travel literature and poetry and on the ethics and praxis of hospitality in Anglophone literature.

SHANAAZ MOHAMMED is assistant professor of French at Marist University. She received her PhD in French from Florida State University. Her research focuses on representations of the South Asian diaspora in Francophone Caribbean and Indian Ocean literatures. Her work has appeared in the *Journal of Indian Ocean World Studies*, *Romance Notes*, and *Chimères*.

MARTIN MUNRO is Winthrop-King Professor of French and Francophone Studies at Florida State University. His publications include *The Music of the Future: Sound and Vision in the Caribbean*; *Listening to the Caribbean: Sounds of Slavery, Revolt, and Race*; and *Tropical Apocalypse: Haiti and the Caribbean End Times*. He has also published translations of Michaël Ferrier's *Mémoires d'outre mer*, *Scrabble* and *François, portrait d'un absent*; Édouard Glissant's *Une nouvelle région du monde*; and Laura Alcoba's *Par la forêt*. In 2020–21 he was a fellow at the National Humanities Center in North Carolina, and he was a 2024–25 Guggenheim Fellow.

SUPRIYA M. NAIR is professor in the Department of English Language and Literature at the University of Michigan, Ann Arbor. She is the author of two monographs, *Caliban's Curse: George Lamming and the Revisioning of History* and *Pathologies of Paradise: Caribbean Detours*. She is also coeditor of *Postcolonialisms: An Anthology of Cultural Theory and Criticism* and editor of *Teaching Anglophone Caribbean Literature*. Her research and teaching interests include postcolonial, feminist, diaspora (Caribbean, African, South Asian), environmental, and cultural studies. She is currently working on a book related to postcolonial environmentalism.

AARON PINNIX is a researcher focusing on how contemporary poetry evokes, imagines, and responds to the Anthropocene, especially regarding the ocean and ocean life. Recent work can be found in *The Routledge Companion to Ecopoetics*, *Shima Journal*, and *Rethinking Infrastructure Across the Humanities*.

NATHALIE ROELENS is professor of Literary Theory at the University of Luxembourg, where she heads the Institute of Romance Studies, Media and the Arts, and affiliate at the Luxembourg School of Religion and Society. Her publications include *Éloge du dépaysement: Du voyage au tourisme* and *Le lecteur, ce voyeur absolu*, and she has edited multiple volumes, including *Di Melusine e di Gorgone*; *Mode modeste: Entre éthique et esthétique*; *"Breaking the Waves": Water (Issues) in Contemporary Arts*; and

Water and Sea in Word and Image. She cohosts the Écologie de la mode seminar at the Collège des Bernardins in Paris.

MARIE SANDOZ is a media historian with a special interest in satellite communications and "useful television" and the author of *De l'orbite au territoire helvétique: Une histoire des communications par satellite en Suisse des années 1960 à nos jours*. Sandoz is a postdoc at the University of Lausanne researching twentieth-century uses of audiovisual closed circuits. Sandoz has published articles on (Swiss) media history, contributed to the volume *History of the International Telecommunication Union*, and coedited with Anne-Katrin Weber a special issue of the journal *Transbordeur: Photographie, Histoire, Société* devoted to the history and politics of aerial photography.

PHILIP STEINBERG is UArctic Chair in Political Geography at Durham University, where he directs IBRU: Durham University's Centre for Borders Research, the Durham Arctic Research Centre for Training and Interdisciplinary Collaboration (DurhamARCTIC), and the Northeast England / Northern Ireland Doctoral Training Partnership. He has published widely on legal, artistic, phenomenological, remotely sensed, and material perspectives on the sea, especially in Arctic regions. His publications include *The Social Construction of the Ocean* and the coedited volumes *The Routledge Handbook of Ocean Space* and *Territory Beyond Terra*.

BRADLEY STEPHENS is professor of French Literature at the University of Bristol. He has coedited five publications in these fields, including *"Les Misérables" and its Afterlives: Between Page, Stage, and Screen*. He is also the author of *Victor Hugo* in Reaktion's Critical Lives series; *Victor Hugo, Jean-Paul Sartre, and the Liability of Liberty*; and multiple pieces in *The Conversation*, *The Guardian*, and *The Huffington Post*. He is currently completing a book on configurations of patriarchy in Hugo's work and has launched a new project on masculinity in twenty-first-century French popular fiction.

EDWIGE TAMALET TALBAYEV is associate professor of French, and affiliated faculty in Environmental Studies and Middle East and North African Studies at Tulane University and professor extraordinarius at the Institute for Social and Health Sciences, University of South Africa. She is the author of *The Transcontinental Maghreb: Francophone Literature Across the Mediterranean* (2017) and coeditor of several edited volumes—most recently, *Re-Membering Hospitality in the Mediterranean* (2025) and *Ecocritical Terrains: Rethinking Tamazghan and Middle Eastern Environments* (forthcoming). She is currently at work on several projects that explore the materiality of water as a site of alternative epistemologies. She is editor of the journal

Expressions maghrébines and coeditor of the Passagen book series for Georg Olms Verlag.

ANNE-KATRIN WEBER is assistant professor of Television Studies at the University of Lausanne. She is the author of *Television Before TV: New Media and Exhibition Culture in Europe and the USA, 1928–1939*. She is also the editor and coeditor of several journal issues, including *La Guerre des drones* (*A Contrario*, 2019) and *L'Image verticale: Politiques de la vue aérienne* (*Transbordeur*, 2022, with Marie Sandoz), and edited volumes, such as *Towards an Expanded History of Television*. Her current project, *Operative TV*, investigates the history of closed-circuit television (CCTV) from the 1930s to the 1990s.

INDEX

aesthetics, 73, 75, 76, 80, 84, 85, 156n9, 178, 181, 185, 237, 257, 265, 298; as "aesthetic regime" (Heller and Pezzani), 162–67, 174, 175

Africanity, 203

Agamben, Giorgio, 78, 148, 207; "bare life," 147, 148

agency: human, 143, 145, 147, 162, 174, 188, 191, 294; more-than-human, 13, 53, 56, 62, 112, 179, 180, 190, 259, 271; relational, 11, 154, 257

Alaimo, Stacy, 11, 12, 13, 156n9, 188. *See also* "transcorporeality" (Alaimo)

Alexis, Jacques-Stephen, 202–4

Amimoto Ingersoll, Karin, 11, 12, 57, 101, 102. *See also* epistemology

Anthropocene, 88, 91, 110, 128, 201, 234, 250

anthropocentrism, 11, 135, 190, 256, 261, 277

Antillanité, 181

appearance, 105, 189. *See also* disappearance

archipelago, 30, 209, 210

archive, 15, 126, 186, 189, 194, 241

assemblage, 10, 149, 151, 163, 170, 217, 259, 292, 295

Atlantic, 7, 22, 73, 74, 108–10, 114, 123, 137n6, 155n7, 184, 198, 201, 202, 225, 233, 238, 264, 301, 302. *See also* Gilroy, Paul

Bachelard, Gaston, 7, 73, 74, 261, 308

Barad, Karen, 2; "agential realism," 257; "diffraction," 14, 16n5; "intra-activity," 16n6

"bare life" (Agamben). *See* Agamben, Giorgio

Bauman, Zygmunt, 259

becoming, 12, 15, 60, 103, 143, 149, 153, 154, 180, 257, 262, 291, 292. *See also* Deleuze, Gilles

Benítez Rojo, Antonio, 209

Bergson, Henri, 60, 80

biopolitics, 10, 11, 138n13, 143, 147, 148, 153, 154, 156n8. *See also* necropolitics

Bishop, Elizabeth, 10–12

Black, 97, 98, 102, 108, 109, 114, 115, 116n3, 123, 127, 128, 133, 145n7, 184,

Black (*continued*)
   203. *See also* Gilroy, Paul: "Black Atlantic"
blue humanities. *See* humanities
Blum, Hester, 2, 4, 10, 107, 117n5, 177, 235, 290
body. *See* corporeality
bone, 127, 129, 136n1, 146, 184, 186, 190, 192, 194, 261
border, 3, 13, 15, 26–28, 52, 102, 123–24, 127, 130, 136n5, 137n9, 142–55, 160–69, 171, 175, 304; borderland, 23; borderscape, 144, 145, 150. *See also* Mbembe, Achille
Brathwaite, Kamau, 102, 109, 114, 198. *See also* "tidalectics"
Braudel, Fernand, 238
Burke, Edmund. *See* sublime, the
Butler, Judith, 130, 147

cabotage, 74
Caillois, Roger, 86, 87
Calvino, Italo, 79–80, 84, 86
camp, 32, 135, 146–49, 174
Campanella, Richard, 33, 34, 38, 44n6, 45nn19–20, 306
capitalism, 3, 98, 99, 124, 128, 132, 145, 146, 149, 201, 234, 238, 240, 243, 250, 284, 298. *See also* "hydrocapitalism" (Pritchard)
capture, 5–6, 8, 10, 14, 15, 55, 76, 103, 129, 163, 164, 202, 209, 242, 286. *See also* Chow, Rey
Caribbean, 13, 25, 27, 38, 101, 109, 126, 127, 138n11, 178, 185, 187, 198–201, 207–10
cartography, 12, 127, 160, 172, 249
Cassano, Franco, 74

Césaire, Aimé, 185, 186, 187; "Négritude," 185, 187
Chambers, Iain, 277, 278, 285, 286, 287, 288, 293, 294, 295
chaos, 38, 86, 132, 209, 210, 221, 279, 285
Chow, Rey: "capture," 5, 6; "interventional creativity," 6
circulation, 14, 124, 136n1, 151, 153, 175, 182, 214, 221, 222, 224–27, 236, 243, 257, 259
clandestine, 125, 127, 136n5, 142–44, 159, 162, 166
Cohen, Margaret, 235, 277
commemoration. *See* memory: as memorialization
condensation, 6, 267
connectivity, 23, 26, 27, 34, 96, 152, 182, 183, 234. *See also* relationality
containment, 2, 4, 6, 14, 17, 50, 54, 89, 103, 143, 146, 147, 149, 150, 154, 167, 206, 216, 220, 229n8, 242, 247, 257, 297, 305, 308
convergence, 9, 11, 23, 27, 35, 66, 186, 198, 215, 290, 294, 303
"Coolitude" (Torabully), 171, 181, 185–88, 194
coral, 177–95; "coralization" (Mohammed), 8, 177–95
corporeality, 7, 81, 149, 152, 191, 193, 260, 263. *See also* dissolution; "transcorporeality" (Alaimo)
"*corps-frontière*" (Mbembe), 149, 152, 154
creativity, 1, 6, 62, 105, 131, 132, 184, 209, 257, 260, 265, 308, 309. *See also* Chow, Rey
Créolité, 181; creolization, 23, 181, 183, 185, 194, 195n1, 204. *See also* Glissant, Édouard

crisis, 38, 146, 149, 207, 209, 234, 238, 240, 241, 250, 276, 301, 306; migrant, 82, 124. *See also* hydrosocial: crisis

Danticat, Edwidge, 137n9, 207, 208
data, 167, 168, 170–72
death, 14, 35, 38, 39, 41, 46nn29–30, 82, 99, 115, 123–39, 142–56, 159–75, 192, 193, 198, 203, 205, 206, 208, 245, 248, 271, 279, 281, 283, 284, 288, 304
Deleuze, Gilles: "becoming," 60; and Pierre Boulez, 7; and Félix Guattari, 7–8, 117n6, 186, 277–78, 282, 292, 308; "movement-image," 60, 80; "rhizome," 186; "smoothness and striation," 7–8, 277, 308; "territorialization," 117n6
deliquescence, 11, 215, 218, 221, 228, 261. *See also* dissolution
DeLoughrey, Elizabeth, 4, 12, 13, 101, 107, 109, 113, 117n3, 177, 201, 202, 211n3, 277, 278. *See also* "tidalectics"
depth, 12–13, 28, 68, 73, 86, 99, 128, 151, 178–79, 199, 217, 244, 259, 261, 269–70, 290, 293, 298. *See also* surface
Derrida, Jacques, 133, 139n18, 229n3; "*différance*," 217; "hospitality," 135
detour, 209, 272
Didi-Huberman, Georges, 76, 79, 82, 87
digital, 56, 58, 67, 80, 172, 218, 226–30; poetry, 218, 225
disappearance, 15, 76, 143, 144, 149, 153, 154, 221, 280, 289. *See also* appearance

disaster, 10, 52, 54, 65, 80, 137, 200, 205, 236, 301
discipline, 3, 4, 86, 98, 124, 136n1, 238, 308–9; and "indisciplinarity" (Edwards), 2, 308–9; and interdisciplinarity, 86, 189, 190
dissolution, 5, 11, 15, 148–54, 156, 271, 278, 282, 288, 290, 296–97. *See also* body; deliquescence; ontology: as "dissolutive ontologies" (Talbayev)
drowning, 74, 123, 124, 127, 133, 143, 145, 146, 149, 150, 151, 160, 161, 164, 171, 174, 190, 283, 293

ecocriticism, 2, 7, 256, 257, 258, 271; material, 2, 178–80, 184, 190, 194
ecology, 4, 23, 25, 35, 38, 41, 73, 88, 90, 91, 98, 103, 112, 124, 179, 201, 204, 234, 260, 301; political, 179, 234, 236, 237
ecosystem, 13, 23, 135, 171, 181, 260
ecotone, 23, 28, 35, 42, 43n3
edge, 12, 14, 24–28, 30, 38, 41, 42, 43n3, 67, 130, 136n5, 142, 143, 147, 149, 159, 188, 284, 303–5
empire. *See* imperialism
empirical, 60, 68, 83
energy, 58, 63, 66, 72, 76, 81, 83, 87, 133, 167, 214–16, 224, 289. *See also* oil
engineering, 50–70, 75, 99, 234, 239, 240, 249
epistemology, 5, 72, 80, 84, 101–2, 104, 178–81, 185, 257, 271, 286, 289–90, 292, 298; and "epistemic hybrids" (Helmreich), 83; materialist, 2; as "seascape epistemology" (Ingersoll), 12, 57, 101
Euclidian geometry, 69n3, 84, 291

evaporation, 113, 267
extractivism, 124, 132, 237

feminism, 7, 102, 117n3, 143, 156n9, 217, 259, 260
flesh, 128, 129, 137n9, 146, 149, 151, 152, 187, 188, 190, 191, 193, 196, 264
fluidity, 9, 11, 13, 24, 26, 30, 35, 54, 72, 76, 77, 80, 94, 109, 127, 128, 145, 152, 177, 181, 183, 186, 195n1, 198, 199, 209, 215, 216, 218, 224, 229n3, 229n9, 234, 260, 261, 264, 268, 271, 295, 307
flux, 83–84, 151, 166, 257, 263, 270. *See also* reflux
fold, 76, 209, 276–99
force, 5, 10, 37, 61, 84–85, 124, 179, 185, 193, 221, 236, 255, 257
forensics, 131–33, 137n8, 169–70; as "forensic oceanography" (Heller and Pezzani), 3, 15, 160; and storytelling, 126, 138n13
Freud, Sigmund: and melancholia, 134; and "oceanic feeling," 107–8, 117n9, 271

Gascoyne, David, 276–99
gender, 179; and bodies of water, 7; fluidity, 271; and hierarchies, 8, 259, 264, 271; as identity, 271; as linguistic distinction, 221, 307; of waves, 82
geographer, 97, 102, 114, 150; Black, 98, 115, 117n3
geography, 2, 4, 5, 7, 21, 23–28, 32, 34, 41–42, 43n1, 45n20, 94, 96, 98, 100, 103, 108–10, 112, 117n3, 135, 163, 238–39, 258, 288; and determinism, 42; dynamic, 13; fluid, 26
geology, 12, 53, 128, 137n9
geophysics, 95, 96, 98, 100–106, 112, 113, 138n13, 146, 151, 153–55, 177, 181, 236, 296
gestation, 88, 261, 268, 272
ghost, 79, 127, 135, 204, 278; as zombie, 53, 127, 144
Gilroy, Paul, 108–12, 114, 116; "Black Atlantic," 108–10, 114, 116n3; "offshore humanism," 111–16
Glissant, Édouard, 117, 123, 135, 137n6, 185, 189, 197, 198, 200, 201, 204, 209–10; "*créolisation*," 181, 183; "*Relation*," 109; "rhizome," 185, 186
grave, 14, 39, 128–30, 135, 138n11, 146, 150, 190, 191, 270, 272n1, 282
grief, 124, 130, 132, 136, 138nn14–16, 165, 171
Grosz, Elizabeth, 154
Guattari, Félix. *See* Deleuze, Gilles

Haraway, Donna, 16n5, 153, 175, 257, 260
harbor. *See* port
Hau'ofa, Epeli, 117n3, 136n6
Heidegger, Martin, 256, 292–94
Heller, Charles, and Lorenzo Pezzani, 15, 100, 138n13, 145, 149–75. *See also* aesthetics; forensics; liquid
Helmreich, Stefan, 4, 9, 50–70, 76, 80, 82, 83, 86, 88–90, 96, 179, 217, 218
Hessler, Stefanie. *See* "tidalectics"
Hofmeyr, Isabel, 4, 236, 237
Horden, Peregrine, and Nicholas Purcell, 3, 238

hospitality, 130, 135, 148, 149. *See also* Derrida, Jacques
Hugo, Victor, 72, 76–77, 82–83, 87, 255–73
humanitarianism, 138n13, 147, 164, 165, 171
humanities, 2, 234, 235, 257; blue, 97, 113, 277
humankind, 146, 148, 256–57, 259, 261–63, 267–68, 271
"hydrocapitalism" (Pritchard), 236
"hydrocolonialism" (Bystrom and Hofmeyr), 236
hydrocommons, 153, 255, 268, 271; Neimanis, 259–61
hydrodynamics, 50
"hydroimperialism" (Pritchard), 236
hydrology, 2, 3, 5, 42, 233–39, 245, 247, 255, 260–65, 267, 271, 278, 280–82, 285, 289–90, 292, 294; as "hydrologics" (Keller-Privat), 8, 278–94
"hydropoetics" (Brauer), 234, 237–38, 240–48
"hydropower," 236, 237, 239–40, 242–43, 248–50; Brauer, 236; Talbayev, 236
hydrosocial, 239–40, 242, 247, 249; crisis, 240–41; cycle, 234, 236–38, 241, 243–46, 248

ice, 90, 113
imperialism, 21–36, 42, 43, 101, 124, 134, 198, 201, 234, 236, 238–40, 242, 248, 250, 263, 269
indentureship, 177–95, 208
Indianité, 181
Indian Ocean, 51, 65, 68, 137

indigeneity, 11–13, 25, 26, 102, 117n3, 199, 306
indigenism, 202–4
infrastructure, 33, 35, 36, 40, 41, 50, 52, 56, 61, 63, 127, 131, 138n13, 161, 170, 236, 239, 248, 249, 302, 307, 308, 309nn1–2
inhuman, 80, 89, 156n9, 292. *See also* more-than-human
invisibility, 2, 15, 16n4, 76, 103, 137n6, 147, 148, 162, 178, 284, 285, 288, 289, 290, 292. *See also* legibility
invisible, 2, 16n4, 76, 137n6, 162, 178, 284–85, 288–92
Irigaray, Luce, 260–61
irrigation, 234, 236–39, 244–45, 249
island, 13, 25, 47, 74, 82, 96, 101–2, 117n3, 134–35, 137n6, 137n9, 164, 178, 191, 197, 199–201, 209, 238–39, 263, 301–2
iteration, 128, 218, 224, 234, 247

James, C. L. R., 105–7, 111, 117n7
Jue, Melody, 4, 58, 61

Kant, Immanuel. *See* sublime, the
khôra. *See* Plato, and *khôra*
knowledge, 2, 4, 7, 10, 12, 57, 58, 67, 74, 96, 97, 101, 104, 115, 117n4, 131, 133, 137n8, 167, 169, 170, 178, 180, 181, 184, 194, 195n1, 199, 237, 239, 257, 261, 262, 267, 296

laboratory, 4, 50–56, 65, 66, 68, 160, 229n9
Laferrière, Dany, 207–8

lake, 3, 8, 15, 25, 37, 38, 44n6, 128, 235, 245, 256, 258, 265, 266, 277, 302, 303
language, 1, 2, 5, 6, 10, 11, 56, 79, 163, 175, 187, 210, 234, 237, 238, 240, 243–46, 249, 256, 260, 276, 278, 281, 285, 292–95, 306, 307, 309; as "liquid language" (Pinnix), 214–30
law, 11, 135, 143, 146, 149, 155n3, 155n4, 162, 169, 175, 236, 268; of nature, 78, 262
legibility, 61, 125, 160, 169, 210. See also invisibility
liminal, 12, 14, 23, 24, 26, 28, 79, 111, 144, 145, 151, 184, 235
liquid, 3–9, 14, 15, 74, 80, 83, 109, 112, 134, 137n9, 138n13, 152; "liquid mortuaries" (Nair), 123, 128, 129; "liquid violence" (Heller and Pezzani), 145, 161–66, 170, 172, 173, 199, 235, 247, 249, 259, 260, 269, 285. See also language
Loichot, Valérie, 138n11, 184, 195n1, 201, 202
loss, 6, 7, 11, 12, 15, 124, 126, 130, 134, 138n15, 145, 188, 191, 192, 200, 220, 224, 260
lyrical, 129, 255, 265, 286, 291

Mallarmé, Stéphane, 215, 218, 219–30
Mars, Kettly, 205–7
material ecocriticism. See ecocriticism
materiality, 2, 4, 5, 7–15, 54, 56, 77, 79, 87, 88, 100, 103, 105, 110, 131, 134, 152, 159, 161, 165, 177–95, 217, 218, 224, 234, 235, 237, 253, 256, 257, 258, 282, 290
matrix, 10, 14, 59, 76, 82, 123, 124, 135, 214, 217, 224, 225
Mattawa, Khaled, 125, 131, 132, 138n13
matter, 2, 4, 5, 9–12, 14, 15, 69n3, 90, 116, 136n1, 138n16, 153–55, 178, 180–84, 187, 188, 190, 193, 194, 237, 279, 285, 290, 291, 293
Mazzantini, Margaret, 14, 125, 127, 128, 131, 132, 134, 136n1, 137n9
Mbembe, Achille: "borderization," 143, 145; "*corps-frontière*," 149, 152, 154; "necropolitics," 143, 145
McKittrick, Katherine, 98, 109, 110, 112
Mediterranean, 3, 7, 11, 22, 25, 31, 45n13, 73, 123–39, 142–46, 148, 151, 155n3, 159–70, 238, 299n6, 301, 302
medium, 1, 3, 4, 5–11, 12, 14, 15, 16n2, 73, 76, 79, 80, 234, 237, 243, 285
melancholia, 14, 132, 134, 138n15. See also Freud, Sigmund
Melville, Herman, 88, 102–8, 111, 117nn4–5, 218, 225, 228, 230n12
memory, 4, 5, 8, 11, 12–15, 109, 115, 129, 132–34, 136n1, 137n9, 149, 177, 186–94, 197, 208, 209, 237, 257, 263, 272n10, 282, 289, 292, 295, 306; as collective memory, 241–46; as memorialization, 124, 126, 128, 136n4, 139n17, 151, 198–203; as oceanic memory, 94, 96, 97, 101, 117n3
metaphor, 4, 8, 10, 59, 80, 89, 94, 103, 104, 107, 109, 112, 116, 137, 177–81, 184, 185, 194, 195n1, 198, 199, 202, 210, 217, 243, 256, 258, 259, 262, 263, 266, 268, 269, 277, 278, 285, 288, 295
metaphysics, 79, 256, 257, 291, 292
methodology, 2, 4, 9, 13, 14, 54, 86, 87, 138, 160–61, 243, 259, 268, 290

migration, 1, 11, 14, 24, 28, 31, 32, 82, 89, 92n4, 100, 101, 123–39, 142–55, 159–75, 184, 191, 225, 249, 295, 303, 304; as immigration, 26, 27, 33, 38, 40, 177. *See also* residue: "residual migrant" (Talbayev)

model, 9–14, 83–84, 88, 90, 113, 146, 154, 195n1, 204, 215, 221, 227, 229n3, 237, 244, 257, 265; as cartography, 167–72; as wave modeling, 50–69

molecule, 3–4, 9–14, 61, 84, 112–14, 146, 150, 152–54, 183, 214–18, 225, 228

Montfort, Nick, and Stephanie Strickland, 215, 218, 225–27, 229n9, 230n12

more-than-human, 11, 12, 94, 96, 102, 110, 112, 151–54. *See also* inhuman

mourning, 130–39, 145, 207, 270

multispecies, 99, 101, 177, 178, 181

myth, 73–74, 80, 82, 91, 132, 202, 204, 288

nature, 45n18, 55, 58, 61, 73, 81, 88, 91, 103, 107, 111–13, 179, 206, 236, 258–61

necropolitics, 3, 127; "water necropolitics" (Talbayev), 142–56, 304. *See also* Mbembe, Achille

Négritude, 181, 185, 187, 194. *See also* Césaire, Aimé

Neimanis, Astrida, 117n3, 151, 152, 217, 218, 259–61. *See also* hydrocommons

New Orleans, 21–47, 302–3, 305, 306, 307; as borderland, 23; as ecotone, 23, 28, 35, 42, 43n3; as edge-zone, 23, 305; and empire, 22, 23, 25, 26, 27, 41, 42, 44; as port-city, 305

nostalgia, 138n15, 188, 257

Nuttall, Sarah, 234, 235, 237

"oceanic feeling" (Freud). *See* Freud, Sigmund

oceanography, 50, 58, 89, 104, 117n4, 167, 170. *See also* forensics

Odessa, 21–47, 305; as borderland, 23; as ecotone, 23, 28, 35, 42, 43n3; as edge-zone, 23, 305; and empire, 22, 23, 25, 26, 27, 28, 31, 40, 41, 42, 44; as port-city, 305

oil, 51, 99, 125, 128–29, 134, 237, 269

Ollivier, Émile, 204

ontology, 2, 76, 99, 101–11, 151–54, 159, 177–78, 184, 187, 257, 260, 262, 264, 270–71, 276, 278, 284; as "archaeontology" (Domanska), 125, 137n8; as "dissolutive ontology" (Talbayev), 11, 149, 151–54; as "wet ontology" (Steinberg and Peters), 13, 100, 150, 278, 290, 291, 292

Orcel, Makenzy, 205

passage, 9, 14, 109, 127, 133, 204, 235, 278, 283, 289, 298; as Middle Passage, 97, 108–9, 123, 126, 201

pelagic, 111

Perelman, Bob, 214, 215, 218, 222–24, 229n6; and Shaw, Francie, 222

permeability, 12, 27, 144, 151, 152, 183, 259

Peters, Kimberley, 9, 13, 95, 96, 100, 101, 112, 113, 116n1, 117n8, 117n11, 150, 278, 287, 290–94. *See also* ontology phenomenology, 83, 110, 256, 259, 260, 282

Plato, and *khôra*, 14–15, 16n4, 133

poetics, 1, 5, 8, 10, 73, 76, 84, 87, 111, 123, 126, 171, 177, 178, 183, 185–94, 200, 215, 218, 220, 227, 228, 229nn5–6, 234, 237, 238, 240, 241–49, 256–58, 262, 264, 266, 267, 271, 276–98. *See also* "hydropoetics" (Brauer)

poetry, 1, 177–94, 203, 205, 214–30, 243–45, 247, 249, 258, 259, 261, 262, 266, 276–99

porosity, 3, 23, 24, 26, 34, 35, 39, 42, 43n3, 53, 151, 152, 183, 259, 279, 291

port, 2, 21–46, 66, 112, 113, 128, 135, 177, 191, 206, 234, 235, 238, 239, 242; as "port-city" (Edwards and Ksikes), 301–9. *See also* New Orleans; Odessa

posthuman, 256, 257, 259

posthumanism, 102, 110

Povinelli, Elizabeth, 93, 100, 114

precipitation, 245, 267

race, 3, 180, 203

racism, 111, 124, 127, 128, 179, 187

reflux, 83, 263, 272n5. *See also* flux

relationality, 112, 154, 182, 198, 272, 306. *See also* agency; connectivity; Glissant, Édouard

remains, 15, 125, 126, 129, 130, 135, 136n1, 152, 178, 183, 188, 191, 194, 243

reparative, 132, 133, 138n15, 155n6

residue, 153, 154, 155; "residual migrant" (Talbayev), 143, 149, 153

rhizome, 182, 185, 186, 188, 195n1, 282, 284, 295. *See also* Deleuze, Gilles; Glissant, Édouard

rhythm, 2, 9, 76, 84–87, 95, 100, 185, 200, 206–9, 233, 235, 262, 265, 277, 283, 289, 296

ritual, 125, 150. *See also* "unritual" (Loichot)

river, 3, 21, 22–30, 33–38, 43n1, 44n6, 44n9, 50, 63, 65, 68, 69, 75, 90, 155, 203, 233, 235, 239, 244, 245, 247, 254–58, 262–70, 279, 288, 297, 302–3, 305, 306, 309

Roumain, Jacques, 202–4

rupture, 4, 15, 132, 155n5, 164, 165, 200, 203, 205, 216, 217, 226, 228, 282, 283

sand, 80, 128, 129, 155, 233, 258, 287, 298

scale, 4, 5, 9, 10, 29, 46n27, 50–70, 88, 109, 137n9, 151, 152, 153, 161, 215, 226, 227, 236, 245, 249, 278, 285

Schmitt, Carl, 103

seascape, 3, 12, 24, 25, 57, 95, 101, 129, 210, 265. *See also* epistemology

seawater, 11, 80, 84, 86, 143, 151, 153, 154, 155nn7–8, 217, 264, 285

sediment, 3, 4, 27, 66, 80, 183, 234

Sharpe, Christina, 108, 113, 155n7; "residence time," 114

shipwreck, 74, 111, 112, 145, 164, 165, 192, 220

shore, 12, 13, 21, 22, 33, 42, 44n9, 51, 53, 60, 66, 69, 74, 81, 82, 99, 101, 102, 111, 112, 114, 116, 129, 134, 137n6, 142, 146, 147, 148, 164, 205, 224, 225, 226, 227, 233, 235, 239, 276, 280, 282, 286

slavery, 14, 25, 33, 37, 40, 44n5, 46nn22–23, 100, 102, 110, 111, 113,

114, 123, 127, 128, 138n11, 155n7, 174, 184, 197, 198, 199, 200, 201, 204, 206, 305, 308
Sloterdijk, Peter, 82
solid, 11, 76, 77, 87, 100, 106, 117, 118, 137n9, 182, 183, 199, 202, 205, 206, 215, 260, 264, 267, 279, 295
sound, 5, 6, 15, 104, 107, 199, 206, 224, 286, 295, 296, 299n8
spectacularization, 159, 164, 165, 171, 172
spiral, 84, 86
stability, 10, 12, 14, 15, 27, 28, 41, 44n6, 46n31, 54, 79, 96, 114, 125, 137n9, 144, 161, 179, 195n3, 198, 205, 226, 241, 286, 287, 291, 292
Steinberg, Philip, 4, 7, 9, 12, 13, 94–117, 137n9, 150, 177, 183, 217, 218, 278, 287, 290, 291, 292, 293, 294; "world-ocean," 9. *See also* ontology
striation. *See* Deleuze, Gilles
sublime, the: Edmund Burke, 74, 256; Immanuel Kant, 74, 255
submarine, 151, 178–79, 182, 184, 187, 192, 194, 195n3, 198
submersion, 73, 88, 97, 101, 126, 128, 134, 142, 151–52, 187, 189, 234, 238, 242–44, 282–83, 305
surface, 9–10, 39, 76, 84, 89, 95, 100–101, 106, 128, 150–51, 159, 167, 169–70, 177, 199, 215–17, 220, 227, 234, 238, 243–44, 259, 264, 267, 269, 278, 281, 288, 290–91. *See also* depth
surrealism, 281
surveillance, 130, 142, 146, 147, 159–75
sustainability, 73, 88, 90, 250, 271
swell, 9, 76, 83, 90, 95, 105, 233, 264, 268, 270
symbiosis, 269, 282

technology, 7, 31, 32, 34, 55, 60, 67, 80, 106, 107, 144, 160, 162–70, 172, 175, 179, 227
temporality, 3, 62, 94, 95, 96, 100, 101, 114, 115, 144, 152, 155n5, 172, 207, 234, 235, 247, 250, 277, 290, 303
terrestrial, 3, 117n8, 124, 128, 209, 233–50, 258, 281
territory, 22, 25, 26, 27, 29, 33, 34, 106, 145, 166, 242, 244, 245, 247, 291, 292
text, 54, 80, 126, 129, 134, 180, 186, 187, 188, 210, 219, 220, 221, 225–29, 289, 298n4
thalassic, 124, 134, 264
"tidalectics": Brathwaite, 13, 16n1, 101; DeLoughrey, 13, 101; Hessler, 13, 101
tide, 83, 152, 166, 210, 216, 233, 235, 267, 284, 290
Tinsley, Omise'eke Natasha, 7, 109, 110, 112
topography, 25, 67, 128, 171, 255, 262
Torabully, Khal, 8, 177–95
Toufiq, Ahmed, 233–50
trace, 4, 12, 14, 15, 55, 82, 130, 131–34, 152, 161, 169, 172, 173, 188, 205, 282, 289
"transcorporeality" (Alaimo), 11, 15, 188
trash, 127, 130, 138n10
trauma, 62, 82, 94, 96, 99, 101, 108, 127, 129, 132, 138n15, 155n6, 178, 181, 184, 188, 191–93, 196–99
Trouillot, Lyonel, 208
tsunami, 51–55, 60–69, 80, 88–90

underwater, 8, 53, 81, 143, 150–51, 170–71, 178–79, 189–91, 195, 198

unfathomable, 156n9, 221, 264, 290, 296
"unritual" (Loichot), 201

Valéry, Paul, 84–85
vibrant, 8, 178, 180, 258
Victor, Gary, 202, 206
Victor, Marvin, 205
violence, 8, 12, 15, 37, 73, 82, 115, 134, 138n13, 143, 145–48, 152, 159, 160–75, 179, 201, 202, 205, 216, 242, 262, 294. *See also* liquid
volume, 76, 95, 100, 102–4, 143, 150, 170, 290, 292
vortex, 9, 76, 84

Walcott, Derek, 103, 109, 126, 129, 133, 136n6, 197, 198, 204, 209, 210
Waldrop, Keith, 8, 15
waste, 128, 130, 131, 146, 149, 154, 259, 279, 301, 309n1
water cycle, 234, 235, 236, 238, 240, 244, 245, 246, 249, 258, 259, 266. *See also* hydrosocial: cycle

water logics, 1–15, 16n1, 21–28, 32–35, 39, 41–43, 56, 69, 73, 238, 250, 278, 305, 309
watermark, 1–3, 8, 9
water rights, 237, 238, 241
watershed, 24, 26, 236, 244
waterway, 27, 29, 31, 33, 44n9, 50, 258, 265
wave, 1, 2, 3, 5, 6, 8, 9, 27, 50–70, 72–92, 95, 96, 103, 104, 112, 113, 126, 131, 182, 197, 205, 206, 209, 214–28, 263, 267, 270, 279, 282, 283, 284, 286, 287, 289, 294, 296, 301
witness, 1, 14, 130, 133, 136, 165, 166, 172, 276
Wittig, Monique, 7, 16n3
women, 143, 145, 246–47, 264, 282; Black, 184

Yusoff, Kathryn, 4

Zukofsky, Louis, 1, 6, 7

Recent books in the series
UNDER THE SIGN OF NATURE: EXPLORATIONS IN ENVIRONMENTAL HUMANITIES

Irish Ecomedia: Empire and Environmental Justice in the Modernization of Postcolonial Ireland
KATHERINE M. HUBER

The Ecological Plot: How Stories Gave Rise to a Science
JOHN MACNEILL MILLER

Cli-Fi and Class: Socioeconomic Justice in Contemporary American Climate Fiction
DEBRA J. ROSENTHAL AND JASON DE LARA MOLESKY, EDITORS

Thoreau's Botany: Thinking and Writing with Plants
JAMES PERRIN WARREN

Climate Change and Original Sin: The Moral Ecology of John Milton's Poetry
KATHERINE COX

The Queerness of Water: Troubled Ecologies in the Eighteenth Century
JEREMY CHOW

Toxic Matters: Narrating Italy's Dioxin
MONICA SEGER

Unsettling Nature: Ecology, Phenomenology, and the Settler Colonial Imagination
TAYLOR A. EGGAN

Basura: Cultures of Waste in Contemporary Spain
SAMUEL AMAGO

Narrating the Mesh: Form and Story in the Anthropocene
MARCO CARACCIOLO

Magnificent Decay: Melville and Ecology
TOM NURMI

Eden's Endemics: Narratives of Biodiversity on Earth and Beyond
ELIZABETH CALLAWAY

New Woman Ecologies: From Arts and Crafts to the Great War and Beyond
ALICIA CARROLL

Of Land, Bones, and Money: Toward a South African Ecopoetics
EMILY MCGIFFIN

Novel Cultivations: Plants in British Literature of the Global Nineteenth Century
ELIZABETH HOPE CHANG

Evergreen Ash: Ecology and Catastrophe in Old Norse Myth and Literature
CHRISTOPHER ABRAM

Italy and the Environmental Humanities: Landscapes, Natures, Ecologies
SERENELLA IOVINO, ENRICO CESARETTI, AND ELENA PAST, EDITORS

Building Natures: Modern American Poetry, Landscape Architecture, and City Planning
JULIA E. DANIEL

Recomposing Ecopoetics: North American Poetry of the Self-Conscious Anthropocene
LYNN KELLER

"The Best Read Naturalist": Nature Writings of Ralph Waldo Emerson
MICHAEL P. BRANCH AND CLINTON MOHS, EDITORS

www.ingramcontent.com/pod-product-compliance
Lightning Source LLC
Chambersburg PA
CBHW030606230426
43661CB00053B/1861